The Impatient American

In Egypt
Where Two Cultures Clash

By
Patrick J. Roelle Sr.
Mr. Pat

The Impatient American

The Impatient American

Contents

Prologue – July 1986

This is a true story. The names are not changed to protect the innocent because, when it came to the Americans and the Egyptians involved, there were none, most of all me. Humor, empathy, sarcasm, pugnacity, personal reflections, regret, and, at times, literary license all played a part.

In the summer of 1986, EGICON, an American-Egyptian joint venture, hired me as Project Director to oversee the construction of a military computer facility for the Egyptian Army. U.S. Military Aid funded the project, the U.S. Army Corps of Engineers administered it, and the U.S. Office of Military Cooperation ran interference.

Throughout the following pages, I have allowed myself the luxury of a writer's license—manipulating circumstances depending on my attitude. I could have edited out what others might consider blatant errors. Still, although correcting the text may save me criticism from history and political science scholars, it would be self-defeating. Reality is what we are emotionally willing to deal with at the time.

Some say these were the good times for *modern Egypt: That is a play on words*. Since the 1980s, agriculture's share of GDP has halved. The sector now accounts for 11% of GDP and 22% of Egypt's employment, 30% and 40% lower than the African average.

Egypt is mostly desert. The Nile Delta hosts most agricultural land; only 2.8% of the country's territory is arable. With limited resources, low productivity, and a rapidly growing population, Egypt must import more than 50% of its food and agricultural product needs, or the people will starve.

The government subsidizes some, but food is not free. In response to rising oil and food prices, Egyptian President Abdel

Fattah el-Sisi recently said, "*Prophet Muhammad and his companions ate tree leaves when they were trapped in the outskirts of Makkah for three years,*" insinuating Egyptians should "*eat tree leaves*" to survive under the country's deteriorating economic conditions. Sisi's remarks came amid soaring inflation, a shrinking middle class, and price hikes on subsidized goods, all of which have caused Egypt's poor to struggle to access basic commodities.

When Cesar, the owner of the American company, offered me the job, although my family, friends, and I agreed I needed a change, I accepted the assignment with misgivings. Relocating to the Middle East seemed drastic; Egypt was in turmoil, and the surrounding countries were in flames.

Cairo promised fulfillment and the chance of a lifetime for me. When Cesar offered me the opportunity to work and live within the society, Egypt brought visions of enchantment generated by books and history lessons. However, I was blissfully unaware of reality at the time.

There was not much in the news about Egypt. My mind wandered to the movie Lawrence of Arabia and thoughts of Arabian nights, billowing tents, majestic stallions, and nomadic tribes seeking protection in an oasis littered with sheltering palms and life-giving waters.

I bought an atlas and looked up Cairo. The Nile River, the lifeblood and lifeline of North Africa, cuts the city in half. Once a gift of the Almighty, it is now a river ravaged by man and polluted by civilization.

Cairo is known as the City of the Pharaohs. The Sphinx guards the entrance to the Great Pyramids. Egypt has seven thousand years of history, but much of the culture is frozen in time, and it is struggling to emerge and set aside its *Third World* image.

The circumstances of my being there and my inability to deal with my past placed me in limbo as an observer. I accepted as unchangeable the culture, poverty, indifference of the rulers, and the apparent lack of concern by the leaders of the free world.

Although not always socially or politically correct, the following pages describe people I met and situations within a way of life that was polar opposite to mine. I have related them as I viewed them, not necessarily as others might see them.

Filming tourist traps and the villages around Cairo was a way to spend an afternoon. Filming within villages bordering the desert where fundamental Muslim ideology has deep roots is difficult and often impossible for anyone who is not Muslim.

What bothered me the most was the underlying attitude that life has little meaning; what counts is pleasing Islam's God, Allah, and that all things happen, only inshallah, the Arabic term for the phrase: *If Allah, Islam's God, wills it*.

Although I managed to photograph some village life on one or two occasions, try to read between the lines, and trust me when I say that the smiling faces mask the reality of the Third World.

The Third World has become a convenient catchphrase that refers collectively to the heterogeneous societies, cultures, and civilizations: Most of which lies in the tropics, have experienced Colonial Rule, whose economies are less industrialized or not wholly modernized, and a majority of whose population have the lowest standards of living, or are considered, or consider themselves poor relative to those of the First and Second Worlds.

The Third World includes all countries of Africa except South Africa and Asia, except Japan, Latin America, the Caribbean, and some states and territories of Oceania.

This is about Egypt. Egypt defines poverty as anyone making less than $2.50 a day. As for the rest, the Second World, it depends on who you ask. For this exercise in today's dollars, China defines the poverty line as anyone making less than $2.25 daily. In India, eighty million people out of 1.2 billion, roughly 6.7% of India's population, live below the poverty line of $1.25 a day, and 84% live on less than $6.85 per day. Russia's poverty line is said to be $5.50 per day. Put it in perspective: 11.6% of the population in the U.S. live below the U.S. poverty line of $40.80 per day.

The Impatient American

This book places secular Western civilization alongside theological social norms widely observed within Egypt's culture. When it comes to religion, Egypt is the most moderate Muslim-ruled country on the planet. In addition to religion, one must understand politics to comprehend my mindset.

The religion of Islam drives politics in the Muslim world. Life in Egypt, like the rest of the Middle Eastern countries except for Israel, revolves around Islamic Sharia law. The basis of that law is the Qur'an, Islam's bible.

Egyptians are predominantly Muslim. I am a lax Christian, and I have some Jewish friends: Pagans, well…., not so much. I think people should get along. Some will say that disqualifies me as an independent thinker. Bullshit, I have Google. *Trust me, you cannot rely on Google. I am sorry to burst that bubble. People with the most to gain are usually at the top of Google's list.*

Joseph Goebbels, propaganda expert and Reich Minister of Public Enlightenment and Education for Nazi Germany, said: "If you tell a lie big enough *and keep repeating it, people will eventually come to believe it."*

Benjamin Franklin said: *"Half of the truth is usually a great lie."* Joseph Goebbels would have liked Google. Benjamin Franklin would have figured it out.

I did not have a clue when I arrived in the Middle East. Like most Americans, I had some *irrevocable* opinions about things I knew absolutely nothing about. *You must dig deeper.* I have, and my *irrevocable* opinions have changed. I am not taking sides; I am trying to understand the mindset.

Islamic tradition claims Muhammad, the founder of Islam, had a revelation in 610 AD. During this time, he was visited by the Archangel Gabriel, who revealed to him the beginnings of what would later become the Qur'an.

The Qur'an relies on Hadith in addition to Muhammad's revelations. Technically, Hadith means the narration of Muhammad's sayings, deeds, or approvals.

Muhammed started preaching Islam as a religion of peace, but after thirteen years, he had less than one hundred converts. He then migrated to Medina, a town with a large Jewish population and two Arab tribes. Since his religion, Islam was based on the Jewish faith, Muhammed anticipated more empathy and support from the Jews. However, the Jews rejected Islam's peaceful methods.

Soon afterward, Muhammed changed his tune and started raiding caravans and surrounding villages. Forced conversions followed as he gained confidence. In the meantime, he slaughtered or expelled all the Jews in Medina while his followers mushroomed into thousands.

When his tribe's boundaries were insufficient to provide basic food and shelter for an expanding population, some moved on to greener pastures.

By 629, after eight years of fighting with the Meccan tribes, Muhammad had raised an army of 10,000 converts and marched on the city of Mecca. By his death on June 8, 632, he was the effective ruler of all southern Arabia, and his armies were invading the Eastern Empires of Persia and Ethiopia.

By 732, the Muslim empire stretched from India across the Middle East and North Africa and up through Western Europe's Iberian Peninsula. The spread of Islam continued into Africa and Asia.

The problem was that many of those new pastures were inhabited by other tribes reluctant to give up their land or share diminishing resources with ethnic strangers. As a result, migration became the driving force of war. Throughout history, the strong have subjugated the weak in their quest for wealth and power. Many surrendered without a fight, joined with the invader, and enslaved their own to avoid suppression.

The Egyptian-Arab heritage was confusing and contradictory. Muslims are not a race of people; they are members of Islam's family, the Ummah, which means *The Nation* in Arabic. The Egyptians I was dealing with were Muslims. They believed they were descendants of the Pharaohs and not remotely related to an Arab or African tribe.

Beginning with the reign of the Pharaohs, Egypt reflects some of the earliest recorded history of man's enslavement of a tribe they considered subhuman.

Biblical events in Egypt occur almost exclusively in Lower Egypt, where the Israelites settled in Goshen. Abraham, Joseph, Jacob, and Moses all lived in the eastern delta of the Nile River. Jeremiah and the Holy Family visited the region. The Gospel of Matthew describes how Joseph, Mary, and Jesus went to Egypt to escape from Herod the Great's slaughter of the baby boys in Bethlehem.

Color, origin, and religious affiliation were prominent in how Dr. Osmond's relatives dealt with subcontractors and the working class. Upper Egyptians, with ancestors born in areas around Cairo, are lighter in color. Many light-skinned Egyptians consider themselves *pure Egyptians* and believe their skin color places them in a class above all others.

Upper Egyptians believe lower Egyptians are descendants of African intruders and the Pharaoh's slaves who remained behind when Moses led the Jews out of Egypt. Lower Egyptians are darker in color, smaller in stature, and used to toiling long hours under the blazing sun.

Those who consider themselves *Pure Upper Egyptians* are lightest in color and consist mainly of the elite and upper middle class. Money breeds money, so there are marriages between close family members. Both the men and women give the impression that they consider themselves the masters and the darker-colored servants.

The Egyptian Generals and most of Doctor Osmond's staff, whom you will meet later, treated me and the other expats assigned to this project as if we were an unnecessary nuisance. I also dealt with the peasant class of Egypt, who, for the most part, welcomed me into their villages and treated me with curiosity, friendship, and respect.

It became apparent it was beneath the Abbouds, Anwars, and Hamids to soil their hands by doing physical labor. Many aristocratic males grow the nail on the pinky finger of the left hand to a length of an inch or longer as a sign that physical labor is beneath them. I do not like Doctor Abboud, Anwar, or Hamid, who, for the most part, either patronized or ignored me.

After our initial meeting, I made it a point to spend my free time detached from the Egyptians assigned to the project. I entertained myself with visits to the pyramids, Luxor's Valley of the Kings, and a dozen or so other antiquities advertised in tourist brochures.

Although generally friendly, the people I encountered in the tourist attractions were only interested in separating me from my money by pawning off trinkets produced in sweatshops hidden in slums nestled in bazaars, and by children working for less than a dollar a day.

Sightseeing took a month; I had eleven more ahead of me. I was fed up with the project and ready to call it quits. But, as I will explain later, I did not have that choice. I was trapped by circumstance and could not return to the States indefinitely; I needed to make do.

I was also ensnared in the culture. However, I was not ready to judge Middle Eastern society based on the upper class's inability to tell the truth or that words like honor, sanitation, organization, fair play, safety, law and order, maintenance, or finish are not in their vocabulary.

After the first month, I made it a point to avoid the tourist traps and spend my free time in the rural villages and obscure communities scattered along the Nile River and the Red Sea, getting to know the people.

Chapter 1

I left the U.S. to avoid a final domestic confrontation at home, and the IRS agent who believed I owed $600,000 in payroll taxes. I needed to remain out of the country for at least a year to gain tax-free status and another year or two to avoid the young, aggressive IRS agent assigned to my case.

I incurred the liability as the owner of a company doing business with the U.S. government on projects for the military. I did not think I owed the money. I tried to sort it out through the American legal system, which is a lot like a modern-day Jew in Israel trying to convince a Hamas lawyer that his homestead rights are valid. Like the Israeli and Muslim conflict, it would go on forever. The only way it could be resolved would be if the IRS disbanded or I left the country. I ended up halfway across the world.

The IRS agent assigned to my case was aware that I knew it is not against the law to fail to pay taxes, and he could not throw me in prison simply because I did not have the money. There is a law against failure to report income, so he attached all my future earnings. He figured I would hide my income, which would give him the excuse he was looking for to throw me in jail.

During the 1980s, the IRS experienced problems of its own. While they replaced the computers at the IRS home office, my file ended up in cyberspace. The IRS forgot about me while they harassed all the people who paid their taxes. It was an opportunity; I avoided them long enough to research a career change.

I fabricated a new resume that included my expertise in construction management and my experience with the U.S. Army Core of Engineers. Although I neglected the part about the taxes the IRS was looking for, the reference to the COE gave me credibility with a company desperate for a Project Director in Egypt managed by the COE.

It was that time of year when the IRS agent would be making his annual appearance. The contract Cesar signed with the COE said my overseas income was tax-free. I signed a contract with Cesar's company, which said I was tax-free. The contract the Egyptian Army signed with the Office of Military Cooperation said I was tax-free, and my accountant confirmed it. The IRS agent ignored my logic and demanded that I attend another meeting.

Cesar, thinking I knew what I was doing, never entered my mind, and, in the end, it did not matter. I am only bringing it up to point out that I have dealt with the American government before. Cesar felt that personal experience with the COE gave me an edge over others who had taken actual college courses in construction management.

When I told my family and friends I was taking a job in Egypt, most of them shook their heads in disbelief. They figured my mid-life crisis had not run a full cycle, and my intent may have been to put the IRS behind me permanently.

None of us knew where Cairo was. All we knew was that it was somewhere in Egypt, in North Africa, near all those friendly places we read about, such as Israel, Palestine, Iran, Iraq, Sudan, and Saudi Arabia. To us, it was a nondescript part of the world covered by the sand of the Sahara Desert and engulfed by five thousand years of war.

My friends and I acquired knowledge by watching the movies Moses and Cleopatra and reading news reports that overseas correspondents managed to get to their respective editors. The real news took time to decipher. Americans are fair game for either side in the Middle East conflict because no one knows which side we will take next or, for that matter, whose side we are on.

At the time, Iran and Iraq were engaged in a bloody ten-year war. Congress and the White House supported Saddam Hussein by providing Iraq with military equipment, while Oliver North and his buddies from the CIA were supplying arms to Iran.

One of the issues was the method of travel to get to Egypt. The consensus was that it was not safe to take a plane because

Muslim terrorists were hijacking those Americans were traveling on or trying to blow them out of the sky.

The war between Iran and Iraq was in full swing. It was not safe to take a ship by way of the Mediterranean because Muslim terrorists were pitching American passengers into the sea as a protest of the U.S. involvement in that war.

There was no guaranteed safe route. I was thinking my friends were right. I was also seriously considering calling the IRS agent and trying to negotiate one last time. But, in the end, the exercise had been a waste of time. It was simple; the U.S. Government guaranteed my wages in the event terrorists hijacked the plane for as long as it took to get me released, identify my body, or have proof of my death, whichever occurred first.

They also stipulated that the company would not be reimbursed for my travel expenses unless I traveled by a U.S. carrier. The travel expense item was the decisive factor. Cesar bought me a ticket on TWA and told me the plane left on Monday.

Cesar hired me on a Wednesday. I settled the affairs the IRS left me with on Thursday, kissed my wife and kids' goodbye on Friday, and then spent the weekend in a hotel to get away from the well-wishers until I hit the friendly skies on Monday.

My flight from Seattle took me to Washington, DC, then Cairo via New York and the security checks in Paris. On the way to Washington, where I was to meet some of the players from the COE, I reviewed the project plans. I had spent the prior twenty-four years in the construction business. My experience told me the assignment would be the piece of cake Cesar promised.

It was an uncomplicated pre-engineered metal building with some gingerbread; one Acme Construction could build in the States in ninety days; I had a year. My mind wandered while I dreamed of trips on the enchanting Nile, visits to antiquities, and a few picture-taking safaris in other areas of Africa.

A COE project helped cause my financial problems. Before I arrived at the office in Washington, I noted several plan errors and omissions on the drawings and tried to make my entrance with a get-even start.

If you have not figured it out already, I am an expert on planning, errors, and omissions. Not everyone agreed. At the time, Joe, my attorney, told me my planning was not worth a shit, or I would have kept the $600,000 the IRS was looking for. The VP at the bank lost his job because he could not find the errors I was putting in my financial statement, and because of the omissions in my personal life, my wife was seriously considering a divorce.

I survived my mid-life crisis. The IRS was still hounding me, but the statute of limitations was running. The banker found a new job. The divorce…, well, that comes later.

I was looking forward to meeting the players from the COE because I intended to tell them they forgot to put steel in the building foundation drawings, and the first order of business was a big extra to the contract.

The Contracting Officer introduced me to the Chief of Engineering; I asked.

"Fred, is there some reason you left the steel out of the concrete in the foundation drawings?"

Fred did not think it was funny and ignored the question. The CO asked me what I was talking about. I told him it would be my first trip to Egypt, and I was trying to familiarize myself with Egyptian building methods. It did not appear we were communicating. The CO wanted a direct answer. I told him I thought it unusual for the COE to design a building without reinforcing steel in the foundations.

That got his attention. Fred asked if I had taken plan reading courses and then suggested it might help if I were to take a refresher before I continued my journey east. Continuing the discussion would have led to a delayed departure. The contract said Fred could accept or reject the PD if he did it before I left the States for Egypt.

I had plenty of time after I settled into my new job. I left the COE's office and headed for New York to meet with Cesar and

Doctor Abboud, one of the Egyptian partners, before continuing my journey east. Abboud never showed. Cesar came to introduce me to his wife and told me that due to a slight error in his financial planning, he would not be able to make my first month's paycheck good until the second month.

There was not much time for a decision; the plane was boarding. Under the circumstances, it was an easy decision. I have been guilty of a few errors and omissions myself, I had never been to Egypt, I had a round-trip ticket, and Cesar's American Express card. Worst case, I would get an expense-paid trip to Cairo.

A little advice is in order at this point. If you travel to a foreign country, take a short course in the language. The only country that gives you a choice is the U.S., and I must admit, I resent it when someone in the States asks me if I want to hear the options in English.

When I arrived in Paris, I had no idea the security police were telling me to take my carry-on with me when I went to the toilet or the coffee shop while they checked the plane for bombs.

Bathrooms are called toilets in France and most of the world. I do not know what a toilet is called. That changes from country to country. The only word I understood was bombs, and since that scared the crap out of me, I left my carry-on on one of the empty seats next to the boarding gate and headed for the toilet. I was relieved when I came out, and since no one else seemed excited, I assumed the bomb scare was a false alarm.

I headed back to pick up my bag; there was a commotion coming from the waiting area where I left it. The security police were preparing to dump my carry-on into a steel container. This was 1986, and, like most white male Americans, the police did not intimidate me. I yelled some obscenity; the French police took offense and escorted me to a private room.

It took a while, but with the help of a woman who spoke English, we sorted through the mess. An hour later, they escorted me back to the plane, where I waited until the rest of the passengers cleared the new security check. The incident delayed our departure by two hours. It was evident from the looks of the other passengers that I had not improved American foreign relations.

Cesar neglected to tell me who I was to meet or where I was to meet them. Before we boarded, I called the Portland office. Cesar was still in New York. Doctor Abboud never did show up. The company secretary suggested I play it by ear and call when I reached Cairo.

I settled in my seat and decided it was time to read the book of helpful hints the travel agent in the States had enclosed with my tickets. The book explained how airport security would change as we approached the high-risk areas of the Middle East.

The flight was uneventful; the plane arrived in Cairo five hours later. The minute I got off the plane, I started to feel uneasy. I looked around and suddenly realized that if there were any order in my life, I would not be in Egypt.

I followed the crowd meandering through the airport. Military guards were stationed every few meters, mostly huddled in groups. (*We are now in Egypt, so we will try to use the metric system.*) They were not paying much attention to the passengers. Had they not been carrying automatic weapons; I would have ignored their presence. The guns made me nervous. It was a common sight in Egypt but one I never became comfortable with.

I was five hundred meters down the hall when I realized I left my camera on the plane. Shit….! I had just purchased a new Minolta with all the bells and whistles; it was expensive. I started back. When I rounded the first corner, three guards blocked my way. None spoke English. I had not been in Egypt long enough to realize the rules in the States had no bearing on a situation anywhere in the Middle East or Africa. The guards would not allow me to return to the plane.

It was futile to continue conversing in a language I could not understand. I felt it best to address the problem with the airline and try to recover the camera later. I turned back toward customs and baggage claim. As I turned to leave, a fourth soldier approached. He spoke Arabic-English and instructed me, in a rather firm voice, to remain where I was. *Arabic-English: A term for the language between an English expat and a local who spoke some English.*

He continued a conversation with the other guards while I stood in 100-degree sweltering heat and then turned to ask what caused me to return to the arrival gate. I told him I had left my camera on the plane. He told me to follow him. When we approached the gate, he escorted me to a group of soldiers huddled around a desk and then left me standing outside the circle.

It had been a long day. I was having my first attack of impatience in Egypt when one of the guards gestured for me to join the group. There was a lot of excitement at the table: Egypt's that way, not much thought process, but a lot of excitement. Thought process is challenging for me too at times; I never realized how many parts there were to an automatic camera until I saw my new Minolta dissected on the desk.

The guard asked why I had left the camera on the plane. I explained that it was an oversight. He turned to his friends, laughing as he gathered the parts into the case and handed them to me. He then told me it was not very smart to leave packages on the aircraft, that I was free to go, and to follow the signs to the customs and baggage area.

The signs were in Arabic, which should not have surprised me, although Egyptians are not Arabs, Egyptians speak Arabic. Passengers were arriving from another flight as I entered the hallway leading to the immigration area. I joined the group, merging into the makings of a line. Soon, I was not sure it was a line; no one was waiting. More excitement: Everyone was pushing and yelling in a variety of languages.

When, after 45 minutes, I had not moved an inch, and new arrivals kept crowding in ahead, what little patience I had left dissolved. I am six feet and two hundred pounds, bigger than most Egyptians. I did some pushing and shoving of my own to the front of the line, where I handed my passport to the clerk.

I was in the wrong line! Another shit! The man behind the desk silently pointed me to a line at the other side of the terminal. I walked to the end of the other, much longer line and started a push to the front. It took an hour to get to the window. It was the visa line.

What the fuck…? It took a minute. I planned that part of the trip. I made a special trip to the Egyptian embassy in Washington, DC, and paid for a ninety-day visa, which they had stamped in my passport. It did not count in Cairo. Egypt immigration passed new rules while I was in transit. Before entering the country, I had to convert $150 into LE (*Egyptian Pounds*) to validate the Visa.

The Egyptian government desperately needed foreign currency because they refused to float the Egyptian Pound to the dollar's value. Due to Egypt's inflation rate, the currency was worthless outside of Egypt. It was not easy to decipher Arabic-English, but I caught on, took out my American Express traveler's checks, and handed the clerk $150.

They did not accept traveler's checks, and I did not have $150 in cash. He directed me to another line where I could get the checks cashed. Three hours had passed since I arrived, and I was at the end of another line. I made it to the third window, where the cashier exchanged my traveler's checks for LE, less a 5% fee.

I went back to the second line to get my visa stamped. What the hell? This is a book about patience, right? I fought to the head of the line and got the visa stamp. I then returned to the first line, where I started three and a half hours earlier, and after another forty-five minutes, I entered the baggage area. The rest of the passengers on my flight left hours earlier. My luggage was set off to the side of the conveyor.

I had been at the airport for four hours. I loaded my luggage and the crate containing my computer onto a cart and headed for customs and what I hoped would be no more delays.

There were two exit lines. Each had signs in English below the Arabic. One said, *"Nothing to Declare," and* the other, "*Customs Entry."* I did not think I brought anything I needed to declare. Wrong fucking line! I was supposed to declare my computer. I am running out of shit. It was against the law to bring a computer into Egypt without paying duty on it. I moved to the end of the other line. It took a while; I was wearing down and had not been in Egypt for a day.

"No problem; how much is the duty?"

The customs officer spoke Arabic-English. He asked me if it was a new or used computer. I did not see what difference it would make, so I told him it was used, because it was. I handed him the papers.

"Forty-five hundred, U.S."

I should have said new because there was a penalty for bringing a used anything into the country.

"Not a fucking chance!"

The man did not like my attitude. He escorted me to another desk, where an officer who spoke better Arabic-English explained that if the computer were new, I would only have to pay a 10% duty. However, since mine was used and I tried to pass it off as new by first going to the Nothing to Declare line, I had to pay a penalty. This did not make sense to me at the time; it never did.

I learned later that the Egyptian government had passed a law requiring foreigners in Egypt to exchange their hard currency (Currency that is not likely to depreciate suddenly or fluctuate greatly in value) for L.E (Egyptian pounds). Converting dollars to LE at the rate the Egyptian banks were offering diluted the dollar's value. Banks and hotels where you could make a legal exchange paid less than half what the black market was willing to pay.

A few months earlier there was no duty on used personal belongings. However, the locals were in the habit of buying items unavailable in Egypt while on holiday and then trying to pass them off as used when they returned home. To stop the practice, the government passed a law to penalize anyone who tried to pass something new off as used. There was a list, in Arabic, of personal belongings that were exempt. Laptops were on the list but were rare in those days; mine was a Dell tower; it was not on the list.

I was bringing the computer into Egypt to work on a duty-free military project run by the Americans. I was not aware of the rules.

We argued the point for a while, but it was futile. I gave in and started to negotiate a deal. Egyptian customs had my paperwork. I insured the computer for $3000 when I checked it in at the airport in the States, so I agreed to the value. If I wanted to bring it into Egypt, I would have to pay $4,500. The Egyptian government misjudged me. I had nowhere near that much money in my wallet.

I told him it was not worth that much and that I would arrange to ship it back to the States and buy a new one duty-free after I settled in Cairo. He said that would be okay, but to get it released so I could export it I would have to pay the penalty for having tried to *smuggle* it into the country.

"How much?"

"Forty-five hundred."

"Keep it!"

I did not have a clue what the rules were. I left the computer at the desk, gathered the rest of my luggage, and headed for the exit. The customs official yelled something, causing me to turn around, and then he handed me a receipt written in Arabic. By that time, another two hours had passed. The Arabs had my computer, but I had my freedom. A few minutes later, I was standing on the concrete in front of the airport, trying to flag down a taxi to take me to a hotel.

After I called the office from Paris, the secretary sent a telex to the Egyptian JV partner with my flight schedule. They had called the airline and knew I had arrived. A lost American trying to get a taxi's attention garnered attention.

People often ask why I use the name Mr. Pat. Hazem was standing on the sidewalk holding a sign; *Mr. Pat*. Hazem introduced himself as my assistant assigned by the Egyptian JV Partner.

At first, I thought that expat men (foreign nationals working in the country) were addressed by their first names, with a Mr. in front of them as a sign of respect. Later, I would realize that when they used an Ah, as in, "*Ah, Mr. Pat*," it was often a swear word. I stuck with it anyway. It would be my name for the remainder of my international career.

Chapter 2

Hazem was familiar with local delays. He checked with airport security and knew I had arrived on the flight from Paris seven hours earlier. After he crammed my luggage into the back of his minicar, Hazem offered me the front passenger seat. We then pulled from the airport onto the main road leading into Cairo.

2. Cairo Traffic

I drive down the road with cars five abreast.
It's my patience they are trying to test.
The lanes in the road are designed for two.
A woman forcing an eight into a size six shoe.

The car on the right is inches away.
The one on the left is starting to sway.
The driver in front missed his turn.
For a quiet country road, I'm starting to yearn.

My patience is waning as the sun starts to set.
Those out of line are starting to fret.

The Impatient American

The lights shine in my eyes.
The rules I have learned are nothing but lies.

I shift gears and feign to the right.
The car on my left has moved in tight.
The man alongside yields a second or two.
I squeezed my eight into a size six shoe.

Hazem drives as if he is escaping from a holdup with New York's finest in pursuit. I told him to slow down; he increased his speed. It was dark; he was driving without lights. I kept asking him to turn them on because I wanted to be able to find my way back to the airport when I left for the States in the morning. Hazem paid no attention.

A few drivers had their lights on, but most did not. There were two lanes in each direction, but three cars abreast on each side, traveling one hundred klicks (*Kilometers*) an hour, fighting for position.

Whoever survives wins. I wrote off being ignored by Hazem to the Arabic-English and braced myself for the ride to the hotel. We passed the Sheraton, Hilton, and a half-dozen other brand names. It was dark. Hazem continued, and then pulled off the main road into a side street leading to a shabby part of town and parked in front of a hotel that had seen better days. Options were limited; mine was to check in and get some sleep.

I assumed the rest of the world worked the same hours I did. I wanted to get settled at the office. I told Hazem to pick me up at eight;"

"Yes, Mr. Pat, *Inshallah*."

Now, about the word *inshallah*, and without the intention of making light of the Muslim religion. It is a God thing. It means *if God wills it.*

I never figured out what they all tried to win, but after I started driving, I joined the game. I always tried to win, too; the slightest hesitation could have meant spending time in a hospital.

On a scale of one to ten, terrorists were a low priority. Driving is the most dangerous part of living in the Middle East. There is no courtesy or quarter given to living things. If there are two lanes, they make it three. Nobody pays attention to traffic lights, even when they do work, which is seldom. People drive one hundred klicks an hour dodging trash, pedestrians, donkeys, and horses pulling carts.

When it was picked up, Garbage was picked up by Kids.

Wrecks abound! Most drivers do not use their lights at night. I asked. Why? It wears out the battery. They also ignore one-way streets. As I established new driving habits, patience was the secret, but controlled rage was the reality. After I started driving and no longer had to gauge Hazem's reactions, I felt safer and less confined. The car the Egyptian company gave me had dozens of dents; no one noticed occasional new ones.

My teenage son would have loved it, just as I would at sixteen. There were no rules, just survive. No one notices if it means driving on the sidewalk or the wrong way down a one-way street. Most police were on foot or in a tower at the corner of an intersection. If you committed a traffic violation, I have not got a clue what that might be; the police write down your license number and issue the car a ticket. When it comes time to renew the registration, the owner pays all the fines at once.

Driving is not the only challenge for an American in Cairo. I take certain necessities for granted that are missing in most of the Middle East, which causes an American on assignment grave discomfort. I thought toilets and toilet paper were basic and have never considered them a real issue. *Now, folks, it is ingrained. I call a toilet a toilet.*

A toilet in Egypt is called a *shatafa*. In Egypt, *squat,* use your immigration for a squat toilet*, handles on the side walls, and a pan you squat over,* and sit-down toilets are sometimes available. The Western sit-down is more common; that is where it ends. Most *shatafas* are designed with a metal tube that focuses on the user's anus that sprays water, think *bidet*. Most four and five-star restaurants and hotels have facilities with these basic items.

Toilet paper, well…, that is an issue all its own. When you find it, whoever manufactured it in Egypt glued the last flap to the roll with a wallpaper brush. By the time you separate a handful, you are down to the core. That can be frustrating when you are in a hurry to finish the paperwork and another tourist is banging on the door who will blame you for the shreds of paper scattered on the floor, and the empty spool.

Those of us who lived in Cairo learned local customs. If you have a good sense of feel, there is a valve on the toilet. Just hope your arms are long enough to reach it without getting off the seat. That is, if you have the courage to sit on the seat and you are not trying to balance yourself while holding your pants off the floor and away from the last guy's shitty aim. Then again, many times, that is not a problem because there is no seat.

Squat or sit down; either way, if you find the valve handle and it works, be sure you are in a comfortable position because you get a first-class ass washing. That is unless the last foreigner managed to get some of the paper off the roll. If they did, it is usually stuck on the piece of pipe you cannot see, and it sprays water everywhere except where you need it. Then, instead of your shit on your ass, you have someone else's used paper plastered all over your backside.

After you manage to clean yourself up, which is probably why the Arabs think the left hand is unclean, you have to rely on the drip-dry method. If you are not prepared, it can be embarrassing when you sneak back into the dining room looking like you have just sat down in a bucket of water.

Typical Arab laborer's Dress.

Locals had their solution. It is a matter of dress. Many of the local outfits look like a nightgown. The correct name is a thobe, an ankle-length, long-sleeve garment worn chiefly by men in the Middle East, which allows some to squat and shit anywhere they please.

I refused to wear traditional clothes, so I had to devise my method of solving the paper shortage. I made it a point to steal napkins off dining room tables whenever I had the opportunity. I am not the only foreigner who thought of the idea, which could explain why most dinner napkins in restaurants are the size of an American cocktail napkin.

Oh! By the way, sometimes the water does not work, and there are no napkins on the tables. After the reaction an expat's body has to the food in Egypt, many of us do not have time to check for necessities. So, most expats make sure to keep their laundry up to date.

Chapter 3

Scheduling anything in Egypt is a complicated process, even if you only have to deal with local laws and customs. It is nearly impossible if you are trying to coordinate your work with an office on the West Coast of the U.S. when the coordinator does not give a shit.

Friday is a Muslim holiday; Saturday and Sunday are Christian holidays. There is a ten-hour time difference between Cairo and the home office in Portland, Oregon. I could not reach anyone by phone on Monday until after six p.m., Cairo time, which is eight a.m. Tuesday in Portland.

My contract said I worked eight to five, which left Tuesday and Wednesday to try to get something done because, on Thursday, everybody was getting ready for the long weekend. The home office never figured out the problem.

I tried to explain to Cesar that today is my Friday, which is his Thursday, and tomorrow is my Saturday, which is his Friday. He will be having breakfast; I will be having dinner. I will be going to bed when he is ordering lunch, and I will be having breakfast about the time he crawls in bed.

Language is also a problem for an American in Egypt. Not just Arabic; for me, that was easy. The contract the OMC signed with the Egyptian military requires English-speaking representatives. That seems plain enough; rules are rules. I simply ignore Arabic when it comes to my project.

It is the English that is upsetting. The British have been in Cairo for over two hundred years. Trust me, U.S. English and British English may spell and sound alike, but they sure as shit do not mean the same.

If I wanted a lift they pointed me to the elevator. If I asked for a tablet, they brought me a pill. If I said I was sick, they would think I was tired. If I were to ask for a rubber, I would get an eraser. If I knocked you up, I rang your doorbell. My mate is my friend. If I said I was pissed, they thought I meant drunk.

When it came to the Egyptians, after each day, when nothing, or at the most, little was done, someone would tell me *we had not wasted one second of tomorrow*. Now…, *think about it*; that makes sense and is true.

A devout Muslim's relationship with Allah is the driving force of all things. Muslims are required to pray five times a day. The favorite expression in the Arab world is "Momkin bookra *inshallah*." (*Tomorrow, if Allah (God) wills it.)* How do you argue with someone on their knees who needs permission from God to do your bidding?

I never knew when prayer time was. It was never the same. Someone told me it was according to where the moon was each night, where it was the night before, or where it might be after tomorrow. In the end, it did not seem to make much difference when prayer time was. It seemed to be whenever I wanted somebody in the Egyptian organization to do something or when I was winning an argument.

****

After Hazem dropped me off I sent a telex to Ceasar telling him I had arrived and was checked in. When the desk clerk returned, he told me they had misplaced the key to my room. It took a while; by then it was 10:30.

I had been sitting upright since I left Washington, DC, three days earlier. I was ready for a shower and bed. The room was a mess; it had not been cleaned, and the toilet seat was missing. It took another two hours to find me a room that had been cleaned that day and had a toilet seat, but hot water was still an issue. Whatever, I was too fucking worn out to care, I crashed.

I was expecting him at eight. Hazem arrived the next morning at 10:30 and gave me some excuse, and then:

"Where can I drive you?"

I was dumbfounded, absolutely fucking dumbfounded! I am a product of the times. Let us deal with this upfront. Sometimes I just cannot control myself. However, devout Muslims strongly object to what is considered foul language and are familiar with American euphemisms. In America today, the f-word can be very hurtful, offensive, mean, or vulgar. In adults' conversations and certain situations, it can be a comic relief, a colorful method of expressing frustration, surprise, astonishment, or a friendly exclamation. You did not walk in my shoes; get used to it.

"The office, Hazem, where the fuck else!"

I was pissed; he was two and a half hours late. Hazem paused and shrunk back as if I had slapped him. I remembered Hazem's parting comment when I told him to pick me up at eight. "*Yes, Mr. Pat, inshallah.*" I did not understand the *inshallah* bit at the time. It was not Hazem's fault, God was busy.

I do not speak much Arabic, but I never heard devout Muslims who speak Arabic-English swear or use foul language, and since it is always up to Allah, they never accept blame. On the other side of the scale, they seldom raise their voice unless they are chanting in the tower of a mosque or condemning America for insulting Allah. I did not realize it then, but I soon learned that when I swore or raised my voice in anger, it was an instant turn-off. I cooled down and tried a novel approach.

"Hazem, you are two and a half hours late. Please, take me to the office."

"The office is closed, Mr. Pat."

"You have got to be fucking kidding me!"

Thought: *So much for resolve. I had told Hazem to call me Patrick or Pat. The Mr. Pat thing was beginning to drive me nuts. I was beginning to feel it condescending.*

"You're early, Mr. Pat."

I instinctively looked at my watch. I had to think about how I would respond without interjecting my real attitude.

"Early, Hazem? It's almost eleven. Is it some sort of holiday?"

"We prepare for Muhammad's birthday, Mr. Pat."

Muhammad was an Arab religious, social, and political leader and the founder of Islam.

I believed that although not all Muslims are terrorists, the majority of terrorists are Muslim. Muhammad had something to do with the religion; other than that, I was clueless about Islam.

Dr. Osmond, Cesar's partner, told Hazem to send a message to postpone my arrival until the following week. The message arrived while I was at the Paris airport.

The birthday thing was over my head. It was not a holiday in the States. I told Hazem to take me to the COE's office in Madi, a Cairo suburb. Hazem pulled out into traffic for the 40-klick trip.

I did not have the courage to sit in the front seat. Sitting in the back, I tried to adjust to Cairo drivers' habits. Hazem was in the game, constantly poised to breed his mini car to an assortment of donkey carts, cars, buses, and trucks pulling into traffic without looking.

After the introductions, I visited with Tom, the COE CO I would be working with on the project. He spent the next hour giving me a rundown on the Egyptian players. He said I would not find Egypt on par with the States when it came to organization, but he felt that with a little cooperation on both sides, we could get the project finished in the time stipulated in the contract.

I asked Tom to describe the other players, but he passed. He said I would soon become acquainted with them myself. He thought I should form my own opinions. He did not want to influence me adversely. The word, *adversely,* slipped in at the end of the conversation. I started to ask, but I let it slide. I wrote the players' names in my diary, and we adjourned our first meeting.

As I was leaving, Tom asked me if I liked to fish and then told me how good fishing was in the Red Sea; it took an hour. I mentioned where I was staying and asked him if he could recommend a clean, reasonable hotel in Heliopolis near the office.

Tom called his secretary. She made reservations for me at the Sonesta Hotel, where Tom had breakfast a few times a week. The Sonesta was a clean three-star hotel, but it was a little over my budget.

When Hazem dropped me off that afternoon, I asked if the office would be open the next day. He told me it would, but no one would be in until after 11:00. I told him I liked to start my day at eight and asked him to get me a key to my office and, this time, to pick me up at 7:45. He agreed, *inshallah*.

By the time I checked out of Ceasar's budget hotel and into the Sonesta, it was 9:30 p.m. The Sonesta was clean, the staff pleasant, and the food was close to edible.

I sent Cesar a telex telling him I had relocated, why, and to where. By then, it was midnight. Ceasar sent me back a telex asking what the room rate was and reminded me I had an allowance; by then, I was asleep.

Hazem showed up at 11:00, which was okay because I overslept and did not wake up until after ten. When we arrived at the office he showed me to a desk with no phone. I asked if he had a key, his answer:

"I will have one after tomorrow, inshallah."

"What does that mean, Hazem?"

"We are out of spare keys, Mr. Pat."

Hazem left. At 12:30, an old man and Sarha, a woman whom I believed to be a secretary, arrived. They were not expecting me. We got acquainted with a few hand signals. The old guy turned out to be Abraham. He was in his seventies. He made tea, which was his job. The tea guy brought me tea; Sarha ignored me.

Hazem's brother, Hatem, arrived at about four. Hatem was my go-between with the Egyptian Army. He told me he had set up a meeting with a General Sayer and that he would have Hazem pick me up at the hotel in the morning at eight, *inshallah*.

The Impatient American

General Sayer was in charge of the military base where we would build the computer center. We needed passes to get through the gate. I assumed that was prearranged.

I have not got a clue what happened to Hazem. Hatem's driver showed up the next morning at 9:15 and took me to the office. Hatem arrived at 10:30 and, like Hazem, provided an English-Arabic explanation of why he was late. I mentioned the meeting with General Sayer. It was canceled. Dr. Osmond, the owner of the Egyptian half of the JV, wanted me to meet him and the staff.

Hatem disappeared, and Dr. Osmond was delayed. I sat at my desk for two hours, fuming until Hatem returned. We spoke for a few minutes; he told me he had set a meeting with General Aziz for 8:30 the next day, and if it were okay with me, he would have a driver pick me up at the hotel at eight.

I looked at my notes. General Aziz was a new player. Hatem told me the day before that we would meet with General Sayer. I wrote it off to the Arabic-English thinking things were improving. General Aziz would be in charge of the computer center. It could not be anyone from the JV. I assumed eight was General Aziz's idea. Someone in Cairo worked the same hours I did. I was looking forward to the meeting.

The driver arrived the next morning at 9:30 and drove me to the office. Hatem arrived at 10:30. I was managing to contain it, *barely*. I mentioned that I was under the impression we were to meet with General Aziz, and that we were late. Hatem told me the General rescheduled the meeting, and then he abruptly left my office. He did not tell me when. I was too pissed off to stop him and ask.

A half-hour later, Hatem returned and led me to an office to introduce me to the man in charge.

"Ah, Mr. Pat, it's good to meet you, but you're early."

I glanced at my watch; it was almost two. I let it slide while Dr. Osmond and Hatem carried on a 30-minute conversation in Arabic. It was apparent Dr. Osmond was not happy; I butt in.

"Dr. Osmond."

Dr. Osmond appeared irritated. He turned from Hatim and settled in his chair.

"What is it, Mr. Pat?"

"The Corps of Engineers wants a schedule; I must visit the site and meet with General Aziz."

"We have a contract, the schedule is already set, and ten percent was due when you arrived in Egypt."

I thought it was an interesting introduction. It was an $11 million project. The contract called for a 10% release when the company was mobilized in Egypt. $1.1 million was a lot of money for a plane ticket and a few nights in a hotel.

Dr. Osmond and Ceasar interrupted mobilization to mean my arrival. Cesar had billed the COE in advance. The COE responded, telling them the pay estimates would have to come through me and the Cairo COE office.

"Yes, Dr. Osmond, I realize that, but my arrival in Egypt is just part of it. I may get them to release a small portion, but mobilization means the project security fence, ours, and the COE's offices set up, equipment on site, and ready to start the site work. If you want to get paid, the COE wants a revised schedule with milestones tied to a budget and a breakdown of costs for mobilization."

Hatim had interpreted the documents for Dr. Osmond. Dr. Osmond sidetracked into a heated conversation with Hatim. A few minutes later, two men entered the room and joined the fray. There was more Egyptian excitement.

On that note, most of Dr. Osmond's employees are relatives. Ten minutes into their conversation Dr. Osmond abruptly sent them from the room. He sat silently for a moment. After one last brisk word to Hatim, he turned to me. It was apparent he was livid, but he was calm. He just sat there.

"Doctor Osmond, I need to get on-site and meet with General Aziz."

"We will meet with General Aziz, inshallah, Mr. Pat."

"I'm sorry; I'm working on my Arabic, Doctor Osmond. The word, inshallah, what does that mean?"

"If Allah wills it, Mr. Pat."

"You mean God?"

"Yes, Mr. Pat."

He was dead serious! Thought: *Really, how the fuck do I check with God?*

"Okay? When will you be available."

"After tomorrow, inshallah."

Thought, *What the fuck? Someday, after tomorrow, if it's okay with God.*

"I'm sorry, Dr. Osmond, what does that mean?"

"Ah, Mr. Pat, I'm busy tomorrow."

Thought: *I was getting the point. What Dr. Osmond means is. It is my country, asshole. Do not fucking bother me with this shit, my nephew will deal with it, and your only job is to get us paid.*

The two men returned with a stack of papers. Cesar's name was mentioned, so I assumed it was the contract between Dr. Osmond's company and Cesars. I was left out while Dr. Osmond was yapping with his nephews in Arabic. It would be twenty minutes and often happened with all the Egyptian players.

As for me, I sat twiddling my thumbs while they cut their deals in Arabic. However, it is about patience. You are invited to join the class, and the first lesson is to cool down before you sound off. I waited until the men left the room.

"Let's plan on Friday, Dr. Osmond.'

"This is Egypt, Mr. Pat. Friday is our holy day; I'll be at the mosque. Cesar told me you would bill the Corps when you arrived."

Shit….! Back to the money thing. I brought the subject up with Tom at our first meeting. As far as the COE was concerned, the only costs incurred to date were my plane ticket and expenses. Tom would not deal with processing an invoice for a few thousand dollars.

"Dr. Osmond, the Core of Engineers and Caesar's offices are closed on Saturday; I'm off Sunday. I can probably talk the COE into releasing some money if they see some progress. But you and Cesar won't get a dime until we are on the site. What would be a good day to meet General Aziz?"

"After Saturday, inshallah."

Thought: *He is not listening; that would be Sunday; I am a Catholic; maybe I could find God. Bullshit....! Sunday was my day off. I had made plans and paid for the tour. It was becoming obvious that the weekend and time difference with the States would be an issue.*

"Dr. Osmond, I need to visit the site, but I can't do that until General Aziz and I meet. How about Monday?"

"Patience, Mr. Pat; you just arrived."

"Does Tuesday work?"

"Check my schedule with Sarha."

"Sarha doesn't speak English, Doctor Osmond.

Dr. Osmond gave me a stern look and then called Sarha.

"Yes, Mr. Pat, I will be here Tuesday, inshallah."

"Will ten work?"

"Yes, inshallah."

Dr. Osmond dismissed me from his mind and lapsed into an Arabic conversation with his nephews.

When I arrived in Cairo, I did not know the rules; I did not ask. Caesar did not know the rules either, but like the Muslims, he prayed all the time, so maybe God would intervene.

I was under the impression that Dr. Osmond and I had settled on a date. Whether the General and God would agree was still up in the air. I put it out of my mind when four men entered the room and joined the conversation.

I never fully understood what inshallah meant. In this case, Dr. Osmond meant I set a date, he agreed, and they would show up if it were okay with God. Dr. Osmond and General Aziz had both agreed, inshallah.

I arrived for the meeting ten minutes early. God had been busy and had not gotten back to General Aziz. Dr. Osmond was in London.

Dr. Osmond returned a few days later. I was pissed but tried not to show it. He introduced me to three of his nephews. They were the engineers assigned to the project.

Mohammad spoke a little Arabic-English. He left after the introduction and would show up at the site now and then. The other two disappeared; I never saw either of them again. Hatim had also disappeared.

****

Name consistency in this book.

Not that it matters, but 200 million - 1 out of 10 Muslims are named Mohammad, meaning 'praiseworthy' or 'commendable.' The name has its ties to the founder of Islam—the prophet Muhammad.

****

"Dr. Osmond, I need to meet with General Aziz."

"Ah, Mr. Pat, General Aziz and I met yesterday."

The son of bitch! Self-control was becoming an issue, but I managed.

"It was a we thing, Dr. Osmond."

"You were invited, Mr. Pat. Sarha said you were busy, but Malish (*no problem*), we worked it out.

"Worked what out? And, no! I wasn't invited."

"Sarha left you a message."

"Dr. Osmond, Sarha doesn't speak or write English."

"Ah, Mr. Pat, you're in Egypt. You must work on your Arabic."

Resigned: sitting…., forehead resting on my hand; regaining control.

"Dr. Osmond, what did you work out with General Aziz?"

Mohammad and Hatim had reentered the office. It seemed everyone agreed. To what? I did not have a clue.

Dr. Osmond and Hatim abruptly got up and left the room. Hatim left me a note, this time in English. He rescheduled the meeting but did not say when.

I heard about security problems at the military bases in Egypt from British expats at the hotel bar. I could not locate Hatim. I caught Dr. Osmond in the hall and asked about security and my getting on the base without a pass. Dr. Osmond was unconcerned; Hatim would work out security clearances.

Ceasar's telex had been out of order since I changed hotels. Text, email, and Zoom were years away. Snail mail took two weeks. DHL and FedEx were available, but in traffic, it was an hour and a half to the drops.

I had been out of contact with the home office since I left the States. It was obvious something would have to give. That meant me. I changed my schedule to Sunday through Thursday. Convincing someone in the home office would be another issue.

Caesar was a saintly man who would not abide foul language or, even worse, take the Lord's name in vain. Not having texting and email with an instant send key was a blessing; it gave me time to compose, cool off, recompose, and edit.

Fax machines were invented in 1964 but were a rarity in Egypt. With 100% duty, they were expensive. Dr. Osmond did buy one once I told him it would be duty-free, but it needed modern paper. Paper was expensive. When one of the staff used some for scratch, he had Sarha lock it in a closet and dole it out, one fucking piece at a time. When they ran out, it took a while to convince the accountant to buy more; he was gone and would return after tomorrow, inshallah.

I needed support from the home office, and a change of schedule. Dr. Osmond disappeared, and I could not convince Sarha to give me the paper without the accountant's permission. I tried the phone, but Cesar would not pick it up. Ceasar would be upset, but I bit the bullet and paid 50 LE to send a fax from the hotel.

Cesar: Please explain to the U.S. staff the time difference with Egypt. Ask them to pick a time between 4 p.m. and 6 p.m., their time, which is 6 a.m. to 8 a.m. my time, on Mondays, Tuesdays, or Wednesdays, for a weekly conference call.

PS / By the way, has Don ordered the anchor bolts; it will take time to clear them through customs.

Caesar passed it on to Don, the stateside Project Manager. Worth noting that Don and I both applied for my position in Egypt. Don was pissed; two days after I boarded the plane, his summons arrived; the judge raised his alimony.

Dr. Osmond saw that there was paper in the fax machine for incoming, but the drawer was locked. I borrowed some paper from the COE and locked it in my desk. Don's answer arrived the next morning. At least now we were in contact.

Mr. Roelle.

The office opens Monday through Friday at 8 a.m. and closes at 5 p.m. Pacific Time. We're paying you to work it out.

Buy the fucking anchor bolts in Egypt. Don't bother me with this shit.

Caesar wants to know when we're going to get paid.

Don.

Dr. Osmond summoned me when he arrived in the office. I set the fax aside, knowing I was on my own. I was also under the impression that Dr. Osmond, Hatim, and I had settled on a new date for a meeting with the Generals. Whether the Generals and God would agree was still up in the air. I put it out of my mind when four men entered the room, and Dr. Osmond took a detour. They disappeared; I went back to my office.

I lost track. We visited General Aziz after the second or third scheduled meeting. It was just a social call, so there was no hurry. They wanted to get the players together to introduce me to the Egyptian Army personnel.

I was emphatic with Hatem, telling him to make sure we had security clearance before arriving. I understood that Hatem cleared the red tape, and we were expected. When we approached the entrance to the base, the guard at the gate leveled his rifle and told me to get out of the car. He looked fifteen years old and nervous.

It appeared Hatim's papers were in order. He left me in the guard's custody to sort the problem out with General Aziz. Hatem was gone twenty minutes. The soldier signaled me to follow him to a room in the guard shack.

Thought: *Oh! My God! When did collecting trash become a hobby? And the smell! Grandpa's hog pen on the farm was cleaner.*

The guard did not speak English. He chirped a little, smiling while pointing, I thought, to a door in the back.

"Shay?" he said. I assumed it was a toilet. *Now, you readers need to keep track.* To an Egyptian, toilet meant the bathroom, and I did need to pee.

"Okay," I said and started toward the door. Oh….! Shit….! Not me, the room. The Jews had been kicking their ass for years; it explained it. Now I knew why they called a room a toilet. These guys could hit everything in the room but the toilet. I could hold it; I turned around. The guard was squatting on the floor, staring in my direction. My hand signals, and loud, no!

He looked disappointed and pointed to the middle of the room, where he had placed a chair with the springs exposed. This was another language barrier. I thought he was offering me a place to sit; it did not look comfortable, but the rifle leaning against the wall convinced me.

"Qahaw." He said. Now…., pause for a moment and visualize the circumstance. You would recognize the look if you have ever had a good dog. There is a toy at your feet that you refuse to pick up. The dog persists, paces a little, kind of pleading.

My yellow lab, Brandy, always brought me sticks to throw for her to chase. If I dropped one, she would never give up. Brandy would tilt her head and give me that look. No matter what I was doing or how busy, I always set everything aside and picked up the fucking stick.

"Okay," I said and walked to the chair. He left for a few minutes, returning with a Colman camp stove, a rusty can of water, a small filthy bag of what turned out to be coffee, and two what looked like shot glasses.

Time was passing; I was curious. The water was simmering. He filled the can to the rim with coffee, mixed it until it was sludge, filled the glasses, and offered me Qahaw.

Shay is tea. It is a tradition in Egypt to offer your guest tea, which I misunderstood when we first entered the room. Qahaw is the word for Turkish coffee. Six-parts grounds, one part water; you strain it through your teeth. I never developed a taste for the delicacy. He looked around, I poured it into the wet spot on the floor the guards were using for a urinal. A half-hour later, a soldier came and escorted me to General Aziz's office.

More culture shock. The grounds and the building I entered gave me cause to think of the Los Angeles slums after the Watts riots.

"Ah, Mr. Pat, welcome to Cairo."

The *Ah, Mr. Pat* thing was beginning to irritate me. General Aziz was pleasant; he offered me a cup of shay and then asked how I liked Cairo. I was somewhat in control of my senses; I did not feel I should insult a two-star General the first day we met.

"Egypt is charming, General. But I understood I was expected, why the delay at the gate?"

"Colonel Sabin was to meet you; he was doing his morning prayers."

Morning prayers? That was a new one! I let it pass. The General and I carried on a typical Arabic-English conversation I was getting used to. I was getting bored, and my patience waned when the General's English improved.

I would realize later that English was a second language for many Egyptians assigned to the project. If they were not flustered, did not want to confuse me intentionally, or were not flat-out lying, they spoke it pretty damned good.

"Ah, Mr. Pat, would you like to see the construction area?"

Hallelujah! He knew the reason I came to Egypt.

"General Aziz, it would be a pleasure if you would show me around."

"Ah, Mr. Pat, it's time for my prayers. Colonel Sabin will show you to the site, inshallah."

Colonel Sabin was not on Tom's list. I wondered who the new player was while I sipped the second glass of shay the General ordered for me before he left. Twenty minutes later, my patience ebbed. I waited another 30 minutes until one of Genera Aziz's aids could round up Colonel Sabin.

God agreed 30 minutes later. General Aziz returned from his prayer room at the same time Colonel Sabin made his appearance. General Aziz made the introductions and told me the Colonel would be my contact with the Egyptian Army personnel assigned to the site for the project's duration. Colonel Sabin held out his hand.

"Saeidt biliqayiy, min fadlik atabieni." He said.

"General Aziz, I'm sorry, I don't speak Arabic."

"Ah, Mr. Pat, Colonel Sabin doesn't speak English. I have ordered him to learn. Perhaps you could meet him halfway."

"Sure thing, General, at least we're starting even."

The COE told me it was an English-speaking contract. So far, the only people I have met who spoke English were the people from the COE: Dr. Osmond, Hazem, Hatem, and General Aziz. Hatem was supposed to be my interpreter, but I had not seen him since he left me in the custody of the guard at the gate. A few minutes later, Hatem entered the room.

"Mr. Pat, how are things going?"

"Not worth a shit, Hatem, where the fuck have you been?"

"Kan waqt alsalat." He said.

"Hatim, in English, please!"

Hatim could see I was upset. Now, it was his prayer time; he turned and left the room.

I arrived at the gate almost three hours earlier. Twenty minutes later, Hatem returned and said something about getting my security pass sorted out. I told him it would have been better if he thought about that when I mentioned it the day before.

We finally left General Aziz's office. Colonel Sabin led us through the Army base to the site. I was under the impression we would build the Computer Center on the same base I entered two hours earlier. I also thought Hatim was referring to the security pass for General Aziz's base. I was wrong on both counts; it was becoming a habit.

As we meandered through the base, I tried comparing it to military installations in the U.S. It was a brief exercise, perhaps, modern-day Central East City of Los Angeles. There was trash everywhere: rotting bags of garbage, dismantled vehicles littered the ground, and parts of military hardware were scattered throughout the area.

The buildings were in complete disrepair. Most windows were cracked. Someone had carelessly nailed cardboard in places where the glass had fallen out of frames. Fungus covered walls where leaking plumbing pipes were hanging from buildings. Shallow ponds at the base of the buildings reminded me of a neglected sewage treatment plant. Thick sludge had formed, and fermenting liquid was seeping back into the building's basements.

A group of men were bathing in a shallow pond scraped out in an area where one of the overhead pipes was leaking in a slow but steady shower.

The base was crowded with soldiers, mostly young, in their teens. The uniforms were rags of cotton cloth in the military gray-green color of the Middle East; fitting clothes was not an issue.

I followed Colonel Sabin to a gate, picking my way around human shit splattered on fractured concrete paths next to the pissed-on wall enclosing the base. The gate was locked from the other side. No one seemed surprised. The guard positioned himself in front of us, barring the way with his assault rifle. We stood around for a few minutes, looking at one another.

I was more than uncomfortable when Colonel Sabin pushed the guard aside, started pounding on the gate, and yelled at someone on the other side, more Egyptian excitement! Hatem turned to me.

"Mr. Pat, we will have to come back tomorrow."

General Sayer's guards would not let us in. The building on the other side of the wall housed the Egyptian Technical Institute, which General Sayer, another two-star general, was in charge of. The guard wanted to see security papers from that base.

"No, Hatim, let's go see General Aziz."

After a few minutes of heated English-Arabic, ignoring Hatem, the Colonel, and the guard's protests, I headed back to General Aziz's office. I did not bother to knock; General Aziz was expecting me.

"Ah, Mr. Pat, we have a security problem."

"General Aziz, what's going on?"

"Patience, Mr. Pat. Your papers are for this base. General Sayer wants you to fill out security papers for the Technical Institute and return them tomorrow."

I did not have a clue. I was under the impression we would be building on General Aziz's base. I took the inch-thick stack of papers, thinking Hatem and I needed to have a heart-to-heart.

"What time tomorrow, General?"

"Malish, (No problem) any time, you are always welcome, Mr. Pat."

"Is ten okay, General?"

"Ten is fine, Mr. Pat, inshallah."

I steamed back to the car, the Cairo traffic, and the office. When I exited the car, I handed Hatem the papers.

"Hatem, please fill these out and sort it out with the General before we get to the base tomorrow."

It was almost five. I walked to the office door, which was locked. I turned back to catch Hatem before he drove off. I waved, but he ignored me and pulled into traffic leaving me steaming in the 100-degree heat.

I cooled a bit during the four-block walk to the hotel, *mentally*. By the time I reached the hotel, sweat was running out of every pore.

I did not see Hatim again for a week, and I did not hear from anyone in the company for a week.

Chapter 4

After a day in the heat, I was looking forward to a shower, but I stopped in the bar to cool down. My mood settled as the sweat dried.

My stomach had not adjusted to the diet or the water. Most of it gives a newcomer liquid shits. My stomach was growling. I had not eaten that day; I was hungry. As far as the food in Egypt is concerned, I did not recognize most of it, but I knew I had to get accustomed and had been experimenting. The first week I learned ice cream is not bad if the milk had been boiled first, which the Sonesta did.

Hot soup appeared to be safe. If you are not fussy about what is in the soup and it is hot, soup and ice cream is a safe dinner for a beginner at the better hotels in Cairo.

You might notice that I seldom mention restaurants other than those in hotels, at least not those owned and operated by one of the locals. A word of advice: if you visit a Middle Eastern country, stick with the international hotel chains or be sure to pack a lot of Kaopectate.

The most exciting part of the day my first week was picking a place for dinner. There are countless international hotels in the area including the Sheraton, Marriott, and Hilton; each has a restaurant specializing in something different.

At the time, the Sheraton's specialty was German, the Hilton Italian, the Marriott Chinese, and what the Egyptians call American. They all had a buffet, but they were Egyptian in content, and except for the centerpiece, they all appeared to be the same.

I was struggling to find enough napkins, so I gave up on the buffets and returned to my favorites. European coffee, strong and thick, the only way the Egyptians brew it. Steak, if you do not care what animal they just butchered, and vegetables, if they had skin on them, like tomatoes or cucumbers that you can peel yourself. Whole fruit, also peeled at your table, is always good, as is ice cream.

My Local Butcher Shop

After dinner, I fell asleep, dreading my second trip to the Army base. I was dressed by six. I was the only one in the dining room. There was coffee and pastries on a side table. By eight, I started to wonder where everyone was.

I had complained to Dr. Osmond about the office hours; he had assured me mine would be open by eight every day. When Hatim's driver did not show up by 9:30, I walked the few blocks. I tried the locked door. There was not any indication of when they would return, so I headed back to the hotel, taking a different route.

Shepherds herding sheep and goats were milling in the streets around carts filled with chickens in wood cages. I had seen a few of each in the outskirts on my trip to Maadi the first day I was in Cairo, but none in the city.

When I arrived back at the hotel, a set of car keys and a note that the car was in the lot were in my mailbox. There was an explanation *in Arabic*. I resigned myself. I would deal with Hatim when he showed up.

I did not have a clue where to go from there. It was after ten p.m. Portland time. I called Cesar's emergency phone. He was getting ready for bed and did not appreciate my call. Apparently, he heard from his Egyptian partner. He was aware I was having difficulty communicating with Dr. Osmond.

"I'm getting ready for bed, and this is costing four dollars a minute. Doctor Abboud says you need to learn patience and some Arabic. I'm paying you. Deal with it."

Click…., end of discussion. Baffled, I stood at the desk with the phone in my hand. Dr. Abboud was a player I had not met. I did not understand the attitude of either Ceasar or his Egyptian partners. There had to be more to this. After the call, I reviewed the prequalification Cesar submitted to the COE. It was enlightening. I dug deeper.

Cesar was born in the Philippines. In 1898, the Philippine Republic claimed sovereignty based on its declaration of independence from Spain.

The U.S. claimed the Philippines when Spain ceded its colony of the Philippines to the U.S. in the Treaty of Paris at the end of the Spanish-American war. In 1899, the United States' drive to extend its influence across the Pacific resulted in clashes between the Americans and Filipino revolutionaries. The Philippine-American War lasted three years. As many as 200,000 civilians died from violence, famine, and disease. Ceasar's father was the lone survivor of a rice and sugar dynasty that traced its roots to the 16th century.

Serving its self-interest, the U.S. gave the Philippines economic aid in return for 99-year leases for military bases and free trade privileges to help get the ravaged nation back on track. Cesar held title to a substantial tract of land leased to the U.S.

Cesar built a company during the reconstruction process after WW2, during which time he worked as a subcontractor for American companies. The money was in running the show, not in leftovers from the Americans. Cesar now maintains dual citizenship and an office in the States, which gives him the ability to work directly for the American government. As a minority, he was entitled to special considerations.

It was his first American Government contract offshore from the Philippines. Now Ceasar was running the show, or so he thought. Cesar had a full staff of managers and engineers in Manila but had not read the fine print when he bid on the Egypt project. I surmised he resented the clause in his contract that he had to hire Americans to run the Egypt project.

I returned to the coffee shop, thinking the word patience seemed to be the most common word in everyone's vocabulary. After reading Cesar's resume, I decided to try to exercise a little more of it.

A British expat was alone at a table and the only one in the dining room. English conversation had been scarce since I arrived. I picked a table next to him, hoping we might strike up a conversation. As I was sitting down, I asked him where everyone was. John introduced himself and invited me to join him. John was in Cairo to oversee the installation of new machinery in a bus factory thirty klicks from Cairo. He explained that it was the beginning of a religious Holiday.

"What Holiday?"

"It's the Prophet Muhammed's birthday. It's the Muslim's Christmas."

"Who the hell is Muhammad?"

I had to look it up myself. Muhammad was, according to Islam, the last prophet and the final messenger of Allah, Islam's

God. He was the founder of Islam and the proclaimer of the Qur'an, Islam's sacred scripture. The Qur'an is the driving force behind a devout Muslim's way of life.

The Muslim calendar relies on the movements of the moon. It has 354, sometimes 355 days, which is about 11 days shorter than the solar Gregorian calendar, which has 365 days.

Mawlid an-Nabi: Prophet Muhammad's birthday begins on a Monday evening and ends on a Tuesday, but with preparations and the effect lasts about seven days.

Eid-ul-Adha or Bakra Eid, also known as the *Festival of Sacrifice*, commemorates the act of sacrifice by Prophet Abraham, as in the Bible, and his willingness to offer his son as an act of obedience to Allah. For some followers of Islam, the date for Eid is based on the appearance of a new crescent moon rising above the horizon, which changes year to year. Eid-ul-Adha lasts four days, but once again, with preparations, the after-effect usually lasts about ten days.

Eid al-Fitr means *The Feast of Breaking the Fast*. The Fast is Ramadan, which recalls the revealing of the Qur'an to Muhammad and requires Muslims to fast from sunrise to sunset. Ramadan lasts 30 days and ends with a feast on the final day.

Of the three, Ramadan has the most effect on the daily life in Egypt. After 30 days of fasting from sunup to sundown and then partying all night, it takes months for some to transition back to a nine-to-five. Most in Egypt never do.

John also told me the reason there were so many sheep and goats on the streets was that Muslim tradition is to have them for their celebration dinners. Those who cannot afford a sheep or goat settle for chicken. They pick them out of flocks' shepherds bring into town and then butcher on the sidewalks at home.

"Not that I object to Christmas, but at least someone could have told me. How long does the holiday last?"

"In Egypt, a week, maybe ten days."

"You have got to be kidding?"

The telegram Hazem sent to Cesar informed him of the holiday, but Cesar neglected to pass on the information. Reflecting on it, I mellowed. If someone showed up on my doorstep in the States before Christmas and expected me to work through New Year's, I would probably ignore them, just as the Egyptians were ignoring me.

Plain and simple, Cesar needed me in Egypt to satisfy the COE and thought he would receive the first payment as soon as I arrived. He lied and ignored Dr. Osmond when he asked to delay my arrival.

Cesar did not have a clue. He's Catholic. However, he did know they would all be off for a holiday. I showed up eager and ready to go, oblivious to the country's culture. I was the prick as far as the Egyptian company was concerned.

I concluded it was my fault for taking the culture for granted, not the Egyptians who had neglected to explain it. John asked me what I planned for the holiday.

"Nothing, John. I didn't have a clue. I didn't come for a holiday. I have work to do."

"So do I; I came for two weeks and want to go home."

"When did you arrive?"

"April sixth."

"April? This is the middle of August."

"I know, this is Egypt, I hope to be finished by our Christmas."

Things were not any different for John than they were for me. My contract was for one year. I did not like the comparison, but I was not ready to deal with it at that moment.

I could not do anything about the holidays, but I am a fan of our Christmas. Since none of the Egyptians would be working and Ceasar did not seem concerned, I decided to make the most of it.

"John, I don't have anything planned. I have deadlines, but what the fuck, no one else is working. How about some sightseeing?"

"I'm game, where to first."

"I haven't a clue. Let's play it by ear. My car's in the lot, but I'm new here. You want to drive?"

"No thanks, I take taxis. Those guys know the rules."

We paid our bill, gathered our cameras, and headed for the car. John took one look at what the Egyptians had given me for transportation and turned back toward the hotel.

"John, do you speak Arabic."

"I have enough trouble with their brand of English. The bellhop tells them where I want to go."

"He's not here. Look, it's a piece of shit, but what the hell? Wouldn't it be better than trying to give directions to a taxi driver?"

"That's not a car. It's a wreck. I would rather walk the local area, there are some street shops a few klicks from the hotel."

I understood John's concern because I felt the same way. I told John I feel better driving a car that was already wrecked, so when, not if I pile it up, I will not have as much explaining to do. John would not budge. He was probably right; it would have been my first time driving in Cairo.

We headed for the business section of Heliopolis. When we turned the first corner, it was apparent that the taxis would be busy hauling goats and sheep. After a few blocks, we decided walking was not the answer. Women were butchering animals on sidewalks, and the blood mixing with sewage boiling from open manholes was affecting our stomachs.

As John stumbled, trying to step over some entrails a few stray cats were picking through, he mumbled something about the car.

"You ready to try the car?"

"Anything is better than this."

I was not sure what that was.

Everyone was celebrating the holiday; the main roads were deserted. Neither of us had driven in Cairo, but I thought I could follow a map to the Cheops Pyramids. After the first turn, the map was useless.

Most streets were unmarked. I circled the hotel three times. All sense of direction was gone. The rivers in the U.S. run north to south, east, or west. The Nile River runs south to north. The sun in Cairo appeared to come up in the west.

Language was a barrier. John had been in Cairo for four months; he was no better at it than I was. We never did find the Pyramids that day; we ended up at the Citadel, the largest Mosque in Egypt. It was one of the other places on the sightseeing list we picked up in the lobby of the hotel. We parked, paid the parking attendant a fee of two LE each, and approached the entrance.

The buildings on the Mosque grounds that were open to tourists had an English sign on the gate: *Closed for the Holidays*. We walked back to the parking area to find the attendant and get our money back; he was gone.

We had been wandering the streets for almost four hours. We gave up sightseeing for the day and left to find another map and someone who could give us proper directions.

The hotel staff was off celebrating Muhammad's birthday. John and I searched the lobby but could not find another map. The next day, we started by taking the first right turn in the road and following it.

John and I spent the next week wandering the side streets of Cairo and the surrounding villages. Although we stumbled upon places tourists do patronize, we found a great deal more than the tourists who take taxis or tour buses.

The culture shock was beyond imagination. Nothing could have prepared me for what I was to experience. Horses were pulling 20,000-pound loads up hills, and a half dozen people were sitting on the carts, adding to the load.

Count the bags– two horses - 22,000 lbs.

Egypt is a Muslim country trying to merge into modern day, while some still maintain seventh-century tradition. Old ways mingle with new. People in traditional dress scowled at those dressed in Western clothing.

Men kiss men when greeting and ignore women. Women kiss women and ignore men. Men and women were holding hands with members of their own sex. Both sexes showed little affection for the opposite sex but a great deal for their own.

Single Egyptian women are tolerated on the streets and in the shops but are not allowed to mingle socially with men outside their families. In the bazaars, women in traditional dress are ignored, while shopkeepers fawn over foreign women.

Due to two hundred years of colonial occupation, middle-class Egyptians despise the English and most other foreigners. The English on assignment treats Egyptians the same in return. Fundamental Muslims consider all English and American expats i*nfidel* intruders. *A person who does not believe in religion or who adheres to a religion other than one's own.*

I learned early on to avoid fundamental Muslim strongholds. When it comes to an infidel, there are two types of Muslims. One would put a gun to my head and pull the trigger if he thought he could get away with it. The second would pull the trigger no matter what.

Devout Muslims tolerate expats and tourists only because of the billions the U.S. keeps bribing them with, and the tourist dollars that keep local economies afloat.

There are few American expats in Egypt; there are thousands of British. The attitude of both the British and Americans seems universal: how stupid and unmotivated Arabs are.

I was new; it was a choice. At the time, it seemed to me that if the Egyptians did not need help from expats like me, we would not have had the high-paying jobs that allowed us a lifestyle of luxury in their world of poverty and indifference, which we chose to make our home.

I mentioned earlier that Egyptians are not Arabs. Although it may be true, only the Egyptians themselves make that distinction.

Iran is Persian, not Arab. The British and Americans assigned to Africa and the Middle East lump all Arabic-speaking people into one category: Arabs. It is a little conflicting at times.

Other than the occasional tourist, there are few white women in the Middle East. Most expat jobs are single status. When it can be found, housing to American or European standards is expensive. Most American and European women find the country filthy and socially unacceptable.

Most American men on extended tours were married to Asian women. Women born in poverty adjust better to the culture, and because of their darker skin, they are more acceptable to Muslim women on the street. Egyptian men treat Asian women more as servants than as equals.

Devout Muslims of both sexes treat white women as they would a prostitute. Some Muslim women will spit on any woman who shows too much skin. Some men will molest them when given the slightest opportunity, no matter how they dress.

Few places in the Middle East, outside the opulence of the elite's homes and international hotels, are clean or comfortable.

The weather in the suburbs surrounding Cairo is similar to Arizona's, but hotter and grossly polluted. On summer days in the desert near Cairo, 110 degrees is common, with days as high as 120.

The locals consider it a cool day if the temperature drops below 80. After a few months in the continuous heat, my body adjusted. I needed to wear a sweater when the temperature dropped below 70.

Religion is a way of life. Imams in Mosques chant prayers into microphones connected to outdoor loudspeakers five times a day. Prayer shatters the silence of early morning and drowns out the honking horns during the middle of the day.

Many Muslim men carry prayer rugs and kneel toward Mecca Province in the Hejaz region of western Saudi Arabia, the holiest city in Islam, during prayer time, wherever they happen to be.

One excuse I often heard for why the Egyptians were invariably late for meetings was that if they missed a specific prayer time, they must make it up before the next call to prayer.

My experience was that prayer time was usually when one of them was due for a meeting, or something was supposed to be finished at a specific time, when I was winning an argument, or I was pissed off.

A black callous on the forehead from beating their heads on the ground gives the enthusiastic believers away. They are also the first in a group to cross a busy street. They believe they will make it to the other side, inshallah.

Traffic and pedestrians in a city of twenty-two million where traffic rules are ignored are in constant conflict. It is a disaster in a Muslim country where life has little meaning. Many on foot dodging through 50 MPH traffic do not make it to the other side. I am sure they were there, but I cannot remember seeing an ambulance on the streets of Cairo.

Sometimes, relatives or authorities scrape them up right away. Relatives are hard to find in a community without working phones or an address on the body. Sometimes, they simply move them to the side of the road, and then the body disappears.

Known locally as the City of the Dead, Cairo's cemetery was seven klicks square and growing. The buildings were made of mud, brick, cardboard, or a combination of some or all.

I became acquainted with the cemetery, thinking it was simply another suburb of Cairo. I entered the area looking for a shop to buy cigarettes. As I drove through, beggars crowded around my car, something the military tries to control in Egypt where tourists congregate.

The City of the Dead was a melting pot crammed with refugees from Sub-Saharan countries, the poorest of the poor in Egypt. Military police avoided it. Expats and tourists made it a point to skirt the area. It was definitely a place where an infidel does not belong.

To most, reality is personal experience or simply what they want it to be based on exposure to their surroundings. I spent my first few weeks in Egypt, becoming familiar with a culture foreign to my experience.

It was impossible for me to accept the plight of the multitudes for what it is. When I reflect, I was reluctant to relate life as I saw it, because in telling it, it becomes real. Once I accepted that a Third World existed, I had to face the people in the confines of my ego. When I did, I wondered what twist of fate gave me the life I have and forced such misery on the subjugated masses surrounding me.

Most Americans refuse to accept the truth about the plight of those who reside in Third World countries. It is outside their realm of existence and has little or no effect on their lives.

The Third World exists within its own time limits, combining the poverty of the masses with the luxurious life of those in power. Life for multitudes beyond our borders is a reality that is no longer acceptable to me, but like most whose daily lives are unaffected, I have done nothing about it. Nonetheless, denying it is not going to change it.

John and I entered the City of the Dead by accident. We were returning from the Citadel on the day we found it open. I took a wrong turn; it was a common occurrence for me, at the time not worth getting too excited about. The first sign that something was amiss was the smell. It was unlike anything I have experienced in the West.

Think of *Someone's vomit, decaying garbage, raw sewage, and rotting flesh, then wash your clothes in it and wear them for a day or two.*

The traffic was unusually heavy, even for Cairo. As we turned the first corner, the reason for the congestion and the smell became obvious. A foul liquid was boiling out of manholes and running a foot deep in the street. People dodged traffic, crossing everywhere, but no one was paying attention to the sewage.

A school bus stopped to let the kids out; those crossing the street were wading to their knees. Donkey and horse-drawn carts were pulling their way through the deeper areas. Cars and buses crowded on higher shoulders. I rolled the window up to escape the spray from passing traffic, but then John and I were suffocating in a car without air conditioning.

The thermometer read 120, and although I was reluctant to roll the window down for fear of being drenched by cars traveling in the opposite direction, I had no other choice. I told John it was better than cooking in the heat. When we opened the windows, a spray of slime came from both directions.

The traffic jam grew worse as impatient drivers pulled out of line and blocked oncoming traffic. We waited it out for over an hour while factory workers and kids found their way home. There was no option to turn around and go back the way we came. We followed the main street, hoping it would lead us back to an area we recognized. In the end, the spray of muck mixed with wind blowing in from the desert had a cooling effect.

Shops and vendors lined the streets. Hundreds of thousands, mostly refugees from impoverished villages of Egypt, along with the migration of displaced refugees from Ethiopia, Sudan, and other unstable countries of Africa, had removed the residue and moved into tombs to set up housekeeping.

Police and military skirted the area. The Egyptian government simply cannot deal with the multitudes without having to annihilate them, which would be bad public relations for the Government of Egypt.

There is a higher concentration of expats in Cairo than in other heavily populated Third World countries because foreign governments fund military projects. That, combined with foreign aid, keeps Egypt's economy afloat, *barely*.

At the time, the U.S. and Russia were competing. Both countries provided equipment and training to the Egyptian army to maintain a military presence in the region. Since then, Russia has gone broke. A number of European countries and Japan have stepped up in an effort to maintain stability in the region.

I call it tacit approval. Most Americans, Europeans…., *Nuts, it is too long a list*. History proves that to many, *in every layer of society*, genocide is an acceptable method of dealing with disagreeable populations, or with those holding values they simply disagree with, some even within their borders.

Some, in every country, have been guilty at one time or another. Think *Indian tribes in America and the Jews in Germany.* At present, Egypt is too dependent on foreign aid and tourist dollars to take a chance that one of the local news correspondences might actually leave their hotel long enough to report the real news to the West. The Egyptian government decided it was better to ignore the problem and leave the people in the cemetery alone.

****

2024 - That has changed with time. Cairo's City of the Dead, a vast cemetery that has been used for more than a millennium, is now being destroyed to clear space for new highways. Authorities have already razed thousands of tombs and mausoleums as they carry out plans to build a network of multi-lane roads. What has or will happen to the multitudes living in the tombs is anybody's guess.

****

Those in the shops ignored the filth. Many were sitting at tables ankle-deep in sludge too thick to drink and too thin to plow. None of them paid attention, and they sat eating beans and bread or smoking water pipes filled with drugs to dull their senses.

The Egyptian Government denies drug use in Egypt just as they deny the filth, poverty, and rubbish piled in every corner of the country. I am not, but for those who are interested, drugs are easy to obtain. Expats approached me often, inviting me to join the party. Smoke shops were on every street. Opium was the drug of choice. Men gather in the shops to socialize just as some gather in taverns back home to drink beer and play pool.

The stench in the cemetery's air was nauseating. I could describe it when I was in Cairo because I experienced it a little each time I entered a congested area of the city. The smell was always fresh in my mind when I was in Egypt, but I have never experienced it back home; as the saying goes, out of sight, or in this case, *smell,* out of mind.

John and I returned to the hotel later than usual. The combination of sweat and whatever else splashed through the car windows stuck our clothes to our bodies. We were anxious for a shower before the dining room closed.

When we approached the desk to retrieve our room keys, we found that they had been misplaced. John and I joined other expats in the bar who were also locked out of their rooms, but the smell as we entered the room caused a few to request that we wait outside on the patio.

John and I eventually found our way to the Great Pyramids. The Cheops Pyramid is considered the last remaining of the Seven Wonders of the Ancient World. From the outside looking in, it is an amazing feat of engineering. I am not a tourist guide, but I suggest those visiting Cairo do their sightseeing from the outside and leave the crypt to the dead.

The entrance to the Cheops tomb is eighteen meters up from the base. The day I was there, the outside temperature was a blistering 100-degrees. A sloping corridor leads through the pyramid's interior masonry, penetrates the rocky soil on which the structure rests, and ends in an unfinished chamber.

I stretched and looked with expectations generated from reading about the opulence of Pharaohs who lived 6,000 years in the past. It was a stark stone room, ten meters square, with a pendant light bulb hanging above an open stone casket, twenty-five watts, so much for great expectations.

The 500-mile stretch of arable land that borders both sides of the Nile River covers approximately 200,000 sq miles, about Nebraska's size. It is home to over 50% of Egypt's population of over 114 million, mostly extremely poor people. Oh, and yes! Flies, billions and billions of flies, which expats refer to as the national bird of Egypt.

It is difficult to get used to because they crowd your ears, nose, and eyes. If you try to eat anywhere except in an air-conditioned room, you have to learn to time your fork and mouth as you brush flies from your food. One solution that helped was to let my hair and beard grow until they covered my face, ears, and the back of my neck.

Fly Resistant

John and I drove one afternoon to the project he was working on in the Tenth of Ramadan City. We arrived as the boab (*caretaker*) was preparing his afternoon meal; he insisted we join him. The meal consisted of flat, unsalted bread, soft-boiled eggs, and goat cheese.

The boab laid the food out on the bare ground. Flies covered the food, just as sand covered a beach. The boab did not seem to notice. When we excused ourselves, he simply smiled and offered his hand in friendship.

There is a great deal of camouflage in Egypt. I quickly became immune to the hustle of the vendors in the tourist shops and on the streets. I avoided areas frequented by foreign visitors, preferring back street shops and village bazaars.

Cairo was a city of twenty-two million; like most big cities of the world, *including those in America*, it had become a melting pot for the poverty-stricken.

I expected outlying suburbs and villages would be more affluent and perhaps cleaner; I was wrong. The landscape in all but a few of the small, oil-rich communities in the Middle East is the same everywhere, poverty and filth in the streets, indifference in the air.

Utilities: power, water, and sewers, where they do exist, are unreliable. Where they do not exist women wash their kids, clothes, and dishes in canals swollen from discharging waste of factories and settlements, then carry water home for cooking meals and brewing tea.

I had not seen a star or breathed clean air since I arrived. I had been in Cairo for over a month and told John I needed a change. Ismailia, on the banks of the Suez Canal, was an hour and a half's drive. There were no factories, the air was clean, and the hot breeze coming off the Sinai cooled itself as it crossed the Canal.

We had directions to the Etap hotel, which took us along back roads, more like cart paths and alleys. I left the highway and traveled a few meters until the clutter of rubbish blocked the road, forcing me to stop while John moved the trash, and where groups of children were playing in the street. There were also beggars waiting at intermittent crossroads leading to the line of tourist shops a few streets from the hotel.

Unlike the first few weeks in Egypt, kids and beggars paid little attention to me. The poor can tell the difference between a tourist and an expat. Beggars and swarms of kids approached often the first few weeks. It did not happen much after the first month. The plight of the people did not directly affect me. I had become adjusted to the sight and the status of the poor. With a simple gesture of my hand, I would simply wave them off.

Like most tourists, I was unaffected by the Muslim onslaught that has brutalized humanity, as well as the tide of indifference to the plight of those living in the shadow of the Muslim sword. It simply is not our problem, and we would soon be gone on a first-class flight out of the country.

The Etap hotel is two-star but clean by Egypt standards. John and I decided to stay the night and watch ships passing against the background of a starry desert night.

Ismailia became a favored place where I could escape Cairo's pollution every few weeks and enjoy peace and serenity next to the canal. I would leave the tourist sections and wander through the back streets to visit stands where the villagers themselves shopped. I became familiar with the town and friendly with some of the shopkeepers.

Egypt was once close to the heart of Judaism and Christianity. Moses was born a Hebrew slave in Egypt between 1300 and 1500 years before Christ was born. The history of Christians in Egypt started with a visit by Mary and Joseph after the Christ Child was born. Saint Thomas founded the Christian Church in Alexandria shortly after the Ascension of Jesus Christ.

In 451 AD, Coptic Christianity in the Middle East split from the Church of Rome over the true nature of Christ. Coptic Christians had survived persecution by the Roman pagans, but crusading Christians from the Church of Rome plagued them after the split.

By the time Muslim Arabs invaded Egypt in the mid-seventh century, they met little resistance from the Coptic Christians. Their numbers had already been decimated; too weak to resist, Islam's sword prevailed.

The remaining Christian population throughout all Muslim countries is still under siege. At the time, there were Muslim uprisings in the southern cities and demonstrations around the college campuses targeting Christians. Ismailia contained a pocket of the few remaining Christians in Egypt.

I felt safe in Upper Egypt, where the cities are concentrated on the Nile delta, and many devote Muslims are unaware of the dark side of their religion. The tourist dollar reigns supreme, and it is an incentive for the Government to keep the militants at bay. Even so, I was a rare expat visitor to the back streets of villages along the Gulf of Suez.

The Impatient American

Egypt is 90% Muslim and 10% Christian and others. An infidel is the enemy in Islam's goal of enslaving or eradicating all others from the earth. Muslim Jahid, a crusade against infidels and heretics, makes all infidels fair game. Although some consider it a republic, Egypt is a Muslim military state. Security checks and proper papers are an everyday part of life. Soldiers casually wandered Ismailia's side streets in pairs or groups of up to ten. They would often approach, testing my resolve.

Given the slightest provocation, infidels are treated with contempt and intimidated at the first opportunity. There are no personal rights, bleeding-heart public defenders, or judges. There are just rooms without windows, locked doors, and interrogators used to getting truthful answers.

The police and the military profile foreigners. Those of us assigned to positions of authority realized the rules only apply to the masses, not the people in charge. Once I understood the system I realized the residents, including those in the military fear and respect authority more than anything else in their lives.

Those of us on foreign assignments willing to take some risk and exercise the authority our positions placed us in believe we would survive. It was an important early lesson because of my connection to the military in the country. Once I understood the system, I simply looked the aggressor in the eye, flashed my Egyptian military identification, and passed on by.

Although times are rapidly changing, as an American, I was used to the rights and protection the Stars and Stripes afforded me. When I am home, I am outspoken and not one to consider the political correctness of a situation. I know better in a foreign country. However, I forget myself at times, voicing my observations and opinions publicly.

The British and Americans maintain a strong presence in Egypt. Many of the locals who own shops patronized by expats speak fluent English. On one occasion, John and I entered a tobacco shop. The shopkeeper looked up when I mentioned to John the *After Tomorrow, inshallah attitude* I was faced with daily, and that I could not understand how anyone could exist as the poor in the Middle East seemed to, without caring about tomorrow, and in no hurry to change their circumstance.

Not all Muslims are militants. The majority, unexposed beyond their own four walls, try to live their lives in Allah's grace while letting others live theirs. The shopkeeper was a moderate, devout Muslim who catered to expats passing through the Suez Canal. He seemed a pleasant but resigned old man. He was amused at my observations and joined our conversation.

"Allah is infinite; He determines our destiny. Heaven awaits only those who serve and worship Allah. For us, things move slowly, but our fleeting time on earth is of no importance. Compared to infinity, life here has little meaning. We have no control. All things will be done, but only if Allah wills it."

John and I shrugged it off; he continued.

"Americans ignore Allah and only serve themselves. It's your choice. You better your lives here but condemn yourself for eternity. Time to you here on earth is much more important than time is to an Egyptian of Islamic faith."

The sole purpose of a Muslim's existence is to please Allah. To some, the best way to please him is to die in the service of Allah while exporting the religion of Islam. It does not make moral sense to me, but morality is simply a moray (*a social norm that is widely observed within a particular society or culture*). It explains religious fanatics willing to give their lives in what we call a terrorist act, which to them is striking a blow for Allah in a holy war. The old man went on to explain.

"Life for the poor in Egypt is hard. It is also short compared to the afterlife with Allah, which will be good for eternity if you live your life in his graces. Life beyond, if you live your life outside Allah's graces, will be worse than that of a donkey on the streets of Cairo."

The old man began to make sense as I became familiar with the customs and daily life of the Egyptian people. I was to learn later that after the death of his son, the Prophet Muhammad is reported to have said: *The eyes shed tears, and the heart is grieved, but we will not say anything except what pleases our Lord.*

Devout Muslims instruct their children that they may not question what happens. It happens only if Allah wills it. As a result, the value of life is not apparent in how they live. There does not appear to be a concern for their own lives, let alone others; they will survive only *inshallah*.

Life does have meaning to me. I cringe to this day at the lack of consideration for life in the Middle East and elsewhere in the Muslim World. However, it was the kids who bothered me the most. If I appeared nervous or offended, beggars and children swarmed around me. When children in groups approached and the village elders shooed them away, I envisioned my own.

My Bowl is Empty

To this day, it is difficult for me to imagine my kids, or now, one of my grandchildren or great-grandchildren, hungry, crying without tears because flies soak them up before they have a chance to run down their cheeks.

I could not watch my son working in 100-degree heat, without shoes or gloves, digging with prehistoric tools for a dollar a day. Worse yet, knowing that is all the future holds for him.

Many young American women have rejected all authority. Would they look forward to being circumcised without an anesthetic at the age of eight, then sold by their family to work in the cotton fields or forced into a life of slavery to a man four times their age, not because their families did not love them, but because they simply cannot afford to feed them.

She would rather be a ballerina.

How would a new American bride, with all her expectations, take to wearing black from head to toe, restricted to following with her sister wives behind her husband, who forces her to bear a child a year and still work eighteen hours doing all her chores by prehistoric methods every day for the rest of her life.

I wonder how my daughter, who loves horses, would react to seeing an aging Arab stallion pulling a 10,000-pound load and then being beaten for his efforts when he stalls.

I left the Third World behind. When others complain about trivial problems in their lives, I have little sympathy. I tell my kids and friends how good their lives are in comparison to those living in the Third World. It makes me wish all the overprivileged could have an opportunity to view the reality of a Middle Eastern village. Most think me callous to what they consider *their plight*.

Chapter 5

Inconveniences are a way of life for expats living in Egypt, but reading about the issues will not prepare anyone for the experience. I have not hit one of the thousands of donkeys, wooden carts, buses, horses, camels, or pedestrians that make an expat driver's life miserable on the streets of Egypt. There are a few more dents in the car from obstacles in the road, but nobody at the office has noticed.

Driving was just one of the headaches. Problems riddled my first two months, one of which was finding a decent flat for the allowance in my contract.

The contract I signed said EGICON would furnish living quarters to American standards. There were about 8,000 suitable apartments and 30,000 expats living there who had the same clause in their contracts; they all arrived before me.

Companies that find decent quarters for employees are reluctant to release them when an employee leaves or is transferred. They pay the rent and hold decent flats for people coming in on future assignments. Like the local paper shortage, I had to learn to make do.

Cesar was complaining about the cost. I was tired of living in a hotel. I kept lowering my standards until I found suitable quarters. The refrigerator worked. There was no hot water in the kitchen, but it only took a few minutes to boil water on the stove. There was an air conditioning unit, which did not work, but that was okay because I got used to the heat, and as long as it stayed above 70-degrees in the flat, the cockroaches remained in the drains, and I wasn't crunching them under my bare feet when I got up in the morning.

The flat was close to work, and to a hotel that had halfway decent coffee, food, and toilet paper that one of the locals managed to unroll past the glued flap most of the time.

Dr. Abboud's idea of American Standards

I prefer to use a hotel toilet when I can wait because the toilet flange at my flat leaks when I flush it. I need to keep a broom handy; after I use the toilet, I sweep the water into a drain in the middle of the floor.

My body never became accustomed to local food. Whatever waste I manufactured was discharged in liquid form. Maintaining sanitation in the bathroom was a constant challenge. I do not think the floor drain was hooked up below my flat. I live on the floor above my landlord. It had to be a bigger problem for him than for me.

The toilet leaked from the day I moved in. I made sure it was flushed each morning before I left, the floor mopped, and the water turned off. When I came home today, I went in to use the toilet and take a shower. Out of habit, I reached down to turn the toilet on. I turned the wrong handle, missing the knob that filled the bowl and opening the valve for the ass washer. The stream of water hit me in the chest.

Trivial things in Egypt sometimes have a positive result. Most of the water went into the bathtub, which saved time rinsing out the cockroaches that appear every evening when the lights are out and the room cools down.

Andy, the QC manager for my project, arrived and moved into the flat. I hired him for his knowledge of quality control and gave him the toilet duties.

****

It was less than two weeks from the time I read Ceasar's ad until I caught the plane. I did not have time to explain my new plan to the rest of my siblings or my mother. She found out when she called one of my daughters to wish her a happy birthday. Between the two of them, they traced me to my hotel, but by that time, I had moved out.

Mom was worried. Phone calls were hit-and-miss, and it took another week. I tried to explain how I was handling the IRS. She was not happy, so I told her I would send a picture of the Pyramids and the Nile River and that Egypt was safe.

My call set off mom's maternal instincts. She did a little investigating on her own. Most of what she found was in newspapers and magazines. Like the rest of us, Mom kept finding conflicting information. I received a concerned letter from her with questions about what was going on over here. She added a few comments about my sanity and some other maternal concerns because she could not figure out why her son of forty-four years, with a marriage of twenty-two years and four kids, would do something so foolish in the first place.

I sent her a brief note telling her not to worry and that it was for therapeutic reasons. I also told her she was watching too much television and reading reports on the Middle East American correspondents sent to their home office.

Alcohol and gambling are available to infidels but not to Muslims because it is against Allah's laws. I do not think most expat correspondents ever leave their hotels. They gather their information from sources at bars and casinos.

Off the subject: *I was in a hotel bar in Peshawar, Pakistan. The bartender brought me a sworn statement to sign certifying I was not Muslim before he poured me a drink. You go figure.*

Correspondents send reports to their editors, who manipulate facts to further their agendas or simply publish whatever comes across their desks if it is in line with their political affiliations.

It appears U.S. military reports generated in the field are being sent to the White House Press Secretary. She manipulates the facts based on what the current tenant at the White House thinks the American public has a right to know.

It does not make sense for anyone to look to the TV or newspapers. I suggested Mom quit listening to all the lies, stick to Dear Abbey and the comics, and treat the rest of the news as I do, an entertaining way to spend a few minutes over morning coffee.

Most of my mail goes through the Office of Military Cooperation. I know they are reading it, but Colonel Baker, who fronts for the OMC in Egypt, denies it. The last time we spoke he asked me to confine my foreign correspondence to tourist-related activities and refrain from discussing the project with anyone except assigned players.

Yes, they read my mail, which is why some of it never reached home. I do not think secrecy is a part of my contract. I think I should be able to voice my opinion, so I ignore him. I now give my mail to expats who are going on holiday. They send it by regular mail. Once in a while, I send a copy through the OMC just to needle Colonel Baker.

American Aid to Egypt is a peace offering to offset money America gives to their Israeli neighbors. It falls under the Camp David Accord: Jimmy Carter's solution.

I came to believe the American government did not give a shit whether we finished the project. As a result, planning was almost nonexistent, and there was never a chance of finishing on time.

Local politics were an issue for Mom. War was raging across the border between Israel and Palestine. *As I write this in 2024, Thirty-seven years later, it still is.* Mom's letters continued to question my good sense.

I explained that my observations were pure speculation based on firsthand experience. She should keep them between her and me. American editors will never print my opinion unless somebody captures me and makes me an instant hero giving the White House an excuse to bomb the crap out of somebody to keep things stirred up.

Our correspondence was crossing in the mail. Mother's questions boiled down to the basics. *What the hell is going on over there?*

I knew Mom well enough to know neither of us would have peace until I gave her some answers. I was not sure myself. It appeared I relayed too much culture shock in my earlier letters. I decided to take my own advice, ignore the local correspondents, and do a little investigation on my own. Mom has not traveled much, so some geography and a little history were in order.

This is where those of you who have irrevocable opinions and are not interested in politics or history might want to skip a few pages and move on to the story. Mom wanted to know what was going on and why I was there.

It has to do with the Camp David Accord. The Camp David Accords were agreements between Israel and Egypt signed in 1978. The accords led to a 1979 peace treaty between the two countries. It was the first such treaty between Israel and any of its Arab neighbors. Under the terms negotiated, Egypt receives $1.3 billion annually in military aid from the United States, while Israel receives $3 billion. The Project I was working on was funded as part of that agreement.

Mom did not understand. She wanted to know the history.

Middle Eastern History 102

Mom's a believer. Anyone who takes the Bible seriously imagines the Middle East as the land of milk and honey, and the birthplace of modern civilization.

The milk and honey are gone because grass and flowers will not grow when you substitute blood and oil for water. As for modern civilization…., *my ass! Based on the Muslim calendar, it is the year 1445.* I decided to go along with that because I was living in the Middle Ages.

I do need to get my geography right. I keep referring to the Middle East, but Egypt, Sudan, and Somalia are in Africa. Actually, the Middle East is a region—it is part of Asia.

Understanding the heritage is a real bitch. We do not need to deal with it, just understand it. There are twenty-two Arab countries. They do not include Egypt, Iran, or Turkey.

I lump all Muslim countries from Sudan to Pakistan into one. There are also many other African countries under Muslim rule, but I do not have time to deal with that much shit.

Except for Israel, Muslim monarchies or military dictators make up *My Muslim Middle East*. It encompasses an area larger than the land mass of Europe. Egypt borders Israel with Saudi Arabia, Iran, Iraq, Kuwait, and Palestine in the vicinity, which are some of the quiet places Mom has been reading about.

The Egyptians hate the Israelis and are not fond of their own relatives in neighboring countries, kind of like the inner-city gangs in the States. None of the Arabs trusted the Americans, who claimed to be friends to some, but, at the time, supported Israel above all others.

President Reagan must have thought he was on a movie set instead of at the White House. Oliver North and his friends were caught selling arms to Persian Iran while Reagan was sending munitions to Arab Iraq. It was an unpopular decision because the Persians and Arabs hated each other.

It was 1986, the year I arrived in Egypt. Regan's administration was prolonging the Iranian war with Iraq to keep the Arab attention diverted from Israel. It is not difficult to understand the attitude of Muslim power brokers.

Iran and Turkey are not Arab or under Arab domination. It is what is left of the Persian Empire. Iran also differs from Turkey and the Arab countries in that most Iranians are of the minority Shiite Muslim sect rather than the Sunni. As far as Shiite are concerned, the Sunni are their mortal enemies. The Sunni Arabs feel the same way about the Shiite Iranians. That is all about family inheritance, which is a dissertation by itself.

Both sects follow the teachings of the Qur'an. *I am going to pass; the Qur'an requires another book, and I will deal with it then.* Suffice it to say that although Shiite and Sunni despise one another, when it is in their interest and given the opportunity, they come together to focus against the People of the Book: Jews, Christians, and Pagans,

The U.S. has been in an undeclared war with Iran since the day Iran overran the American Embassy in 1979, and the French gave Ayatollah Ruhollah Khomeini a one-way ticket home. Since then, the U.S. has sided with the Iranians against Iraq, with Iraq against Iran, with Kuwait against Iraq, and invaded Libya and Iraq twice.

America is currently (*2024 under Biden*) waffling but has sided with Israel against everybody. As a result, the Shiites and the Sunnis have come together in a common cause and have now sided against the Americans.

Modern Jews from Europe plunked themselves down in the middle of the mess, claiming preexisting rights because the Judeo-Christian God, Yahweh, told Abraham to move his tribe to the Land of Canaan (modern-day *Israel*) about 4,000 years ago.

It took until 1897 for Zionism, *the development and protection of a Jewish nation,* to finally take root. The State of Israel would take another fifty years to become a reality.

After 1933 and the construction of the Dachau concentration camp by the Nazis, Zionism became a rallying call for the Jews. The modern-day Exodus picked up steam. When it came to facing Hitler's Nazi regime, European Jews decided to take the more direct route home and bought tickets on boats leaving Germany. Many did not make it. Britain turned them back and refused to let them offload in Israel.

Britain was not alone. By September 1938, the waiting list for a German visa in the U.S. had reached 220,000. Even if the State Department issued the maximum number of visas each year that it could have under the existing laws, new German and Austrian-born applicants could anticipate at least a nine-year wait for a U.S. immigration visa.

Muslim nationalism was also accelerating. Millions of Arab Christians and Jews, under Muslim duress, began to flee their ancestral homelands. Many migrated toward Palestine. Palestine is a poor land, which intermittent conquerors have subjugated since the time Moses sent Joshua ahead after the first Jewish Exodus from Egypt.

Muhammad arrived much later than Joshua. He neglected to explain to the Muslims that God gave Moses the map to the Promised Land 1200 years before Muhammad was born and Allah showed up. The Muslim Palestinians do not understand why they had to vacate their homesteads so Jews can resettle in Palestine.

Although Palestine does produce oil, it ranks 125th in the world when it comes to reserves. No one in the West was too concerned about the turmoil.

Like the Jews leaving the concentration camps in Germany, who at the time were not welcome anywhere, when the Jews arrived in Palestine, the Palestinians willing to leave were not welcome anywhere either.

Americans should be familiar with the attitude. If not, check your history books and compare it to what blacks, yellows, reds, and Jews went through trying to get into an American country club until about 1970, and some even today.

I hate to backtrack, but I need to go back to when the Jews quit their contract building the pyramids for the Pharaohs in Egypt and headed toward the Promised Land.

Moses was short on supplies and running out of water. Bible Numbers 20:8-13. - Yahweh (*God*) told Moses. *Take the rod; you and your brother Aaron assemble the congregation and speak to the rock before their eyes, that it may yield its water. You shall thus bring forth water for them out of the rock and let the congregation and their beasts drink:*

Bible Numbers 20:10. Instead of speaking to the rock, Moses strikes it, but it still produces water. Not only does Moses do something other than what Yahweh told him to do, he suggests that he and Aaron are responsible for producing the water:

While the incident may seem relatively small, Moses is following in the tradition of Adam and Eve, who failed to follow Yahweh's orders. Yahweh's word is life for humanity, and to ignore it brings death. The way that Yahweh responds to Moses reveals that Moses' choice was intentional rebellion, and Yahweh forbids them from entering the promised land (Bible Numbers 20:1).

If you are not already there, this is where it may get confusing: If you question the history, do your own homework.

Moses broke the law, and Yahweh refused to issue his entrance visa. Moses wandered the desert skirting the Land of Canaan, but he sent Joshua ahead with stonemasons with hammers, chisels, and wedges, but no swords, to drive the Canaanites off the land. The Canaanites were the third people of the Bible, the Pagans. Some scholars claim Canaanites, Judaism, and Islam trace their lineage to Abraham. *Worthy to note, 1200 years later, Muhammad decided to join the family and claim lineage to Abraham through Ishmael, Abraham's bastard son.*

Canaan is the term for the ancient region of what is now Israel, the West Bank, and the Gaza Strip, as well as parts of Lebanon, Syria, and Jordan.

The Canaanites were detailed in the ancient texts of Mesopotamia, Phoenicia, and Egypt. The land of Canaan was inhabited as early as 8,000 BC. *Semitic peoples, those who speak Hebrew,* Arabic, and Aramaic, were known to have settled the land around 2,000 BC.

The Bible refers to Canaan as the Promised Land Yahweh gave to Abraham and his descendants. The Canaanites were mentioned as licentious and wicked due to their polytheistic religion. The Bible also characterized the Canaanites as idolatrous and immoral because they practiced polytheism, the worship of multiple gods (Canaanite religion, Mythology, and Practices).

There were only a few livable areas and no Jewish lawyers. The Canaanites put up a pretty damned good fight defending their water rights. According to the Biblical Book of Joshua, Yahweh assists Joshua by calling up a powerful storm to bombard the Canaanites with rain and hailstones. Following this battle, Joshua confiscated the Canaanites' swords and led the Israelites to several more victories, ultimately conquering much of Canaan.

Over the next few centuries, one Middle East power displaced another. The Romans moved in a few thousand years ago and kept the lid on things until, with the help of the Jews, they crucified a carpenter by the name of Jesus. Christians changed Yahweh's name to God as being Father, Son, and Spirit. A few hundred years later, Christianity became the downfall of the Roman Empire as well as a bitter enemy of the Jewish race.

Muhammad was born in 570 AD. He disliked Jews, Christians, and Pagans. He formed the religion of Islam and united the Arabian Peninsula under Islamic law. From then until the 10th century Muslims were killing or enslaving infidels, Jews, Christians, and Pagans while expanding toward Europe and Asia.

In 1063, Roman pagans were in charge. The Muslim Caliph sent his forces into Jerusalem and leveled the Church of the Holy Sepulcher, which was built over the site where Jesus was entombed and from where he resurrected. It is one of the holiest shrines in Christianity. By then, Muslims outnumbered the Romans. The Romans enlisted the Church of Rome for help. Pope

Alexandra II, who claimed to be Christ's successor and wanted to rule the world, joined his Pagan enemies, and went on a crusade to find Christianity's roots.

For the next four hundred years, Christian crusaders took a few detours, enslaving or slaughtering Muslim, Jewish, and Pagan inhabitants along the way. The Crusaders eventually made it to the Middle East, and then in 1099 AD to Jerusalem, which Israel, and Palestine both still claim.

Islam and Christianity have a lot in common. Muhammad founded Islam, which means peace, and then set out to conquer the rest of the world by killing or enslaving anyone who disagreed. The religion took root as the Muslim armies killed off or enslaved those who refused to accept their teachings, which pretty much describes the activities of the Church of Rome during the Christian Crusades.

Eventually, most of the Crusaders returned to Europe, but when it comes to conversion, Muslims killing Jews, Christians, and Pagans remains a successful tactic, even to this day.

As the Christian Crusades were winding down, the Ottoman Empire, an Islamic Caliphate, was expanding. It ruled the Middle East from about 1299 AD until the end of WWI, expanding as far north as Spain.

When the Muslims arrived on the border of France, they finally got the attention of Europe. British and French armies moved back in and began a colonization process in the Middle East and North Africa to contain the Muslims.

The guns and cannons of the invading armies from Europe proved you do not take knives and swords to a gunfight. The French and English had guns and cannon. The Arabs and Persians, as well as the African tribes, had knives and swords; they never had a sporting chance.

France and England fought forty-one wars against each other between the first Anglo-French War in 1109 and the Hundred Days War in 1815. On average that is a war every 17.3 years. In total, France won twenty-four, England-Britain won eleven, and six were tied. The point is that France and Britain simply did not get along.

The English and French enslaved the Muslims, what was left of the Christians and Pagans, and divided the territory. After Napoleon left, the French proclaimed all Arabs subhuman because they would not move their tents out of the way of the rebuilding project on the Suez Canal.

There were no oil wells. The Arabs did not need the Suez Canal. However, the French did because they were stealing the wealth from the Near and East Asia and losing it to the British in the Atlantic. The Canal was a much shorter and safer way to get the treasure back to France without having to enter the Atlantic.

125,000 Arabs died after the French enslaved anybody who could pick up a shovel and put them to work building the Canal, which is probably why the Arabs still have adversity to tools of any kind, and another reason my project was running late.

However, there was a conflict with Britian. British ships maintained control of the seaborne paths to India; they did not need the canal. The British moved in before the French could finish off the nomads or the Canal and paid the remaining Arab nomadic tribes in the Sinai to sabotage the French project.

By the Middle of the 18th century, the French and English had settled their differences and had split North Africa. They also enslaved the village-dwelling Arabs and made a significant dent in the population of the nomadic tribes. As far as the rest of Europe was concerned, if halting the wave of the Muslim Ottoman Empire at the borders of Spain meant butchering a few million locals, so be it.

It was not just Muslims who were targeted. Many of the Jews driven from their homes in Arabia lost their way to Palestine and ended up in Europe.

Pogroms (*organized slaughter of the Jews*) started in Russia and then spread to Europe during the 17th century. The Jews were seriously thinking about going back to Palestine. At that time, the colonization process had started, which led to North Africa and the Middle East becoming the training ground for the armies of Europe; more Jews were not welcome.

By 1930, the Jews who left Russia to avoid the Pogroms owned most of Germany. Hitler's cronies were jealous. The Germans followed the lead of the French and British. Hitler was convinced Jews were subhuman. He decided to purify the Aryan race by annihilating not only the Jews but the gypsies and homosexuals as well. By 1933, with the completion of the first Nazi death camp in Dacca, the Jews were seriously looking for a place to go, which is when Zionism, the idea of a Jewish Homeland in Palestine, finally took root.

America had its own prejudices (*once again, even to this day).* Think *about The reaction to the October 2023 Hamas invasion of Israel; they* slipped into a state of denial and looked the other way along with Europe as the slaughter of Jews and Christians continued during the twentieth century, and now, the ongoing bloodshed in the modern-day Middle East, Sudan, and central Africa.

Hitler got off to a damned good start killing six million, over half the world's remaining Jewish population before a few Jews chose to argue with the British landlords in the Land of Milk and Honey over facing the concentration camps Germans were building all over Europe. It was a new time in history. The Jews won the argument with the British and survived the first battles with the Muslim Arabs.

Americans were, are, still fussy about whom they were going to let join their country clubs and realized that more Jews who went to Israel would mean fewer making applications at home. They decided to make up for their lack of attention in Germany by helping the European Jews convert to Israelis.

After World War II, America supplied the State of Israel with enough arms, munitions, and money to evict the Arabs from half of Palestine. Since the prophet Mohammed has not come back to explain the situation to the Muslim world, the proverbial flies are in the soup. This brings us to the present time and the fact the Palestinian Arabs feel they still have some homestead rights.

Personally, I think they should all get along, but that is never going to happen.

The Egyptians, Syrians, Saudis, Iranians, and Iraqis do not like the Palestinians. However, they are all Muslims under the guidance of the prophet Mohammed, who never agreed that Allah gave Moses permission to send Joshua to settle there in the first place.

Chapter 6

Along with construction, customs, security, safety, and attitude problems, students assigned to the Computer Center are in the U.S. training. They can get better-paying jobs and remain simply by marrying an American; most, if not all, will not be coming back to Egypt.

It also seems Moses told the Egyptians not to do anything until he got back, and since nothing else has been finished since he quit his job at the pyramids, the lack of local concern does not surprise me. In the end, the exercise did not matter to anyone except me because I wanted to go home.

Cesar's Egyptian JV partners assured me they were aware of the schedule and would have no problem finishing on time. They also did not believe I should be concerned about their building methods because they were the direct descendants of the Pharaohs.

Dr. Abboud repeatedly told me their ancestors built the pyramids and I should not be concerned about their ability to meet the specs or time limits. During one of our conversations, Abboud claimed the Egyptians had a civilization dating over 7,000 years and knew more about construction than either the COE or me. The Pyramids and other antiquities of the past tend to enforce his claim. However, as I became familiar with Arab construction, I questioned who built what. I think the 7,000-year estimate is a result of tracking the growing size of the garbage piles.

I am also writing history and political science lectures while trying to get my project off the ground; time passes quickly. The religious holidays are over. It is time to have another meeting with General Aziz. I would prefer to postpone it, but a meeting is important because the get-even contract I had in mind when I left the States was not going my way.

I was supposed to be mobilized on the site by October 4th. It is the first week in September, and I am not sure if the Egyptian Army will let me enter the site, let alone allow the equipment I need to come through the gate.

The COE secretary just called asking me why I was not at the groundbreaking ceremony scheduled to start twenty minutes ago. I arrived thirty minutes late. Egyptian time worked for a change. Tom met me at the gate; the ceremony was reset for an hour later. It was scheduled that morning when some politicians flew in unexpectedly from the States, and the COE thought it would be a nice gesture.

I was not included in the ceremony except for introductory purposes. I sat back, listening while everyone lied to one another. General Olsen, the man in charge of the local office of the OMC, explained.

The U.S. bribed Egypt with billions in military aid and economic assistance to maintain peace between Egypt and Israel. The computer center would track the military hardware America was supplying.

The Egyptians would have the finest military logistics computer in the world. He was looking forward to the cooperation of those involved in the project and expected everything online and on schedule. I sat there asking myself why the American military could not keep track of their own shipments. I also think the American taxpayer would be put out if they knew their own military would usurp their technological superiority.

Tom introduced me as the person responsible for constructing the building. IBM would be installing the computers twelve months from the date the COE signed the contract with Cesar, now less than ten months away.

The COE approved the project two years earlier. General Aziz would be in charge. He handpicked thirty local computer whiz kids and sent them to the States to study. However, in 1986 a trained computer programmer fresh out of most any college commanded $60,000 a year. Those from Ivy League schools with advanced degrees made substantially more. Wages in the service of the Egyptian Government would be a meager 5,000 LE, or at the time, the equivalent of $2,500 a year.

The students scheduled to graduate from such schools as Harvard, Berkeley, and Southern Cal., and who attended at the American taxpayer's expense were accepting job offers from American companies. Some had already married Americans and applied for citizenship. Others were simply accepting positions and refusing to come back.

Political handshaking went on after the speeches. Tom took me aside and asked if I would step outside to meet with Generals Aziz and General Sayer. There was a problem brewing between General Aziz, who ran the Army base next door, and General Sayer, who ran the Technical Institute where the ceremonies were taking place. Tom would be boarding a flight for Hong Kong that evening. He smiled when he told me it was an issue that only *Mr. Pat might be able to resolve*.

The courtyard looked like West Point on graduation day. The brass was gathered around a rickety tin shed with cars parked under it. One of the cars was General Sayer's Mercedes. The problem appeared to be General Sayer's Technical Institute never agreed to give up land to General Aziz's Army battalion, which accounts for the attitude at the gate between the two bases a few weeks earlier.

I was under the impression that the Egyptian Army had settled the issues regarding where to build before the OMC and the COE awarded the contract. However, General Sayer and General Aziz were of equal rank. Neither had the authority to tell the other what to do. Hosni Mubarak, the Egyptian President, did. He was too busy conning the Americans for more money to bother with the projects underway.

Colonel Baker, who worked for the OMC, told me General Aziz petitioned Mubarak for the money, and Mubarak talked the American Government into funding it. I think the CIA conceived the project because, although the idea was to track U.S. arms moving in and out of Egypt, there was as much Russian military equipment coming in as there was American. It would also be tracked with the new software. The Americans have agreed to staff the center with American personnel if the students fail to return. It sounded to me like more CIA spy shit.

The headaches started when General Aziz made the request, and the OMC got involved. He did not have spare land on his base. The adjoining Technical Institute under General Sayer's control had a large, mostly unused area, which included the parking shed and General Sayer's garden.

General Aziz told the Americans he would build the center there. The Americans agreed, but General Aziz and the OMC did not bother to consult his neighbor, General Sayer. General Aziz invited General Sayer to the dedication ceremony, which took place on General Sayer's base. He accepted the invitation, thinking it was a ceremony to honor him.

He seemed perplexed when, instead of someone pinning a medal on his chest, Mr. Pat was going to take away his parking lot. The first order of business was for him to move his car so I could demolish his parking shed.

We spent the next hour sorting through the mess. To move forward, Colonel Baker compromised. He told Tom to instruct me to draw up a new mobilization plan and leave the car shed alone until General Sayer could be persuaded. Tom headed for the airport to catch his flight to Thailand. General Olsen left for the American Embassy. General Sayer and I left mad.

When I got back to my car, Colonel Baker and Glen, the COE Area Engineer, were waiting. They told me to sort it out and let them know what happened.

"Glen, how do you expect me to sort it out? I can't even get back on the fucking base?"

Tom was out of sight. I was under the impression that the contract instructed me how and where to start. I was not aware of anything requiring me to fight with the Egyptian Army over where

I was supposed to build the building. The discussion became a little testy.

Glen told me, as he and Tom would many times in the following months, that the contract documents directed me to *diligently pursue the work and to file a claim if I encountered a problem with the Egyptian military if it resulted in added cost.*

Colonel Baker and Glen left me standing in the heat. I thought back to the CO in Dahlgren, Virginia, who had helped cause my headache with the IRS a few years earlier. He gave me an order to *diligently pursue the diving system or else*! I balked and ended up in Egypt. Egypt was far enough south; I did not want to end up in Sudan.

Tom had the right idea. Thailand, or any place else on earth, looked good, but I could not leave the country without my passport. The OMC conned me out of it the first week I arrived, and they know I cannot leave without it.

Cesar's contract said the OMC would sort out my security pass and secure a resident visa. Colonel Baker promised me a resolution on my visa ten days after my arrival. I was still waiting. Both were tiresome issues I did not want to have to deal with.

I spent the next two days in the office with the telephone and telex out of order, the project going down the toilet, and no plan.

Cesar hired me because I marketed myself as an expert at resolving plan errors. After the second day without contact with the outside world, I changed tactics. The first issue I had to deal with was the place to build the building. A change was in order.

Preparing the request for more money meant solving the security problem and getting back on site. Hatem had not been much help. It was time to enlist the help of those Americans assigned to the project with the title OMC.

The phones came back online long enough for me to call General Olsen and ask him to request a meeting with General Aziz and Colonel Baker the following morning at ten, and not to mention that I would be there. As luck would have it, the phones went dead *again*. I was not sure anyone would show.

General Olsen and I arrived at the base gate at 9:45. Colonel Baker had other business to deal with and would be along later. I told the General I had a plan, and although it went against the policy, it was in the best interest of the project that we bend the rules a little.

American Generals are scarce in the Middle East. Usually, when one shows up, money is involved. General Olsen carried a lot of weight with the local military brass. He was able to come and go as he pleased.

My decision to impersonate a military officer was a spur of the moment. Still, since none of the American Generals wear uniforms in the Middle East unless they are on a U.S. base, and I knew the Egyptian soldiers could not read English, I believed I might get away with it.

I asked the General to let me join him in the Embassy limo and deal with the guard. General Olsen started to protest but agreed when I reminded him his retirement was less than a year away, which coincided with the time I was to finish the building. I also told him I was aware he was in charge of military cooperation, and if someone did not start cooperating with me soon, I was heading for the Israeli border, with or without a passport.

The General was not an officer who could be intimidated, but he had a sense of humor. I think he agreed to let me try it my way out of curiosity.

I needed an interpreter, but I did not bother to explain. I told Hazem to meet me at the base at 9. knowing he would be at least two hours late. If Hazem knew what I had in mind he would disappear for good.

As the General and I approached the gate, Hazem arrived on schedule. It was easier than I anticipated. The guard knew General Olsen on sight. When he asked for my identification, I gave him the only official-looking thing I had in my wallet: my Oregon driver's license.

I told Hazem to tell the guard I was an American general, and like General Olsen, I never wore a uniform. We were in an embassy limo; the soldier let us through the gate.

The Gate between the two bases was unlocked. It gave me the impression the Generals had sorted out the site issue. I picked a soldier out of the crowd and told Hazem to assign him as a guard to a post by the gate to General Sayer's base. Hazem was a little dumbfounded.

General Olsen was a busy man.

"It seems they have resolved your access themselves. Was there anything else?"

Like Hazem, I, too, was confused.

"No, General. I'll take it from here."

General Olsen turned and left without a backward glance.

"Hazem, stay here and tell the guard General Aziz wants him to keep the rest of the soldiers away from me."

Hazem stuck around. The guard ignored Hazem and wandered off. Strangely, he returned later and took up a post by the gate. I am not sure what assignment the guard is supposed to be doing. For all I know, General Aziz may have gone along and assigned him to the post to keep an eye on me. Whatever the reason, I come and go as I please to General Aziz's base and to the internal gate to the Technical Institute without the red tape that would otherwise take two hours every day.

I found out later General Olsen had explained to General Aziz that whatever costs we incurred because of the feud between him and General Sayer would come out of the budget for the computer center. Aziz settled my pass to his base. The issues between him and General Sayer would take a while.

General Olsen never mentioned it again. He salutes the guard every time he arrives. I do not bother. No one is supposed to know I am a general.

General Olsen was wrong about the Generals sorting out their issues. The next time I tried to enter General Sayer's base, the guards from the Technical Institute stopped me at the gate. It took another week before I reentered General Sayer's base. On the day I finally managed to get to the site, General Sayer met me there and told me I could begin mobilizing, but the car shed was unresolved, so we could not start the work.

If the car shed were the problem, it was the responsibility of the COE to pay me to build General Sayer a new one with the materials I could salvage.

One thing at a time. The next order of business was to pick a site where General Sayer would allow me to set up a site office and then figure out how to get the COE to pay for the lost time and added expense.

I spent the next week supervising a few of Doctor Abboud's laborers while they cleaned up the area, and I drew up a new mobilization plan. It was time to present it to the Generals.

The meeting ended after four frustrating hours, which required two prayer breaks. When we adjourned, we had an agreement. I could take the shed down, and the COE agreed to pay me to put it back up in a new location. General Sayer would allow me to fence the construction area, but I had to put in a gate for his men's access.

This would mean I could not access the building site by the gate designated in the contract documents or get to the site at all without going through General Aziz's base. However, General Aziz would allow me to use his gate, and both Generals would allow us to use the gate in between.

More bullshit….! My mistake was not building a permanent wall between the site and General Sayer's base at the first opportunity and definitely before we tore the shed down. After the laborers stacked the debris, General Sayer's soldiers arrived and confiscated the materials.

I was not getting combat pay. When men showed up in field dress, I sat back and told Hamid, my Egyptian superintendent, to let them take anything they wanted. The truck was being loaded; I took a few pictures before going to General Aziz's office to call Gary, who was taking Tom's place in his absence.

Stealing the car shed - So much for planning.

In the meantime, somebody told General Sayer I smuggled a camera onto his base and took pictures of the army truck loaded with the shed materials. The contract documents clearly stated that cameras were not allowed on the base.

I was sitting in the shade under a tree when Gary, General Olsen, and Colonel Baker showed up. By then, everyone on General Sayer's base was looking for the camera. I had not bothered to tell them I had given it to my driver, who had left to get the film developed. I decided to use one of General Aziz's tactics. I lied and told them the soldiers were imagining things.

When they finally allowed me to leave, the brass were arguing about the shed materials, which had also disappeared. Gary grabbed me as I was going out the gate; he wanted a copy of the pictures.

“Pat, where’s the camera?”

“What camera? My contract doesn’t require I take pictures, and cameras aren’t allowed on the fucking base, Gary.”

“Don’t give me that bullshit.”

“Gary, we both know General Sayer ordered his men to steal that junk. Most of it is scrap. There isn’t enough salvage for a carport, let alone a parking shed for six cars.”

“Yes, but you’re responsible for the shed materials. We’re going to need a copy of those pictures when it comes time to rebuild.”

“Look, if I give you the pictures everybody will have proof I broke the rules. Ask Glen, he can add a codicil requiring monthly pictures, which will get me off the hook.”

Glen could not revise the existing contract; he told Gary to backdate a one-time change order so I would provide a copy of the pictures to the COE. The next day I traded a set of the pictures to Glen for a case of American beer, which I cannot get because I still do not have duty-free privileges.

Alcohol has been a problem. Gary is in charge of issuing duty-free privileges to expats. He is a Mormon and does not approve of alcohol. Since alcohol is my only reason for wanting the privileges, Gary is dragging his feet.

Glen had someone from the OMC deliver the pictures to Sayer and Aziz. The car shed is still an issue, but no one has brought up the camera.

The next order of business was to get men, materials, and equipment through General Sayer’s gate and onto the construction site, but as usual, planning lacked purpose. Every time the guards changed, so did the rules.

I negotiated the two bases as I pleased, but as for the rest, crossing the first barrier took two hours a day. Once they did get to General Aziz’s base, they waited for an army escort to the gate leading to General Sayer’s base. Depending on prayer time, which could take another hour.

Once at the gate to General Sayer's base, the rules depended on the guard's frame of mind, so it often took another hour. The workday was nine hours. It would take another hour for one of the men to find a bucket, collect water, and make tea. It would take at least two more hours for them to reenter General Aziz's base to leave, which took up the remainder of the day. I call that a well-planned public employee day, but we did not get much work done.

I needed to find another way. Four roads led to entrances through General Sayer's base. One went by the Mosque; using it would disturb prayer time. Another passed by the General's office; more traffic would disturb his meetings. Police had closed two of the access roads leading to the base to heavy truck traffic.

My next meeting with General Sayer went on and on. Four hours later, after two prayer breaks, General Sayer grew tired, conceded, and agreed to a gate at the far end of the base. I would later find out it was a man gate too narrow to get the equipment through.

After inspecting the designated access, I went back to General Sayer's office. He was gone and would be out of the office until after tomorrow, inshallah.

Security problems plagued us the week General Sayer was away. For the first few days, the Egyptian Army would not let laborers on the site at all. Then General Aziz restricted the equipment from passing through his base because it was disturbing his prayers. Besides, the contract said I was to use the gate on General Sayer's base until a new permanent gate on our site was installed.

The COE and the OMC could not or would not help. I was not sure which. I had run out of patience and was calling Glen daily. Tom showed up unexpectedly. Glen contacted him and asked him to return and try to sort out the site access problems with the Generals. Tom was not happy about cutting his holiday short. He was also anxious when he realized I had been in Cairo for almost two months and was six weeks behind schedule.

The next day, he arrived at my office in Heliopolis mad. The contract agreement was that we use General Sayer's gate. When he tried to call him, General Sayer had left, and he would be back after tomorrow, inshallah.

Tom needed a new schedule. I was in a foul mood and told him I had not bothered and at that moment, did not give a shit if the building was ever built. Tom broke out a six-pack of American beer. Tom had talked to General Olsen but had not come up with any ideas of his own. He asked me if I had any ideas.

"What's with these assholes, Tom? This project was their idea. From how they're acting, you would think I was with the Israeli Mossad building a spy station."

Tom was in a lousy mood himself, but he called General Aziz and set up a meeting. It took two days to get the players together. The meeting went as I expected. General Aziz lied about the help he was giving me, and although he had returned, General Sayer refused to attend. Tom and I decided if we were ever going to get the project past go, we had to deal with General Sayer ourselves. To do that, we felt we needed to enlist the aid of the OMC.

I asked Tom to set up a meeting on the site for the next day, but not to mention it to the Generals. The COE and the OMC had access to the site. I hoped to surprise General Sayer and catch him in his office before he found out we were coming. I did not want him to disappear again.

There was a new security officer on Aziz's base. He wanted new paperwork. I still refused to fill out forms, but they allowed me access. Colonel Baker, Tom, Glen, and General Olsen arrived in the same embassy car shortly after I entered the base.

Glen joked about how diligently I was pursuing the contract. Two men were working on the fence; the rest were sitting under a shade tree in the middle of the site. We did not have many tools on site, which was another issue. I said something about him still having my passport and that it would be nice if he would find a way to get it back to me so I could leave.

When the handshaking was over, I presented Tom with an overblown change order reflecting my mood, along with a new construction plan. The bill worked out to a little over $1.2 million.

Tom thought it was a nice figure and suggested we present it to General Aziz since the money would have to come out of his budget.

The OMC would not agree. Colonel Baker started to protest, but I had learned about military cooperation from him regarding my visa and passport; I ignored him.

When Tom gave the bill to General Aziz, I thought the General would choke on his tea. Time is of no consideration to a Muslim with an inshallah attitude. He could not see the problem and why it should cost so much.

Tom explained the contract. We were supposed to play by American rules. If the Egyptian Army causes extras, which include added time for things not covered in the contract, the cost will have to come out of the construction funds.

General Aziz's budget was shrinking as students in the States married Americans and jumped ship. There was a construction cushion, but it was for work done, not for delays caused by the Egyptian Army.

“Ah, Mr. Pat, you must have more patience. I am working on the security issues with General Sayer.”

General Aziz insisted it was just a foul-up in security. I said something about getting security off my ass. Colonel Baker told me to quit swearing and shouting at the General.

Things settled; Colonel Baker did start to negotiate with General Aziz by telling him we might have some money coming if the problems I outlined did exist. I thought the Colonel was having memory failure until I remembered he was from the OMC, and military people stuck together. We never told Colonel Baker I was an acting General, so he could lie to me all he wanted.

Hazem arrived. I did not have a clue how he got on site. He came with the front-end loader I ordered, which was at the front gate, but General Aziz’s guards refused to let it through. It was parked on the street, so I turned to General Olsen.

"How about showing me how military cooperation works and getting that loader through the gate so we can go to work."

He was pissed. The Colonel spoke fluent Arabic. He said something to General Aziz, taking the proverbial bull by the horns. General Olsen and I stood by the window and watched as Colonel Baker jogged to the gate, pushed the guard out of the way, got on the loader, and drove it to the site.

"General Olsen, if I had known that was all there was to military cooperation, I would have solved my own security problems."

Colonel Baker reentered the office, steaming.

"Now, why didn't I think of that, Colonel?"

Colonel Baker ignored me. He lit into General Aziz in Arabic-English, which was mostly swear words. I thought about getting security under control. I reminded the Colonel; he told me it was impolite to yell at a general with the soldiers around.

General Aziz decided things were getting out of hand when Colonel Baker loudly suggested I keep my fucking mouth shut. General Aziz ordered some tea and told us he had to leave because it was prayer time. I might have been upset with the Colonel if I had not been trying so hard to keep from laughing. I whispered something to General Olsen about penalties for colonels who were disrespectful to generals.

Everyone calmed down after Aziz left the office. General Olsen and I knew I meant me, but the Colonel thought I meant General Aziz. He apologized and took the tea General Aziz's aid offered.

"Colonel Baker, I'm not getting paid to take on the Egyptian Army, and I have no intention of messing around with the guards and guns."

"Why don't you take General Aziz's advice, Patrick? This is Egypt, not Oregon. You're taking it too personally. Be patient. I'll sort out the security problem with the Generals."

"Patience, my fucking ass, Colonel! I'm a month behind schedule. If you don't fix it soon, you can kiss your deadline goodbye."

Tom decided we needed a diversion and suggested it was time to pay General Sayer a visit. As we were leaving, General Aziz was returning from prayers. As he entered his office, his phone started ringing. He reached for it, but Tom took him aside and said something to him in Arabic.

Tom tells me he does not understand and that he refuses to learn Arabic. He refused to answer the Generals, or for that matter, anyone else he knows speaks English when they address him in Arabic. Tom simply ignores them until they change their questions or answers to English. It is seldom, but every once in a while, when he gets really, really pissed, Tom has an epiphany. I whispered to Tom.

"What did you tell General Aziz."

"Nothing!"

"I heard you; you said something in Arabic."

"I don't speak Arabic; you're hearing things."

General Aziz turned and mumbled something in Arabic that gave Colonel Baker a reason to pause. General Aziz left his office. Colonel Baker was shaking his head when we headed for General Sayer's office.

The car shed was gone, and both Generals had the pictures. As we were leaving, General Aziz returned and told Colonel Baker that he and General Sayer had settled the location of the new computer center and that General Sayer would not object to using the original mobilization site.

Tom was not in the mood, but whatever he told General Aziz got his and General Sayer's attention. General Sayer was obviously distraught when we entered his office, but he offered us tea. Before it arrived, he handed me a list scribbled in Arabic-English. It was hit-and-miss, but I got the gist as he stammered through it.

General Aziz was right. General Sayer did not object to the original site. He did object to the hours we were working, the location of the proposed storage area, the noise we were making which was disturbing his prayers, and the fact we had not yet begun to rebuild his car shed.

He did not object to Colonel Baker delivering the loader to the site. I figured Tom probably had something to do with that due to whatever it was he said to General Aziz. At least that was a step in the right direction. I figured it was an opportune time to assess the mood, deal with more equipment, and get permanent site access without going through General Aziz's base.

"General Sayer, I need to bring an excavator on site to remove the old building foundations. The gate you designated for access and the one between yours and General Aziz's base is too narrow. May I have your permission to use the gate up the road or start building our own access?"

It was a simple solution. Two hundred meters from the site, there was an adequate access gate. It should not have been a problem. It was narrower and temporary until we put in our own gate, but it would do. Nobody could object except General Sayer.

General Sayer had been studying the contract between the Egyptian Army and the COE, and regardless of his orders, he did not intend to allow us to build on his land without putting up a fight; he was only getting started.

General Aziz had contacted General Sayer before our arrival and told him I had complained to the OMC and to him that General Sayer was costing the JV money. I wanted the Egyptian Army to pay the bill. At that moment, it dawned on me that both Generals were upset because I ignored another Egyptian custom. I reversed the roles. It is usually the contractor who pays off the Generals. In this case, I was asking them to pay me. It was a new experience for both of them.

"General Sayer, what about the gate?"

"Ah, Mr. Pat, you have many problems. I, too, have a problem. I have no place to park my car."

"General, I have an idea. I've been going over the plans. When we finish the project, I think there will be enough materials left over from the computer center to build you a new garage. Maybe we can make a deal if it's all right with the COE and General Aziz."

Colonel Baker bolted from his seat and started for the door.

"If you're going to offer the General a bribe, do it when we aren't here."

"Colonel, don't be so fucking sensitive. I'm not offering a bribe. I want to get the car shed resolved. Tom has already agreed to pay us to rebuild it. The only problem is a lack of materials. There should be enough left over for a lousy car shed."

Tom entered the conversation.

"It's a bribe, forget it. Look, Patrick, you've only been here a few months. Don't let the culture rub off on you."

Tom turned to the General.

"General Sayer, let's forget the shed for now. I'm sure the missing materials will turn up before the building is finished. We'll see to it the shed is reconstructed. That's our agreement; we need to go on to other things.

General Sayer was still pissed that I brought the loader on-site. It helped, but the construction site was built over fill covering ribbon footings from old barracks the British had built. Some were four feet wide and three thick; all were fortified with steel.

"General, please, I need to bring an excavator to the site."

"Ah, Mr. Pat, I have been reading the contract between the Egyptian Army and your company. An excavator will take work and wages away from Egyptian laborers."

Two in a row. The *Ah, Mr. Pat shit* was an omen, but it had not settled in. I did not recall a clause in our contract saying anything specifying using Egyptian labor in place of equipment. I was wondering where he came up with that shit.

"General, I have three thousand cubic meters of material to move. Most of it is concrete. It would take the forty laborers I have a year to clean up that mess."

"The Egyptians built the Pyramids, Mr. Pat. They did it with labor and oxen."

The General was at it again. I was trying to figure out where he expected me to get oxen and a few thousand slaves.

"General, the pharaohs used a-hundred-thousand slaves, and it took seventy years. I only have ten months to finish this project."

"Forty men are not enough, Mr. Pat."

"General, hiring a hundred more will still take two or three months."

"Mr. Pat, an Egyptian laborer can move one cubic meter daily. You have three thousand meters to take out. Is that right?"

"No, General. We are talking concrete and steel; we first need to break it up."

I was thinking I got my point across when the General got up from his chair and headed for the door. Shit….! It was prayer time.

"General, wait a minute! I need this resolved."

"I have resolved it for you, Mr. Pat. Forty men are not enough. If need be, hire a thousand men; it should only take a few weeks."

The audience was over. As the General was leaving for his prayer room, I could hear Colonel Baker muttering to Tom in the background that perhaps a new garage might be an idea.

"Forget it, let's get the fuck out of here!"

We headed back to the site. I was protesting to Tom and the Colonel about another delay. Tom told me to read the specs, which said it was the contractor's responsibility to diligently pursue the work and follow the laws of Egypt.

"That's fucking bullshit, Tom, and you know it! How about it, General Olsen; we haven't heard anything from you today."

General Olsen did not say anything until we approached the site, and he saluted the guard.

"Patrick, do the best you can. We'll look into it, but as Tom says, it's a construction scheduling problem, and that's your responsibility."

"It's a scheduling problem, my ass! General, do you really expect me to hire a-thousand laborers to move that pile of shit?"

"No, but you'll think of something."

General Olsen waved to the guard and asked if we would take time out for lunch.

"Why not?"

Tom and I made a deal. We do not discuss business on our time off. Thoughts: *If General Olsen and Colonel Baker would settle some of the arguments with the Egyptian army, it would make the job a lot easier for all of us.*

I could not understand why they were dragging their feet, and I was inclined to start taking a hardball position on some of the issues, which I knew would not set well with Tom. Then, again, I thought back to my CO friend in Dahlgren, Virginia, who I argued with and lost. The thought settled me. Besides, I liked Tom and knew he was just doing his job. If I kept my nose clean, part of that job would be to pay for the delays caused by the Egyptian army, which would come later.

On the way to Herfy's, which was Cairo's answer to McDonald's at the time, I was almost ready to give in. I thought about General Sayer's suggestion. It would take at least a month to line up the labor and six months more to get them cleared through security. If I managed to succeed in hiring a-thousand laborers, with that many men on the site without proper sanitation, there would be more shit to deal with than concrete and sand. No, that was not going to work, plan B, after lunch.

After we ordered, Tom started telling us about his latest fishing trip. By the time the waiter brought the food I had forgotten the Egyptian Army. As Tom was biting into his second burger, the door opened. An Egyptian soldier came in dragging a hose connected to a sprayer outside. It was time to spray the restaurant for flies. He did before we had a chance to move.

Cairo fly control

By the time we got to the door, we were all soaked to the skin. I wondered if General Sayer had sent the Army spray unit to follow us. Tom left for his office; I headed for my flat to shower and change. When I finished, I went back to Tom's office to see if anyone had a suggestion. By the time I arrived, everyone had left for the day except for Gary.

Tom called earlier and told him about the situation at the site and at the burger house. Gary did not want to deal with my ranting about the project and decided to divert my attention by offering me a late lunch at his flat. Why not? I was still hungry, and Gary's cooking could not be worse than what I had become accustomed to.

Gary was a Morman. I knew he did not have American beer or other alcohol, so I did not bother to ask. He did have American whole wheat bread, ham, fresh tomatoes, Best Foods mayonnaise, Nally's potato chips, grape soda, and Twinkies, compliments of the American commissary. It was marvelous and the best meal I had since I left the States.

Gary kept me occupied with tales of other construction headaches the COE was dealing with in Egypt. By the time he finished, I quit feeling sorry for myself and started feeling sorry for the COE.

During the drive back to my flat, I wondered why the COE had pawned the problem with the Egyptian army off on me. The JV did not have the money to bribe the Generals, and even if they did, I had no chance of recovering it from the COE.

I was seriously thinking about giving the whole thing up, heading for the airport, and going home to face the IRS. Going home defeated was a depressing thought. It was Thursday, which is my Friday. I figured a day off and time to clear my head would put me in a better frame of mind. For the next 24 hours, I would forget about the COE, the Generals, and the project. On Saturday, I would work on a new plan.

Chapter 7

The thermometer would redline at 110. I left my flat at 9:30. Some hotels in the area opened their pools to nonresidents. I figured a little poolside relaxation was the order of the day. I had been trying to work on my tan; I bought a book and headed for the Sheraton.

There were five or six Arab families and a few expats by the pool. I thought the heat was a bit much for the tourists, and perhaps they were staying cool in the shade, but it soon became apparent why the place was so empty.

The flies if I were Alfred Hitchcock I would write another book. It was impossible to sit still. I gave up reading, the flies would not bother me neck-deep in water. As I approached the edge of the pool a young Arab mother was reaching to pick her toddler son out of the pool. He was as naked as the day he was born. As she lifted him out of the water the kid shit in the pool.

It did not appear the day was going to be better than the previous weeks. It was still early and damned hot. I did not feel like going back to the flat. I wandered around Cairo's back streets for the rest of the morning dodging traffic and waving at taxi drivers. I stopped at the Marriott Hotel for lunch and then headed back to my flat in Heliopolis.

I left the Marriott at two. At 4:30 it was hopeless. I wandered around but my navigation was not panning out. I admitted defeat and flagged down a taxi to lead me back to Heliopolis. After one stopped, I could not figure out how to tell him I wanted to remain in my car, and for him to lead me home.

I know my way home from the Pyramids, and every taxi driver in Cairo would understand Pyramids. I tried a few hand signals. When that did not work, I drew a picture on the back of one of my business cards. The taxi driver nodded his head and then turned laughing with some local pedestrians.

We settled on a price of ten LE, which is a high fare in Cairo considering two will get you all the way across town. I did not argue, the sooner I left the area, the less of a fool I would feel. I tore the note in two and gave the driver half. I would give him the other half when we arrived at the Pyramids.

He smiled and headed down the road. I followed him as he took off through traffic. We traveled about five hundred meters when he made a turn into the entrance to the parking lot. At a width of seven hundred feet and a height of over four-fifty everyone else could see it for five klicks around the area. I had left the Marriott for my flat in the direction of Heliopolis. The Pyramids are 180 degrees in the opposite direction. The short distance should have been a 50-piaster (*cents*) ride, but I was lost, and the road I was on led me to Alexandria. I gave the driver the rest of the note.

It had been a long day; the sun would soon set. As I circled the Pyramids I longed for quiet and solitude. I had heard a stable next to the pyramids rents horses to tourists for evening rides in the desert.

I was involved with horses as a teenager, as were two of my daughters. I also owned a ranch for a time and raised horses. I had been planning to search for a blooded Arabian. My daughter wanted me to ship one back to the States. I had looked into export and shipping, but the process would be more of a financial burden than I could afford.

The stable was next to the Sphinx where the city meets the edge of the desert. Finding it was a matter of trailing a group of tourists on horses who were on their way back to the stable. The stable was one of those suited to the urban cowboy who had seen a few western movies and thought he would like to give horseback riding a try.

The horses were old, ill-kept, wind-broke from too much running, and head shy from the novice's flaying attempts to keep them from heading back to the barn.

The one on the right could barely walk.

I wandered through the private barns avoiding the commercial crowd where Arab grooms were barking at tourists trying to con a few LE from them for an hour's ride. I was surprised, the horses in the inner barns were in clean stalls, well-fed, exercised, and groomed daily.

There was little light in the stable. I startled a stallion that was reaching over through his half-open split door nibbling at a bale of hay lying next to the stall. Startled he bolted back, pawing at the sand, a warning so to speak. One of the grooms approached and entered the stall to calm him down. I watched them in the shadows until the animal settled.

The groom removed his halter, closed the door behind him, and with a smile pointed toward a paddock behind the barn. I took him to mean it was time for me to leave.

I was returning to my car by way of the rentals hoping to find a horse I would be willing to ride. At first glance, I wished I had not bothered and was planning my next day off at one of the hotel pools to do a little fly swatting. Then, I noticed a man exercising what I thought to be a yearling colt. They were in a paddock, the one the groom pointed to and that I passed leaving the barn.

The gate to the paddock was locked, there were signs posted in Arabic. Another entrance nearby meant climbing over the last few years' manure pile. I had not done anything about the scuff marks and lack of polish on my boots since I left the States, I thought, what the hell?

Once more, planning lacked purpose. I thought it was mostly hay until I sank up to my knees in liquid shit. It was dripping from my pant legs when I finally managed to break the suction hold of the fermenting pile.

It had been another wrong decision in Cairo. I was covered to my knees with horse, camel, and donkey dung. I was also thinking I should take the patience class everyone was suggesting when I saw there was an entrance with an open gate on the other side of the corral.

The man and the colt had disappeared. I surrendered to the thought that it was a lack of planning causing the rest of my problems in Cairo. I also saw my first observation might have been wrong about the houseboy cleaning my clothes. It looked like I ruined one of the few pairs of Levis I brought with me, and the boots were going to need more than polishing.

I searched the area for a water hose. I was surprised when I found one, more so when it was connected to a working hose bib. I rinsed the foul liquid off my pants and started on my boots. I looked around to find a stick to clean the notch between heel and sole; my fault, but I was pissed, it had been, literally, a shitty day.

I found a stick, looked up, and stopped, staring. At that moment, the man and the yearling were coming back up the alley between the barns toward the corral.

The man waived me over. When I approached, the groom I met earlier in the stable entered the paddock; he took the lead and proudly showed him off. Egyptian Arabians grow slowly and do not fully mature until their 5th or 6th year. The colt was about two, maybe a little younger. His head and features were classic Arabian. Black as the walls of a coalmine, without a speck of white or other markings, he was stunning.

The young stallion carried himself arrogantly, *much too light a word*, acting as if he just won the Arab Classic at the Madison Square Garden; he was magnificent.

As I was inspecting him the boab of the stable joined us. He and the groom conversed for a moment, pausing to look towards me. Language was not a problem for a change. The boab recognized I admired good horseflesh, and he was proud of the colt. I finished and turned to leave, regretting I had left my camera in the flat. They called me back, but it was late; I waved them off.

I exited the area through the gate the boab entered and meandered back toward my car by way of the front of the stable. Several of the hawkers tried to pawn rejects from the glue factory on me; I was ignoring them. As I was reaching for the door handle the friendly boab, now accompanied by a young Arab approached and called out to me.

I thought they wanted to try to sell me the colt. I remembered my daughter and stood for a moment, there was no way I could swing it. I smiled, casually waved them off, and opened the door to my car.

The young man's fluent English surprised me; I turned back.

"Mr., you seem to know and like good Arabians, ours are exceptional."

"Yes, they are, at least the black is."

"The black colt is for sale."

"Sorry, I checked; Egypt frowns on exporting blooded stock. Fees are over fifty thousand U.S., and then there's shipping. Even if I could afford the colt, it's far beyond my means."

"If not the black, there is another way."

"No thank you, I don't want to go to jail."

"We can freeze a stallion's sperm. There are Arabian mares in America."

I thought I was immune, but I was caught up in it. The boy was out of place. For that matter so was the colt. I knew there were breeders in Egypt, but I thought they were on remote ranches on the upper Nile. Most were in the oil-rich countries of the sheik kingdoms. I was now thinking it was a scam.

"Who the hell are you, and where did you learn English?"

"My name is Omar. I was educated at Princeton. My father is in Iraq. He sent me here to live with my uncle; he sent me to school in America.

"Who's your father?

"He is one of the leaders the Americans don't trust. I am here with my brother. We cannot return to Iraq, or to America. My father's accounts are frozen, this is his way of providing for me and my brother."

We talked for a while, his story had a few holes when it came to the reason his father was on the outs with the Americans, but the rest seemed plausible. As unrealistic as it was, I was caught up. Sperm was only halfway there.

"I would need to find a mare."

"We have friends in America with a ranch where we board a few Arabian mares."

"That's some story, this makes no sense, but if you are on the level, how much?"

"For sperm, a guaranteed foal, no guarantee on the sex. Five thousand U.S. for a filly, ten if it's a colt. If you pick one of our mares another twenty-five. Colt or filly, it would be worth twice what you pay."

"I would want to see the stallion and know he is sound; I would also want to be there when you collect the sperm."

"Americans have little trust. Gestation is eleven to twelve months. A foal must be born early in the year to compete. The stallion is here; we only collect in February. If you are here that can be arranged. But to prove him sound one must ride him; can you ride an unruly stallion?"

“Unruly, that’s a strange word for an Egyptian, Omar. As for the rest, trust is a fool's game. I would have no recourse. If I agree, five for a live filly, ten for a colt, born in the States. I pick the mare, someone to witness the collection, transfer it to the States, observe the breeding, and be there when the foal drops.

“You must pay the five thousand when the sperm is collected.”

“No, money would be deposited in a U.S. escrow, payment on delivery.”

Omar turned to the boab, and after a moment:

”Agreed: Now once again, if you are interested, can you ride a stallion?

“Yes, to both.”

“Then, please, come follow us.”

As for the money, Omar was right. A pure Egyptian Arabian foal from a blooded stallion and a decent mare would fetch not twice, but four times the investment. At this point, the question was why, there had to be a catch; I was sure that would come later.

I locked the car and followed them to the stable courtyard. Egyptian Arabians are some of the most prized in the world. I had seen them in exclusive show arenas in the States, never up this close. As we approached the barns the groom came out leading one of the most majestic stallions I have ever seen. Then I realized it was the gray I had startled earlier in the barn. In full light he was black but turning dapple gray.

He was in his prime, about five years old. His head was classic Arabian, his eyes clear, but wild, seemingly untamed. He pranced, neck bowed, his small ears twitching in the direction of the gasps and stares of tourists who were frantically trying to keep out of reach of his rearing and striking legs.

Saddled in delicately dyed leather of English design, and bridled in a polished sterling snaffle, I thought he and I were out of place. He would demand applause in the most exclusive Western arenas.

I could not help thinking back thirty years to the days of my youth when I was living in California, and I rode my blooded stallion across those desert sands.

The groom disconnected the lead from the bit and offered me the reins. With his other hand he pointed toward the dunes behind the pyramids. I moved back out of the way; Omar approached.

"He will settle, take him to the desert?"

I was well past my prime. Thought: *I suffered, sometimes for weeks, while my body mended from broken bones lesser animals had given me.*

While I debated the area became crowded with tourists, who, with cameras in hand, had moved in too close. I looked around, noticed the patronizing smirk on the face of a British tourist, and then remembered, I was wearing levies, cowboy boots, and a western belt. I overheard another one make a crack about Americans and urban cowboys. Omar heard him, he tapped me on the shoulder, and then turned to the Brits and flipped them the bird. The Brits were laughing.

"Omar, you have got to be kidding; not a fucking chance!"

"Fuck the Brits, what's the worst, he dumps you on your ass. The sand is soft, he won't step on you, he will come home, and we will come get you."

More thinking*: I started riding when I was thirteen and my father bought a hobby farm. By my late teens I was exercising polo ponies and blooded thoroughbreds. I was thirty when I bought a ranch of my own where I raised and trained quarter horses. It had been a while, but there was a time I could handle an unruly stallion. Like the animal in front of me, I too have pride, and damn that Brit,* I really wanted to give it a try.

"What the hell? Yes, I would be honored to take him into the desert."

I really do need to quit thinking. I let myself believe it was a reasonably good idea, however like the rest of my ideas in Cairo, once again, my planning was not worth a shit. Mounting the gray might not have been too difficult if he was contained in a Brahma chute at a rodeo, but all I had was a short rein and 1200 pounds of uneasy horseflesh.

Damn the English, and the scraps of leather they call saddles, I was wishing I were in Texas, where they made saddles a man can hang onto. We danced around, clearing the courtyard of tourists who had moved in too close. The closest I could get was a handful of mane and one foot in the stirrup.

There was laughter coming from the direction of the tourists in the background. It was a really dumb idea after all. I stepped back, sweat pouring off me in rivets, my lungs heaving from the effort of the strain, the Cairo air, and my last pack of cigarettes.

I was ready to concede defeat and head for home. I looked around; the group of spectators had doubled in size, some cheering, the Brits laughing. I turned back to give it one more try, but it was useless. By then, I had excited the animal, and simply moving toward him caused him to rear and strike out in defiance.

I had given up when another Egyptian entered the courtyard and approached the gray. Gentleness and patience are not traits I was familiar with in Egypt. But, as the man approached, the gray sensed a change. He settled, nuzzling at the trainer's hand as he offered him some sort of treat. The man moved his hand to the stallion's neck, and as he stroked and quieted him, he turned and gestured for me to mount.

I stepped forward cautiously. Taking a grip on his mane, and then, after placing one foot in a stirrup, the trainer helped lift me to the saddle, he then quickly tightened the cinch and adjusted the stirrups. The gray stood quietly as the trainer rechecked the girth, released the bridal, stepped away, and gestured toward the sun setting behind the dunes.

I hesitated, not knowing what to expect. The gray stood quietly at first, but I could feel the twitching of his muscles, and sense his excitement building once again. I put pressure on him using the calves of my legs as I learned to do many years before; raw power and energy surged back into his body. He came alive, reared, then lunged toward the shadows behind the Pyramids.

I somehow managed to stay on board and regain control. We sidestepped through the area scattering the tourists, who, with cameras in hand, had moved in too close.

I was thinking I was too damned old to risk broken bones just to show off to a Brit I never met. However, the gray quickly settled. As we crossed the threshold separating the desert from the stables I looked back and saw Omar and the boab had smiles as wide as the Nile; the Brit was shaking his head.

I turned and settled in the saddle as we moved toward the brilliant colors of the setting sun. Soon, the moon cleared the tips of the pyramids, beckoning us to enter a world private to men less blessed.

The gray moved toward the desert as if crossing a field littered with the bones of his ancestors, carefully at first, picking his way out of the chaotic life of man, and into the Arabian nights of yesteryear.

As we cleared the glow of stable lights and the fading sounds of honking horns he began to surge, moving into the frail bit holding him back. The sun had set. We soon became accustomed to the shadows cast by a rising moon; our eyes adjusted, deciphering fact from fantasy. My confidence grew until I gave him his head and allowed him to roam at will, at whatever pace he chose.

The gray was not soured to a barn. Stretching his strides he headed into the desert leaving behind his chains to men and misery. As he reached further into the world of his ancestors, I moved my hand to stroke beneath his flying mane wanting to calm him to the fact that I was still on board. It was a needless gesture. My own age and anxieties had melted with the setting sun, and the fear I felt had disappeared, as had the quivering of the gray.

The colors cast on the horizon began to lose their brilliance. My mind substituted reality with thoughts of fabled Arabian nights and flowing tents; past dreams surfaced. As we reached the crown of dunes and the lights of the distant city emerged we paused for a moment, bringing life to the books and movies I had fantasized about while crossing the California desert as a youth.

The vision of city lights blurred from rising heat caused by multitudes and the pollution of a civilization buried in waste. I fantasize about clear skies and desert campfires surrounded by nomads of the Sahara gathering their clans and animals around them for protection against the night and their warring enemies.

We moved on, the gray striding effortlessly for what seemed but a few short minutes. As the moon rose high into the night skies and the blackness of the valleys behind the dunes disturbed my dreams of yesteryear, I sensed a time of concern that those we left behind may have already passed.

I reached beneath his mane to stroke his muscled neck and began to draw him down. The gray seemed to understand. Soon, he stood quietly looking into distant shadows, as reluctant as I to turn and head for home.

We watched the lights of the city for a time and then turned back. I gave him his head, but he stopped and stood a while longer, gazing at artificial lights cast on the Pyramids for the benefit of western man. I nudged him with my knees, he moved forward, but once again hesitated. It seemed like me, he too resented modern man's intrusion on reality.

Prancing, then settling, it took a few minutes before the gray seemed satisfied to have been allowed to run at his own pace with me letting him take whatever course he chose. He was quiet, no, more like subdued. I turned him for another look toward the freedom the desert offered, and then again back toward the stable.

At times dunes blocked our view; the gray allowed me to guide him, somewhat careless in his trust. We wandered a while; it was long past tourist time when we reentered the stable courtyard. The gray and I had cooled our ardent feelings and were once again back among mortals and reality. After having waited patiently the trainer stood to take the bridle; I dismounted.

The boab and the trainer approached. The trainer spoke Arabic-English. I thanked them. As I reached for my wallet, they gestured in such a way to tell me, but then quietly:

"Omar will contact you, after tomorrow, inshallah. This part was a gift."

"Tell Omar I will try to find a way."

It was September. After tomorrow would be a while, but this time I would try to find God. I thanked them again, and then turned for one last moment to approach the gray, wanting to let him know I understood that he too would look forward to another time.

Chapter 8

The fleeting hours of tranquility dissolved into the smell of auto fumes, crowded roads, and honking horns as I fought the traffic back to my flat.

The memories of my youth, combined with the solitude of the desert, made the night long and lonely. I lay awake for hours thinking of those I loved back home whom I had treated so carelessly over the years.

It had been a while, but there was a time when love mattered. I was beginning to realize one of the reasons I found myself so far away was that my ambitions had taken precedence over my family.

I dreamed of times and moments past.
The hours passed in thoughts of yesterday.
I rose from sleep and tried to make them last.
No matter, my mind awoke and made me pay.

New dreams held times and memories so dear.
The loneliness was gone a while, it seemed.
Then I woke to find that all was clear.
The room, the same, as empty as my dreams.

Those moments so long past I cherish now.
Had you asked me then they seemed so small.
Give me another chance tonight I'll take a vow.
To treat them as the coming of a fall.

I prayed to make this dream come true.
To somehow wake tonight and find you here.
It could only be a dream how good I'd feel.
When morning comes, this room you'll share.

The next morning, I shook the sleepless night out of my mind. I was beginning to understand the reasons for my being in Egypt had more to do with my personal life than with the IRS. It had been a coward's choice. When given the opportunity to leave my life in Oregon behind, I simply left without making the conscious decision to deal with my domestic situation for good.

The culture shock and the project had taken its toll. The contrast in the desert brought me back to reality. It was a turning point. On the way to work that morning I began to adjust. I was going to be here for a while, much longer than I had anticipated. It was time I began to accept this was Egypt, not America, if it was perplexing to me, I must be disconcerting to them, and some adjustments in my attitude were in order.

I met Tom at the Sonesta Hotel for breakfast. He asked me if I had bothered to read the COE safety manual.

"That's off the subject; why do you ask?"

"Look, over there."

Tom was pointing to an army base a short distance from the hotel. A man was standing on the top of a ten-foot wall with a 100-pound sack of cement on his shoulder. I started to say something to Tom about not seeing what it had to do with my project when the man dropped from the wall, still clutching the sack.

He hit the pavement, disappearing in a cloud of dust as the impact split the bag. The thief was still out cold when the police showed up and packed him off in a truck. I knew I needed to follow up on Tom's question. I had seen enough in Cairo to know safety was not an Egyptian priority. Tom dropped the subject after the police left and then headed for his office.

****

Off-the-track social issues.

The picture of the thief jumping from the wall gave me cause to think about accidents I see every day. I come across beggars with deformed or missing limbs. Deformities were not always due to an accident. There are traffic accidents daily and catastrophic construction mishaps are common, but most beggars are born sound of body. Sometimes, when a child is born into a beggar's family, the parents break and then twist the child's limbs to deform them, thereby ensuring the child's livelihood in later years.

Where are those crippled and deformed as a result of an accident? I have seen scars, but few crutches and no wheelchairs. Later, when I brought it up to Tom, he shrugged.

"People simply die. There is little or no medical care available for those who cannot afford to pay."

"What about for those of us who can?"

"Stay away from the hospitals. They're eighteenth-century when it comes to cleanliness. Don't deal with it yourself; infection is the biggest killer; washing a wound with Cairo water could be a death sentence. Leave instructions in your passport to be taken to the Embassy or the American medical clinic in Madi."

That was fine for Tom and the COE staff, who carried diplomatic passports. For the rest, the Embassy was an iffy option. None of my American staff or I ever needed medical attention. It was one of those issues better left to procrastination than resolution, since in Cairo for me, there was none. I followed Tom's advice and inserted instructions, both in Arabic and in English, in my passport to take me to the medical facilities at the American College at Maadi or the U.S. Embassy in the event of an accident or major illness.

The Aids epidemic sweeping the world hit Egypt during my stay. A few months after my arrival, the Egyptian Army insisted all expats had to have an HIV test to maintain their security passes. It was not a requirement for the Egyptian personnel.

I learned the Egyptian doctors taking the blood tests did not believe in disposable needles. I refused to go in, as did all the other expats. After a few days, when none of the Americans or Brits showed up on their projects, the Egyptian military compromised and allowed expats to supply tests from their own doctors. The American Embassy set up a medical plan for Americans. As time passed and new arrivals entered the country, the Egyptians conceded that foreign test certificates were acceptable, but they could not be more than two years old.

Egypt was a learning experience. Now, when I am in a foreign country, I simply assimilate into the culture without spending much time dissecting it. After living within an unfamiliar society for any length of time, the differences simply sink in; some rub off as the diverse aspects become apparent, and I need to adjust.

The villages of Egypt are crowded with children of both sexes. However, there is an obvious absence of girls or young unmarried women between the ages of eight and twenty on the city streets or in other public areas. When a girl or young woman does appear in public an adult female accompanies her.

Muslim laws forbid any physical contact before marriage. For a Muslim, virginity is a requirement for a suitable marriage. Keeping money in the family is a goal in Egypt, and the surrounding Arab countries where arranged marriages and marriages to first cousins are common.

Arranged marriage is not always forced in Egypt but is strongly encouraged. In upper-class families, engagements can last from one to two years to allow couples to become acquainted. It does not always work out in Egypt's middle and upper class where there is Western influence, and the girl wants out.

It is different in the villages where arranged marriage is the rule. A female child in a village is often forced to marry shortly after she has her first menstrual cycle, sometimes as young as eight or nine or by the time she is thirteen.

Doctor Osmond, the senior partner in the Egyptian half of EGICON, was educated in the States and earned a Ph.D. He and I never became friends, but we developed a mutual respect. I had been on the project for almost a year. The only Arab female I met associated with Doctor Osmond's company was Sarha, Doctor Osmond's secretary.

I entered Doctor Osmond's office one evening much later than usual. There was a woman dressed in expensive, stylish European clothes standing off to the side of his desk. She appeared to be in her early forties. She was one of the most stunning, beautiful women I have ever seen. I realized I was staring before I turned away. Doctor Osmond caught my look and introduced me to his wife. She offered her hand, which was unusual for a Muslim woman, and then excused herself in clear and precise English as she turned to leave the room.

The door was ajar. I had entered Dr. Osmond's office without knocking. Doctor Osmond stood up, turning his back to me; he moved to the window as the door closed behind his wife. The gesture seemed like a reprimand. I had been in Cairo long enough to know better, and I knew it best to wait until his mood settled before addressing the reason for my visit.

I stood next to him by the window watching as his wife entered the limo. He waited until it pulled away from the curb; when he turned back, he was smiling. It seemed I had misjudged his mood. What followed was the only personal conversation I had with Doctor Osmond, or for that matter, any of the Egyptians the entire time I was in Cairo.

"My wife is leaving for Paris; I always miss her when she's gone."

"Does she go to Europe often?"

Doctor Osmond was a wealthy member of society. I was stumbling; personal chitchat with one of Egypt's elites was an abnormal situation for me.

"We will be going on holiday to Spain next month. She wears European clothes when we travel, and she prefers to shop in Paris."

Doctor Osmond was a devout Muslim; he kept his prayer rug next to his desk. There had been times when he would excuse himself from a meeting to perform his daily prayers. I was a little embarrassed at my obvious ill-mannered stare and felt obliged.

"I'm sorry, Doctor Osmond, I didn't mean to stare, but your wife is very beautiful."

"Yes, she is, Mr. Pat."

I thought the conversation ended nicely; I was preparing to move on when he continued.

"You wouldn't understand."

"Why is that, Doctor Osmond?"

"Many men stare at my wife. She is much younger, and when we travel, she is often mistaken for my daughter. I would prefer she wore our traditional clothes, but she was educated in Switzerland and is hard to control."

I was stumped. Doctor Osmond and I were not friends, and our backgrounds were separated by centuries. As far as I am concerned, Muslims live in the 14th century, and their beliefs regarding the subjugation of women in society are criminal. At a loss for anything else to say.

"How long have you been married?"

"Almost twenty years, Mr. Pat, but you wouldn't understand."

It was the second time he invited me to pry. I have been in this situation before but could not remember how to end a conversation that I knew would end badly, without ending it, badly.

"Why is that, Doctor?"

"Because she is my sister."

I sat silently for a moment, then, given the situation, as tactfully as I could.

"That's not for me to judge, Doctor Osmond. I'm an outsider in your society."

"Normally, it is not allowed, Mr. Pat, but we can't have children, so it should be acceptable to you."

****

Thought: One of those constant contradictions in the Islamic world. From all outward appearances, Dr. Osmond was a devout Muslim. However, the Qur'an, Surah An-Nisa 4, 23, specifically forbids marriage between brother and sister. *"Forbidden to you are your mothers, your daughters, your sisters, your father's sisters and your mother's sisters, your brother's daughters and your sister's daughters."*

Zina is an Islamic legal term, including illicit sexual relations, in Dr. Osmond's case, with his sister, which can also be found in the Qur'an and the hadith. Qur'an, hadith, and law uniformly state that punishments for zina are the same for men and women. The death penalty is in use in many Muslim-majority countries, where it is utilized as sharia-prescribed punishment for crimes such as apostasy from Islam, adultery, witchcraft, and murder.

However, Surah 39.53 says, *"Say, O Prophet, that Allah says, O My servants who have exceeded the limits against their souls! Do not lose hope in Allah's mercy, for Allah certainly forgives all sins. He is indeed the All-Forgiving, Most Merciful."*

I suppose this was one of those times when Dr. Osmond found Allah.

Our conversation moved to the business at hand. I saw Doctor Osmond's wife once more before I left Cairo. It was the night before my final departure and the only time Doctor Osmond invited me to his home. Doctor Osmond's servants and wives prepared and served a buffet.

Dr. Osmond had the four wives the Muslim religion allows. His sister stood off to the side dressed in a stylish but traditional hooded Abaya, which covered her hair and all of her skin except for her hands and face. Only the men comingled.

****

Islam forbids alcohol consumption. You would never see a Muslim couple in a bar. Unmarried couples dancing together is haram, *anything that is forbidden by Islamic law.*

Although tourists would forget themselves at times, I never once saw a Muslim man kiss a woman in public. Men kiss men on the cheek and might shake a woman's hand; women kiss women.

Muslim women marrying non-Muslim men is forbidden. On the other hand, the Quran allows Muslim men to marry non-Muslim women.

In most Muslim countries, unmarried couples are forbidden to spend time together alone. As a rule, there is no public commingling of the sexes. At the time, Egypt was far laxer than the surrounding Muslim countries. I observed unmarried couples holding hands and talking, but except for a few whispers and an occasional giggle, there was no other physical sign of affection.

According to some interpretations of the Qur'an, Islamic Arabia considered infanticide a means for the prevention of poverty and was considered to be the solution for the liability of a female child. Muslim male children were revered; traditions were carried forward. Muslim male children do almost anything they please.

Only once have I seen an Arab discipline a child, male or female, and even then, it was a mild rebuke. Arab children are like many American kids; teens are the worst and rude beyond description. They are never taught respect for anyone or anything, which explains their attitudes as they grow into adults.

Islam forbids abortion. I prefer that part of their religion to the changing American values, which in some states allow killing a child up to the instant of birth as a convenience, or because it might have a physical defect, or simply be the wrong sex.

I stopped for breakfast at the Mena House, one of the oldest and most beautiful hotels in Cairo. Thirty minutes after placing my order, I was arguing with the waiter because I had just seen him gather glasses from a table where a group of tourists had left, pour the leftover orange juice into one glass, and bring it to me.

On the other side of the room, a child, about six years old, was throwing his leftovers around the restaurant. I was trying to convince the waiter I was not interested in recycled juice when a part of the kid's breakfast landed on the shoulder of the only clean shirt my houseboy managed to iron that week. The waiter apologized. I sat patiently while he scraped it from my shoulder and then tried to rub the stain from my shirt with the rag he used to wipe the tables.

A few minutes later, I had forgotten about the incident and was reading a week-old copy of an English newspaper while I waited for the waiter to bring oranges and a juicer from the kitchen. As the waiter approached, another blob of goop from the kid's plate landed on the placemat in front of me. I had no idea what the goop consisted of, but I lost my appetite.

I looked up; my waiter had stopped to take an order at another table and then carried the oranges back to the kitchen. My patience dissolved into a feeling of futility. I placed a five-LE note on the table and headed for the door. I had to pass the table where the brat and his family were sitting. As I was walking by the buffet, I noticed the scrambled eggs looked green and runny, much like the mess that landed on my shirt.

I scooped a handful out of the tray and paused at the table where the kid was reaching for the leftovers on his father's plate. I deposited the handful I was carrying in the lap of the man who seemed humored by his son's activities. In his haste to extricate himself from the dissolving mess in his lap, he overturned the pitcher on the table, spilling the contents in the direction of his wife and two other kids. The confusion made it possible for me to disappear into the crowd without having to face an unpleasant confrontation.

In the early morning hours, the road to Alexandria is an hour-and-a-half drive of monotony. Along the way, I reflected on other aspects of the culture. It is difficult to guess the ages of the Egyptians. Middle Eastern men usually wait until their mid to late thirties to marry because middle-class marriage in the Muslim world is a costly undertaking.

It requires a substantial dowry for the prospective bride. There is little credit available. Islam does not allow a person making a loan to charge interest. It is haram, which means prohibited, as it is considered usurious and exploitative. Most men wait until they are financially secure and then marry women twelve to fifteen years younger.

The Muslim religion allows men to have four wives. Some followed the tradition of Muhammad when he took Aisha, a nine-year-old child, for his bride. In today's Muslim societies, the youngest allowable age of the girl for a Muslim man to consummate a marriage is the day after she has her first menstrual cycle, which can be as young as eight or nine.

A Muslim man may divorce his wife simply by saying, *"I divorce you,"* three times. The most common term is Talaq. Which literally means release. Talaq is a unilateral repudiation of the wife by the husband and does not require the wife's consent. She must observe a waiting period of approximately three months to be sure she is not pregnant; then, she is free to remarry.

Temporary marriage for girls between the ages of nine and twelve is common in villages. By the time the child wife approaches the age of sixteen, she has had three or four children and is then often divorced and retired to a farmer's field or household chores and replaced by another temporary wife.

Sarha, Doctor Osmond's secretary, is twenty-five. She has never been married. She is a beautiful woman whom, on sight, many Western men would pursue. Talking to Sarha is like talking to a 12-year-old. It is not so much in what she says. I cannot understand most of it. It is her tone of voice and expressions that reflect an absence of maturity.

Young Middle-class men react to criticism by pouting. They shrink back from the anger in my voice that results from frustration with the *After Tomorrow, inshallah* attitude, and the lack of respect for the contract rules. Nevertheless, when you praise a young Egyptian it is as though you took off the training wheels.

I have always been a man who's enjoyed watching beautiful women. What better place than a swimming pool where I can hide the lechery in my eyes behind a pair of dark sunglasses? The pools in Egypt were a disappointment. Hotel pools patronized by the locals are for children and men. Mature Muslim women seldom enter the water.

It is rare, but when they do, young Muslim women approach the pool fully wrapped in a towel or ankle-length robe covering a modest swimsuit. Her husband takes the robe from her as she enters the pool and wraps it around her as she leaves the water.

Unlike some Muslim countries where you seldom see a woman dressed in anything besides basic black, Egypt is different. Egypt's population is 10% Coptic Christian and others who do not follow Muslim tradition. The British have also influenced the culture, as have the millions of tourists who visit the tombs of the Pharaohs.

Young women in a village field.

Not all Egyptian Muslim women are devout. Those who are single stray from traditions. As most Egyptian Muslim women age, married or single, they migrate back to basic black. The colors young Egyptian women seem to prefer are mostly reds and yellows in floral prints. The brighter the better, are most in style for those who depart from traditional Muslim clothes. It seems they try to imitate European and Western women who dress as they please in Egypt, so long as it is modest. Even so, you will not see much bare skin in a Muslim country, even Egypt.

During English and French rule, it was forbidden. However, circumcision for girls was and is widely practiced in the fundamental Muslim world. The middle and upper classes are reluctant to admit it, but as Islam takes deeper roots in the old traditions, the practice is expanding.

The Imam Shafi and Imam Ahmed Ibn Hanbal schools, two of the four major schools of Islamic jurisprudence, uphold that circumcision is obligatory for both males and females.

In Egypt, 86 percent of women and girls aged 15-49 have undergone some form of FGM. (*Cutting and other procedures that injure the female genital organs.*)

In June of 2008, the Egyptian Parliament agreed to criminalize FGM in the Penal Code, establishing a minimum custodial sentence of three months and a maximum of two years or an alternative minimum penalty of 1,000 Egyptian pounds (LE) and a maximum of 5,000 LE. As of yet no one has been convicted according to this law.

It is common in the villages where they perform the surgery under less-than-ideal conditions. The surgeon is usually one of the religious leaders assisted by a senior wife. The surgery is done without administering a painkiller. They remove the external genitals, including the clitoris. Some sew the opening shut so there is just enough left for the child to pee. The surgery leaves the girls scarred mentally and physically. The blood on the bedclothes resulting from the tear to reopen the passage on her wedding night is displayed to the wedding party and is a reason for rejoicing.

The best description I can use to describe most Muslim women is that they are sexless. Many are beautiful, but something is missing. It could be maturity from a Western man's point of view. However, perhaps I simply compare them too much to the liberated women of the West.

****

Regardless of the local culture, I knew Tom expected me to conform to American standards of safety and sanitation, *fat chance*. Tom usually has a reason for bringing up a point. I reread the COE safety manual and the safety plan I drafted when I first arrived in Cairo.

I could see Tom's point. I was letting the culture influence my decisions. To bring myself back to reality, I listed a few of the basic violations, which were an everyday part of my project, so I could have Hamid *try* to address them.

- Buy shoes, shirts, and pants for everyone. *Fuck that*, most will not wear them.
- No more heating tea with a cutting torch. *That is a maybe*.
- Put shoring in the excavation that is twelve feet deep and was caving in yesterday. *That is a reality*, but only if I can get Dr. Abboud to buy the material.
- Toilets, not bathrooms! *I do not care what they call them. They are fucking toilets*. We never did get the portable toilets I asked Abboud for the first week I was in Cairo. *That is a bitch*; it makes no difference if I get them, *they will not use them*, but it will make Tom think I tried.

The COE safety manual addresses sanitation as one of the highest priorities. As I was working on the list, Fathie, Dr. Osmond's purchasing agent, who does not speak, read, or write a word of English, entered the room. It seemed a suitable time to bring up safety and sanitation. I called Doctor Abboud and asked him to join me.

"Doctor Abboud, would you please tell Fathie to buy the portable toilets I asked you for weeks ago."

"They are expensive, and the laborers won't use them."

"I can't have the men relieving themselves in the middle of the construction site, Doctor Abboud. The COE is insisting we get the sanitation and the proper clothing resolved before they approve more payments."

"Have the men dig a hole in the corner of the site and put a piece of plywood over it with a hole in it. Tell Tom they won't wear the shoes or pants."

"Doctor Abboud, Dr. Osmond won't get any more money until we comply with the safety requirements. Sanitation is at the top of the list."

Doctor Abboud did not answer. I think he was reflecting on the phone conversation I overheard between him and Cesar. Abboud was insisting Caesar fund a larger share of the upfront costs. After a long pause and me thinking this was going to be another long day, Abboud shrugged his shoulders and gave Fathie some direction.

The portables were still in question. Abboud did agree to have a toilet put in the construction trailer. When I arrived at the site that afternoon, Hamid had installed one in the closet over a gaping hole dug in the sand.

"Andy, what are you using for a toilet?"

"General Aziz lets me use the one by his office."

"What about the rest of the crew?"

"Beats me."

"Andy, sanitation is part of safety; that's your job."

"Fuck that; shit is below my paygrade. There isn't a god damned thing I can do about it if you can't get the portable shitters; give me a fucking break. Literally, Pat, I've just about had enough of this shit! Abboud is not going to give in. This is their country…... Look, tell Tom to kiss your ass and Hamid to build the fucking outhouse."

I lit his fuse. Andy was pretty easygoing, but both Tom and I had been on his ass about sanitation issues. In reality, Andy's hands were tied. He submitted the requisition. When Abboud ignored them, Andy gave them to me.

"What the fuck? You and Abboud think alike, Andy? Two out of three. That works for me. Clever idea: now, why didn't I think of that?"

Actually, it was Abboud's idea when Andy ordered the portables. Andy thought it was a good compromise. Andy was right; it was my headache. We had fifty laborers on the site. I could imagine what the walls of the Army base smelled like.

I went back to the office and told Abboud his construction methods were unacceptable and that sewers needed to go somewhere besides a hole in the ground under the place where I intend to put my desk. Abboud could not understand why it was an issue.

“It’s a temporary office. You won’t be using it much.”

“Doctor Abboud, I’ve had enough of this shit. We will do some of it your way if you do part of it mine. Tell Fathie to order some plywood and a holding tank so I can have Hamid build an outhouse for the crew and order a holding tank and some pipe for the office.

“We don’t need a tank for the outhouse, and we can use mud bricks instead of plywood.”

"I’m done with this; if you don’t, I will, and I will back-charge Dr. Osmond."

It went on for a while. I told Abboud I would not move to the site until there was proper sanitation installed. It was absurd enough to be funny, except I have had to face enough emergency runs since I have been eating Egyptian food to know it was no laughing matter. He shrugged; it was prayer time. He told me to have Hamid deal with the problem.

Let me clarify when prayer time is. By testifying that there is one God and Muhammad is His Prophet, an individual distinguishes himself or herself as a Muslim by praying, which is salat. Muslims are required to pray five times a day: at dawn, noon, mid-afternoon, sunset, and evening.

Call dawn at 6 a.m. They are never awake, so change that to 9:00, noon works, afternoon 3 p.m. Sunset 6:00 p.m. Evening any time before midnight. If you miss one you have to make it up before the next one. That usually happens when I am in the room. Obviously, God takes precedence.

I returned to the site and told Hamid to put in a septic tank and run the sewer line from the toilet in the trailer. I gave in on the plywood outhouse and ordered mud bricks.

“Hamid, I’m meeting Tom tomorrow to get the pay estimate approved. Tell Doctor Abboud I expect to find my toilet working before the meeting, or Doctor Osmond is not going to get paid.”

Hamid would check with Abboud; it would get done inshallah. I gave up for the day and headed for my flat. Andy was home doing laundry. I was not in the mood for conversation. I went straight for the bathtub.

I was just relaxing when the washing machine discharged. I forgot the landlord had hooked the washing machine into the showerhead because it was easier than breaking into the concrete floor and installing a proper drain.

I stood up to let the water drain, and then I shut the washer down and took a shower. With Andy's load of wash and my bath, I was out of hot water. It was another typical ending to a day in Cairo.

Chapter 9

Today was a milestone and perhaps a turning point. Tom and I had spent the last few days arguing with Generals Olsen, Aziz, and Sayer, along with Colonel Baker and a few others I would rather forget about. The topic was still site access and security. We had been coming and going through General Aziz's base without issues, but it was still taking two hours a day to get the crew admitted to the site on General Sayer's base.

Tom was supposed to meet with the Generals that morning. I thought he might iron out access with General Sayer himself if I was not there. I sent Andy on ahead and pulled the covers over my head to drown out the chanting of the Mosque next door. Since nobody was paying attention to me, they would not miss me for a day. Andy was back in less than an hour.

"We can't get on the site."

"Who can't get on the site?"

"Nobody. Hamid is outside the gate to General Aziz's base with the laborers, and the guards won't let me in to see Aziz."

"I've really had enough of this bullshit, Andy. Call Tom; he's meeting with the Generals this morning."

"I did; the meeting was canceled. General Aziz didn't return his call."

"Fuck! Give me a few minutes to get dressed."

It had been weeks since we had problems with the entrance to General Aziz's base. I thought we were over that and dealing with access to General Sayer's base. When we reached the site, Hamid was sending the laborers home for the day.

"Hamid, where do you think you're going?"

"Colonel Sabin told us security wanted more information. We have to wait for new passes before we can go back to work."

"Get the crew over here."

Imitating Colonel Baker, I walked up to the gate, pushed past the guard, and led the crew toward the site. The guard was having a fit. Colonel Sabin was coming across the compound in my direction.

"Hamid, ask Colonel Sabin what the problem is."

Colonel Sabin sent the guard back to his post. He and Hamid spent the next ten minutes arguing while I stood in the heat. I grew tired of being left out.

"Hamid, ask the Colonel. Where is General Aziz?"

"Colonel Sabin said he didn't know."

"That's bullshit, and I know it. Tell the Colonel to tell General Aziz I'm going to take the crew onto the site, and I have no intention of filling out more fucking papers. Also, tell him I'm fed up; we've done it a dozen times."

I left Hamid to argue with Colonel Sabin. General Sayer must have known General Aziz had barred us from his base, so our guard was the only one at the gate between the bases.

I had called Tom before I left Abboud's office. He said he would call General Aziz and meet me at the site. Hamid, Andy, and I spent the next two hours sorting out some of the safety and quality control problems. Tom never showed.

I was really fed up. My belligerent entrance to the base had caused a stir with the military. When I tried to leave the construction site there were six of General Sayer's soldiers barring the way; I called out to Hamid.

"Find out what the hell is going on now!"

Well…., I finally really pissed off the General. General Sayer heard we entered the base without new passes, which he and General Aziz had agreed to the day before. He sent his security force with orders not to let anyone else enter or for us to leave the site until they had clearance from him. This time, it included me.

"This could take days, Hamid. See if you can talk one of the soldiers into finding General Aziz and ask him to come to the site."

I went back to the site office. I had all I was willing to take. Whatever resolve I had developed previously was diminishing as rapidly as my patience. I stepped outside reflecting on the current problem. While gazing out at the lack of progress I spotted the 980-loader Colonel Baker brought on site a few weeks earlier parked off to the side. The operator was asleep behind the wheel.

Hamid returned a few minutes later with Colonel Sabin in tow. By then, I cooled off enough to try to exercise a little patience.

"Well?"

"General Aziz says it's General Sayer's base."

"I know that, and?"

"You can't leave until General Sayer agrees."

So much for patience, the office was next to an eight-foot concrete block wall separating the base from the rest of Cairo.

"Hamid, I've had enough of this crap. Tell Colonel Sabin I know there's a road on the other side of that wall. Ask him if he's familiar with it."

Hamid asked the question. The Colonel shook his head in agreement. It was the main road past the base.

"Ask the Colonel if he thinks the loader is big enough to make a hole in the wall."

"Mr. Pat, you wouldn't!"

"Ask the prick!"

Hamid was arguing with Colonel Sabin. I sent Andy over to wake up the operator and have him bring the loader to where we were standing. The Colonel was getting the message by the time the loader arrived; his dark skin was turning pale. He turned to Hamid and said something in a significantly raised voice. The loader operator stopped in front of us as I turned to the Colonel and Hamid.

"Tell him, if General Aziz doesn't straighten out this mess so we can leave, I'm going to put in my own fucking gate."

The Colonel was getting the drift without more comments from Hamid but had not quite figured it out. Andy rejoined the conference. He had been sipping tea on the front steps of the office a few meters away and overheard enough to believe I was serious.

He and Hamid both started in on me about what Egyptian jails were like, and that I needed to calm down. Hamid added some shit about patience. I was livid. No! I was fucking livid! I looked over at the Colonel, who was meandering nearby.

"I'm not here to take a fucking patience course, Hamid. I don't care if you are Doctor Osmond's nephew. If you don't tell Colonel Sabin what I just said, I'm going to fire your ass and hire a Brit who will do what the fuck he's told!"

Hamid, more than a little reluctantly and then with some prodding from Andy, gave the message to Colonel Sabin, who then looked at me as if I had declared war on the Egyptian Army.

He thought about it for a minute, shrugged his shoulders, and headed for General Aziz's office. Ten minutes later General Aziz came through the gate surrounded by a dozen of his soldiers. I did not need to deal with more military personnel. I started in on him before he could start on me.

"General, don't bring your soldiers on my site? You know this is off limits to your personnel."

He stopped cold with a puzzled expression on his face.

"General, we have an agreement. I stay off the Army's land, and the Army is supposed to stay off my land, so if you don't mind, get them out the hell of here!"

Aziz turned and sent the soldiers back to the gate. Great…., now I had two groups of soldiers milling around my only exit from the site.

"Ah, Mr. Pat, what's the problem?"

"Don't give me that Ah, shit, General Aziz. You know damned well what the problem is. General Sayer won't let me leave, and you assured me there would be no more security problems."

"You need to calm down, Mr. Pat. I don't have authority on this base; General Sayer is in charge. There have been protests at the college and threats against the military. General Sayer issued orders to clear everyone before they can return to this base, and I can't have them wandering around my base in the meantime. You should not have brought them here."

"General, I'm well aware of the trouble with the religious groups. The Embassy posted a travel warning, but the riots are four hundred kilometers south of Cairo. General Sayer is just using it as an excuse to stall the project. Talk to him because I am going to leave here today, and if I have to build my own entrance to the site to do that, I will."

General Aziz said something to Hamid in Arabic. Hamid merely pointed to the loader, and then he and Andy headed for his office. General Aziz looked at me and shook his head.

"General, we're leaving this fucking site today, one way or another!"

"You must learn patience, Mr. Pat. I'll talk to General Sayer."

General Aziz left for General Sayer's office. I went over to sit down in the shade and wait. Andy was coming back out of his office. He and Hamid were approaching with concerned looks on their faces.

"Pat, you need…."

"Don't fucking say it, Andy."

"Say what? That I think you're nuts, and you're going to get us all shot. He's a general in the fucking Egyptian Army for Christ's sake. The men at the gate are armed; they weren't yesterday; General Sayer is serious."

"The Generals won't let his soldiers shoot anybody. If he does, the COE will cancel the project for good, and they will be answering to their military. Andy, this has become a fucking game with those two. We're in the middle. Today is as good a time as any. Nothing else is working. It's been months. Something has to give. If I do the project will go down the toilet. One way or the other, we are all leaving this base today."

"That's some consultation. Why don't you call the Embassy and let Colonel Baker sort it out."

"You call him, or did you forget we don't have phones on site? They've had weeks. General Olsen and the Colonel keep telling me it's my problem. At least this way, maybe I can finally make it theirs."

The discussion went on for fifteen minutes. I glanced toward General Sayer's office wondering what was taking Aziz so long. Dammed! Aziz was sneaking through the gate back toward his own office and taking his soldiers with him. I started to follow. General Sayer's soldiers closed the gate behind him and stood in front, baring the way.

"That does it. Hamid, tell the loader operator I want a six-meter-wide hole in the wall."

Hamid went over to the operator and had a brief conversation with him.

"Mr. Pat, he refuses."

"I'm not surprised. Tell him to get off and go to the tea shed."

The operator was off the cat and in the shed before Hamid got through explaining.

"Hamid, tell the laborers to get out of the way." "Andy, you and Hamid go wait in the office."

I climbed on and headed for the wall, which was another example of Egyptian construction methods. The wall was no match for the five-yard bucket of the thirty-five ton machine. All it took was one pass.

A few minutes later, there was a new entrance to the site. I was a little over-anxious and made a bigger mess than I meant to. Traffic was backing up where debris from the wall was blocking one lane, the rest of the traffic was slowing to dodge chunks of concrete, which were scattered over the other two lanes.

*Big **F** in my Patience Class.*

Some of the construction crew were leaving out the hole in the wall at a run as I moved the loader back. I forgot for a few minutes that Egypt is like the U.S. Police are apt to grab anyone in sight when an unfamiliar situation occurs. An American tearing down a maximum-security wall to an Army base in Cairo would certainly be an unfamiliar situation for the Egyptian police.

I looked back toward the old entrance. Two of General Sayers's men were jogging toward his office; the rest were approaching me at a run.

Lots of excitement. Hamid and Andy joined the fray. General Sayer's men spoke to Hamid, then posted themselves along the street barring sightseers from entering the area. One of them pointed Andy and me to a bench we had set by a tree on the site. It appeared they would wait for General Sayer before dealing with us.

I told Hamid to have the remaining laborers clean up the mess and then get the guard from the entrance gate to General Aziz's base and post him inside the new opening. There were no soldiers left at the gate between General Aziz and Sayer's base.

I knew I would have to face General Sayer eventually. Andy and I went to the bench in the shade, sat down, and waited. I told

Andy if he and Hamid wanted to leave it was time. I have to give Andy and Hamid credit. Neither of them left. Hamid brought me a fresh cup of tea and joined us by the tree.

"How long do you think it will take, Pat?"

"I don't know, Andy, but it won't be long?"

A few minutes later, Colonel Sabin was approaching with a half-dozen of Aziz's soldiers. I started to say something but thought better of it. The Colonel stopped, staring at the breach in the wall, and then called Hamid.

"General Sayer has sent for you."

"Yes, Hamid, I thought he might."

Colonel Sabin was escorting me to General Sayer's office. General Aziz arrived and posted his men next to the hole in the wall. Andy and Hamid started to join the parade when General Aziz joined the crowd.

General Aziz stopped and took Colonel Sabin aside. Colonel Sabin was livid. Aziz did not appear too upset. It was more like he was smirking when he turned to me, thought better of it, and then turned and left without another word. That did not quite settle on me.

Colonel Sabin was really pissed. He graphically told Hamid that General Sayer wanted to see only Mr. Pat. I told Andy to follow Aziz to his office and call General Olsen and Tom. I felt I might need some military cooperation.

When we got to the hall leading to Sayer's office, Colonel Sabin pointed me to a bench. There was a guard on either side; it was not a time to argue. Ten minutes later, the Colonel returned and escorted me to Sayer's office. I do not know how he did it, but General Aziz beat us there.

General Sayer and General Aziz were engaged in a heated conversation near a map of the base posted on the wall. It was apparent Aziz was trying to calm Sayer down. Sayer was pacing, glancing from me to General Aziz. He was mad as hell, struggling not to show it. He took a breath and sat down at his desk. He did not offer me tea.

It took a few minutes. General Aziz said something. More excitement, the Generals were back at it. This was not going the way I expected. Mr. Pat was mentioned a number of times. General Aziz moved back, General Sayer, and the mood in the room calmed down.

"Ah, Mr. Pat. We seem to have a problem."

Sometimes, it is simply better to play Gomer Pyle.

"We do, I'm sorry to hear that, General. What's the problem?"

"We have had a breach of security, but General Aziz and I have a way to solve it."

"What do you suggest, General?"

He was a little shaky when he took out plans for his base.

"Our solution, Mr. Pat, is you should put in your gate here. That way, you won't have to come through General Aziz's gate, and your people won't have to cross my property and deal with our security."

Not at all what I expected. It was the location where I just breached his security.

"General, what a great idea. Why didn't I think of it?"

If it helps to make him the hero, why not? The General never did mention my causing the breach in security. After a few more minutes, while he and General Aziz were still holding a heated discussion, I excused myself.

"General, is there anything else? I need to go."

General Sayer looked toward me. He had a sullen expression and was shaking his head.

"No, Mr. Pat, but you must remember you are a guest in my country; we have rules, very strict rules. You must learn to follow them. You have made this decision, so I will hold you responsible for everyone who enters the site. I suggest you make sure they stay off the rest of my base."

"I'll build the wall between the site and your base now that I can get the material on site, General; will there be anything else?"

"No, Mr. Pat."

I left the generals to sort out whatever they had to sort out. As I approached the site, Colonel Baker, General Olsen, flanked by Tom, Andy, Hamid, and Colonel Sabin, were standing by the hole in the wall.

"What are all you people doing here?"

"What the fuck were you thinking?"

"About what? General Sayer and I settled the security issues. Now, we have our gate. What the fuck are you doing here, Colonel?"

Utter confusion, everybody talking at once.

"One at a time, what's the problem, Colonel?"

"Andy called; he said General Sayer placed you under arrest."

"You know how it is in Cairo, Colonel." "Sorry, Andy." "Colonel, messages sometimes get turned around in translation. I told Andy to let you know General Sayer solved the security access by asking me to put in a new entrance to the site for our exclusive use."

I explained the lead-up and the outcome of the conversation with General Sayer. Tom and the Colonel were a bit miffed at my methods and said so.

"Look, Tom, why not just report it as I've explained it? General Sayer will be happy because it will look like he's working with us. Colonel Baker will be happy because he won't have to lead a rescue squad. General Aziz will be happy because I won't bother him every day with security issues, and I'm damned happy because my boss will think I'm learning some patience and have successfully worked out the security problems with the Egyptian Army."

The laborers finished cleaning up the street. I told Hamid to have an iron gate installed in the morning. Colonel Baker mumbled the only squad he was going to lead was one escorting me to the airport if I pulled another stunt like this one.

General Olsen smiled and saluted the guard as he went out of the new entrance. Tom stuck around.

"That was ballsy, Andy's right, you're lucky you're not in jail, or worse. How did Aziz take it?"

General Aziz was coming from General Sayer's office and on the way back to his. He stopped for a moment and then approached Tom and me.

"Ah, Mr. Pat, General Sayer is angry, you must learn some patience."

"Yes, General, I'll enroll in a course in the morning. Thank you for resolving the access problem with General Sayer."

"The soldiers will remain until you have a proper gate installed. You must also build the wall and secure the area quickly."

"Yes, General, I'll get right on that."

General Aziz was smiling when he left for his office. Tom gave me a quizzical look. I, too, was a little perplexed. I had watched the banter between the Generals; it had me thinking.

"Tom, it's beginning to make sense. General Aziz almost couldn't contain himself in front of Sayer. Sayer was pissed, yes. But I don't think it was at me. I'm beginning to think this all started as a game of sorts, a sparring match between the Generals."

"You can't be serious."

"Think about it. None of this has made sense. General Aziz annexed his land without his permission. Maybe he did ask, and General Sayer objected. Aziz's base is a postage stamp compared to Sayer's. Aziz doesn't have the land. It was really no big deal because there was more than enough vacant land on Sayer's base, but Aziz didn't have to include the area where he parked his car and planted his garden. General Sayer had a barbecue and a picnic table under the tree next to the garden. We are going to have to remove both. It was his favorite spot, and there aren't any other shade trees in the vicinity. I think it got out of hand over the car shed. The garden and picnic areas compounded it. With their bookra inshallah attitudes, time doesn't mean a fucking thing; you and the OMC know that."

"That doesn't explain why they let you get away with a stunt like this."

"No but putting in the gate has been a subject at every meeting since we started this. It's in the minutes."

"Yes, it is, and we were working on it. This reflects on both the COE and the OMC. When this gets back to DC, they are liable to have us both escorted out of Egypt."

"About you, me, and the OMC? Shit…., Tom, we've been the fucking patsy. They both had to know it was getting out of hand. They also knew I was more than a little pissed at all the bullshit and that something had to give, and soon, otherwise, this project would go down the toilet. They were caught up in the game. Locking me on the site was the last straw. Not that I'm so damned important, but it finally lit my fuse. So, yes, I went off the reservation, and yes, I do know I'm lucky I'm not in the guard house. We were all just pawns. It was over when General Sayer no longer controlled access to the site. Checkmate, General Aziz wins."

"That's farfetched and more than a little bullshit. The wall is on Sayer's base. All he has to do is post guards to keep you from using it until it's repaired. In the meantime, he could have thrown your ass in jail."

"That's not going to happen. I've been thinking about this since the loader arrived. The hole is where the plans show the new gate. The Ministry of Defense approved the location, and so did General Aziz. It's on the drawings and is part of our contract. General Sayer can't argue with that. This is an internal military issue between two feuding generals. Write up the report the way I explained it. With site access settled, Glen and General Olsen will sign off on it."

"It's in your ballpark. Put it in writing. Draft minutes for a meeting, date it yesterday. I'll call General Olsen and clear it up with the OMC."

Reality: The COE, OMC, and everyone on the JV side, including Andy, were more than a little aggravated. However, we were all relieved the security issues were finally resolved and we could get on with the project.

In Tom's mind, the gate was history when General Sayer did not arrest me and throw me out of Egypt. Tom reached for his briefcase.

"By the way, here's the letter you need for the Department of Transportation."

"Tom, my Oregon license is good in Egypt. I don't need an Egyptian driver's license."

"You need a resident visa. Once you apply for it, you need a local license. Get it and leave a copy with the OMC. Nobody avoids a wreck in this country forever. If you don't have a valid driver's license, even the embassy staff won't be able to fix that mess."

In Cairo, the foreigner is always at fault; if he had not been in the area, he would not have been involved in the accident. They would impound the car and throw a foreigner in jail until the fines and bills were paid.

"I'll try to take care of it in the morning; how about that fishing trip we've talked about?"

"When you get your license. I'm not going to do all the driving, and you're not driving my car without one. We could take yours, but you surprise me every morning when you make it to work in that piece of shit."

Tom flipped me the bird as he drove out the hole in the wall. I laughed. No, not really. Actually, I breathed a sigh of relief. I had lost control. I knew I was damned lucky not to be sitting in General Sayers's guardhouse.

Chapter 10

A driver's license could take the better part of the morning. Hazem had disappeared with the laborers during the gate incident. I did not want to wait for Hazem and deal with the traffic or the crowds in the middle of the day.

Government agencies dealing with ex-pats usually had someone who spoke Arabic-English. I decided to try to handle the issue myself. When I arrived at the station, the place was typical of Egypt. I was pushing my way to the head of the line like the rest of the crowd when I bumped into a Brit who introduced himself as Oscar. Oscar told me it was his third trip. We decided to make it a team effort.

Pushing and shoving, we finally made it to the head of the line. The clerk gave us a stack of papers; they were in Arabic. *Yes, I know*; we should not have been surprised. It was after 11:00, about the time Hazem got to the office. I suggested we have Hazem translate them.

Hazem met me with an apology of sorts for disappearing as soon as I broke through the wall. Hazem translated and we filled in the blanks. There were a few extra requirements. We had to have a medical doctor certify our health and get an eye test. It was the middle of the following day by the time we had the papers filled out. We decided to give it a shot the next morning.

My planning was getting better. The traffic was lighter in the early morning. We were the first to arrive at the window. The clerk took one look and handed back our applications. More Arabic-English. An impatient British expat waiting in line behind us stepped in and translated.

"What the hell's the matter with you two idiots? The papers must be filled out in Arabic."

"Shit….! Good point."

I wondered why I had not thought of that. The only country that provides paperwork in another language is the U.S. It was back to Hazem, who did not arrive at the office until noon. Oscar and I decided not to try again that day and arranged to meet the following morning. When the door opened, and after we made it to the front of the line, we learned it was the morning for the motorcycle tests. We would have to wait until ten before we could take our driving tests.

While we waited, a young Egyptian fluent in English approached. The test was simple. Driving a car down a straight line and then back up to the starting point, about twenty meters in all. The yellow cones were far enough apart to drive a Mac truck through.

We flipped a coin. Oscar lost; he went first as he approached the cones the man at the other end of the course still taking his motorcycle test aimed for Oscar's headlights. They met in the middle. Oscar stopped. The motorcycle swerved and continued the course. Oscar started again, finished, and approached the man giving the test.

Oscar failed. He was not supposed to stop the car in the middle of the course. The men giving the tests do not care if they get their signals crossed; arguing was not going to change the guy's mind.

Our translator had stuck around. My turn, or so I thought. When I approached, he waved me off. We both failed because we were driving the same car. We would have to come back another time. I asked if that is why they gave the car the traffic tickets, and what would have happened if Oscar had passed the test.

"They don't like white expats, especially Brits. There's no way either of you is going to pass unless you speak Arabic and know the rules, not the driving rules, their rules. He could probably be talked into waving the test."

The kid's game sunk in. He was collaborating with the guys giving the test.

"How much?"

I took out a 20-LE note.

"Fifty each, U.S."

"No fucking way!"

One more time around the conversation we settled on fifty total. The driver's license ordeal was over.

As Oscar and I started to leave, there was more excitement in the test area. It was too late to go to work. It looked like the best entertainment in town. I suggested we stay and watch the show.

The next driver started by backing into a motorcycle. There is always excitement in Egypt, not a lot of logic, just excitement. I was cracking up. Hitting the motorcycle did not count because it was not in the test area.

The next contestant was a young, attractive Asian woman in her early twenties. The racket stopped. She knew she was the object of attention and seemed to be enjoying it.

She smiled and performed the task without a hitch. She got out of the car and walked up to get her license stamped. The guy told her she failed and would have to come back the following day. More excitement, our translator approached the woman; Oscar and I left. I had not been to the site for three days.

I called Tom to tell him I had the license, and we could plan the fishing trip. When I told him about the trouble I had to go through to get it he asked me why I did not get an international driver's license before I left the States. Five bucks and five minutes would have saved the three-day hassle. He then asked me how the construction schedule was coming along.

There were new issues, but I did not feel like bringing them up just yet. Tom told me if I did not have the schedule done that week, he could not approve the current payment. I had enough headaches without the JV partners bitching about money.

I told Tom a construction schedule based on reality would show we would be late; Glen would hold up payment for sure. Tom told me to follow the directions in the documents.

We needed a starting point. A baseline schedule starting with the date the contract was awarded was due when I arrived. Cesar failed to provide it. Tom told me to do the schedule based on what I knew before I left the States. I could update it when I submitted the next pay estimate and, at that time, request added time and money for the delays.

I hated to take time preparing a schedule I knew from the start was full of holes, but I had enough experience with the American government to know Tom was not kidding.

When I arrived back at the site, Andy was at the front desk. Hamid was at mine with someone I did not recognize.

"Andy, who's that with Hamid?"

"Anwar."

"Who the fuck is Anwar, and why is the tree still standing? It's been three days."

"Don't jump on me, and don't be so impatient; the tree seems to be an issue."

"What's this patience crap coming from you? I get enough of that shit from everyone else."

"I know, but you're the one running this zoo. I don't know who he is. He was here when I arrived. I think he works for Abboud."

"What's it about?"

"Haven't a clue; something about the tree. They both ignored me when I asked."

Abboud mentioned someone by the name of Anwar was working in Kuwait; that project was winding down. Anwar would be the construction manager in charge of scheduling the subcontractors when he returned. I thought I nipped that in the bud when I told Abboud the schedule, and dealing with subs was in my job description. I did not get a straight response. Abboud slipped back into Arabic and then disappeared.

It had only been a few weeks. Andy may have been right about the patience bit, but so far, other than Hamid and Hazem, the Egyptians had refused to come to the site. We were meeting at the head office. I was fed up with being ignored and then patronized by Egyptian players already assigned to the contract. The site was mine, and I sure as shit did not need Anwar.

"Hamid, I told you to have the loader take the tree out three days ago?"

The tree was a large willow in the middle of the construction site. It was about one and a half meters in diameter and forty meters tall. It was one of the first tasks on my list once I saw the site, but it was in General Sayers picnic area. I had been putting it off. The tree was in the way; it had to come down, and after the incident with the gate, the sooner, the better.

I had done some logging in Oregon and would have cut the damned thing down myself. It would have taken all of ten minutes. Hamid and I had been discussing methods since the first day we managed to get a crew on site. Explaining I needed a chainsaw was beyond the grasp of both Abboud and Hamid; when the loader arrived on site, it was a moot issue, *I thought*.

"I'm sorry, Mr. Pat. Anwar says it's too dangerous to push over with the loader."

"He did? Who's Anwar, Hamid?"

"Sorry, Mr. Pat. This is Anwar. He's the construction manager for Doctor Abboud's company."

That was a switch. I thought Abboud was a partner in Dr. Osmond's company.

"Hello, Mr. Pat, it's good to meet you."

"Sorry, I can't say the same, Anwar. I think you and I should have a little chat."

"Can we do it later, Mr. Pat? I need to go over some things with Hamid ….."

"That's enough, Anwar. We need to talk."

Anwar turned to Hamid and said something in Arabic.

"Hamid, Anwar, use English in this office. Hamid, get out there and take the tree out the way I told you to."

Hamid just stood there. He was having a problem taking directions. It was obvious there was a question of authority. I thought Hamid, Anwar, and I should start the conversation over.

"Anwar, how do you want to take the tree out?"

"The subcontractor will take it out with his laborers, Mr. Pat. They will dig a hole around it, cut the roots, and it will fall."

"That works, Anwar, but tell me, how is the subcontractor going to make sure the tree doesn't fall on one of his workmen or across the new security fence we just built?"

"The subcontractor has agreed to take the tree out in exchange for the wood. If one of his workmen is hurt, or the fence is damaged, it is his responsibility."

"Patience, my ass, Andy." "Hamid, get out there and tell the operator to push the fucking tree down with the loader and then drag it out of our way."

I was not sure how I should handle another boss giving me orders, but I concluded a direct approach would be best.

"Look, Anwar, whatever happens on this site is my responsibility. Get rid of that subcontractor and then go back to wherever it is you came from. If you can't do that, leave Hamid alone. If you have suggestions about construction methods on this site, bring them to me. I'll decide what to do about it."

"I am just trying to help, Mr. Pat."

"Don't."

Anwar did not leave. He wandered around the site with his clipboard in hand and a sour look on his face. Hamid was busy with the loader operator. I was on my way to the construction office when Tom arrived.

I forgot Tom and I had scheduled a meeting with General Aziz. I was not looking forward to it. General Aziz was a little miffed that I had ignored General Sayer's orders when I brought the loader back and, with it, a dozer without clearing it with General Sayer. General Sayer was complaining to Aziz. It seemed the noise of the equipment was disturbing his prayers.

Tom and I were entering Aziz's office when Anwar joined the party. It seemed they knew each other. Muslims generally do not make physical contact with members of the opposite gender. However, on greeting, a man may side kiss the other man's cheek two or three times, or hug.

General Aziz ordered tea before I could say anything to Anwar. Anwar and the General were huddled in a conversation. Twenty minutes later, Anwar was still discussing whatever it was he was discussing with General Aziz in Arabic. Tom lost his patience and entered the conversation.

"General, can we get on with the meeting?"

"Anwar and I have settled it."

Tom gave me one of his funny looks. I shrugged my shoulders. It was going to be the hard way.

"General Aziz, Anwar has no authority on this project and no business discussing anything with you. Whatever it is you two have agreed to, forget it."

"But, Mr. Pat, General Aziz has ………"

"Anwar, I'm warning you, if you don't stay out of this, I'm going to ask Tom to have you barred from the site."

Anwar sulked through the rest of the meeting. Tom and I did not accomplish anything, but Anwar got the General's mind off the equipment complaint. The meeting adjourned. Tom and I headed back to the site. Anwar was trailing behind.

Tom walked straight to his car and then mumbled something about enforcing the American requirements of the contract if I did not get Anwar off the site. Tom was upset. The Egyptians ignored us and discussed anything they felt like with us around, thinking none of us understood.

Tom heard enough to realize Anwar was cutting a deal with the General. That could mean Anwar offered the General a bribe. Tom left. The tree was still standing. Hamid and Anwar were ignoring me.

"Anwar, what did you offer General Aziz?"

"Nothing, Mr. Pat."

"Don't give me that shit, Anwar, and stay away from Hamid and the Generals." "Hamid, I've had enough of this shit. Get back to work. I want that tree down before I leave today."

"Mr. Pat. General Aziz asked if we would give him the tree."

Things were coming together. Wood in Egypt is scarce and expensive. The lumber from the tree was worth at least 4,000 LE. It appeared Genera Aziz had his eye set on it from the start. He was not alone. When we buried the garden and moved the picnic equipment, General Sayer sent word that when the tree came down, it was to be cut up, and he would have it removed from the site.

"Anwar, you said you didn't make a deal with the General. The tree is on General Sayer's land. It is not going to be General Aziz's property until this building is finished. The tree belongs to General Sayer unless he says General Aziz can have it, do you understand?'

"But, Mr. Pat, General Aziz agreed to forget about the gate and the pictures."

"Anwar, stay out of this! How the hell do you know General Aziz? Shit….! Never mind. Go tell General Aziz he can't have the tree unless General Sayer and the COE agree."

I turned around and stormed off. I was out of patience with both Anwar and Hamid. I also had a feeling my problems with Anwar were just beginning. I did not trust Anwar or General Aziz.

I waited until the tree hit the ground and then told Hamid to stack the logs and larger limbs in a corner of the site as far away from the gate between the two sites as possible and to post a guard on it. I then headed for the office and a discussion with Abboud about Anwar.

When we built the temporary fence separating the area from General Sayer's base, we installed a man gate. As I was getting into my car, two groups of soldiers, one from General Aziz's base and one from the Technical Institute, were approaching the tree. As I watched, forty soldiers in field dress pushed Hamid and the workers out of the way and then surrounded the tree.

Everybody wanted patio furniture.

"*Now what*? .... Andy, Hamid, go see what's going on."

Andy was waved off by the military when he approached the area. Hamid was trotting my way.

"Mr. Pat, the soldiers don't want us there."

More excitement: There was not a lot of discussion. The soldiers from different sides were pushing and shoving each other.

"Hamid, go find Colonel Sabin or General Aziz."

Hamid ignored me. He headed for the soldiers rather than face the Generals. I waited until Hamid managed to get General

Sayer's men on one side of the tree and General Aziz's men on the other.

General Sayer's men were wearing black armbands. It appeared General Sayer was anticipating a problem and had drawn the lines of battle by making sure his men recognized one another if the argument became physical. Hamid trotted back to me.

"Hamid, what the hell is going on?"

"General Aziz sent his men to get the tree, and so did General Sayer."

"Hamid, go tell them the tree belongs to me and to get off my site."

It was too late. Generals Aziz and Sayer were approaching the guards surrounding the tree.

"Hamid, it's teatime; let the Generals sort it out."

We left the Generals alone with their men. I thought they would settle it themselves, and we could all go back to work. I waited an hour, watching the excitement from my office. It was obvious from the arm-waving that the argument would continue until someone besides generals of equal rank could sort through it. No such luck; Fuck...., it was up to me.

"Good afternoon, General Sayer, General Aziz. What seems to be the problem?"

The Generals started in on me, in Arabic.

"One at a time, and in English, please."

Neither answered. They turned and headed for their offices. Hamid wandered over; I asked him to see if he could find out what the argument was about.

"By the way, Hamid, where did Anwar go?"

"He left when the soldiers arrived."

"That figures."

Colonel Sabin arrived a few minutes later.

"Hamid, see if he has some answers."

Colonel Sabin was raising his voice; Hamid was backtracking.

"Well?

"Colonel Sabin says to tell you the tree has been placed under military arrest."

"What? What the hell does that mean?"

Both Generals felt the tree belonged to them. Thanks, Anwar! They directed their men to remain on guard until its ownership was established. That could take some time, and the tree was in the middle of where I was supposed to build the building.

The tree came down on Wednesday. Tom and I took off Friday and Saturday. On Sunday, when Tom and I arrived at the site, the tree was still under armed guard.

"Hello, Tom; are you ready for the meeting?"

Tom did not know about the tree. I had not bothered to tell him because I thought it would be resolved by the time we came back to the site. Besides, I was not sure how to explain it. When he saw the soldiers around the tree, he stopped.

"Don't ask, Tom. Let's go see Aziz."

The meeting was routine. It did not appear Aziz was going to bring the tree up in front of Tom. I would also have liked to avoid it. I knew Anwar made a deal with the General and I was not able to find out what it was. The General was getting ready to adjourn the meeting.

"General, what do you want me to do with the tree?"

"Ah yes, Mr. Pat, the tree is a problem."

"Yes, General, it appears it is. General, what's up with the tree?'

General Aziz fidgeted a few moments before he answered.

"Mr. Pat, you were supposed to build the wall between the bases first. It's still his land. General Sayer owns the tree because the wall is not finished."

"Great, it appears it's settled. Will you please remove your guards?"

"Mr. Pat, the tree is on this side of where the new wall will be. Build the wall, and the tree will belong to me."

The contract documents allowed me to use local concrete and concrete blocks. There was no reason I could not build the wall. However, after I installed the gate, Doctor Osmond told me not to spend the money until we received the check for mobilization. I had installed a temporary wire fence.

"I'm sorry, General Aziz, there won't be any money to build a permanent wall until the rest of the staging area is finished."

I thought Tom was going to gag on his tea.

"What are you talking about?'

"Tom, please, stay out of this one."

"Mr. Pat, if I call back my men, so will General Sayer. You could move the tree to my base tonight.

"General, if you think for one minute that I'm going to try to steal the tree, you're crazier than I think you are."

The crazy comment was a slip-up. It pissed the General off; he decided it was his prayer time.

"Pat, what's going on?"

It was too ridiculous to explain.

"Tom, ask the General when he cools off. I've had enough of the tree. Also, explain to him that if this project is still held up by the tree tomorrow, I'm going to give you a bill for time that will make the last one look like pocket change."

I stormed out the door, leaving Tom to deal with the General. Tom had no clue what the problem was. As for me, I could not wrap my mind around it. When I returned to the site, General

Olsen and Colonel Baker were talking to Andy. General Olsen was having a tough time containing his laughter. Colonel Baker was shaking his head.

"Hi, Andy, General, Colonel." "Andy, did you explain our current delay?"

"Briefly."

Tom came back to the site, mumbling to himself about the Red Sea and a fishing trip. When he reached us, he broke the news to General Olsen and the Colonel. General Aziz refused to budge. It would be his computer center. As far as he was concerned, it was his tree. His soldiers would remain until General Sayer gave him the tree or when General Sayer had to concede and remove his troops when I built the new wall. In the meantime, the other work was at a standstill. It was too much for Colonel Baker.

"A fucking tree is holding up a project I've spent four years on. Great!"

"Look, Colonel, the Camera, and the hole in the wall, well…., that was my doing. I'm lucky I'm still here and not sitting in a military jail. I am not, repeat! Not going to move that fucking tree until the Egyptian army agrees. What I am going to do is follow everyone's advice and exercise some patience. As far as I'm concerned, the tree is the Egyptian Army's and the COE's problem. I'm going to send everybody home and then go to the Heliopolis office. I'll return to the site when you guys get it sorted out."

Chapter 11

I cooled off, but I did not go back to the office that day. I knew Tom would be looking for me and try to con me back into the argument. I gave it three days. The guards still had the tree under arrest. With no end in sight, I decided to try to negotiate a truce.

The Generals were more amicable than I had anticipated. It seemed they were working on a compromise, and the issue would soon be settled, inshallah. In the meantime, the tree would remain on the site, and so would the guards. The best I could do was to convince them to let me drag the tree out of the way so we could get something done on the site.

My patience course was telling me I had to take one thing at a time. I figured the tree was probably pretty low on Allah's list of things to do, and it could take a while. In the meantime, the Generals decided to have their soldiers cut it up and stack it until Allah agreed.

It was still in the way, but we were managing. Managing meant I had two new problems to deal with. We needed to relocate a telephone cable and a six-inch water line that was crossing through the building's footprint. They were not on the site plan the COE furnished. We had to relocate, or cap and abandon them. If they were live, we needed to notify the utility companies and get permission to interrupt the services. No one could or would tell me if they were in use, where they originated, or the buildings they fed.

It appeared to me they fed services to General Aziz's base, but I could not be certain. I instructed Hamid to have them surveyed and locate where they entered and left the site. A survey and utility relocation were not part of our contract. It would mean added cost, time, and a change order with the COE. That would also take time.

Normally, I would notify Tom. He would permit me to proceed, and we would settle in due course. I had enough on my plate. I decided to ignore it for the time being and settled the construction schedule with Tom.

Hopefully, Tom would approve the pay estimate for mobilization and what little work we had in place so Dr. Osmond and Cesar would get off my ass about money.

Although I was reluctant to provide a schedule I knew was flawed from the start, I took Tom's advice and ignored the facts. When I was finished it was full of holes. The partners and the COE, other than Tom, might believe I was on schedule. I also knew it would cause me bigger problems down the road.

I analyzed the delays and thought if I warned everyone the project was going to be late, it would be easier for them to explain now rather than later. The actual construction work was not an issue. Based on the scope of work, a year was more than sufficient to build the building anywhere in the world, provided the bureaucracy stayed out of the way and materials were available.

That was not going to happen. I had to deal with laws Egypt passed to conserve their foreign currency after the COE awarded the contract. Shortly after Cesar signed the contract it became impossible for anyone to import anything without paying duties of up to 100% of value. The law was intended to protect manufacturing jobs in Egypt.

There were few modern factories in the country at the time. As a result of the tariffs, a dozen new manufacturing plants were under construction in the vicinity of Cairo. In the long run, it was a benefit to the economy, but it would be a year or two before they were operational. The reality was that other than rebar and cement products, the majority of materials we needed were not produced in Egypt.

Foreign materials were readily available. European machinery and equipment were on par with the U.S. The majority of materials coming into Egypt were produced in Japan, China, and Australia and were substantially cheaper than U.S. and European products.

The American taxpayer was paying the bill. Congress imposed the Buy American Act on projects funded by the American taxpayer. The law is simple. Purchase American-made materials, or if not made in America through an American source in the U.S. There were a few exceptions. Concrete and concrete products were exempt, as was rebar.

The law also requires American citizens to manage and oversee construction to ensure standards meet U.S. building codes. This would work in the States, and Acme Construction could finish the project in about ninety days. We have been given a year. Even with the coordination of shipping materials from the U.S., no one thought it would be a problem in Egypt.

The COE awarded the contract on August 4th. I arrived in Cairo on the ninth and tried to mobilize on the site. At the time locals were preparing for the holidays and were awaiting notice from the religious leaders that the moon was in the right place so the Feast could get underway.

Preparations took one or two days, and the Feast lasted ten. It took three days for the flooding sewers to rinse the blood off the streets and for cats, rats, and flies to clean up the leftovers before I would venture back to the office. By then, it was August 25th.

I spent a month convincing the Generals I wanted to build the building on the site the COE described in the contract documents, which took until September 24th. It was October 9th before I found a suitable area to build a new gate and four days to patch the hole, which brings me to the tree and to today, which is October 31.

It is Friday, and the long weekend is underway; it will be Monday before I can contact the office in the States. It takes an overseas contractor at least ninety days to get permission from the Corps of Engineers to purchase the materials because the COE insists on reviewing a submittal. Cesar received the contract on August 4th, which was the day the process started.

So far, everyone is working along the same lines because it will be November 4th on Monday, ninety days since the contract was awarded, and no construction work has begun.

In addition to purchasing and shipping materials from the States, we must submit shop drawings for review and approval before starting the work. Shop drawings, when done by engineers in the States, take about sixty days. The government has thirty days to review and approve them. Once they are approved, we will need to deposit a letter of credit with the building manufacturer. Manufacturing takes sixty days.

As of today, I have not received the drawings, but if I assume I will in another thirty days and I submit them on December 4th the COE should return them by January 4th.

Buying the building was Dr. Osmond's responsibility, but you needed the government's permission to move hard currency out of the country. I addressed this problem with Dr. Osmond. If it is illegal to, as Dr. Osmond's banker indicated, *smuggle* the material into the country without paying duty, it is also illegal for an Egyptian bank to issue a letter of credit to buy it. I gave the bank a copy of the contract between the JV and the COE with the duty-free clause, but the contract was with the COE, not the Egyptian army.

The Egyptian bank wants a copy of the agreement between the COE and the Egyptian Army. The COE has refused because it is classified secret. The Egyptian Army has refused because the COE is giving the building to the Egyptian Army. The Army has not figured out that Dr. Osmond has to purchase it and then give it to the COE. Without a letter from the Army, customs say it is against the law; the banker has refused.

I suggested to Caeser that he supply the letter of credit. The JV agreement says the building is Doctor Osmond's responsibility. Doctor Osmond referenced a few accounts in Europe that listed sufficient funds to cover the purchase. Cesar refuses to get involved.

Dr. Osmond promised we would have the letter of credit by the time the COE reviews the drawings, which should be by January 4th, or 150 days into the contract. The manufacturer has a backlog, so it will take sixty days to manufacture the building and turn it over to the COE's freight forwarder. The Freight company has eighty days to deliver and unload materials at the Port of Alexandria, where the Egyptian Army will pick them up and bring them to the site. By then, we will have used up three hundred days of the contract time.

Once the building arrives, and by the time the crew opens, inspects, sorts, stores, and repairs the damage the Egyptian Army caused in loading and transport, the COE inspects it, and Andy fills out the paperwork, it will be 360 days into the contract. That will leave five days for construction, and I do not give a shit what anybody says, even Acme Construction is not that good.

By then it will be the religious Holidays again, which is an opportunity for a fishing trip with Tom. When the holidays are over, we can call those fifteen days; it takes ACME 90 days to build the building in the U.S.

We are not in the U.S., and EGICON is not nearly as good as ACME. Based on performance to date, my best guess is we should finish sometime around March of 1988, which is about eight months late. When I finished preparing the logic did not fit the 365 days in the contract. If I gave it to Tom, the COE would not pay Cesar and Doctor Osmond.

I thought back to the CO in Dahlgren, Virginia. Tom was right. I prepared a simple bar chart assuming I was still in the States and both the COE and the JV partners knew what they were doing. When I finished the first draft, I felt like calling home and telling my family about my early arrival. It worked out to be Thanksgiving, which was just a few weeks away and about what I would expect of Acme Construction.

I needed to stay out of the States long enough to ensure my tax-free status. I refined the schedule to show we would finish up on the 349th day, about two weeks early. It did not make me look too good, but it was within everyone else's time limit. All the other players would be happy until reality set in a few months down the road.

My day was finished by the time I drew the charts and put the schedule in proper order. Tom was expecting me the next morning.

"I finished the schedule."

"Great, how does it look?"

"All things considered, not bad, about two weeks early. Do me a favor, approve the pay estimate, and get everyone off my ass?"

Tom reviewed the schedule. He felt it might be a little optimistic, but for the time being, it would do. He and I discussed it while he made a few notes for his report. I then told Tom that since everything was on schedule, I would be taking a few days off.

As I was leaving Tom said somebody by the name of Mike from Washington called and wanted to know if we could finish by July. It seemed the COE wanted to award a follow-up contract to IBM, and IBM needed a few extra weeks to meet their schedule.

"Sure, Tom, why not? By the way, I have another schedule with some contingencies if your boss is interested."

"Forget it. I just finished arranging the fishing trip. We depart two weeks from Friday. We'll review it when we get back."

It did not make one bit of difference to either Tom or me. The rules had been around longer than either one of us. They are not going to change during the life of this contract. The project would finish when it finished, *inshallah*; Tom and I both knew it.

A twenty-month time limit was a real possibility. I also knew not all things are finished in Egypt, at least not in one man's lifetime. One of the British ex-pats is being paid through the end of his contract and going home a few months early, even though his work is incomplete; lucky him.

Cairn arrived six months ago as a supervisor for a British-Egyptian JV to install a telephone transmission line between Hurghada, Tom's fishing village on the Red Sea, and Cairo.

Although they manufacture steel poles in Egypt, they are too short. If they were to use them, all the nomads had to do to steal the wire was to bring a camel with a tall hump.

The British contract called for the installation of wood poles. The contract specified them because you cannot import steel poles into Egypt. The Brits did not argue.

They had been building in Egypt for two hundred years. The Brits knew termite infestations were common, and termites love wood. Untreated poles would rot in less than five years. What they did not take into consideration is that nomads use dried camel dung for their fires, and they do not mind the smell of creosote. I can understand the lack of concern by the nomads because I lived in Egypt. I have also become accustomed to the air drifting over the desert from Cairo, which pollutes even the smell of their campfires.

The poles arrived four months late because it took that long for Egyptian customs to accept proof that no one in Egypt manufactured the coating on the poles. If it were available in Egypt, it would be a wood pole with an illegal coating. A company in Helwan made a similar coating. It would work, but when it gets wet, it bleeds and smells like Helwan air, and the ground around it looks like the top of creeks leading into an Egyptian village.

What the hell, why argue? The Brits agreed to use local material. When the poles arrived, Cairn's crew started in Hurghada, working toward Cairo, drilling holes, setting poles, and stringing lines at a rate of three klicks a day.

Not bad, but on the fourth day, when they returned to Hurghada, the poles installed in the first three klicks had been cut down by nomads, and the wood and wire had been packed off. Steel poles were the answer, but we have been there; it was a useless exercise. Carin's boss did what any contractor working for an American agency spending taxpayer's money would do. He instructed Carin to continue the work.

The next day Carin started where he left off and continued to install three klicks of poles and line a day. The nomads followed behind, keeping up. There was always a three-klick stretch of finished work in between, which gave the inspector from Cairo the impression work was progressing on schedule.

After one of Caren's trucks hit a mine leftover from the Six-Day War with Israel, the inspector decided it was safer to inspect the material on the trucks before they left the port of Alexandria rather than after it was installed in the desert.

Carin decided stockpiling the poles and wire in the desert instead of transporting them each day to the site would make the job easier for both him and the nomads. When the nomads stole the materials and stripped the trucks, everybody was happy except the people in Hurghada who needed the transmission lines. The Aid agency solved that problem by moving its office back to Cairo.

Chapter 12

My days never start the same in Egypt as they do at home. Usually, the alarm shatters my sleep when the room is still dark. I get up, go into the bathroom, pee, shower, shave, brush my teeth, and get started on a new day. Cairo is different. When the alarm goes off, I wake up thinking perhaps this is all a nightmare and maybe I am just living a fantasy.

I am beginning to understand the *after tomorrow, if Allah wills it* attitude, so I try to ignore yesterday. After I finish my morning routine, I head out the door thinking we have not, as Hamid is prone to remind me, *wasted one second of tomorrow*.

It never takes long before my hopes for the day disappear. I either trip over the neighbor's trash, step in some dog shit on the unlit stairs or slip in the waste that has leaked through the wall from my toilet into the hall.

I refuse to fix the toilet because the landlord lives in the flat below me, and even if he does not know where it is coming from, I know water mixed with shit runs downhill. Like most everything else in Cairo, the lights do not work, and it is hard to see the trash or the dog crap on the floors.

I solved the problem this morning. I took the mirror down in the bathroom. Now, I let the landlord know I am awake by flushing my toilet. The next thing I notice is the mirror is missing and it reminds me I should not take anything for granted.

I was careful going down the stairs. I did not step in dog shit or trip over the trash. The puddle in the hall got me off to a smiling start wondering how long it would take my landlord to figure out water runs downhill, and the leak must be coming from my flat.

My stomach was also feeling better because I was adjusting to the food in Cairo. Dinnertime is the one time of day I look forward to, and now that I have been here a while, I have a few favorite restaurants.

The German restaurant in the Heliopolis Sheraton has a chicken special every Sunday. I get half a chicken, a pot of decent coffee, freshly baked bread, a glass of wine, and a Cuban cigar for dessert, all for eleven LE. Based on the current black market rate of exchange, a little over $5.

I have been going there every Sunday for the last six weeks. The waiters call me Mr. Pat, like everyone else. I know what the special is, and I do not have to look at a menu and decipher the Arabic. Unlike my experience at some of the other restaurants, when they give me a bill that includes charges not on the menu and then tell me the Ministry of Tourism has raised taxes, and they have not had time to change the price, I do not feel cheated.

Overall, it is a little better than average and a pleasant place to spend a few quiet hours. However, in addition to the hassle with the project and at my flat, some British tourists tried to ruin my Sunday chicken dinner.

I had reservations. The tables are in close quarters; the room was crowded when I arrived. Mohammad, the Matre'd showed me to my table. Three young Brits were seated at the table next to mine. The girls with them were dark, slim, and attractive, with Italian accents, I thought, *stewardesses.*

I knew the men were tourists because their shoes were clean, and there was not sand falling on the table when their heads shook from the laughter and gaiety.

I did not mind the close quarters because English conversation is scarce in Cairo. Even if I could not join in, I could eavesdrop. The group looked over as I adjusted my chair to avoid rubbing elbows with the man next to me. When I caught their odd stares, I thought it was because I was an American who was friendly with the Egyptian staff.

The waiter brought me soup, which is not part of my Sunday meal, and something I did not order, which should have been an omen. I gave up trying to identify the meat and tested the vegetable. It was tasty, so I tried the meat. I thought, *water buffalo*.

As I concentrated on the soup, the Brit next to me stretched, bumping my arm spilling the continents down my chin and onto my shirt.

As I started to wipe the soup off my chin, I understood the odd looks. I had not shaved or gotten a haircut since I left the States. I looked down and realized my boots looked like I had been busting broncs on a ranch in Montana.

Topping it off, my houseboy was doing the laundry when I got home, so I had not taken a shower. Sand from the dust at the construction site, which had accumulated in my hair, was sprinkling into my soup. I was ignoring the sand by stirring it to settle it to the bottom of the bowl. I realized I was beginning to adjust to the culture, and I probably did appear a little strange.

The waiter asked about the soup. My accent was obviously American, which I think annoyed the Brits. Their conversation turned into loud opinions about the U.S. Some Brits have the same attitude as the French. Both have forgotten if the Americans had not saved their ass, they would all be eating sausages and sauerkraut.

I am not excessively thin-skinned, and since the waiter retrieved my soup and placed the chicken in front of me, I decided to keep my mouth occupied by biting into the only breast I had seen since I arrived in Egypt. I mention that because one of the chicks sitting with the Brits was rather well-endowed, and I noticed. I was admiring the view when the man stretched again, tipping my glass of wine into my plate of chicken. This time, he apologized as I sat back to avoid the wine spilling over onto my pants.

The girls were smirking, and Mohammed was rushing to my table. Little did they know. I was flunking a test in my patience course. There were three of them. I was in a nice hotel; it was my Sunday night out, and I was not looking for trouble. I talked myself into believing it was an accident after the Brit patronized me with a second apology and offered to replace the wine. The truth is, I was a little out of shape, and as I said, there were three of them. I decided to let the matter rest and settled back to finish dinner.

The waiter brought me another plate of chicken; this time, I managed to get through to the bones. When I finished, he brought my after-dinner coffee. I was forgetting about the soup and wine when the jerk next to me felt another tired spell coming on. My coffee cup was four inches from my mouth when he stretched again. This time, I was ready. I calmly moved my cup out of the way, leaned back in my chair, and asked.

"Do you Brits like baseball?"

"It's British, and what the fuck do you care if we like baseball?"

"Because that's your third fucking strike, asshole."

I had been thinking, no, more like brooding, about how I was going to handle a third stretch all through my second plate of chicken.

I debated; I knew it would stir things up if I poured my hot coffee in his lap. What the hell? He grabbed his crotch. His loud obscenities garnered attention from the surrounding tables and the hotel staff.

I rose from my chair; he was a young man, obviously in shape… Shit! He stood up, but he was not too big; *that worked. I pushed him back down and then bent over to whisper to him and his partners that if any of them stood up,* one of us would end up either in the hospital or jail.

Brave words for an out-of-shape 44-year-old grandfather. He looked around, the security police were coming at a brisk pace. The Brit sat back down and settled. Mohammed had been watching and was approaching the table with an amused look on his face. When it turned out they were a couple of wimps, it was funny.

The young Brit was subdued. I sat back down, looked toward Mohammad, who did not want any part of it, and turned to greet

Achmed, the head of security; his men were surrounding the tables.

"Malish." *No problem.*

It was that Arabic-English thing again. At first, it did not appear things were going my way. Security was always on patrol, but they did not see the first two stretches. It would appear we had some words and I intentionally poured hot coffee in his lap.

Mohammad introduced Achmed. He spoke Arabic-English, but he was confused. I knew the men were new in town; I had some experience dealing with the Egyptians. I decided to sort the matter out myself. I turned back to Mohammad and asked him to tell the chief of security that accidents happen and that we would pay to clean up the mess. I figured the Brit had enough sense to go along.

Mohammad told him I was a regular. I took Achmed off to one side. Nobody saw me slip him twenty LE. Mohammad approached; the two of them moved off and had a brief discussion before security left, and Mohammad returned to my table.

"Mr. Pat, the waiters, they are clumsy."

"Malish, Mohammad."

I sat back down and asked the waiter to bring me fresh coffee. The Brit who started the ruckus was still in his chair soaking up the last of the coffee; the girls were gone. Mohammad was standing in the background.

"Mohammed, ask the waiter to bring me a fresh cigar and tell him this gentleman has offered to pay for my dinner and for cleaning up the mess."

I gave Muhammad a ten-LE note before I left. With the twenty I gave Achmed, it came to an extra fifteen for the night, which is not bad considering most places that have entertainment in Cairo charge an entertainment tax, and, after all, I had been entertained. I do not know what the Brit's bill came to, but you can bet your ass he paid it and left a generous tip of his own.

Chapter 13

I always feel better after a relaxing night out. I called Tom before I went to dinner the night before, and we arranged to meet for breakfast. I was going to avoid the office, Anwar, Abboud, and the other unpleasant aspects of my job for the day to see if Tom and I could sort a few of the problems out ourselves. Tom was waiting when I arrived.

"Good morning, I came by way of your site; your friends still have the tree surrounded."

"Tom, the tree has already cost me five days, and who knows how much longer it will take the Generals to sort it out. Why don't we start planning the fishing trip?"

"Not yet, we have a slight problem."

"You sound like General Aziz, what's the problem?"

"Colonel Baker called. The Embassy hasn't got your work visa, and you can't go to the Red Sea without your passport."

"Great, Tom, I can't go anywhere without my passport. I've already got one extension. I'm getting the feeling Colonel Baker has a lot to do with me not getting it back. Tell him my visa expires in three days, and I have no intention of staying around illegally."

"Relax, it's a temporary problem. He assured me it would be taken care of next month. In the meantime, you have to get another thirty-day extension."

"It takes two days to renew a tourist visa. Besides, it's the COE's and OMC's responsibility. How come you keep pawning this crap off on me?"

Tom and I ate in silence. *Light bulb! Okay, their game. My solution.*

"Tom, tell Baker that as far as the government of Egypt is concerned, my tourist status expires next week. They do make an exception if a tourist is willing to meet their terms. We both know what that means. If it's not resolved, I'll have to leave the country for at least two weeks and then reenter. The visa is the OMC's responsibility, but it falls to the COE and the contract, it will be up to you to approve an extra to pay the bill."

The terms I was referring to were a willing civil servant and the amount of money I was willing to part with.

"I'll commit to that if it happens, but only if you make the effort and renew it one more time."

"Paris."

"What the fuck?"

"I'm going to Paris. First class flight and a hotel in the old quarter near the Seine."

"That's fucking blackmail, not a chance."

"Tom, I mean it. I've had all the shit I'm going to take. This is an OMC headache, not mine. Oh, and by the way, a five-star, not one of those shitty three-hundred-year-old flats on a back alley, three flights up with six-foot ceilings."

"You can't really be serious."

"Yes, I am."

Tom brooded for a minute or two.

"Shit! I'd like that deal. Okay, but on the condition you do your best to get the visa and don't fuck it up on purpose."

We both knew there was no guarantee. I was tempted; an outburst with a clerk, or for that matter, any confrontation with immigration, would ensure failure. However, if I were gone for two weeks there was always the possibility immigration would refuse to issue me a new tourist visa when I returned. Tom knew I did not want that.

The Impatient American

Renewing a tourist visa for 90 days in Egypt is a very difficult process. I was not looking forward to the headache, but like the driver's license, I had to get it resolved.

Egyptian LE is worthless for foreign purchases. Egypt is continuously trying to find ways to raise hard currency, such as dollars or English pounds. One of the ways the Egyptian Government controls currency is to make it illegal for anyone to purchase anything with hard currency. A tourist had to change the hard currency for Egyptian LE in order to pay for goods and services.

In order for a foreigner to extend a visa, the Egyptian government required an exchange equal to $6 into LE for every day you were going to be in the country. Other than the hotels, Egyptian citizens were barred from accepting hard currency, but they were always trying to acquire it as a hedge against inflation.

Changing money on the black market is easy, but the rate fluctuated by as much as 20%. The days before a holiday or before a weekend were best because locals leaving the country needed hard currency to buy tickets and make purchases for goods not available in Egypt.

At the time, the government of Egypt refused to float the pound. The black-market rate was almost twice that of what the banks paid. Credit cards worked in hotels and for plane tickets. Nobody took checks in Egypt. Transactions with shopkeepers, subs, and suppliers were always done with LE.

No one except the government asked for proof as to how you obtain the LE. The Egyptian Government made a feeble attempt to put a stop to the black market by planting undercover agents in shopping areas and near roadside stands. Agents approached foreigners as they walked down the streets and asked if they wanted to change money. Everyone in the country was aware of the scheme, so the only people who were caught were tourists.

The on-the-spot fine was the amount of money the tourist tried to exchange and a warning that the next time would mean arrest and detention. The secret was never to exchange money with anyone who offered. Find someone who has been there a while and get a referral.

The tourist who falls for the scam is happy to get off for a few dollars because he does not want to go to an Egyptian jail. The agent who caught him was happy because he exchanged the hard currency he took from the tourist on the real black market.

Arresting tourists in a country dependent on tourism for the majority of its GDP can be problematic. The Government was happy because they did not know anything about the transaction. I was happy because Tom warned me about it the first week I was in Cairo. He gave me a referral to a safe moneychanger.

Ceasar was not aware of the system. What was a less-than-adequate allowance for expenses based on the legal rate of exchange left me with a substantial surplus every month. Overall, it was one of the better systems in Egypt.

Egypt's import bill today, excluding military hardware, is over $61.8 billion a year. They are in dire need of hard currency. Hard currency comes from foreign aid and the tourist industry, which has dropped almost 70% from its high to about $4 billion a year, not nearly enough to cover its debt.

It is a continuous circle. As soon as the Egyptians make a foreign purchase, they deplete their hard currency. When they cannot find a rational solution, Egypt's answer to a dilemma, like all governments, is to pass laws designed to screw the masses and line the pockets of those in charge.

Egyptians are family oriented. Think, *Joe, and Hunter Biden.* What is good for them is also good for their relatives as long as the relatives show their appreciation with a few kickbacks of their own. The corrupt system makes the rich richer and the poor poorer.

Unlike America, Egypt is lacking in almost all natural resources except sun, sand, wind, and water, and has only a little bit of oil. The sun shines every day, but Egyptians nap during the heat of the day. They have not figured out how to maintain power plants, so the lights go out constantly, and they cannot see at night.

As a result, they have not wasted one second of tomorrow, but it will get done *after tomorrow, inshallah*.

God's busy and is hard to find. Left on their own, Arab construction methods are such that the wind blows sand into the factories through cracks in concrete walls, doors that do not close, and openings for windows they are still trying to purchase with hard currency they do not have, that leaves oil.

Middle Eastern oil is a gift from Allah to Arab leaders, their friends, and relatives. They do not give a shit if they pollute the water, block out the sun, turn the sand into sludge, and let the wind blow the crap everywhere. Their religion permits it because they can screw infidels by selling them oil at an inflated price, and when it comes to fucking infidels, Allah can always be found, and he definitely wills it.

The Arabs use oil money to buy the necessities of life to maintain power in the Middle East, which includes planes, tanks, automatic weapons, rockets, limos, billion-dollar yachts, private jets, and scotch.

Four women in charge of one kitchen create havoc. Muslim men leave their squabbling wives at home with the kids and holiday in foreign lands. The more affluent include a line of designer silk Thobes, *an ankle-length, long-sleeved gown-like garment Arab men wear*. This gives them the opportunity to show off their erection abilities, which, in my opinion, are the only construction skills wealthy Arabs have.

What the Government does not bother to buy are luxuries for the masses, such as wheat for bread, sugar for tea, fertilizer, tractors, electric turbines, trash compactors, toilets that work, water pipes that do not leak, fly spray, or medical supplies.

If peasants complain, they simply escalate ongoing wars with their neighbors and send anyone who complains about being out of bread to the front lines.

Middle Eastern History 103

Some of that diversion I mentioned in the beginning, a few pages you might want to skip to get back to the story. Mom would want to know.

On the subject of war. Allah does not like women; he encourages his followers to use rape as a weapon of war. The Holy Qur'an: translation by Abdullah Yusuf Ali. Hadith book 008, # 4. Think of *October 7, 2023, when Hamas attacked Israel*.

From Israel's declaration of independence in May 1948 until 1978, Egypt was the primary Arab staging ground for a continuous cycle of war between the Israelis and the Arab states. The Six-Day War had its origins in disputes between Israel and Egypt over the rights of Israeli shipping to pass through the Suez Canal and the international waters of the Red Sea.

In 1967, Egyptian tanks and army troops were massed across the Suez Canal and in the Sinai Desert, preparing to attack Israel from the west. Syria and Jordan were approaching from the east. Armies of their neighbors, including Iraq, Saudi Arabia, Kuwait, and Algeria, contributed men and arms to the scuffle. Israel was out-manned, out-gunned, and surrounded on three sides with their back against the Mediterranean.

Israel spread the word it had built its first operational nuclear weapon. For a time, the Muslims could not find Allah, and caution prevailed. In the meantime, President Johnson secretly authorized supplying Israel with a variety of arms, even though an embargo on weapons shipments was placed on the entire Middle East.

Things settled, but the Arabs kept poking the bear. Allah was taking a nap. Egypt got impatient and closed the Straits of Tiran, Israel's only remaining access to the Red Sea, the Gulf of Arabia, and the Indian Ocean, essentially cutting Israel off from trade and communication with Asia and Africa. In response, on the morning of June 5, 1967, Israel launched a preemptive strike against the Egyptian forces.

On the first day, Israeli air strikes destroyed 286 of Egypt's 420 combat aircraft. An Israeli ground offensive was also launched in the Sinai Peninsula.

On the third day, Israeli paratroopers and army streamed into the Old City, Jerusalem, to pray at the Western Wall and hang an Israeli flag on the Temple Mount. For the first time in 2,000 years, Jerusalem was reunited under Jewish sovereignty. Israeli troops then began to advance into areas surrounding Jerusalem.

By the sixth day, Israel was in control of the Sinia, Golan Heights, Gaza Strip, and the West Bank. Genocide is the Muslim's long suit. Israel did not have the capacity for capture and detention or to care for thousands of prisoners, so they released them. History books refer to this as the Six-Day War. Arabs celebrate it as a national holiday.

Rumors flourished, but by December 1966, Israel was believed to have possessed a nuclear bomb. They began full-scale production of nuclear weapons following the Six-Day War. The question was: where did Israel get the technology?

In 1973, Richard Nixon requested another $2.2 billion to support Israel's war effort. The obvious answer in the minds of the Arab states was the U.S. That pissed off OPEC, the *Organization of the Petroleum Exporting Countries,* which is Muslim.

In retaliation, OPEC slapped an embargo prohibiting OPEC countries from selling oil to the U.S. However, like mine, Arab planning is not worth a shit, either. The U.S. consumed the majority of *spare oil* production capacity. The U.S. simply increased U.S. production. Iran, which at the time was run by America's puppet, the Shah, and Venezuela made up the rest.

The Embargo failed. It was most devastating to the Arab countries, who gave up billions in revenue during the embargo. The Embargo only lasted a year. The U.S. shrugged it off, shut down domestic production, and took up with OPEC where they left off.

America was once again dependent on Arab countries for oil. Israel has never publicly conducted a nuclear test. Jimmy Carter followed Nixon's lead, but he did not want Israel to start over the Arab oil fields. He sent the American Secretary of State to broker a peace in hopes of dousing the flames.

It did not work. The price of oil kept sliding. When the price dropped below $85 a barrel, OPEC countries could not afford to subsidize bread, and their peasants revolted. The year was 1977. The president of Egypt was Anwar el-Sadat. Nine out of ten Egyptians lived in poverty. Half the male population was unemployed.

When President Sadat cut public subsidies for flour, cooking oil, and other staples, people took to the streets in two days of violent protest. Known as *the bread riots*, the public's rage forced Sadat to restore food subsidies, but when the army stepped in to quell rioters, eight hundred were injured, eighty were killed, and more than a thousand were imprisoned. In his interview with Mike Wallace following the deadly riots, President Sadat insisted.

“I'm proud because I have the full support of the man in the street in Egypt.”

It was all about the money; *it always is*. The solution, help the Arabs raise more foreign currency. The rest is history. America agreed to leave its oil in the ground and to suspend future drilling.

Once America's oil was safely locked below the surface of the earth, POTUS suggested the Arab countries cut production to create a shortage and raise the price of oil.

When the money started flowing again, Egypt, funded by OPEC, refocused on Israel. The U.S. stepped in once again and brokered a new peace. Egypt and Israel signed a treaty in 1979.

As part of the agreement, the U.S. began economic and military aid to Egypt, and political backing for its subsequent governments. Since then, the U.S. has subsidized Egypt with over $80 billion worth of aid.

With money in the bank, the Arabs went shopping. When the American politicians offered to sell them planes and tanks, they ignored the wheat farmers. Jimmy Carter continued to appease the Muslim world with more bribes but retired shortly after relinquishing the American Embassy in Iran to the Muslim extremists without a fight.

President Regan greatly admired Hosni Mubarak, the new Egyptian President, his leadership, and his character. He invited Egypt's diplomats to a speech about how supply-side economics would solve the financial crisis in America. Egypt misunderstood Reaganomics. In Arabic-English, import quotas appeared to be the answer.

George Shultz, Regan's secretary of state, convinced Regan's buddy, Egyptian President Mubarak, whose legacy is mass torture and detention of Egyptian citizens, that the way to conserve foreign currency was to pass laws forcing the people in Egypt to buy only the products his relatives were manufacturing.

The theory was simple. Pass a law prohibiting anyone from buying anything from anyone outside the borders of your own country. Build it yourselves and let your friends and relatives sell it at whatever price they can get. This way you can conserve hard currency, keep the military in toys, and with the leftovers, *maybe buy bread*. This is the period I was there.

But, since you cannot import anything, you need natural resources to manufacture what it is your relatives want to sell. The Middle East does not have natural resources except sun, sand, water, wind, and oil, and we have already covered that subject.

It took the Arabs a few years to discover the mistake in their logic, but it was too late because they already passed the laws. The Muslims take Friday off, and the Christians take Saturday and Sunday off. The moon is usually in the wrong place on Monday. Everyone is resting from the long weekend on Tuesdays; nobody wants to tackle a problem like this on the day before a long weekend, and Allah is resting from the holiday; it takes a very long time to change the laws.

Chapter 14

Renewing a visa for an American tourist past ninety days made all the other bureaucratic problems in Cairo to date child's play.

To exchange money at a bank, I needed to get my passport back from Colonel Baker. The first order of business was a trip downtown. I was not looking forward to the day. Finding a parking place is always the first order of business. What is locally referred to as the Cairo Mafia controls parking on the Streets of Cairo. They dole out territories two or three parking spaces at a time. It is a lifetime position. As long as the family adheres to their rules the territory is passed from generation to generation.

Foreigners get preferential treatment because the Egyptians assume we are not familiar with local parking rates. I know it was supposed to be ten piasters, which is about five cents. They always stiff me for twenty-five, but I never argue because it seems to make their day.

The traffic downtown was heavier than usual. The closer to the diplomatic section the more difficult finding a parking space would be. A short walk was better than circling the area for an hour or more. I began looking three klicks from the Embassy.

As I slowed, parking attendants tried waving me into areas too small for my car. I wished I had waited for my driver, but as I came around a corner, one of the attendants waved me into what looked like adequate space. I felt lucky, it usually takes at least a half-hour, and finding a parking place on the first swing through the area was a bonus.

I pulled in, running over a thick obstacle hidden from view when I made the turn. Thinking, *no big deal, there's trash everywhere in Cairo*, I got out of the car and turned to lock it.

More excitement. When I turned back to pay the attendant, instead of simply holding out his hand and accepting the coin, he was yelling and waving his arms. I mistook the hand signals. I got back in, backed out over the bump, and waited. It was not trash. I had run over the legs of a man who was working under the car in the adjoining space.

There was a crowd gathering, blocking the view. Dammed….! Tom was emphatic when he told me that in the event of an accident, if possible, leave the scene and head for either the COE office or the Embassy, whichever was closer, the Embassy was less than a mile away.

It was an accident, but I had no idea as to the condition of the victim. I could not see; the crowd had shut me out of the area. In the meantime, the milling crowd attracted the attention of police, who were approaching on foot.

Only seconds had passed when the attendant came through the crowd, shouting at the police and pointing in my direction; I followed Tom's advice. I scrambled back into my car, locked it, drove my way through the growing mob, and headed for the OMC.

Leaving the car by the curb, I walked through the front door, cleared security, and went directly to General Olsen's office. The General was in, and so was Colonel Baker. The Colonel opened the conversation, asking about my health.

"I see you haven't upset General Sayer enough for him to have you shot…., yet."

I ignored the Colonel and told General Olsen I was there to pick up my passport. Tom had called the General; it was waiting for me on his desk. Once it was in my pocket, I faced the current problem.

"General, I may have gotten into a little difficulty with the police."

"What do you mean, may have? Either you did, or you didn't."

Colonel Baker again.

“I ran over someone in a parking spot a few klicks from here. He may be seriously hurt.”

“Well, is he, or isn’t he?”

More exact words, he must have watched the same John Wayne movie.

“I don’t know. I left before I found out.”

“Start from the beginning. What happened?”

I felt like using some of the local logic by telling the Colonel it was his fault because if he had taken care of the visa, I would not have come downtown.

“Your car’s parked in front?”

“Yes, Colonel.”

“Give me the keys.”

General Olsen did not appear worried, but where I came from, hit and run is a criminal offense that would land me in jail. I left to use the toilet. When I returned, the General had a bottle of Jack Daniels and two glasses on his desk. Things were looking up, but it took a while.

Colonel Baker was back.

“Pat, you’re becoming a bigger pain in my ass than the project. How do you manage to get into these messes?”

General Olsen started to come to my defense, but the comment pissed me off.

“Do you think I ran over him on purpose?”

The Colonel started laughing.

“What’s so fucking funny?”

It appeared I fell into one of the local scams, but like everything else I was involved in, the results had not gone as planned. The police were watching the attendant and his parking zone, which is why they arrived so quickly. Another expat ran over someone in the same area a few days earlier. The expat paid the attendant a few hundred LE to cover the injured man's medical expenses.

Later, his conscience bothered him, so he had someone check to see how badly the man was hurt. He was told the police thought it was a fraud. There had been some complaints about the attendant faking injuries and collecting side money. I did the unexpected. I was supposed to get out of my car. The attendant would have helped the man out from under the car who was faking injuries. He would then ask me to pay the medical bills. I backed the car out after the man under the car off to the side replaced a bag of trash with his legs. The police knew I was a foreigner, but no one had taken down my license number.

"It serves the son of a bitch right. What now?"

"Nothing, I had your car parked in the embassy lot down the street. You can leave. Since it was a con, the police aren't looking for you."

"Thank you, Colonel."

"General, would you mind asking your aid to get me a bottle of scotch from the commissary? Gary hasn't settled my duty-free privileges, and I can't buy anything with alcohol."

The General called his secretary, who came in a few minutes later with a bottle of Johnny Walker Black. Andy and I finished half the bottle that evening. I fell asleep after agreeing he could bring a roommate into the flat.

I woke the next day, cussing the morning call to prayer from the mosque next door. Andy slipped the question in between the second or third drink and when I stepped out on the balcony to have a cigarette.

The chanting from the mosque mingled with the noise from the passing traffic, drowned out the question. Andy wanted to buy a monkey; he claimed I agreed to let him keep it in the flat. I did not have time to argue, I was due to meet Hazem at the office for a trip to immigration.

A tourist visa in Egypt is good for sixty days. The Government usually allows a seven-day grace period for an expat to have time to sort through the bureaucratic red tape in a country where no one is in charge and everyone is trying to line their own pockets. I was pushing the deadline, and there was no guarantee. If I neglected it, the Egyptian army could bar me from the site.

I also knew that if I did not have a valid visa when I tried to go home, they would not let me leave the country without paying a hefty fine. Since going home had been foremost in my mind since the day I arrived, I had to sort it out.

The first order of business was to make sure I had a police stamp on my passport. Foreigners must register at a hotel with a passport so the police can track them. The hotels are required to stamp the date of arrival and submit the names and identity numbers of their guests.

Those who move into an apartment deal with it differently. The property owner is required to fill out the forms, but they put it off like everything else. Most companies have locals on staff who register new arrivals.

I had turned my passport over to Colonel Baker in order to secure my Egyptian military clearance. To do that, I assumed he would also register me legally in the country, but that did not happen.

The police charge five LE for each set of forms. They do not care how many you mess up. I asked Hazem to accompany me to the police station to make sure I got it right.

One of the questions was my marital status. Mary, my wife, would not have understood if I started denying her existence. I filled in the blank with married. Since I was married, he was convinced I was living with my wife. He wanted to know when she would be coming in to register. The officer would not buy my story. I made another mistake when I admitted to fathering four children. The discussion shot the morning.

It was 1986 before a simple scan transferred your information to every police station in the country. I threw the first set of forms in the trash; we would try another station. By the time we struggled through the line, it was early afternoon. I was in for another session, like the driver's license, and wanted an end to it. When we got to the blanks about my family status, I told Hazem I was going to say I was single with no dependents. Hazem and I argued the point, but I managed to convince him my wife and kids would understand. We approached the window, turned the form in, and waited, and waited, and waited.

"Go see what's taking so long."

Hazem returned with a disappointed look on his face.

"What's the problem, Hazem?"

"In the space where it asks your reason for being in Egypt, we put down Construction Project Director for EGICON."

"Hazem, have you forgotten? That's why I'm here."

Hazem explained: It is against the law to have a tourist visa in my passport if I'm working in Egypt. I would have to get a work permit. *Yes, obviously, I should have already figured that out.*

The problem with a work permit is you have to prove to the Government you are not doing a job that an Egyptian can do, and once you get the permit you become subject to the Egyptian tax system.

The taxes in Egypt for an expat are whatever the local tax collector wants to assess, which is usually 25% of your gross, plus 29% for social insurance. I had been there ninety days, and there would be penalties and late fees.

No Egyptian could do my job because of the requirement for American supervision, which was easy. My contract with the Egyptian Army says I am tax-free, and I want to keep it that way. Having an IRS agent hounding me in one country was enough.

"Hazem, let's find another police station."

"Why a police station, Mr. Pat? We have to go to the Ministry of Labor to apply for the work permit."

"Forget it, Hazem."

We found another police station. It was simple the third time. I took off my wedding ring. I was unmarried; I had no children and no job. I was a snorkeling enthusiast camped by a coral reef on the Red Sea and would be leaving in 30 days.

The next order of business was to convert $180 into Egyptian LE. I needed to go to a local bank. I figured the banking system would probably be too much for Hazem. I decided to enlist help from the man in charge.

"Doctor Osmond, I need to change some dollars for my visa, and I need a legal bank receipt."

"You can get a receipt at my bank, Mr. Pat. I'm going to the bank this morning. Would you like to go with me?"

"Yes, and while we're there, perhaps you could help me open an account so my expense money can be wired in from the States."

Doctor Osmond told me he would be free to leave in a few minutes, inshallah. God must have been taking a nap because we did not arrive at the bank until two the next afternoon.

I chalked up the four-hour wait the day before and the wasted morning off to a few hours of homework for my patience class. Doctor Osmond's driver parked his car in front of the bank and then handed the parking attendant a tip. When we entered the bank Dr. Osmond shook the guard's hand and palmed him five-LE. As we approached the bank President's office he slipped the guard at the door some money.

Customary tea arrived. The banker and Doctor Osmond lapsed into a conversation in Arabic that kept me in my patience class after school. We finally got around to my business an hour after we arrived.

"Dr. Osmond, I have a meeting with Tom this afternoon."

Dr. Osmond turned to the banker, carrying on his conversation for another ten minutes. I was fidgeting with my watch, which appeared to irritate both Dr. Osmond and the Banker. The banker directed his attention to me, *finally*.

"Ah, Mr. Pat, what can I do for you?"

I did not like the way it was starting. Every time someone started a conversation with, "*Ah, Mr. Pat*," I ended up with a new problem. I explained to the banker I needed to open an account to have my expense money transferred from the States, and to change dollars into LE to extend my visa. The banker pressed his intercom, I assume it was his secretary, and then he lapsed back into a conversation with Dr. Osmond.

About a half-hour later, a woman entered the office with a stack of forms. She asked for my passport. To my relief, she sat in a chair and filled them out herself. When she finished, the banker asked how much money I would like to deposit and how much I would like to exchange for LE.

An expat can maintain both an LE and a dollar account in an Egyptian bank. The Egyptian pound was dropping like a stone. The black market rate of exchange was rising daily. Up until then, Dr Osmond had been funding my expenses. If Caeser sent dollars, I could withdraw dollars and change it on the black market when I needed LE. I told him I had $2,000 to deposit and $180 to exchange for a visa renewal.

"Yes, Mr. Pat, may I have the receipt."

"I need a receipt; that's why I'm here."

"Ah, yes, Mr. Pat. I mean the receipt they gave you at the airport when you brought the money into the country. You were supposed to declare it at customs."

"I don't know what you're talking about.'

"Then it's illegal money, Mr. Pat."

I was supposed to declare the hard currency I was bringing into the country. The law was to prevent black market moneychangers and shopkeepers from trying to launder dollars through the local banking system.

During my stay, if a foreigner did not have an official declaration slip for the money they were carrying when they tried to leave Egypt, they would confiscate the cash and prison was a possibility. I never saw the form. I do not think it is readily available, and you probably have to ask for it in Arabic.

Doctor Osmond and the banker lapsed into another conversation while I sipped a fresh cup of tea. It was five p.m. I had lost another day.

"Excuse me, Doctor Osmond, but I'm sure there must be some way to sort this out today. I have to get back to the project."

"Ah, Mr. Pat. Doctor Osmond is a friend. I will sell you a receipt; then, you can deposit your money and make the exchange."

"How much?"

"Ten percent."

I turned to Dr. Osmond.

"Mr. Pat is my friend."

"Five percent."

I handed him American Express traveler's checks.

"Ah, Mr. Pat, traveler's checks."

"How much?"

"Sorry, Mr. Pat, ten percent.'

"I only paid five at the airport."

I shrugged in resignation and began signing over the checks. It was after 10:30 when I entered my flat. I called Hazem and told him to meet me at the office at eight; it was important, and I was not going to be in the mood for explanations if he was late. He assured me he would be there on time.

I arrived at the office at 7:45. Hazem arrived at 9:30. *It was against the law in Egypt to fire anyone if they had worked for a company for ninety days*. Hazem and I made it to the Ministry of Passports at 11:00, just in time for rush hour.

Although most Government offices in Egypt open at nine. Tea is a priority; the Egyptian workers seldom start their days before ten. The workday at most government offices is over by three. That takes three prayer breaks; it does not leave much time for business.

The Ministry of Passports had about twelve employees waiting their turn at the one open window. *No....! They do not have a system.* The wait is an hour or more, depending on how much crowding and pushing you are inclined to do. After the session with the banker the day before, I was inclined, it only took forty-five minutes to reach the front of the line.

Hazem checked the forms as I filled them out. When we finished, he handed the forms and the currency exchange slip to the cashier. We left the line to wait until they called my name. The wait was less than thirty minutes, a record by Egyptian standards. I was thinking something was finally going my way. They handed me the application and said something in Arabic that caused Hazem to collect the forms and step back from the window.

"Hazem, what's he saying?"

Hazem turned back, continuing the conversation.

"Hazem, what's going on?"

"I'm sorry, Mr. Pat, but the receipt is no good."

"Why not?"

"It doesn't say you cashed the money for a visa."

"What fucking difference does that make? I cashed the money at the bank. Nobody said it had to say anything about a fucking visa on the receipt!"

I was pissed, another day shot. I was only one day from my visa expiration, including the grace period. I was knocking on the banker's door two minutes after the bank opened.

"Good morning, Mr. Pat. Would you like some tea?"

"Yes, please. I have a problem with the receipt for the money exchange. You neglected to put a visa stamp on it; the Ministry of Passports won't accept it."

“Ah, Mr. Pat, you didn’t tell me you needed a visa stamp.”

“I told you I was exchanging the money to renew my visa. It’s your country. You do this every day; you know the rules?”

“I’m sorry, Mr. Pat, but rules change too quickly to keep up.”

“It’s simple, please…., just stamp the receipt?”

“I’m sorry, Mr. Pat, but copies of foreign exchange receipts are turned in to the government each day. You will have to exchange more money to get a new receipt.”

Twenty minutes later, I was on my way to the passport office. Three hours later, I had the visa stamped in my passport, but not before I had another argument with the passport office.

I had been in Egypt for ninety days. He was convinced I was working in Egypt. He told me the passport office would not extend tourist visas past 120 days under any circumstances because there were too many foreigners taking Egyptian jobs. I would not get another until I left the country and applied to reenter.

I did not argue, even though it would not have been lying. I was not working in Egypt. I spent the first three months trying to get to work, arguing with Generals, and fighting my way through government offices. He was right about one thing: no tourist in his right mind would stay in Egypt for over 120 days.

The Ministry of Passports was a block from the Embassy. I decided to stop in and see General Olsen. Colonel Baker was in his office.

“Where have you been? No one has been working on the site for four days.”

”Colonel, I’ve been getting my visa extended, which is something this office was supposed to handle. I’ve just been told they will refuse to extend it again, so unless you get it fixed, I’m out of here.”

“Calm down. Leave your passport with my secretary; we’ll sort the permits out before yours expires.”

"General, with all due respect, my passport will stay in my pocket until my resident permit has been granted. The closest anyone is going to get to it again is a photocopy."

Colonel Baker started to say something about trust and then thought better of it. He could tell I was getting a traveling urge, and at that moment, the project was the least of my concerns.

"Pat, you're only one of dozens. Have the secretary make a copy of the passport."

"Thank you, Colonel. What seems to be the problem at the site?"

"You still have a problem with the tree."

I thought the Generals had made a deal. I had forgotten about the tree.

"You have got to be fucking kidding."

I could see the Colonel was not. General Olsen was trying to control his laughter.

"Fuck! I thought it was just the Egyptians, don't you guys give a shit about the schedule, Colonel." "I've had enough of this shit, General. Do you still have Jack in your desk?"

The Colonel left while General Olsen poured me three fingers of Jack.

"Settle down, Colonel Baker is trying to hold it together. IBM has a contract with critical dates. If we don't give them the window they ask for, it will cost millions and could delay the project for years or possibly mean canceling it."

"I'll see what I can do about the tree tomorrow, *inshallah*. Maybe I can find God. General Olsen, if I thought for one fucking minute the COE would cancel the project if I walked away, I'd be gone tomorrow just to pay that prick Aziz back. We both know the COE isn't going to cancel, and I'm going to be stuck here until we get it resolved. Tell Colonel Baker to sort out my permit; I'll find a way to get it done."

"No more holes in walls, and for god's sake, don't steal the fucking tree…… Shit…., well, on second thought, just don't get caught."

Thoughts: *I am beginning to think I was in McHale's Navy, and General Olsen was playing Joe Flynn's part.*

We spent the next hour discussing some of the problems the General thought I might come across that were occurring on other projects in Egypt. Afterward, I decided to break the news to my wife that the one-year contract would definitely take longer. I was not sure how much longer, but it was time to deal with reality.

Chapter 15

I tossed and turned much of the night and slept little the following week. The conversation with General Olsen and the comments John, the Brit, made about a two-week job taking six months was sinking in. The prospects of a piece of cake, get-even with the COE contract were gone. It looked like just one big pain in the ass for the next nine months.

I dreaded getting up in the morning, but Andy was pounding on the door, insisting I go to the site and see what I could do about the tree. The project had been at a virtual standstill since it had been placed under arrest thirteen days earlier.

Hamid did, *finally*, manage to get a permanent gate installed. The guard saluted me when he opened it. At least security issues were solved.

I parked a short distance from the tree, which was still surrounded by army personnel from both sides. I decided since General Aziz agreed the tree belonged to General Sayer I should enlist the help of the owner.

General Sayer's guards let me through to his office without the usual delays.

"Good morning, General Sayer."

"Good morning, Mr. Pat. Would you like some tea?"

"Thank you, General, yes, but just one sugar, please."

The General sent his tea guy out for tea. I hoped he would wash the glass this time, but I smiled at the General and breached the subject.

"General, General Aziz told me the tree belongs to you. Do you know why he still has his guards posted around it?'

The General gave me a funny look and then picked up the phone. I had no idea who he was yelling at, but I heard Aziz's name mentioned. The conversation was still going on when the tea arrived, but the General slammed down the phone, got up from his desk, and left the room without a backward glance. I sat drinking tea. Thought: *Fuck…….., I really do not want to deal with this shit.*

General Sayer did not return. When I got back to the site, Colonel Sabin and Hamid were waiting.

"Good morning, Hamid, Colonel."

"Good morning, Mr. Pat. We have a problem."

"Same shit, different day, Hamid."

"What did you say, Mr. Pat?"

"Nothing, Hamid, what's up?"

The conversation wandered back and forth in English-Arabic between Hamid, me, and Colonel Sabin.

"Hamid, get to the point!"

The point took another twenty minutes. Colonel Sabin was telling Hamid that since I offered to rebuild the car shed, General Sayer wanted it in writing, and a date when it would be completed. Now, I was confused. The subject had gone from the arrested tree to General Sayer's car shed, and Colonel Sabin worked for General Aziz.

"Hamid, tell the Colonel I have put it in writing, but I don't have the materials."

Hamid explained the situation. The Colonel did not like the answer.

"Mr. Pat, General Aziz wants you to write a letter by noon today that you will build the car shed no matter what, or he is going to make us stop work until you do."

"Hamid, we haven't worked on this site for over two weeks."

I looked at my watch. It was after 11:00. We jumped from the tree back to the car shed. I did not have a clue what one had to do with the other except that Sayer had the scraps from the shed, which: Shit….! Thought: *Light bulb time. Fuck…! Which was not going to work for a new building, there were not enough materials to rebuild.* The bastards cut a deal. Sayer wanted a carport, and now I would have to buy the materials.

"Hamid, tell the Colonel nobody will be working on the site until Saturday, and then send everyone home."

"What about the letter, Mr. Pat?"

"What letter, Hamid? Tell the Colonel I didn't understand. I have to leave; I have a lunch appointment with Mr. Tom. I'll see you on Saturday."

I had spent most of the prior week dealing with correspondence from Don, Cesar's purchasing agent. I had a few dozen purchase orders but none of the required submittals, which were past due. I did need a few days off. I figured a little psychological warfare with the Generals was in order. I decided to have lunch with Tom and explain why no one would be at the site for a few days.

"Hello, Tom?"

"Where have you been?"

"Sorry to say, but you are off the hook for Paris. I was getting the visa extension; it took a while."

I was not in the mood. Tom took the hint. A few minutes later, Colonel Baker walked into the restaurant.

"Tom, we need to find a new place to have lunch. We have company."

"Hello, Colonel. Would you like to join us?"

"Why isn't anyone on the site?"

"There are people on the site, Colonel. The Egyptian Army is guarding the tree, and one of my laborers is keeping them in tea. Why don't you show us some of your military cooperation and straighten out the mess so we can go back to work, or haven't you heard? General Aziz threatened to stop the project, and the tree doesn't seem to be the only issue."

"I understand General Aziz asked you for a letter, and you sent everyone home."

"That's not how it happened. Look, Colonel, the car shed is the COE's problem, the tree is the Egyptian Army's problem, and my work permit is your fucking problem. How come everyone is making their problems my problems?"

"You know the contract calls for you to pursue the work until the Army or someone else stops you. So far, that hasn't happened."

This time, it was Tom spouting off. As far as Tom was concerned, interference was not an issue; it was all about the money. The contract allowed me to claim added costs when and if I incurred them.

"Tom, the Egyptian Army is armed. Two generals of the Egyptian Army have the tree surrounded by men hostile to one another. The military has locked me out and locked me in. Just what the fuck do your characters expect me to do?'

"Pat, you drove a loader through an army base wall and blocked the highway to President Mubarak's palace. You put in your gate access, conscripted your guard from General Aziz's army, tore down Sayer's car shed, and destroyed his garden. There has been a lot of rhetoric and fist-shaking, but no one is shooting at you. Why, as you would say, are you so fucking sensitive now?"

"Screw you, Colonel, this is fucking nuts, and you know it. We both know the Generals are playing a game, and I'm not getting much help from my side."

The conversation was not going my way. I was feeling defensive. The Colonel was also interrupting my fishing plans with Tom. The fact was, I was totally fed up and trying to think of anything but the army base.

"OK, Colonel, I agree. I also think the Generals are just making noise, and except for the guard at the gate, the guns probably aren't loaded, but I figure someone is going to have to give in soon. If it's me, I'll be giving in to the Generals for however long it takes to build the building. Give me a chance to do it my way. If the tree issue isn't resolved by Saturday, I'll think about a letter to General Aziz."

"Okay, Saturday. By the way, General Sayer just told me the access road to the Army base that leads to your gate will be closed to truck traffic between the hours of seven a.m. and six p.m. You will need to schedule your deliveries accordingly."

"Shit…., Colonel Sabin did mention something about disturbing his prayers. I didn't think he was serious."

"It appears he is. We got the notice this morning."

"Bullshit, those bastards are at it again. Tell the General it won't work. The contract calls for the Egyptian Army to bring the construction materials from the Port of Alexandria to the site. I don't give a shit what time of day they deliver them. Working at night is a matter of the cost of added supervision to unload, which will be an extra to the contract."

Colonel Baker finished his coffee and said goodbye. Tom started to get up and leave with him until I mentioned dessert was on the way. Tom took the hint and sat back down. After the Colonel was out of the room, I wanted to finish planning the fishing trip, but my heart was not in it.

"Tom, those two won't leave it alone. Can the prick close the roads to truck traffic?"

"Probably, the army has more authority than the police in this part of the world."

"I didn't want to say anything to the Colonel, but I only had to comply with Egyptian laws that were in effect before the contract was signed. If they change the rules, it's going to be a pain in my ass, and it's going to cost them. Let's wait and tell General Sayer on Saturday, or would you like to go over it with him today?"

"Saturday works. Let him enjoy his victory until then."

I was hoping the tree issue would sort itself out. I spent the next few days in my flat trying to catch up on sleep and correspondence to home. I arrived at the site Saturday morning. The crew was back to work, but the Army still had the tree under arrest.

"Hamid, The COE's office trailer is scheduled for delivery tomorrow. General Sayer closed the road to trucks during the day. Reschedule tomorrow's delivery for tomorrow night after six."

"Mr. Pat, the tree problem is solved."

"How's that, Hamid? The tree and army are still on the site."

"General Sayer has agreed to split the tree with General Aziz if General Aziz's soldiers will deliver his half in one of General Aziz's trucks."

I would believe it when I saw the tree leave the site, but I could not help hoping.

"Great! It looks like we're finally getting some military cooperation around here."

It seemed General Sayer did not have access to a truck that could haul the tree. General Aziz did. I did not trust either one of them. Once General Aziz had his hands on the tree, General Sayer could kiss his share goodbye.

When General Aziz's truck came through the gate, it was no longer my problem. As I was leaving, the Egyptian Army was loading the tree. It did not matter to me who ended up with the lumber. I was glad to see the problem resolve itself. Tom showed up with Colonel Baker as the truck hauling the tree was pulling out the gate.

"What happened?"

"I haven't got a fucking clue. The Generals appear to have worked the problem out themselves. Oh, by the way, Colonel, the tree has held us up for nineteen days. I want an extension and reimbursement for the cost."

Tom stepped in.

"That's not in his ballpark. Let's see what we can do about the water line, the phone line, and the closed roads."

The three of us headed over to General Aziz's office for the weekly meeting. Colonel Baker commented on what little had been accomplished to date.

"Good morning, General."

The General had the tree; he was in good spirits. We wandered around our conversation in Arabic-English for a while, not getting a lot accomplished. I grew tired of the one-sided conversation.

"General, you speak English……, please! Have your men figured out if the telephone line is working and what the water line feeds?"

"Malish, Mr. Pat. I have been told the lines are not a problem; you can remove them."

"General, would you put that in writing?"

"I'm sorry, Mr. Pat, but it's not my responsibility. They are on General Sayer's base."

"General, you're in charge of the project. If the lines are dead, what's the problem?"

"Mr. Pat, you can take the line out. If it's a working line, it will be a problem for the engineer who told me it isn't in service."

"Patrick, don't you think you should do some research of your own and let the General know for sure?"

"Colonel, I've given the General my opinion. I think both lines are in use; I have repeatedly asked them to get the utility companies to move them out of the way or shut them down long enough for me to do it. I don't want another tree issue on my hands." "General, can't you get them to shut the water line down for just one day."

"Ah, Mr. Pat, you have so many problems. You are paid to fix problems, not to bring them to me."

"General, I think it's your water line. I can't relocate it until someone shuts the damn water off."

I was not getting anywhere, and General Aziz was leaving for his morning prayers.

"Tom, the General doesn't seem worried about the phone line, and I'm not worried if they run out of tea; let's drop it."

"What do you have in mind?"

"Colonel, the best thing you can do is go study up on military cooperation. After I do what I have in mind, we may need a little of your expertise."

"Pat, is that the truck with the tree coming back on site?"

Oh, shit, it was! There were a half dozen soldiers in the truck. The driver parked the truck and they all left through the gate to General Aziz's base.

"Hamid, go find out what's going on?"

Hamid returned a few minutes later. When General Sayer told the police to close the roads to truck traffic, he neglected to tell them to let the truck with the tree through the checkpoint.

Aziz's guard locked the truck and took the keys. It was not going anywhere soon. The technical institute was a school. The hours on the base varied, but there were very few resident guards, and the gates were locked from eight p.m. until five a.m.

Asking Hamid to follow, I left Tom and the Colonel and headed for my office. I was not in the mood to discuss the truck or the tree with Tom or the Colonel, and I figured they would not want to be part of my solution to getting it off the site for good.

"Hamid, the Army's guards are gone. Bring a truck here tonight with some laborers, load the tree, and get it out of here before they return."

"But Mr. Pat, there is a guard at the gate?"

"Hamid, it's my gate, and the guard works for us. Send him to the tea shed for the night. He'll be asleep. If the Generals don't post soldiers back on the tree, get it out of here before they show up tomorrow."

Hamid started to give me an argument.

"Hamid, I'm fed up. You and Dr. Osmond are more familiar with getting things done in Cairo. Get the damned tree off the site. If it's still here in the morning, Tom's going to insist I comply with the contract documents and replace you with an American."

"Hamid, come back here."

"Yes, Mr. Pat, did you change your mind."

"No, Hamid, get rid of the tree, but when you do, save some of the branches for Tom and me. We're going camping and will need some firewood."

The tree was enough for Hamid to deal with. I let the water and phone lines go for the day. I arrived at Doctor Osmond's office at 11:30 the next morning. I felt a little guilty about sleeping in, but I did not want to go to the site and find the truck and tree still there.

I was settling into my chair when Sarha told me General Aziz called three times. He wanted to see me *immediately*. I was not surprised. Hamid must have followed orders; I was going to have to deal with the missing tree.

"Did the General say what it's about, Sarha?"

Sarha wandered around, searching for an answer. The language barrier was still a problem. I felt lucky to get the message at all. I resigned myself and went to the site. When I arrived, Hamid was not around, and neither was the tree. Thank you, Lord.

Shit! Anwar was there.

"Hello, Anwar, why aren't you in Kuwait?"

"Good morning, Mr. Pat. I'm working with the engineers and stopped by to tell you we're almost finished. I'll have the shop drawings by next week."

"That's great, Anwar. A month late is better than not getting them at all."

Anwar was supposed to see to it the drawings were submitted by milestone dates. I had not seen Anwar since we cut down the tree.

"Anwar, where's Hamid?"

"I sent him to the office to review the drawings, Mr. Pat."

"God dammit, Anwar, I'm supposed to review the drawings. Hamid is supposed to be on the site. Unless I find a way to keep Hamid on the site where he is supposed to be, Tom is going to insist I hire another American. I don't think Doctor Osmond will like that."

"But I am here to take his place, Mr. Pat."

"Anwar, I don't like you, Tom doesn't like you, I don't know anyone who does like you. Go back to the office and tell Hamid to get his ass back here."

Anwar tuned out the Arabic-English. He stood with a grin on his face. I was not getting through. There was no reason to continue the conversation. Anwar started to say something. I ignored him and headed for General Aziz's office; Anwar started to follow.

"Anwar, I'll see what the General wants. Stay here or go find Hamid."

Tom and Colonel Baker were coming through the gate. Tom had a grin on his face, but the Colonel did not look pleased.

"Good morning, Colonel, Tom. What brings you out today? The next meeting isn't scheduled until Tuesday."

"General Aziz called about a missing truck, and General Sayer called about a missing tree. What did you do with the tree?"

"I had Hamid to haul it off after the soldiers left. I have no idea what he did with it, and I really don't give a shit."

"Where's General Aziz's truck?"

"I don't have a fucking clue, Colonel, and I don't give a damned about that either."

I assumed Hamid had followed directions. I did not have a clue about the missing truck. It was time to visit the Generals.

"Good morning, General Aziz."

"Where's my truck?"

The General was pissed; he did not offer tea.

"General, I don't know anything about your truck. I thought you wanted to see me about the tree?"

"The tree doesn't matter, Mr. Pat, the truck matters."

Colonel Baker started to say something, but General Sayer entered the room. Usually, the men argued good-naturedly; this time, they were both angry. I knew the disappearance of the tree and the missing truck was going to end up in my court.

When things quieted down, the story began to unfold. General Aziz did not wait for Sayer to open the road. His men left with the tree without waiting for General Sayer's men. The truck was turned back at the checkpoint.

When General Aziz's truck returned with the tree, General Sayer confiscated the truck because now it was on his side of the temporary fence.

It appeared the Generals sorted out the problem. General Sayer would reopen the road for a day if General Aziz would allow a few of General Sayer's men to go along to make sure he got half the tree.

When General Aziz sent his men for the truck, both it and the tree were missing. General Aziz was accusing General Sayer of stealing the truck and the tree. General Sayer was pawning the blame off on me.

"General Aziz, what makes you think I have anything to do with your missing truck?"

Aziz did not answer. He kept chirping at Colonel Sabin and General Sayer and then turned and started shouting in my direction in Arabic. He started back in on General Sayer as Colonel Baker translated.

The tree was not a military problem. It was a personal issue between the Generals. The truck was another matter. General Aziz used a tank transport truck for the tree. It was one of a few. It was extremely expensive equipment; General Aziz was responsible for it and needed to return it to the tank base. Colonel Baker broke into the conversation, and the argument started over again. It did not appear military cooperation was the answer. I told Tom we should call the meeting off until I had some answers.

Hamid was still unaccounted for. I assumed he had succeeded in loading the tree into one of Dr. Osmond's trucks and moved it off the site. I did not have a clue what happened to the army truck.

It dawned on me that although it might make sense that General Sayer had stolen the truck and the tree, and it was stored somewhere on the base with the shed materials, I knew there was not a chance in hell that General Sayer would steal an empty truck.

A good offense does not always prevail, but it can muddy the water. As I was leaving, I butt into the discussion between the Colonel and the Generals.

"General Aziz, excuse me, but I think if you find the missing shed materials, you will probably find the tree and the missing truck. If you do, you fix both our problems. You will have your truck and your share of the tree, and I'll have the materials to build General Sayer's car shed."

The room became quiet. General Aziz looked pissed. Tom was having a tough time controlling his laughter. Colonel Baker was shaking his head. I took the silence as an opportunity to close the conversation and head for the door. General Aziz was mumbling to General Sayer who was shouting answers.

When General Aziz's door closed behind us Colonel Baker opened the conversation and said what we were all thinking.

"Do you have any idea how much shit you just stirred?"

Colonel Baker was finally laughing. I had an idea of what happened to the truck, but I did not see any sense in not taking advantage of the situation.

Tom and the Colonel decided the truck was the General's problem, and since the tree was gone, there was no need for them to be part of the discussion. I left them in my office with their tea while I went to get some answers from Anwar.

"Anwar, did you make arrangements to have the tree hauled off after Hamid and I left?"

Anwar lapsed into Arabic, looking for an excuse to visit another part of the site.

"Anwar, come back here. The tree is off the site; I don't give a shit what happened; I just want to know if you used the army truck to haul the tree off, and if you did, where the hell is it?"

It took a while. Hamid left the site the day before to find a truck to move the tree. He found Anwar instead, and Anwar decided to sort it out himself.

The Army truck was still loaded with the tree. By nine p.m., the only guard on the gate was the one I conscripted from General Aziz; he was asleep in the tea shed.

Anwar sent Hamid for a driver and someone to hotwire the truck and haul the tree to a dump site. The men were to finish and have the truck back at the site by five while the roads were still open to truck traffic.

After Hamid left, Anwar ran his plan by Dr. Osmond. Doctor Osmond stopped by the site as the truck was leaving; he wanted to have a look at the tree. When he saw the tree, he could not see any sense in sending it to a dumpsite where someone else would salvage it. He ordered the driver to take it to his villa on the Red Sea so his carpenters could make patio furniture.

By the time the driver made the round trip, it was after eight. When he approached the base, the roads to the site were closed to truck traffic. The driver did not want to risk driving a military truck through the checkpoint without papers, so he abandoned it on the highway.

When the driver told Anwar what happened, Anwar went back to move the truck to a safe area until later that night when the roads would be open. In the meantime, the Egyptian police impounded the truck and towed it off because it was blocking traffic.

"Anwar, what the hell am I supposed to do now?"

I did not wait for an answer. I figured the truck incident might be the undoing of Anwar, and besides, there was not a damned thing I could do about it anyway.

"Anwar, forget the truck. When is Hamid coming back?"

"After tomorrow, Mr. Pat."

"What does that mean, Anwar, after tomorrow?"

"He will return after tomorrow, inshallah, Mr. Pat."

"Anwar, that won't cut it. What does after tomorrow mean, the next day, next week, what?"

"I sent him to Alexandria; he will return after tomorrow."

We did not get there that day. To an Arab, *after tomorrow* is something like bookra inshallah. *He will not return tomorrow, but he will return someday if Allah wills it.* I was leaving when a light bulb came on. Anwar on the site was an opportunity; I decided to take advantage of it.

"It's only two. Will you finish Hamid's shift so I can try and sort the truck problem out?"

Anwar was delighted; I had been trying to throw him off the site since the day I met him.

"Yes, Mr. Pat."

"I have something that needs to be fixed today. There are some telephone wires in the way of the new building. I need them removed so the excavation can be finished. Pull them out with the loader and have the laborers put them with the scrap."

I had no doubt Anwar would try to get in my good graces. He did not bother to ask if the phone lines were in use, and he was unaware of the water line. I did not bother to tell him about it or that I thought they were both live. I decided to make it Anwar's problem, and I did not care if General Aziz ran out of tea or could not call me for a few days.

Doctor Osmond had the tree, so I figured the truck was his problem. He had political connections, and if I were in trouble, it was his fault, so he could sort that out. I also figured having Anwar take out the water and telephone lines to the Army base would stir things up enough the next day so the truck might be forgotten until Doctor Osmond could find it.

"Hello, Tom; I think it's time for the fishing trip."

"Forget the fishing trip. What did you do with the truck?"

Colonel Baker did not leave. He entered the room behind me.

"Colonel, I'm not the enemy; don't sneak up on me like that."

"Pat, where's the dammed truck?"

"I don't know, Colonel. It was causing a traffic jam in Cairo, and the police impounded it."

I relayed the story. The Colonel mumbled something about setting military cooperation efforts back a few years, but he was smiling.

"What is it you want me to do, Colonel? This is their country, not mine. I don't make the fucking rules.'

"Why don't you and Tom plan the fishing trip and include me."

I could see the Colonel was weakening.

"I think we're leaving a week from Thursday?"

Tom agreed. The Colonel said it would not be a good time. I was relieved. I did not want the Colonel along. I was looking forward to forgetting about the project for a few days. Before the Colonel left, he asked about the phone and water lines. I said I had a solution and thought it would be resolved in a few days. Tom and the Colonel wanted to know my plans.

"I'm working on it, Colonel. Let's leave it there. In the meantime, I'll make you a deal. I'll sort out the construction problems; you keep up with military cooperation and keep me out of the General's jail."

"That bad?"

"It could be Colonel; it will depend on how long it takes the right agencies to get involved. Let's put it on the shelf until tomorrow."

The Colonel left; Tom did not want to hear it. We got down to some serious planning for the trip. In a way, I was wishing I could leave that day. I knew I had set Anwar up, but still, I was not looking forward to the following morning. I went back to the office to see if Doctor Osmond had the truck issue settled.

"Doctor Osmond, I understand you're going to have some new patio furniture?"

Doctor Osmond did not answer.

"Doctor Osmond, what did you do with the General's truck?"

"Mr. Pat, General Aziz will have his truck back this evening. Please fill out a voucher for 500-LE and charge it to trucking expense."

Doctor Osmond was smiling; 500-LE was a bargain. The lumber in the tree was worth ten times as much. I knew then the tree and truck issues were settled.

"I'll give it to the accountant. By the way, have you sorted it out with Generals Sayer and Aziz?"

"Yes, Mr. Pat. General Aziz and General Sayer are both satisfied. By the way, there's some firewood in the garage; ask Abraham to put it in your trunk."

"Thank you, Doctor Osmond."

What the hell! It was their country and their systems. I did not want to know, so I said goodbye and returned to my office to call Tom and the colonel and leave a message that both the truck and tree issues were behind us.

Abraham loaded the firewood. I was leaving the office when Hamid and Andy came in.

"Pat, we have a problem at the site."

"Same shit, different day. Hamid, can't this wait until tomorrow?"

"It's Anwar; he broke the water line to General Aziz's base."

Thought: *Good work Anwar, right on schedule*.

"Hamid, I told Anwar to take the telephone line out. I didn't say anything about the water line."

"But Mr. Pat, the telephone line was wrapped around the water line?"

"Shit! I forgot to warn him about that, Hamid."

Anwar took the bait. The easiest way to get the phone cable out was to hook it to the cat and pull it out. The phone line was wrapped around the water line, but the sand hid the water line. When Anwar hooked the cable to the loader, the operator never looked back. Anwar and the water line did not have a chance.

"Did the Army shut the water off?"

"They can't find the valve; the site is filling with water."

"Anwar's in charge, Andy; I don't see any reason to interfere. Hamid, go home and let Anwar fix his mess. Andy, let's go to dinner; we'll go to the site later."

"By that time, the excavation area will be flooded. I think we should see if we can do something about it before it overflows into the street."

"Hamid, have a portable pump delivered to the base." "Andy, I'm hungry, let's go eat."

We arrived at the site around 10:00 p.m. Andy was right; the water was just a few inches from flooding General Aziz's parking lot and spilling out into the street. The pump was on a flatbed next to the excavation area that was beginning to overflow. Anwar was in a state of panic and unable to find the words.

"Anwar, call the plumbing contractor and tell him we need a shut-off valve and a coupling for the water line, then go home; I'll deal with it. Before you leave, have the men hook up the pump and run a line over to a manhole. There's no sense in flooding General Sayer's base."

Anwar's fishpond.

The water pressure on the base was low. The pump would overtake the flow by morning and expose the pipe where it was broken. We could deal with it then.

Anwar was giving orders to the laborers when Hamid showed up. Hamid knew about the water line, but he had not been there to warn Anwar. Anwar got the pump hooked up and running, then headed out the gate. The flow was coming from the direction of General Sayer's base; it was feeding General Aziz's. We wandered around for an hour looking for a valve.

The guards following us were getting nervous; we were on General Sayer's base and were not supposed to leave the construction site. I decided to give it up for the night and hope the pump kept up. It never entered my mind the Egyptian Army would not, or for that matter, could not turn off the water.

The plumbing contractor arrived as we were leaving. There would be nothing he could do until the water level dropped. Andy and I stopped at the Sheraton on the way home to have a drink. I needed to come up with the excuse I was going to give the Egyptian Army, the OMC, and the COE. In less than two days, I managed to allow a truck and a tree to disappear, cut the telephone lines, break the water line to General Aziz's base, and flood the construction site.

"This time, you may have gone too far."

"I warned Tom and Colonel Baker, Andy. Look at the good side. Anwar won't show up for a while, so at least I got him off my back. The phone and water lines had to come out. This way, maybe the Generals will take care of the problem themselves."

Andy was not convinced. He also did not want to have to face General Aziz the next day. He decided to take the day off and buy the monkey I agreed to let him bring into the flat.

"Andy, I may have just gotten rid of Anwar. Do we really need another monkey?"

Andy reminded me that I agreed, so I gave in. After all, what harm could a six-pound monkey cause?

The next morning, I decided I had better make Tom aware of the problem before the Egyptian Army called him. I stopped at his office on the way to the site.

"Morning, Tom."

"Where have you been?"

"It's eight a.m. Where the hell do you think I've been?"

Tom was upset. Somebody got General Aziz out of bed. He called General Olsen, who called Tom. My phone was out of order, as usual. I was the only one who slept the night before.

"Don't get excited, Tom. The Army will find a way to shut the water off, or we can install a new valve when the water drops and then fix the phone line. Look at it this way. The General told me the phone line was dead. The water line had to be moved. General Sayer refused to shut it off long enough to reroute it. They would have to find the valve someday. Besides, I think I got Anwar out of my hair for a while."

"What's this got to do with Anwar? I told you to keep him off the site.

"Anwar is one of the owners of the company. I work for him, not the other way around. How the hell do you expect me to keep my boss off his project?"

Tom ignored me. I knew I had to tread lightly on the subject of Anwar. The contract required the site superintendent to be American and approved by the COE. Cesar and Doctor Osmond underbid the project. Tom conceded to Hamid because he knew the expense of another American would be a financial burden I did not want to have to deal with.

We were all trying to deal with the supervision problem in our way. The Egyptian Army did not want to deal with more Americans. Hamid, like Anwar, was a real pain in the ass, but I knew he and Doctor Osmond were probably the ones responsible for keeping the Egyptian Army off my ass and me out of jail.

I also knew I was having fewer problems than other Americans on similar projects when it came to financial demands from the Generals. Doctor Osmond was playing by local rules, which I did not want to know anything about. I did not think another American on the site would help matters.

Tom and I decided to face the music together. General Olsen and Colonel Baker were there when we arrived at the site.

"Good morning, gentlemen. Shall we go see the Generals?"

"Not just yet, Patrick; let's get your story straight."

Oh! Oh! General Olsen was miffed this time. We spent the next hour in my office while I tried to explain that the phone line should not have been a problem because General Aziz said it was not in use, and how was I supposed to know we could not shut off the water?

General Olsen and Colonel Baker were not buying it, but none of us could come up with a more plausible explanation. We took a vote and decided to try it on General Aziz. As we left, Colonel Baker took me aside and said he thought I should move the date of my fishing trip up a week and let things cool off for a while.

"Colonel, where the hell have you been the last three months? Do you think General Sayer was ever going to turn the water line off or that General Aziz even bothered to have the phone line checked out?"

"No, but that's not the point."

"What is the point? Everyone keeps telling me I have to meet a schedule. Then, when I run into a situation requiring a little cooperation, you people disappear. I warned you; it all worked out. With the tree gone and the phone and water line out of the way, there shouldn't be many more headaches for a while."

General Olsen overheard our conversation and told us if we were going to stick to a story, we should try to get along. I was upset with Colonel Baker. The Colonel had not done anything but play politician since I met him. The problems I was having with the Egyptian Army came under his jurisdiction. Tom and the Colonel went on ahead and left General Olsen to see if he could settle me down.

"General, if I left the problems up to Colonel Baker, I would still be trying to get on the site."

"Patrick, sometimes you're a little dense. To you, it's just a building, but the computer center is critical; we need to track the hardware and make sure it remains in Egypt for defense against rogue Arab states, not shipped to the Sini to be used against Israel. If we waited for the Egyptians to respond we would never finish the building. Most American PMs on our projects go with the flow. The projects sometimes take years or are never finished. You're, well.... different and willing to stick your neck out. Colonel Baker knows that."

"I'm about done with that shit; I don't want it chopped off. Colonel Baker needs to get his act together."

"He knows you're going to use some unorthodox methods, methods he can't get away with himself. He's military, remember? So is Tom. It's easier for them to apologize and sort something out after it happens than to plan a solution."

"I understand that, but they keep putting me on the line. General, what are we doing here? This isn't costing the Egyptians a dime. It's a gift from the U.S. taxpayer. Why are they fighting us every step of the way?"

"When you figure out an answer, let me know. In the meantime, I don't want any more surprises. I want to know if there are other problems facing you which we need to address before we meet with the Generals."

"Just one, General Olsen, how do you expect me to build this building on time with all the roads closed to truck access?"

"The Egyptian laws are your problem. Your company agreed to comply with them when they bid on the project. You will have to schedule your deliveries at night."

"You're wrong, General. We agreed to the laws in effect at the time Cesar signed the contract. General Sayer had the roads closed after we started work. If we have to work at night, it's going to cost someone."

"You're up to something; what have you got in mind?"

"If I can get General Aziz and General Sayer into an argument about road access and convince them it's General Aziz's construction money at stake, maybe the broken water line won't be such a big deal."

"Why not? Let me mention it to Colonel Baker. By the way, where do you come up with this shit?"

"I lay awake at night, wouldn't you? Let me surprise him."

I did not give General Olsen a chance to say anything to the Colonel. Regardless of what General Olsen said about Colonel Baker, I still believed he could do a lot more to resolve some of the problems if he wanted to bother with them. I did manage to get Tom aside and ask him to go along.

"Pat, you're going to get thrown out of Egypt if you keep this shit up."

"Relax. It's the only way."

"Good morning, General Aziz, General Sayer."

The General did not offer the customary tea. It seemed he was out of water.

"Ah, Mr. Pat. We have a problem."

"We sure do, General. How do you expect me to build the building when General Sayer closed the truck access to the site?"

The General started to say something, but Tom entered the conversation.

"General. Mr. Pat brought me an estimate of the added cost for a second shift. It means more supervisory personnel; I want Americans. He wants another five hundred thousand."

I was wondering where Tom came up with the figure when Colonel Baker started to say something. It seemed we caught everyone off guard. It was General Aziz's budget, but General Olsen would have to come up with the money.

General Aziz and General Sayer were arguing in Arabic. General Olsen explained to the Colonel that he should leave the problem to Tom and me. I decided to press the advantage.

"General Sayer, we had a little mishap last night. It seems the construction superintendent wasn't aware of the water line and broke it while taking out the old phone lines. I'm sorry about that, but if someone shuts the water off, we will have it fixed in a few hours."

"Mr. Pat, it isn't the water line I'm concerned about. The water line only goes to General Aziz's base."

"What's your problem then, General? I'm sure General Aziz and I can come to an understanding on the water line."

"It's the phone line, Mr. Pat. It's the line into my base!"

General Aziz set me up.

"General, I'm sorry, but General Aziz told us the line was dead."

"No, Mr. Pat. I told you it wasn't the service to my base."

General Aziz was at it again. Cute General, but I could see from the look on Sayer's face he did not get away with it. General Sayer said something to General Aziz and then started to leave.

"Wait a minute, General Sayer. What about the street access for the trucks?"

Colonel Baker started to say something about leaving well enough alone, but I ignored him.

"General, it's like Tom told you. If we don't find a way to let the trucks in during the daytime, it will cost another half a million."

"Not me, Mr. Pat. It's General Aziz's building and his budget."

Thoughts: *Paybacks were a bitch, and General Sayer thought he had just found a way to get even.*

The room was in a stew about the water line. If I worked around the clock relocating it and had it fixed by the next day, General Aziz would see what he could do about the street access and get someone in to fix the phone lines.

The Colonel and I called a truce. Everybody calmed down on the way back to the site. The problem between the Generals was an Egyptian military cooperation problem.

Anwar left that morning for Kuwait; Hamid was back in charge. By the time I got back to the site, the subcontractor had installed a valve on the water line and shut the water off. They would have it relocated in a few hours; General Aziz would be able to brew tea. Things went pretty well for the next few days.

I was sitting at my desk, hoping it was going to be quiet for a while longer. General Sayer's phones were working, the site was secure, and the tree was gone. The subcontractor had fixed the water line to General Aziz's base, and the site was drying out.

I was ready to call Tom and settle the last-minute details of the fishing trip when General Olsen and Colonel Baker entered my office. Something had to be wrong; these people never came to my office unannounced.

"Good morning, General, Colonel."

"Patrick, your phones are out of order."

'No big deal. It happens two or three times a week. What brings you down here?"

"The water line, General Aziz is fuming because it's not fixed, and your men have stopped working on it."

"Colonel, the water line to Aziz's base was repaired the day after it was broken."

"If it's repaired, why is General Aziz still out of water?"

"Remember the problem we had finding the valve to turn the water off in the first place?"

"Yes, what's that got to do with the water still being off?"

"The valve is on General Sayer's base. They found it after we installed the new valve and closed it while we relocated the line. I sent him a notice after we repaired the line and asked him to turn it back on. I have a signed receipt, that was three days ago."

The General and Colonel sat down. I asked them if they would like some tea. General Olsen asked for a copy; he told the Colonel it did not appear to be our problem. He would personally relay the information to General Aziz.

We spent the next few minutes betting on how long it would take General Sayer to give in and turn General Aziz's water back on. The General and Colonel left a few minutes later. I decided to forget about the phones and go to Tom's office.

"When are we leaving, Tom?"

"Thursday morning. Is everything under control so Colonel Baker won't be looking for you when we're gone?"

"No problem."

Tom and I finished a few details, and I headed out to do some last-minute shopping for the trip.

Chapter 16

I met Tom and his wife, Unan, at their flat in Maadi at eight. Unan was operating on Egyptian time, she was still preparing snacks and had not started packing. It was almost 1:30 by the time we left for the Red Sea. The trip was supposed to take six hours. We wanted to be there before dark. Planning was as usual for Cairo; we were starting four hours late.

Tom had made the trip before. We would need to top the tank off before we started to cross the desert. We did not have room for gas cans; we would be fueling in Helwan.

Helwan is a well-named industrial section on the outskirts of Cairo. Cement dust pours out of the stacks of cement factories like mushrooming clouds from an atomic explosion. Channels of raw sewage run along the sides of the highways, and oil slicks hide the banks of the canal. The foul liquid meanders its way into rural sections of the Nile Delta to farmer's fields for irrigation, and to the villages for everyday chores.

The station was out of gas. It was forty minutes back to Cairo. If we went back for gas and then returned, we would need gas again. We tried to ask for directions to another station in the village. I could not speak enough Arabic to locate a working toilet, and Tom was not familiar with the local dialect.

It appeared to be a lost cause. Unan was used to dealing with local shopkeepers. She thought the attendant was telling us to follow a man on a motorcycle who was heading into a village off the main highway. As we meandered through the fields, it did not seem the guy on the motorcycle knew where he was going. He kept stopping to talk to the local farmers, apparently asking for directions. We were driving one of the embassy station wagons. Most station wagons in Cairo were taxis. Every time Tom slowed down, people wanting a ride jumped in front of the car, waving for us to stop.

The road, jammed with people and animals, was not much more than a dike across a farmer's field. Tom had his hands full navigating the human congestion. Camels, donkey carts, and water buffalo going in both directions were adding to the strain. I sat back and watched the scenery.

Without electricity, market day in the villages of Egypt is every day. When we entered the village, the market filled every cranny except for a dirt path just wide enough for traffic. Vendors were hawking everything from fruit to, what do you know?

"It's in old milk containers and probably half water."

Tom did not want any part of it, but we had no choice if we wanted to catch the boat the next morning.

"Tom, they didn't know we were coming. Everyone in the village uses it in their equipment. Besides, it's almost five, and if we don't get back on the road soon, we should go back to Cairo and try another time."

Tom glanced at the fuel gauge. I said something about the desert and us only having enough survival equipment to last three days. We were a long way off the tourist tracks. While Tom was bartering with the petrol vendor, I decided to photograph reality.

Laundry Day in a Village in Egypt.

The culture shock continued. The banks of the creek running through the village were littered with pots, pans, articles of clothing, children in various stages of undress, and women of the village huddled in groups cleaning all of the above in what looked and smelled like it was discharged from an overflow in a sewage treatment plant.

Water buffalo do not seem to mind; a few wallowed in the mud, stirring the banks upstream, adding a brownish cast to the surface already blackened by oily sludge and sewage that filtered its way from the factories of Helwan.

There were few men in the village; polygamy was their way of life, and birth control and abortion were forbidden. While many of the women had moved back, kids began to crowd the area, curious about foreigners in their midst.

Where did the kid on the left get the blonde hair?

The village was miles from the nearest tourist route. These kids were unschooled in the mannerisms of beggars who took up residence at every tourist attraction in Egypt. No one held their hands out when I pointed the camera in their direction.

I had often tried to capture this part of Egypt on film. However, village elders always interfered. I finished the first roll and was busy reloading the camera while moving towards the creek. This was the part of Egypt ignored by politicians and bureaucrats running the country. Even the village leaders preferred I refrain from exposing the indifference and poverty to the outside world.

I lucked out this time. Tom had attracted more attention than I had. While he was trying to pour petrol out of a twenty gallon milk container into the car with a funnel he fashioned from cardboard, I captured some of the sights I hope never to forget.

Waste, some human, some animal, some toxic from the factories of Helwan mixed with the lifeblood of the Nile. Women, young and old, were carrying tubs from shacks, dumping them in the proximity of others who were dipping water for household chores. Others were sweeping the surface of the creek to move Helwan's waste further downstream long enough to dip an article of clothing in the water below the surface.

Children in various stages of undress were bathing or merely frolicking in the shallows. Some male toddlers, naked, were standing at the bank peeing out into the creek, a contest it seemed, to see who had the furthest reach.

I turned back to the car and came face to face with a very upset elder. Gestures tempered with anger are easy to understand in any language. His shouting attracted the attention of other men in the crowd who were joining him, shouting, and threatening.

"When are you going to learn? Get back in the car."

Tom appeared at my elbow with a fistful of money, trying to negotiate a settlement. It was not working. Prodded on by the elder, the crowd continued to shout and point in my direction. Holding my camera in front of me, I approached the crowd; they started to settle.

"I told you to stay in the car!"

"Relax, Tom."

I did not want to give up the exposed film. I had reloaded the camera with a fresh roll. As I approached the man who started the fray, I stripped out the film and then pulled the film from the canister. I then took another roll from my shirt pocket and offered it to the men in the crowd. It had the desired effect. A few ten-LE notes settled the argument.

"You know the rule. Keep the camera in the case when you're in the outer villages."

Tom was referring to some Egyptians who not only resented all foreigners, but believed a picture could capture the soul. In some Islamic societies, photographs are thought to encourage the worship of idols. Others believe they will invalidate their prayers and prevent angels from entering their homes. We left the village the way we came, passing the petrol station we had detoured from two hours earlier. A tanker was filling the storage tank.

"It's just a matter of timing, Tom."

I opened a can of beer and handed it to Tom. Thought: *I have the pictures, a forever reminder that even on the worst day of my life, I will still be better off than the peasants of Egypt on their best day.*

The desert was the next order of business. The Egyptians were building a new highway along the shore of the Red Sea, but it was still a year or more from completion. The road we were on, more like a path at times, was the route the Egyptians thought the Israelis would take when they crossed the Red Sea to attack Cairo.

There are army camps scattered along both sides. Every twenty klicks, there was a military checkpoint. Most of the outposts consist of a few mud shacks manned by less than a half-dozen soldiers.

"First checkpoint coming up, Tom."

The embassy car had diplomatic plates. The soldier did not bother to ask for passports. He spoke Arabic-English and seemed to enjoy the opportunity to show off. He asked us where we were heading. I told him we were going to the Red Sea on a fishing trip. The soldier could not figure out why rich Americans would bother spending time and money chasing fish around in a boat when we could buy anything we like.

Five minutes passed with the man leaning on the edge of Tom's open window. It had been a while since he had a bath; the smell was drifting in. Tom had had enough; he pulled out his diplomatic passport. One look and the conversation about fishing was over. Tom was obviously annoyed. The guard wanted to see my passport.

"Talk about me, Tom; why can't you keep your big mouth shut once in a while?"

I had been through enough security problems to know we could end up spending the night. I handed the guard my passport along with my security pass from the Army base wrapped in a ten-LE note.

Privates in the Egyptian military made seven LE a month. Ten was a monster tip for him. The guard handed back our passports and then asked if we had cigarettes. When I handed him a pack he smiled and waved us on our way.

It was my turn to drive. A mile from the outpost Tom pulled the car over, stopping on the edge of the narrow road. The beer was putting a strain on my kidneys. Tom's wife was in view. I walked to a pile of rocks near a barbed wire fence. Both Tom and Unan started to protest.

I thought this was going to be one hell of a fishing trip if Unan was that much of a prude. We would be camping on islands that did not have rocks big enough to stand behind. Tom yelled; I stopped in stride. Turning toward the car, I noticed a worn sign lying in the sand.

In 1967, in preparation for the Six-Day War, Egypt laced the beaches of the Red Sea and the sides of the connecting road to Cairo with land mines. The skull and crossbones on the downed fences were faded. Intermittent strands of barbed wire installed after the war in the remote areas were still a warning for locals. Many of the minefields had not been cleared. I stood behind the car and did what an Egyptian would do. I hung it out in the middle of the highway.

I had been behind the wheel a few minutes when I figured out why Tom saved the second half of the driving for me. The road was a nightmare of world-class chuckholes. It would have been hard enough to navigate in the daylight; it was a nightmare once the sunset. I settled into a slow, tedious pace. At times, the road ended abruptly, and I had to take off across the desert, following tracts in the sand.

The only maintenance done on a car in Egypt is after a wreck. Half the vehicles do not have working lights. Egyptians who do use their lights play a game; expats refer to it as *blinky light*. They are not used to someone driving with a steady beam, especially of the enhanced quartz variety the Embassy installed on the car we were driving. Their solution is to start blinking their high beams to tell you they want you to turn off your lights. If you refuse, it is a high beam all the way.

Truckers give no quarter. It is a narrow road. They have the right of weight and figure the middle of the road belongs to them. Truck lights that did work were blinding. It is up to the driver of a car to figure out which part of the road the truck is using by determining which of the truck's lights is working.

Unan helped when she took a pair of Tom's sunglasses out of the glove box; they only had one lens. She showed me how they work. Keep the unprotected eye closed when a truck is approaching, and then open it when the truck passes. It took about twenty klicks, but once I got the hang of it, it helped.

A few hours later, we entered the outskirts of Hurghada. Our trip covered five hundred klicks and took thirteen hours, for a little more than thirty-eight klicks an hour (22 mph).

The entrance into town was spotless. Hurghada is a tourist community, and, at first, I thought the people decided the way to keep the foreigners coming back was to keep the trash out of sight.

We checked into the Global Hotel and would board the boat the next morning. The hotel was Egypt standards and cost thirty

LE a night, a little over $12. The rooms were musty. Tom chucked their bed linens out into the hall and unrolled their sleeping bags.

I had been in Egypt long enough to blame myself if I did not have enough sense to plan. I brought along the necessities for travel in rural Egypt. A sleeping bag was a given for camping out. As for the rest, soap, toilet paper, and a can of Raid were purchased at the commissary.

I threw the hotel bedclothes into the hall, sprayed the room and bed with Raid, and then took a shower. The common toilet and shower were down the hall. There was no hot water, but that did not matter. It was past midnight, but the temperature was still over ninety degrees. The plumbing was exposed; the water was warm.

Unan had prepared the food for the trip. Unan was raised in a peasant village in Thailand. She would eat anything that walks, crawls, flies, or swims, and she is not particular about which part or how it is prepared. Tom and Unan had been snacking on the drive from Cairo; they went straight to bed. I had passed. It was not what I was used to, and even by Middle Eastern standards, it was, well, *different*.

I was hungry. It was past midnight. The hub of Hurghada, like the streets of Cairo at that time of night, was busy; restaurants would be open.

Hurghada was a remote destination catering to the budget-minded diving and snorkeling crowd from Europe. Due to the remote access, the shops and restaurants had not yet had the influx of American and European tourists that would expect them to clean their floors and tables more than twice a year. I wandered around the village for an hour before I found a place where I was willing to try the food. The restaurant was on the roof of one of the shabby buildings. Blowing sand from the desert covered the floor.

Keeping dogs in Islam is not permissible except for hunting or guarding livestock and crops. A pack of stray dogs was snarling and sparing over scraps of food where the waiters were scraping leftovers off plates over the side of the building.

I sat at the end of the restaurant with a moonlit view of the ancient harbor. The sky, crystal clear, lit by the stars, was magnificent. It was a pleasant change. Cairo air is always thick with pollution from traffic and the industrial waste of Helwan factories.

The meals were inexpensive, much less than what I was used to paying in Cairo. Red Sea lobster, a spiny species without the pinchers of the Maine variety, was only six-LE. It was the highest-priced item on the menu. I would be on a seafood diet for the next few days. Chicken is usually a safe choice anywhere in Egypt. I settled on chicken.

There was little traffic. I was enjoying a beer I had brought with me and the quiet of the evening. Things were rather pleasant until the waiter brought the chicken; it looked a little strange. Now, I realize the method of preparing some fowl says you should let it ripen a little before you cook it, and I heard somewhere that wild upland game birds should hang by the neck in a cool cellar for a few days while the flesh ripens until the head separates from the body. The chicken was the foulest game anyone ever tried to pawn off on me as chicken. I gagged; if I had not had the bottle of beer to wash the stink out of my mouth, I would have puked on the floor.

The head waiter came over to introduce himself. He could not understand my Arabic-English. He tried French. I could not find words to make him understand, so I threw the chicken, along with the plastic plate, off the roof and into the waiting pack of dogs. I paid for the chicken and gave the waiter an extra LE to retrieve the plate.

My appetite was subdued. I wandered around the village for a while and then entered one of the shops in hopes of finding a souvenir. The first thing I noticed was all the trash I missed when I entered town. I picked through some but gave up when I found the Egyptian method of mounting a fish, turtle, or even a seashell is to leave it out in the sun until the liquids dry and insects remove the meat from the hide.

It had been a long day; I was tired. I went back to the hotel looking forward to clean salt air, a few days of camping on ocean-washed beaches, and definitely some fresh seafood. I sprayed my room again with Raid and then opened the last of the day's allotment of beer. I went outside and stood on the balcony while the insecticide dissipated. The view of stars lighting the night sky and a few puffy clouds casting shadows on the coast of the Red Sea was a refreshing change.

A cool breeze was crossing in from the sea. Crisp, clean sheets felt good after a long day. I was asleep in minutes. Tom woke me at six. When I opened my door, he handed me an ice-cold beer.

Normally, I do not drink beer in the morning, but I forgot to bring toothpaste. My mouth, with the stale taste of yesterday's beer mixed with the decaying smell of the chicken, felt like it was full of cotton balls. I rinsed with salt and gargled with the beer. I entered the dining area feeling better. They did not have coffee. I settled for tea and a light breakfast of soft-boiled eggs and a sweet roll.

$30 a day, with a captain, deckhand, and ice.

When I saw the boat pulled up on the sand, I realized my escaping Egypt by way of this exit would never be an issue. Everyone would take it for granted no one in his right mind would try to cross the Red Sea in a contraption like the one I was about to board. I thought about telling Tom, budgets are one thing, but?

Saudi Arabia is on the opposite shore of the Red Sea, by boat 870 klicks. I had crossed Saudi Arabia off my travel list. They take your passport when you enter the country and do not give it back until you get their permission to leave.

By 1988, the U.S. Army Corps of Engineers had constructed a $14-billion network of military facilities across Saudi Arabia. At that time, an expat working for a Saudi firm had to get the company's permission to leave before the Saudi government would agree.

I heard horror stories from expats who arrived in Saudi Arabia for short tours and then had to bribe their way out when the company they were working for decided not to live up to the terms of their contract.

Expat women who had lived in Saudi could never leave their compounds unless they were dressed in traditional garb for fear of harassment from both Saudi men and women. Like most places in Middle Eastern society, women would spit on them if they showed more flesh than hands and eyes.

We had to go through immigration. It only took a few minutes. Immigration officers in Hurghada were lax. They figured if you were willing to chance it and cross into Saudi Arabia without a proper visa it was your problem. After the boat was loaded, we settled into our respective places. I had the roof; Tom and Unan had the back deck. It was not a bad arrangement; I could see for miles.

The Egyptian government began drilling for oil in the 1860s. Shell started up operations at the Hurghada field in 1911. Satellite pictures going back to 1985 show a brown stain that spreads up to a mile wide, creeping out into the sky-blue water around the sites. The pollution is *produced water*, a byproduct of oil drilling that is pumped ashore from rigs and sits in large ponds before being flushed, barely treated, back out to sea.

The oil rigs were north, closer to land than where we were headed. At the time, coral islands where we would be fishing were still unspoiled, beautiful, and vibrant. Divers from all over the globe flocked to the reefs to view some of the most magnificent sea life in the world.

The color of the water is dependent on its depth and the coral beneath the surface. It ranges from light green to the deepest shades of blue, red, and orange imaginable. With a scuba mask I could see to the bottom in thirty meters of water.

Turtles, dolphins, and exotic fish were abundant. There was life on the surface everywhere as we trolled leisurely, meandering around the islands on a course heading toward the tuna currents Tom and I had been anticipating for the last few months. We caught a variety of fish, none of them over ten kilos. Most were grouper or a sea bass variety.

It was hot, the air dehydrating. We had only brought enough water for cooking; the beer Tom and I had allocated was starting to look good again.

We trolled until noon. Unan decided it was time for a break. I had not eaten since we left Cairo. I was ready to try some of Unan's delicacies. The captain anchored in a sheltered cove within a few meters of the beach. We would be staying through the heat of the afternoon sun.

Unan was preparing lunch; Tom was opening another can of beer. The water looked inviting, and I needed to clear my head from the morning's refreshments. I broke out snorkeling equipment. Leaving 110-degree heat made the 86-degree water feel cool. I headed for the nearest reef. As I approached, thousands of fish, hundreds of species of every color, parted before me in waves. Although Moray eels, some two meters in length, whose massive heads were protruding from coral caves, looked foreboding, they appeared content and made no effort to threaten me as I skimmed the outer edges of their lairs.

I dove to inspect a turtle lying silently on the bottom. As I passed it, I reached for the antenna of a spiny lobster cowering in a shallow cave. I missed, a few would be easy to catch later in the afternoon.

A pack of smokes a day does not help. I was out of breath but relaxed in a world I found beautiful and remote from the chaos of the last few months. I floated lazily back toward the boat, spotting a scorpion fish, white with black stripes. Small in comparison to many fish on the reef. It looked harmless as it meandered along the bottom. I found it hard to believe a prick from one of the spines trailing beside it could send the strongest man home in a plastic bag. I made a mental note to remember Tom's warning. Scorpionfish cruise shallow water feeding on crabs returning from nightly foraging on the beach; it is not a time to wade.

When I reboarded, I looked around. We were alone except for an Army post on one end of the island. The only other sign of human life was a diving boat moving south that had been anchored off the reef when we approached the island.

Egyptian law forbids harvesting coral by foreigners. For a change, I agreed with the Egyptians. However, poaching is rampant by locals selling to unwary tourists, and visiting divers smuggling exotics out of the country to finance their lifestyle. I never saw a police or military boat. Most recreational divers stick to the reefs close to shore near the villages. Poachers work the outer reefs, avoiding tourists and police.

Coral was not the only commodity. Conch, a large tropical marine mollusk, is an expensive delicacy worldwide. Due to overharvesting, some species are now endangered. There was a sandy beach at the curve of the cove where we were anchored. Conch shells the size of footballs, some still glistening with flesh attached, littered the beach where the poachers had recently removed the meat. One pile was two meters high. I looked into the distance; the boat had disappeared.

Unan had prepared one of the fish we caught that morning. She seemed pleased with herself and the dish she was offering of raw fish cheeks and chicken livers in a hot pepper curry sauce. Thought: *Thank God for the beer to wash it down.*

Lunch break was over. It was time to continue toward the tuna grounds. We were trolling at about six knots. I thought it was too fast by my standards for grouper, but we were catching fish. We would continue to fish for grouper for the remainder of the first day and camp on an island a few miles from the warmer tuna currents further north.

As we left the lee side of the island, a wave hit us like a small boy swiping at his toy boat in a bathtub. We settled, but the boat lifted again from the force of gale-like winds and came close to pitching me off my perch and into the sea. When I recovered, the captain had the boat running parallel with the growing swells toward the open water.

Tom yelled something and tossed me a fresh beer. As I reached for it, a swell broke into a wave, slamming into the side of the boat; I missed the catch. The can disappeared into another breaking swell.

The island we just left was part of a long coral reef with intermittent islands. They were a little off course but in the right direction. We could pass behind them; that would break the wind and waves.

"Tom, tell the captain to head for the calm water behind the reef."

Tom and Unan were arguing with the captain; the deckhand was seeking shelter in the cabin. I worked my way around the mast and down the ladder to the safety of the deck. The boat was still heading for open water when I reached Tom and the captain; a wave broke over the side.

"Can't he see we're in trouble? Tell him to turn this tub toward shore."

"The captain said he's the captain and knows what he's doing."

"Tell him if he doesn't turn toward shore, I'm going to be the captain."

Tom was turning toward the captain as another wave broke over the side and damn near washed our camping gear overboard. We decided on mutiny. Tom worked his way between the captain and the tiller. I took over and swung the boat in the direction of the lee side of the nearest island.

When things settled Tom sent Unan down with a six-pack to explain to the captain. We were paying the bill; we should be able to choose where we wanted to fish.

The captain was a Muslim; he did not drink alcohol. Beer in Egypt comes in one-liter bottles; he had never seen a can of Coors. Unan told him it was American soda pop. Before we reached the protected water of the nearest island, we had a tipsy, seasick captain puking over the side of the boat.

After we reached calm water, the captain mellowed, and his stomach recovered. Tom made a deal to allow him to return to his duties if he promised to follow our directions. We picked up speed trolling between the islands for the next few hours. Too fast for grouper, we were catching an occasional Barracuda and Wahoo prowling the coral reefs.

The wind subsided as we passed on the lee side of one of the larger islands. The cliffs would protect us from the wind, but there was a manned army post on the island. An hour before sunset, we circled a couple of small islands for one final look to make sure there were no occupied army outposts before settling on one with a shallow, sheltered cove.

Tom was on the deck sorting through wet camping gear. I was on the sundeck enjoying clean salt air and the last of the day's sun while the captain scouted the cove for a decent campsite. By the time we anchored, the wind changed direction. The sun was setting; it would be dark soon. It was too late to move. Tom and I stowed the gear on the beach behind an outcropping of rocks that would give us some protection. By then, it was blowing close to thirty knots.

Tom and I set up camp while Unan scouted the area for driftwood. We had brought firewood and charcoal, but we did not have a lot of space in the car. Although it was a small amount for three days, I thought scouring a desert island was a hopeless exercise.

Sand and barren rock surround the Red Sea. Village huts and livestock corrals are made of mud bricks and straw. Nomads collect scraps of wood or limbs of trees for their campfires. It would be a rare occurrence to find driftwood on the beaches. Unan returned empty-handed except for a thick stick with a knob on the end. She held it in the air and announced she would be preparing dinner.

After we were settled, I sat back to watch the sunset. I did not have to ask what we were having for dinner. I knew it would be some part of one of the fish we caught that day.

I was out of the loop, stoking the fire. Unan and I got into a tug-of-war over the limb she had managed to find. She had set it aside; when I reached for it, she grabbed it and tried to pull it away. I was not sure what the problem was; she kept lapsing into her native language, which she had a habit of doing whenever she was excited.

Unan won the tug of war when Tom cracked open a bottle of Jack Daniels and offered me a drink. I was removing the bottle from my mouth when Unan grabbed the club, jumped up, and ran down the beach, waving it above her head. She stopped after a short distance and brought it down on a crab that came out of the sea to feed.

Unan had been to the Red Sea before. She knew that as the sun set, Red Sea Ghost crabs started their migration to land in search of food. They are the kind I have seen in the movies, one big claw and their eyes standing straight up from their shells. The largest one we encountered on the trip was about four inches across the back. The end of the club Unan was wielding was about four inches and it appeared from all the excitement they were evenly matched. When she let the first one have it between the eyes, I was not concerned that she might add it to the dinner menu; most of it was smeared into the sand.

Tom got up to follow Unan. She was running up and down the beach, swinging the club, and then splashing in the water after the pieces. Tom was following her with a pan.

While Tom and Unan were off on the hunting trip, the blustery wind picked up. None of us were paying attention to the camping gear scattered on the beach. I was enjoying the show when Tom let out a yell. I looked in the direction Tom was pointing. His sleeping bag and pillow were tumbling across the sand, heading for the surf.

I reached for the sleeping bag and Tom's pillow but missed both, tripping over the bottle of Jack. Jack was more important than Tom's bedding. The bag and pillow escaped my grasp. Tom dropped the pan and tackled the sleeping bag. The pillow tumbled into the Red Sea.

Tom was upset because I let his pillow get away. Unan was yelling at Tom because he dropped the crab parts in the surf. It appeared dinner was going to be delayed. I entered the argument because Tom knocked over the lantern while he was putting his sleeping bag under the ice chest. Unan tripped in the dark and kicked Jack in the neck; he was spilling into the sand.

Nobody said much until Unan called a truce. She took another bottle of Jack out of her overnight bag that neither Tom nor I knew she had. Tom lit the lantern, Unan brought Jack to the party, and I promised to help Unan gather more crab if Tom would protect the camping equipment from the wind.

Things mellowed after Jack joined the party. We chased Jack down with the last of our beer allotment for the day, and it appeared Unan had forgotten about the crab hunt. I was also wondering what she had in mind for dinner.

Unan broke out some crunches. I was hungry and convinced the foraging was off. I bit into *something*, then told Unan I thought it was a bit salty. Unan apologized and told me the Egyptians do not know how to fry grasshoppers, and that she would do it herself the next time.

The crunches were not that bad. If Unan had not told me what they were, I would probably have thought they were salted nuts. I needed a diversion, and I ate lots of crabs; the hunt was back on.

I used pots back home. Unan had to give me a quick course on crab hunting. I was to take the flashlight and look for crabs as they came out of the surf to feed. I was then to step aside, making sure to shine the flashlight in its eyes so Unan could thump it with the club. I was to pick up the pieces, rinse them in the surf, and put them in the pan, as they say in Egypt, *Malish*.

It only took a few minutes; I lost interest. The crab migration was in full swing. Live ones were attacking pieces of their relatives and dragging them back to the surf. Others were trying to make my feet their dinner. Although I did not think they could hurt me, stepping on sharp shells and claws would cause nasty cuts to bare feet. Unan was running gleefully up and down the beach, swatting them as fast as she could swing the club. I yelled to Unan that the pan was full and the hunt was over.

"Leave the flashlight."

"Not a chance."

Without the flashlight, the hunt was over. Unan was sulking. I was still hungry. Tom never intended to eat crab. When I got back to camp, he was sitting by the camp stove stirring dinner. Tom and I gorged ourselves on American delicacies: Dinty Moore beef stew, baked beans, and hot dogs. Unan sucked whatever it was she was sucking out of burnt crab shells.

After dinner I prepared my bed by digging a trench in the sand in front of a rock shelf. A barrier of sand and stacked camping equipment would protect me from both the wind and the crab. I crawled into my sleeping bag, lit a smoke, watched the stars, and dozed off to the sounds of the boat captain's drums. I slept the night through. When I woke at five, the wind had subsided, and the crabs had disappeared back into the sea.

Dawn was breaking on the horizon. Tom and Unan were stirring. Tom mumbled something about a beer. Beer for breakfast two days in a row was not appealing. The coals from the night's fire still held enough heat to start a new fire. I could not find the coffee, but in a few minutes, I had a pot of tea simmering. I headed down the beach to find a discrete place to pee. When I returned, Tom and Unan were huddled around the fire.

"What would you like in your tea?"

"Coffee, Tom. Doesn't anyone in this country drink coffee?"

"You're too picky."

Tom reached into the ice chest, took out two cans, opened one, and tossed me the other; the second day of the fishing trip was on.

I crawled back into my sleeping bag, sipped the beer, and settled back to watch the sunrise. I have never seen anything in the world to compare to the brilliance and the beauty of the sun coming up out of the east and reflecting on the colors of the Red Sea.

I timed it from when the first flame of orange showed on the horizon until the sun separated itself from the horizon in an hourglass shape, the color of liquid fire. It took less than five minutes. I thought to myself, regardless of all the setbacks, those minutes were worth the trip to Egypt.

Shaking the sand out of my shorts as I dragged myself out of the sleeping bag, I thought about the sunrise and Muslims who beat their foreheads on the ground in prayer. We were alone on the island with no other human life in sight. The heavens above held a few puffy clouds scattered in a clear blue sky; in the distance were barren islands dotting the surface of the Red Sea.

The shopkeeper is right. Faced with infinity, a man's lifespan has very little meaning on this planet. We are given the opportunity to visit for a split second in the grand scheme of things. Man needs to learn some patience with neighbors he disagrees with. Sometimes we are reminded by acts of nature how fragile the gift is. If we keep it up, our creator will conclude he made a mistake, borrow Unan's club, and the seventh day will set.

When we left the shelter of the cove, the wind picked up. The captain was circling the island, deciding which direction to take.

Tuna currents were a few miles offshore. I was anxious to get on with the day.

"Tom, it's not as rough as yesterday. This boat is big enough if he keeps the bow pointed into the swells and doesn't let it slip sideways in the trough. Let's see if we can talk him into getting on with the program and head for the tuna grounds."

Tom said something to the captain. He looked over at me and Unan, shrugged his shoulders, wrapped a shawl around his head, settled himself on the back deck, and steered the boat into the swells. The sea was rough, but the old boat was more seaworthy than it looked. It did not appear there would be a problem except to time the beer can with my mouth because I did not want to go to a dentist in Cairo.

Our first strike came just as we were entering open water. The hit came on my pole. It wasn't a tuna; it was a big wahoo. The fish stripped about a hundred meters of line. I was settling in for my first game fish of the trip. The fish slowed, and I turned it toward the boat. I was pumping it in when I felt a sudden surge and then a dead weight on the line.

I dragged what was once a 60 to 80-pound Wahoo to the boat. Its head had been sheared from the rest of the body by a shark. I looked around. Thought: *the boat was not nearly as seaworthy as it seemed a few minutes earlier*.

We stripped the shark's leftovers from the jig. I reset the pole and settled back on the top deck. We passed the tip of the outermost island and were entering the tuna currents. A few minutes later, we had a strike on Tom's jig. Tom was fighting the fish; the captain was fighting the wind. He increased the speed, coming off a swell; Tom lost whatever it was.

Tom reset the pole, mumbled something to the captain about taking a swim with the sharks, and headed for the cabin to fill the cooler with the day's supply of beer. Unan was crunching on some of the leftover crab from the night before. I was finishing my breakfast beer and trying to decide if I wanted to go down and argue with the captain, who had turned the boat sidewise to the swells and was sneaking back in the direction of the island we had just passed.

The wind had picked up. Waves were occasionally breaking over the bow, washing over gunnels, and spilling on the back deck. When he turned sidewise to the wind, a breaking wave nearly washed me off my perch. I knew I had made a mistake. As I was working my way down the ladder, I glanced back at the poles.

"Tom, something's ripping the line off your reel."

Tom's pole was bucking in the pole holder; his line was disappearing into the sea. Tom scrambled out of the cabin, grabbed the pole, and the fight was on. I yelled at the captain to slow down and went to see if I could help Tom. The captain ignored me and put the throttle to the floor. The boat only did about ten knots, but the sudden lurch as he turned toward the lee side of the nearest island threw Tom and me into the rail of the boat.

"Pat, take the wheel and line me up with the fish."

Tom followed the fish to the downwind side of the boat. I took the tiller from the captain. Unan slipped and fell on the deck, trying to get out of the way as the captain ducked back into the cabin.

The fish stripped more than half of Tom's line on its first run. Sharks do not usually hit a feather jig, and it was too big for a wahoo. It was a tuna, and I did not want Tom to lose it.

"Keep the boat in a straight line?"

"Lighten up. I'm doing the best I can."

I was having trouble keeping the stern of the boat in line with the fish while steering the bow into the waves. I told Tom I had done a lot of fishing in the Pacific Ocean back home and I had owned a dozen different fishing boats. I did not recall telling Tom I could do much with a 30-foot double-end dory with a tiller in 30-knot winds and 10-foot seas.

I could not see over the cabin. I had to throttle the boat with my foot while standing on the ice chest so I could watch for the next wave that could wash Tom into the sea if I were not careful.

I took the tiller and the gearshift and told Unan to take the throttle. Unan and I had not figured out the timing. Tom kept yelling at me about not running over the fishing line.

I sent Unan to the cabin to get the captain or the deckhand, but she came back mumbling something about both of them kneeling on their prayer rugs.

"Cut him loose, Tom, and let's get out of here!"

"No fucking way, steer the damned boat."

I put my mind to keeping the bow pointed into the waves and Tom's line pointed toward the fish. For the next half-hour, Tom fought the fish, I fought the boat, and Unan ducked back into the cabin to fight with the captain. The sea was fighting us all. Still, Tom managed to bring the fish to the boat.

"Unan, steer the boat while I help Tom land the fish."

Unan took the tiller. I shut the engine down to an idle, reached for the gaff, and went to where Tom was working the fish. As the boat listed toward the fish under the power of the next breaking wave, I sunk the gaff in, and we hauled the fish aboard.

It was a bluefin, about 150 pounds. Not a giant by Red Sea standards, but a nice fish just the same. The captain and deckhand came out waving their arms and smiling. It was the biggest fish ever landed on his boat.

The captain forgave us. He took back control from Unan, looked at me, and pointed to the islands. I nodded my head, and he turned the boat toward shore.

Unan joined Tom inspecting the fish, telling him what a great meal the *good parts* would make. By the time we reached the island, it was time for noon break. Unan told the captain to put into a sheltered cove and make for shore. The island was larger than the one we camped on the night before. I could see a few dilapidated buildings scattered among rock outcroppings; they did not appear inhabited.

The captain crossed the reef and nosed the boat up on the sand. I was hungry but feeling a little queasy from the beer sloshed to foam by the pitching of the boat.

Unan had finished the crab the night before. I was hoping she would break out some of the junk food Tom purchased at the American commissary. When Unan reached in the cooler and took out some of the ripening squid we brought along for bait I picked up the snorkeling equipment and took off for the coral reefs we crossed coming into the cove.

It was magnificent. It was deeper than the day before; viewing sea life was like watching a wide screen at home. The quantity was about the same as the day before, but the fish were larger, colors more varied, and they were now schooled by species. Moray eels are not known to be aggressive to divers unless disturbed or frightened. However, the largest moray eel ever recorded measured 13-feet. They are both ravenous and vicious, ambushing predators and pouncing on prey when it passes by their lairs. At twice my length, and with heads the size of buckets with inch-long teeth I stayed on the surface and out of reach.

The color of the sun reflecting off multi-color coral made everything seem almost artificial. The lobster poking their antenna out of shallow caves were larger than the ones the day before; the depth was deceiving. Had it not been for the eels, I might have attempted to snare a few for dinner.

Reef coral has razor-sharp stony skeletons and will grow until it reaches just below the surface. After an hour drifting, suspended by the buoyancy of the sea, and allowing the currents to carry me in the channels in between, I headed back to the boat, hoping Unan and Tom had finished lunch and she would not be insulted if I fixed something for myself. I also knew Tom was celebrating his catch, and if I did not hurry, he would be into my allotment of beer.

I was wrong about the island being uninhabited. There were three soldiers on the beach in front of the boat engaged in a conversation with the captain. Everyone seemed relaxed, so I joined the party. Unan had the situation in hand. She was passing out sandwiches, squid: *maybe?* The soldiers seemed to be enjoying them. I hoped they would eat them all.

The men were a ragged lot. Their clothes past threadbare, and none was wearing shoes. From the way they were wolfing down the food, it appeared it might have been a few days since their last full meal.

When I climbed into the boat, I noticed my camera case mixed in with the camping supplies. I picked it up to put it in the cabin but stopped to take a few pictures of Unan and her new friends. When I took the camera out of its case, the mood changed. One of the men shouted to the captain as he pointed to me and then to my camera.

I realized the mistake. I was in a tourist mood and, once again, forgot the rules. I put the lens cover back on and placed the camera back in the case. I would wait until we were leaving the cove and far enough offshore not to cause the soldier's concern. With the camera out of sight, the men's mood settled. We were only staying one more night. We gave them some of the fish we caught, along with some of the food we brought with us. It did not enter my mind until later; there was no excuse for the soldiers to be hungry. The island was alive with nesting birds, and the sea was crowded with edible life. I concluded the soldiers were lazier than hungry.

The soldiers left. As everyone else settled for the afternoon break, I took out some of the fishing gear I had brought from the States. The pole was a light six-foot steelhead rod with a level wind reel filled with three hundred yards of twenty-pound test line. It was ideal for fishing in the Pacific Northwest for steelhead, and salmon to forty pounds.

"What do you expect to do with that thing?"

"Fish, what does it look like?"

Tom was chuckling as I baited the hook with some of the squid and then cast it out over the coral reef behind the boat. The bait had hardly settled. I was still taking up the slack when one of the brightly colored reef fish took the bait and headed for the rocks.

"Just like bass fishing back home."

"We'll see. You haven't landed anything yet."

I did not understand Tom's skepticism. The fish weighed about five pounds; it was just a matter of preventing it from cutting itself off in the sharp coral. The fish turned, and I hauled it along the surface, skimming it across the open water.

I was bringing it the last ten meters to the boat when the surface of the water erupted behind it. I reacted with a sudden yank on the pole, pulling what was left out of the mouth of the charging predator.

I did not see a shark fin, but whatever it was severed the body just back of the gills. I retrieved the shreds. Tom was snickering in the background. I was wondering if I could entice another strike out of the marauder, I felt sure was still lurking at the edge of the reef.

"Give it up. You'll never stop it with that gear."

"Bullshit, I've caught forty-pound salmon on this outfit."

"Suit yourself, it's your tackle."

Fish were circling the transom of the boat where Unan had pitched the leftover lunch. I took a 7/0 hook fixed to a wire leader from the tackle box and attached it to my salmon outfit. Then, I made up a drop line to catch one of the fish feeding on the squid behind the boat. A few seconds later, I had one flopping on the deck.

I hooked it behind the dorsal fin so I could cast and then guide it to the edge of the coral, a trick I learned fishing along the kelp beds of Mexico. The bait landed a few meters past the coral. I took up the slack, steering it toward open water, and then free-spooled the line when the fish settled on course.

My planning paid off for a change. A few seconds later, the predator took the bait in a swirl of foam and headed for deep water. I continued to let the line free spool until the fish was clear of the reef, then looked back at Tom. He had a grin on his face and shrugged his shoulders.

I turned my attention to the task, pointing the tip of the pole in the direction of the line disappearing into open water. I engaged the drag and lifted the tip of the pole with enough force to pull the hook out of the back of the baitfish and sink firmly in the jaw of the predator.

"What the fuck….?"

The line continued to disappear toward the open ocean as if hitched to the transom of a retreating yacht. I tightened the drag; it did not help. The line continued to disappear. I hooked my thumbs on the spool in an effort to turn the fish but only succeeded in burning the hide off my thumbs.

Prolonging the inevitable, I continued to exert as much pressure as I could until three hundred yards disappeared into the sea. The line snapped when it came to the knot. I watched as the line I brought 10,000 miles vanished into the Red Sea; Tom was chuckling.

"I have more line. Want to give it another try?"

I have fished since I could walk and have caught thousands. I could not remember hooking one that simply ignored being attached to my reel.

"What do you think it was?"

"It wasn't a shark, too fast. Probably a big Wahoo, eighty, maybe ninety pounds, could have been bigger. I've seen some caught over a hundred-forty when fishing for tuna. They're one of the fastest fish in the sea. You need a lot more line than that reel will hold to turn them. It appears the wind's laid down. Give it up until tonight; it's time to try the tuna grounds again."

The wind in the cove had settled into a light afternoon breeze. We gathered up the gear, waved to the soldiers, pulled anchor, and started toward the open water. We were on the lee side of the island. When the captain turned the boat into the open water, the wind hit us like a gale. The sea was just too damn rough.

Tom thought we should try it because he knew it would be my last chance at a tuna. Not me; there would be another time. I have caught a lot of fish; one more did not matter. I did not intend to become personally acquainted with the shark that stole my Wahoo that morning. We settled for cruising around the islands and more grouper fishing.

Grouper fishing was not nearly as exciting as catching tuna, but we caught a lot more fish than we wanted to clean, and the calm water made it easier to keep from spilling the beer.

We put to shore around three. It was early, but hours in the hot sun had taken a toll. We were tired. I never ate the lunch Unan prepared. I put aside a small grouper I caught that I planned to cook for dinner.

We decided the campsite the night before was as good as we could hope for. I knew if I made it through one night of crab hunting, the second one would be a piece of cake.

We were in camp for an hour. Tom and I were sitting back, recanting the fight with Tom's fish and the one I hooked by the coral reef that got away. I was making a mental note to compare the stories to the ones I would hear from the others back in Cairo after Tom repeated them a few more times. Tom was getting into the part about the captain speeding up the boat while he was yelling at him to slow down when a boat pulled into the cove and settled next to ours.

Coincidentally, the visitors were also Americans escaping from Cairo for a few days. Bill introduced himself and then commented on our fire.

"Where did you find firewood? We've scouted every island for miles; they're all picked clean."

"An army base in Cairo."

Bill looked a little skeptical at what he took as sarcasm. He turned to Tom and asked him if his group could share some of our firewood. This was Bill's first trip to the Red Sea, and like the rest of us embarking on a new experience in Egypt, he neglected some of the planning.

Tom told him we were short ourselves, but he was welcome to join us. Bill hesitated, eyeing the pile of firewood and the extra bag of charcoal stacked next to the fire. I think he expected us to offer to share some with him and his group.

It was going to be a long night, and we would need some for breakfast. Bill relaxed when I suggested they camp and stay the night. One good fire was better than splitting up the wood, and we all ended up with a cold breakfast in the morning. Tom and I thought we planned the trip well. We had packed enough wood and charcoal from Cairo to ensure hot coffee in the mornings, which we forgot to pack.

There were three others with Bill. When I saw them unload a case of Coors, I quit thinking about the intrusion and looked forward to English English-speaking company. Unan told Tom she was hungry and would fix dinner.

"Unan, I have a fish set aside, would you mind if I do the cooking tonight?"

Unan did not like my method of cooking in a frying pan with just butter, salt, and pepper. We compromised. I would cook my dinner, and she would fix theirs. Unan sent Tom to the boat to find a specific grouper; the captain called it a Schrief. It has a light, flaky texture; its snow-white flesh is the best of the local grouper family.

I knew she was partial to the Schrief because I tried to release it when I caught it earlier in the day, and she strongly objected. I was tempted to give Unan's cooking one more chance. The Schrief weighed about eight pounds. It was the color of pink coral with red and black spots on its tail. It was beautiful. I thought it was a shame to keep it. We had more fish than we could eat, and I did not see what one less mattered.

Tom left for the boat. Unan offered me more of her crunches. I declined and started my dinner before I lost my turn at the fire. Everyone was in good humor. It looked like the visiting Americans were going to be excellent company. One of them came over to join me at the fire and asked if I would like to share his bottle of Jack Daniels.

Bill was the PD on another American-Egyptian JV building a diaper factory for Johnson and Johnson. Bill and I were swapping stories about our projects in Cairo. Bill had it easier, being able to use local materials, but I was not the only one frustrated with the rules and customs. I was getting to the story about the arrested tree when Unan let out a piercing yell.

Tom and Unan are newlyweds and are still having difficulty with each other's language. Unan's method of a marital discussion is yelling and arm waving. I was used to Tom and Unan's quarrels, but the newcomers were not. They started to get up to give the couple some privacy. I told them to sit back, relax, and watch the show.

I was picking up enough to know they were fighting about how Tom was going to prepare the fish. Tom wanted to clean it. Unan wanted it to be left intact. Tom was trying to win his case by explaining the fish was too big for the frying pan. Unan said it did not matter because she was just going to lay it on the open fire.

The fire comment and the reflection of burnt crab in the glowing coals the night before were too much for me. My nose and stomach were not ready to deal with Unan picking through all *the good parts*.

"Tom, why don't you just cut it in half? That way, your half will fit in the pan?"

I was only kidding. Unan thought it was a good idea. Tom shrugged his shoulders and gave in. Unan picked the front half, as I knew she would. Tom gave the back half to the deckhand who had come to the beach for more soda pop.

Unan surprised me. After removing the heart and liver, she removed the guts and left them in the surf for the crab. She finished doctoring up the fish and set it in the coals as I finished dinner.

The visitors were setting up their camp, waiting for their turn at the fire. Tom was nipping on the bottle of Jack the Americans left behind, getting his stomach ready for another of Unan's delicacies.

By the time Unan finished preparing dinner, I had crawled into my sleeping bag and was reminiscing about the last 14 hours. It had been a pleasant day, no, a great day, which had turned into a relaxed and enjoyable evening. I lit a cigarette and settled back to watch the sunset. Cairo, the project, and the Egyptians had faded from my mind.

As day melted into night, Tom and Unan patched up their quarrel. The Americans finished setting up camp and joined them at the fire, waiting their turn. I settled in my sleeping bag, leaning against the rocks. I was content and relaxed, an unusual feeling for me in Egypt.

I shifted to remove some rocks from beneath my bedding and was getting comfortable when Tom asked if I wanted dessert. I looked over but was not able to recognize what was in the bowl. I made the mistake of turning my head a little too far and caught a glimpse of Unan munching on the half-cooked fish head.

"Good night, Tom."

Tom and Unan finished dinner and disappeared down the beach on another crab-hunting expedition. They were also going to see if they could find a seabird's nest so Unan could have eggs for breakfast.

The Americans converged on the fire. Bill turned and saw I was still awake. I accepted a chunk of the steak he was grilling over open flames. It was a much better dessert than what Tom offered. I made a mental note to ask Bill where he managed to find choice beef in Cairo.

It was Bill's first time fishing for anything bigger than trout in a lake by the town where he grew up. Johnson and Johnson pay more than Cesar. Bill and his friends had chartered a 45-foot sport fisher, not one of the dories. However, they had neglected to confirm onboard cooking facilities, which accounted for their frantic search for driftwood.

With a boat that big, the wind had not been a problem. They had been fishing for tuna and had found a school. Schools migrate by size. After Bill finished telling me about the excitement of catching 60 to 80-pound fish I unraveled myself from my sleeping bag and took him over to the boat to show him Tom's.

We returned to the fire as Tom and Unan arrived with a pan full of crab parts, which Unan immediately dumped on coals, and a few bird eggs she was saving for breakfast that looked like they were about to hatch. I made a mental note to fix my breakfast and then headed for my bedroll. By the time I settled, Tom and Unan had finished their desert of burnt crab parts and French-fried grasshoppers. As I rolled over to settle for the night, I noticed the stars were gone. The sky had clouded up, and lightning was flashing in the distance.

"Tom, it looks like rain."

"It hasn't rained in Hurghada in six years."

"I don't know, those clouds look like a brewing thunderstorm. Maybe we should consider sleeping under the canopy on the boat."

Tom was not convinced. I turned toward the shelter of the rock outcropping and was asleep immediately. I would have stayed that way all night, but the thunderstorm hit. The rain would have been a refreshing change during the day; it was inconvenient in a sleeping bag.

"Tom, the drought's over!"

Tom woke for a moment and then pulled his sleeping bag over his head.

"Go back to sleep. It won't happen again for another six years."

I gathered my sleeping bag and headed for the boat. It had drifted off the beach during the night tide. The captain had set an anchor a few meters from shore. I waded out and remade my bed under the canopy. I woke up an hour before daylight. The clouds had moved out over Saudi Arabia. Clearing skies and the warm morning air meant our last day was going to be beautiful.

I woke the skipper as I searched the boat for a can of diesel to restart the drenched campfire. He came out of the cabin to see what the ruckus was about and caught me as I was climbing down to wade to shore. He was pointing in the water while tugging on my arm to get me back in the boat. I remembered Tom's warning. Scorpionfish prowl the shoreline in the early morning, searching for retreating crabs. I was anxious to get on with the day. I could not see wasting an hour. I had the captain wake the deckhand and move the boat to shore.

The camp was stirring. Bill said something about coffee. I suggested I would fix it if he supplied it. Fishing trip or not, coffee is better than beer at five a.m.

Our plans for the day were to fish until ten and try to reach port by noon so we could cross the desert in the daylight. We packed our camp, traded the remaining wood and charcoal to Bill and his friends for a bottle of Jack, said our goodbyes, and boarded the boat for the final day. I climbed up to the top deck. The sun was clearing the horizon, warming the morning breeze. It was going to be a scorching, sweltering day.

"Tom, is the ice chest full?"

Tom refilled the cooler and then he and Unan joined me to watch a school of dolphins that joined us and was pacing the boat after we rounded the tip of the island.

We had all the fish we wanted to take home. We chose a scenic route back to port; it would take us along the coral reefs between the islands. It was a surreal setting compared to the months in Cairo. The school of dolphin stayed with us for miles, matching our speed, and playing tag under the bow as it broke the crest of the swells. The colors changed as we crossed varied depths. Turtles were sunning themselves on the surface.

Other boats had passed this way, and we would soon be cleaning our catch. Seabirds flocked to the boat as we approached Hurghada, anticipating a feast. We stopped when the harbor came into view and drifted in the current. It was time to sort the catch, give the captain and deckhand a share, clean those we would take home, and repack our gear for the trip back.

The captain said it was his responsibility to clean the fish. Unan would not hear of it. I offered to help, but Tom was already cutting into the second carcass while Unan was elbow-deep in the tuna, probing for the heart and liver.

There was not room for me. I headed back to my perch to catch a few rays of sun and add to my darkening tan. When I looked back, Unan was stuffing filets, along with a few unwrapped heads, in the new cooler I borrowed from Gary. I made a mental note to see if I could find some Lysol to clean it the minute I got home or buy Gary a new one if he noticed.

Tom and Unan joined me while the deckhand washed the blood and trimmings into the sea. The captain was steering toward the harbor. Circling gulls dove into the wake, which was churning scraps to the surface, screeching at one another as one would fly from the water with one of the morsels and another would try to steal it in the air.

A muffled explosion shattered the silence sending the trailing gulls scattering. We looked in the direction of what sounded like a bomb going off. The captain went to the rail to have a better look. He shook his head in what appeared to be resignation and then turned away. Unan caught him as he took the tiller. He thought it was one of the land minds left on the beach from the war with Israel. A few minutes later, we heard another. This time, a cloud of smoke filled the sky over the harbor; the captain did not seem concerned.

Budget-minded foreigners camping on coral islands were common in Hurghada. Customs would be more concerned with returning tourists than departing ones. Tom was ready because he had been through the camera issue the first time he visited the area. He handed the officer his diplomatic passport and told him the pile of belongings was free from search.

As we were leaving, I picked up my camera. He asked. I said the camera was mine. Tom's immunity covered his belongings. It appeared there was a duty on cameras, it was my problem. I had not left Egypt. We argued back and forth.

"Prove it, or I will confiscate the camera."

I was not getting anywhere; it was an expensive camera. He knew I would not leave it without paying something.

"How much?"

"Fifty-LE."

"Twenty."

We settled on thirty.

Tom walked up as I was handing him the notes.

"I see you're learning Egyptian etiquette."

"It's not that difficult, Tom. Just carry enough ten-pound notes."

Tom and I packed the gear in the car. Unan reached into the ice chest containing the unwrapped fish to retrieve some snacks she set aside for the trip home.

"Tom, we're ahead of schedule; let's stop for lunch before we tackle the highway."

We headed for the Sheraton, knowing we would find a clean restaurant and restroom. At the time, the Sheraton was the only hotel in Hurghada to European standards, but at 350-LE a night, it was outrageously expensive compared to the Globel, where we stayed when we arrived. We heard a third explosion as Tom pulled out of the Sheraton. It was close by; my curiosity replaced reason.

"Tom, let's go see what's going on."

We drove toward a plume of smoke billowing off the beach. It was rising from a construction site where the Egyptians were building new villas. It was behind a fenced area with a faded sign of a skull and crossbones stuck in the sand, warning of an old minefield.

The government does not concern itself with the mines, and the cost of proper locating equipment is far too expensive for the locals.

A warning to invaders.

Contractors clearing land for new roads and developments have devised their methods. One man sits on the front of a truck that has a front extension, much like a reverse plow, to probe the sand as they drive the area in widening circles. This time, the probe was not as thorough as the tires of the Jeep.

When we approached, a soldier blocked our way. There had been an accident; the area was off-limits. The first explosion was when the tire of the truck found one. The second was when another truck entered the area to pick up the injured men. The third was when a ten-year-old laborer stepped on a mine as he ran out to see what was going on.

I got out of the car for a closer look, which was a mistake. When they dragged three mutilated bodies to the road in open tarps, the next sound was an American puking in the street.

The tragedy on the beach put a damper on the mood. The trip back to Cairo was slow and tedious. The difference, we could see the trucks coming at us in daylight, so we knew which side of the road they were on.

It was raining when we entered the outskirts of Helwan. When it rains in Cairo, it rains a mix of water and soot. Tom needed to stop every few klicks to let me wipe the slime off the windshield. Besides dealing with the grime, it was the end of a shift at the factories. Local laborers were coming and going, crossing the highway by the thousands.

The roads, slippery from the mud, were jammed with donkeys pulling carts and thousands of people trying to wave down the few passing taxis and buses.

Tom grew tired of dodging animals and pedestrians; he asked me to take over. It took four hours to cover the last hundred klicks to Maadi. We arrived at Tom's flat at 11:30. Tom and I divided the catch. I left for my flat in Heliopolis.

Andy's Monkey.

The stairway was dark; I was cussing the dog that had shit on the steps. When I entered the flat, I woke Andy and our new roommate, the monkey.

"Anwar's at it again."

"Not tonight, Andy. It's been a long day. By the way, where is the monkey sleeping?"

"On the balcony, I roped an area off for her."

The door to the balcony was ajar. I did not want to get into it with Andy just then, but I did wonder if he established the zoo above or below where we hung our clothes to dry.

Chapter 17

Sarha had been taking English lessons.

"Good morning, Sarha. Has Anwar been here?"

"Yes, Mr. Pat, he's at the construction site."

"Thank you, Sarha. Has any mail arrived for me?"

Sarha gave me a sheepish look and then told me there had not been any calls or mail from the States. It did not make sense. I had not received mail from home for almost a month. I thought it strange. There was correspondence from my Joe, my attorney, and friends getting through, but nothing from home.

"Sarha, leave the key to the international phone with Abraham when you go home tonight. I need to make some calls to the States."

"Yes, Mr. Pat."

I could tell by the sheepish look something was going on. Knowing Sarha, I did not think it could be that important.

"Sarha, I'm going to the site. If I miss Anwar, tell him to wait for me this evening."

Anwar was at the site, at my desk, going through some of my papers. Hamid was dozing in a chair in the corner.

"Anwar, would you mind if I used my desk?"

"Sorry, Mr. Pat. I only use your desk when you aren't here."

"Anwar, leave the shit on my desk alone, and what are you doing here? You're supposed to be working with the staff on the drawings and leaving Hamid alone."

"The drawings will be done soon; I came to help Hamid."

"Hamid, do you need help?"

"No, Mr. Pat."

"Good; go do your daily reports; you're a week behind."

Hamid turned to leave, and Anwar started to follow.

"Anwar, sit down!"

"Hamid, wait. Has General Aziz been around while I was away?

"No, Mr. Pat."

Hamid headed out the door. The General had been absent. The only trouble I needed to sort out was Anwar.

"Anwar, the drawings were supposed to be ready two months ago. Why don't you stick with them? Hamid and I can manage the site."

Anwar left as Doctor Osmond entered the room. It was a bad omen. Doctor Osmond seldom came to the site, and he never got to his own office this early in the morning.

"Good morning, Mr. Pat, when will the money arrive?"

Straight and to the point. It was in my job description and signed off by both companies. I authorized the distribution of the first few checks from the COE by a formula based on a written agreement of the division of responsibility of the partners. It wasn't rocket science. There was a total contract price, and lump sums were agreed to. It did not matter how much either side spent. Ceasar had the lion's share of money spent to date and would until the work on the building actually started.

After the first check arrived, Doctor Osmond complicated things by insisting his accountant review and agree to the figures. Cesar caved in, not realizing the man could neither read nor write English.

I knew it would not work from the start. I gave Sarha the paperwork to give to the accountant after I submitted the pay estimate to Tom three weeks earlier. The last check had been sitting in limbo at Cesar's bank for over a week, waiting for approval from Dr. Osmond's accountant, which Sarha put on my desk the day after Tom and I left on the fishing trip.

I did not mention the delays caused by his accounting staff, the fact that we now needed both mine and his signatures notarized before the funds could be disbursed, or that it was his idea.

"I'm sorry, Doctor Osmond. We need to go to your bank and have our signatures notarized so Cesar's bank can distribute the funds. Can you meet me there tomorrow afternoon around one?"

Doctor Osmond agreed without the customary inshallah. It figured. When it came to getting money, his cooperation was the easiest thing to obtain.

I was not looking forward to a trip to the bank. I planned it for 1:00 on purpose. The president of the bank's doors closed to the public at 2:00. I was hoping the simple task of getting our signatures notarized would take less than an hour.

The Generals had been quiet while Tom and I were on the fishing trip. Colonel Baker was on a trip to the States, and General Olsen was not usually involved unless General Aziz was rattling his cage. It seemed the only pressing problem was splitting up the money and Anwar getting me a set of drawings.

The drawings the COE gave us at the onset of the contract were generic. It was our responsibility to develop shop drawings, which needed to be approved by the COE prior to starting each phase of work. The drawings were long past due. I did not believe Anwar when he said they were close to being finished. I left Dr. Osmond to make a few calls to the States. Sarha was gone, and so was the key to the overseas phone.

Abraham was brewing tea for Doctor Osmond. Abboud was on his way to Doctor Osmond's office. He told me the meeting was important and to tell Abraham they were not to be disturbed.

"Abraham doesn't speak English, Doctor Abboud."

Abraham was a shirttail relative of Doctor Osmond and the only Coptic Christian working for the company. Abboud was not fond of Coptic Christians and avoided them. I liked Abraham; he did not pray five times a day, and I did not trip over him once while I was there. He did not understand a word of English. I figured Abboud could give him whatever message he had in mind. In the meantime, all I had in mind was finding a key to the phone.

I was sitting at Sarha's desk rummaging through trays when Abraham brought tea. With a few hand signals, I explained I was looking for the key to the international phone. It took a few minutes, but he got the message and pointed to the top drawer of Sarha's desk. I tried to open it, but it was locked. It took a while to convince Abraham of the importance of the call. He went to Doctor Osmond's office to see if there was a spare key to Sarha's desk. There was. He returned with Abboud trailing. Abboud was a little miffed; the meeting was not to be disturbed again.

"Thank you, Doctor Abboud, but I really do need to make some calls."

Abboud turned to go back to the office. He stopped to tell me Doctor Osmond had rescheduled the appointment at the bank for 9:30, and that I needed to be on time.

The key was nestled among a stack of letters addressed to me from my wife, my mother, and my daughters, which were lying on top of the opened envelopes. Sarha was learning English; there was a translation dictionary in the drawer.

Sarha was reading my mail, but it took her a while. Some of them arrived two to three weeks earlier. I was pissed beyond measure, but wondering what the hell was going on, I removed the letters.

I spent the next hour trying to get through to my wife. When the phone finally rang, there was no answer. It was becoming a common occurrence. It was impossible to schedule a precise time to make a call. Half the time, the lines were dead, and at other times something always seemed to screw it up.

I was an hour late making the call the last time; Mary was tired of sitting by the phone. I was supposed to call the night before, but Sarha had hidden the key. I did manage to get through to one of my daughters. She was surprised to hear from me. She was also surprised to learn I did not know her mother was on holiday with friends until the end of the week.

I put the key to the phone back in the drawer where I found it, locked Sarha's desk, put the spare key on my key ring, and headed out the door, mad. I was not sure at the time who I was mad at: Sarha for hiding my mail, or my wife, who neglected to tell me about her vacation.

Sarha has always been friendly to Andy and me. As her English improved, our conversations led to her wish to marry an American so she would not have to go through with her wedding. In Egypt, Sarha was considered past her prime. It was an arranged marriage to a man her father chose. I knew Sarha wanted to migrate to the States. I did not have a clue why she would be hiding my mail.

The next morning, Sarha was still on my mind, but the thought of a full day at the banker's office took the edge off my anger at her and directed it at Doctor Osmond. Dr. Osmond never made an appointment before 11:00. I did not think he would be on time, but I had little choice; he might make an exception to collect money.

I arrived at 9:15 and was shown to a chair outside the bank President's office. No explanation: It appeared it would be a while. I entertained myself watching the scene. At the time, an expat making a transaction at an Egyptian bank was a lengthy pain in the ass. There was no filing system. The ledgers were piled on the floor.

There were no computers. All entries were made by hand. There were very few desks. Dozens of employees sat in a line of chairs facing each other with a ledger book in their laps. If a chair became vacant, one of them would use the empty seat of a facing chair as a desktop.

Doctor Osmond showed up at 11:15. Same damned shit, different day. In his mind, he arrived early. It seems he rescheduled the appointment with the banker again. I was obviously irritated.

"Dr. Osmond, I understood the appointment was for nine-thirty; it's after eleven."

He stood there for a minute; he was not used to someone questioning his authority. Now he was obviously pissed.

"Mr. Pat, Doctor Abboud left you a message. You must learn some Arabic."

Abboud was fluent in English, but he resented me being there. I had missed or been late for a number of meetings. Learning to speak Arabic was one thing. Reading, other than numbers so I could shop at the outdoor stands, was beyond my thought process.

Dr. Osmond must have decided it was time for an Arabic lesson. It was up to me to explain. I spent the next five minutes trying. The banker did not respond. Not only had I neglected my Arabic lessons, but I had also neglected to follow protocol. If you want to have a civil conversation with a member of the Egyptian elite, you need to wait for tea.

After the tea arrived, Doctor Osmond explained our needs to the banker. The forms I brought along were simple. All they needed were Doctor Osmond's and my signatures notarized and an official stamp from Doctor Osmond's bank. The banker reviewed the form letters and then called his secretary. He sent the letters out with her. The secretary returned twenty minutes later. When the banker handed me the papers, there was a slight modification.

"Doctor Osmond, the disbursement authorization had a place for both our signatures on the same page. We now have two separate forms. I need one disbursement letter with both signatures."

Doctor Osmond and the banker discussed the problem for the next half-hour. The banker then turned to me.

"Mr. Pat, you have an account with my bank, and Doctor Osmond has an account with my bank. I have no problem witnessing each of your signatures."

I decided to get at least that part done. Doctor Osmond and I each signed our respective forms. When we finished, I explained that the single signature forms were fine for the American bank to verify our signatures, but the disbursement letter required both our signatures and had to be notarized.

"Mr. Pat, you have an account, and Doctor Osmond has an account. We can acknowledge your signatures separately. If you want both of your signatures on the same paper, you must have an account together."

"That's nuts! You just witnessed each of our signatures. All I want you to do is witness them on the same piece of paper so Doctor Osmond can get paid."

The SOB did speak English. Dr. Osmond and the banker lapsed back into Arabic. By then, it was 1:30. So much for my patience course. Thoughts: *Fuck him, it is his money*. I excused myself, telling Doctor Osmond I had to meet with Tom.

Dr. Osmond left the papers on my desk with a note in English asking when he could expect to receive the money. It took an additional two weeks. Not bad by Egyptian standards, but it was having an effect on my relationship with Doctor Osmond who instructed Hamid to slow the site work because he had not been paid.

I never figured out what the cost is for an expat to maintain a bank account in Egypt. I had to go to the bank on my own a few days later. I give 25-piaster to the parking attendant, one LE to the guard who lets me in to see the President, and ten LE to get me a teller who speaks Arabic-English.

It seemed to me that there should be enough tipping, but after an hour of waiting for the teller to acknowledge me, I gave back into the system. It took two LE for the teller to pull the ledger out of the pile in the corner, one to the guy who actually gave me the money and one to have the transaction copied.

I tried to explain it to the company bookkeeper, who checks my monthly expense report. She told me she did not want to try to explain it to the IRS and asked me to collect it from Doctor Osmond. I brought it up to Doctor Osmond, now I pay Doctor Osmond's accountant ten-LE to go to the bank for me because Doctor Osmond felt I was paying too much. I have no idea how much it really does cost, but now it only takes a few minutes each month.

Baksheesh (*a bribe*) is a way of life in Egypt. If I quit fighting it and went along with the system, the Generals would make my life a lot more pleasant, the subcontractors would cut me in, the banker would sign any paper I put in front of him, my toilet would work, and the garbage wouldn't sit out in front of the flat so long. However, I have not figured out how to convince Cesar to reimburse me.

When I left the bank, I realized I still had not developed the patience necessary to deal with day-to-day problems. It was too late to return to the site. I knew Sarha would be gone by the time I made it to the office. I decided I should do what I told Doctor Osmond I was going to do and pay a visit to the COE's office in Madi.

Tom was engrossed in paperwork on the new convention center, which was one of his other projects. It was ten times the size of mine and nonmilitary. Dealing with corrupt bureaucrats was a bigger headache than mine. He breathed a sigh of relief at the opportunity to set it aside.

Access was resolved, the phone and water lines were repaired, and things had settled into a routine. It would be another few months before the first materials would arrive from the States. The excavation was complete. I was waiting for Anwar to bring sand samples so we could do compaction tests and backfill, along with the plans.

Anwar told me the plans would be done yesterday, but then left me an Arabic-English note telling me he did not like something or other and that he was having the engineers redo them. Without the drawings, Anwar did not think I needed the sand.

Tom and I decided I could afford to leave the site in Hamid's hands for a few days while I tried to get submittal information from Don in the States and while I waited for Anwar to get the plans finished. It was after midnight when I got back to my flat. I did not bother to set the alarm.

Chapter 18

Andy left the door to the balcony open where the monkey zoo was set up. The flies woke me at 9:15. I was shaking the sleep out of my eyes and heading for the bathroom when I realized the monkey and I were not alone. It was the houseboy's morning to clean the flat and do laundry.

The washing machine was out of order. The man is gay. When I opened the door, he was in his bikini underwear, dancing around in the bathtub on my laundry, pretending he was an Italian crushing grape.

The plumber finally showed up and fixed the toilet, but now the bathtub leaks. He will be back to fix the bathtub *after tomorrow, inshallah*. I still have not figured out how After tomorrow translates, but it is always followed by inshallah. He must have meant the leak would be fixed when it was on God's to-do list for the day.

The leak started to grow. The bathroom floor is tile, but the water seeps under the door to the wood floor in the bedroom. The floor around the foot of the bed has been damp for over a week, so the growth is twofold. The wood floor is buckling. I noticed it when I stubbed my toe on it a few days earlier. I tried to stomp it back in place, but all that did was break the seal next to it and let the mold escape, which is the second growth.

The bathtub started leaking last week, and now the toilet will not flush. When I got home that night, I intended to give the property owner notice. Since then, the houseboy relocated the bedroom furniture covering the worst spots. I am finally learning a little patience and I did not feel like another domestic argument. I let the problems slide.

I talked to the property owner a few days later about the water leak, the toilet, and a few of the other problems in the flat. He fixed the toilet and promised to make the rest of the repairs *after tomorrow*, inshallah.

I was going to talk to Andy about looking for a new place. When he told me the landlord was complaining about the monkey shitting on his truck parked below our balcony, I decided to pay another month's rent and forget about it. Besides, moving into a new flat in Cairo would be a real pain in the ass. All the available flats have the same problems.

- They are under the flight path of the runway, which is used between the hours of one and three a.m., or when the wind is in the right direction.
- The toilets do not work, and you have to flush them with a bucket.
- The fridge is open because it will not stay shut.
- The elevator works, but only if you use the landlord's key.
- Many Egyptians keep fleas and lice as house pets.
- You have to heat water on the stove to do dishes because the faucet is not connected to the water heater.
- The air conditioner will not work when the lights are on because the fuse is too small.

I looked at enough flats to know I had one of the better bargains, and unless one of the American companies pulled out permanently and gave up one of their units, I was not going to do better on the budget Cesar gave me. I now just complain to the landlord, chisel on the rent every month, and find a way to make do.

Going back to bed with the houseboy in the house was out of the question. Besides, there was a loud racket in the hall. The garbage guy slipped on the water leaking from the bathtub. He is yelling at the landlord because the wind is in the right direction, and the jetliner approaching the runway is drowning out the conversation.

I told Tom I was going to take a few days off, but I wanted to confront Sarha about my mail. When I arrived at the office, I caught Sarha off guard.

"Good morning, Sarha; I need to make a few calls to the States."

"Mr. Pat, Doctor Abboud has the key."

"Sarha, I put the key to the phone back in your desk where I found it the other night. I also found the letters you were saving for me. Why the hell are you reading my mail?"

Sarha disappeared out the front door with her makeup washing away by flowing tears, passing Andy, who was coming up the steps.

"What's the matter with Sarha?"

"Who the fuck knows, Andy. Something about her boyfriend. She's been having some problems planning the wedding. I think the stress is starting to show."

I did not tell Andy. I figured Sarha would recover, and in the future, she would see to it I got my mail. Andy did not leave it alone. He liked Sarha; they were working on Andy's Arabic and her English. He thought Sarha must have misunderstood something I did or said. He dropped the subject when Abboud came through the door.

"Doctor Abboud, have you seen Anwar?"

"Anwar went to Alexandria for a few days. Do you need something?"

"Yes, Doctor Abboud. The plans he's supposed to finish."

"Anwar isn't involved in the plans. The subcontractors will do the plans when we sign the contracts."

"Doctor, you and Anwar have been promising me a set of plans for months. He told me they would be done this week."

"You must have misunderstood. You must learn more Arabic. Each of the subcontractors will prepare the shop drawings for their phase of work."

I ignored the Arabic crack.

"Doctor, that's bullshit, and you know it. I need the drawings now, or at least a realistic date I can tell Tom they will be ready. When will the subcontractors get them done?"

"It won't be long. Have a little patience."

"Doctor Abboud, the plans were due in the COE's office thirty days ago. What am I supposed to tell Tom?"

"Tell Tom we will have them after tomorrow."

"Bullshit, Doctor Abboud, Tom is going to be pissed. What the hell does that mean?"

"Mr. Pat, it means soon, inshallah."

Now he was pissed; he glared at me for a minute and then dismissed me from his mind as he lapsed into Arabic with someone who came in the front door.

I had missed a point. Other than for some site work, I was not aware we hired the subcontractors. Now I was more pissed; Abboud slipped that one by me. I did not want to face Tom. I gave up and headed for the site. I decided to forget about the plans until I met with the subs. Tom was getting tired of my excuses, and I did not want to give him another fictitious date. Abboud could play his games but would come around when Tom shut off the money.

I stopped to buy cigarettes. When I got back to my car, I found what I thought was a parking ticket stuck under the wiper. I returned to the office later that afternoon. Other than the ticket, it was one of my better days.

- Tom came by to bring me a carton of American cigarettes and a bottle of scotch from the commissary.
- General Aziz was still out of town.
- There were no nasty telexes from the States because it was their Sunday.
- When I went home, the toilet in the flat was working.
- I found some bleach; the mildew in the bedroom was turning into a fine powder, and the houseboy had cleaned most of it up.

- The property owner parked his car under the balcony all day; Andy's monkey had the shits.
- The garbage man cleaned up the mess in the hall.
- The dog that had been shitting on the stairs disappeared; one of the Koreans down the street must have celebrated something; they like dogs any time of year.
- The property owner has not bothered about my washing machine, but the bathtub is fixed, so my clothes are clean.

The next morning, I gave Hazem the traffic ticket and told him to fix it. I then went in to try to patch things up with Doctor Abboud. Abboud never prayed; he is what I refer to as a fringe Muslim, someone who does not practice the religion but holds on to the heritage. He was educated in the States. My language did not normally offend him, but he did not like me. I knew that; he knew it was mutual.

After our first meeting, Abboud treated me like a necessary evil or simply ignored me. I thought we had a silent truce. His bullshit was driving me nuts. I was beginning to think he enjoyed prodding me at times.

When we started site excavation, I told Doctor Abboud I needed an excavator, a bulldozer, and a front-end loader. He sent me fifty laborers without shoes, nine picks with five handles, eight shovels, and about sixty meters of rope. The rope attached to the shovels so that when one man would dig, three could pull the shovel full of material out of the hole.

After Colonel Baker brought the loader on site, we managed to move five hundred cubic meters of material before I solved the security problems and made my deal with a subcontractor to bring the rest of the equipment through the new gate. I was hoping Abboud's answer to the plans was not going to be a repeat performance.

Abboud was gone until after tomorrow, inshallah. Nobody could tell me when he would return. When I arrived at the office the following day, Sarha was there with fresh makeup and a new hairdo; she handed me a letter from home.

"Thank you, Sarha."

Sarha smiled at me and said something I did not understand. I did not want a repeat performance and figured I had better find out what it was she was talking about before I answered.

Andy was assimilating into the culture and had turned it around. At that point, he spoke rather good English-Arabic. Andy was one of the most patient men I ever met. After tomorrow, inshallah worked for him. He kept telling me, when I was upset my choice of words offended and intimidated the Egyptians who spoke Arabic-English and that I needed to quit swearing and be more patient with Sarha.

Andy had a conversation with Sarha a few days later and put it together. Most of my mail arrived opened when it came through normal Egyptian channels. The letters Sarha was holding for me were from my wife and daughters. Sarha had a crush on me, and since Muslim men can have four wives, Sarha assumed I could, too; she was curious about my family.

I went into the office to read my mail, but Tom showed up anxious to discuss something about a pain and suffering complaint General Aziz had filed against me with the OMC over the broken water line. He had just entered my office when Hazem returned. I asked Hazem what was so important he had to invade my session with Mr. Tom. Hazem told me he had arranged for my ticket to the ballet.

"Hazem, what the hell are you talking about?"

Tom was laughing; Hazem was backing out the door. He seemed confused, and I could not figure out what Tom thought was so funny.

"Tom, settle."

"Hazem, what are you talking about?"

The parking ticket turned out to be a flier for the Russian ballet. Hazem wanted to tell me he managed to get me a front-row seat.

Tom is big enough to play guard for the NFL. He has his ideas about a man's masculinity. Tom has ignored that; like some males who do not like stuffing things in their pockets, I sometimes carry a leather bag, which looks like a purse. He has also never breached the subject of my houseboy, whom he has met.

I told Tom I was a grandfather, and I was sure I had clarified which direction I leaned. However, he has never seen me with a woman besides Unan and Sarha, which does not count. My going to the ballet could be a turning point in our relationship.

Tom was still laughing and starting to get up to leave. I did not want to trade my fishing partner for a picture-taking trip with Andy and his monkey.

"Tom, sit down and shut the fuck up." "Hazem, come back here."

"Yes, Mr. Pat."

"All right, once more, what's with the ballet?"

I put Hazem in charge of the important things. He takes care of arranging for my fishing trips, dinner reservations, horseback riding, and now, ballet seats. He is fairly good at it, and most of the time, I end up close to the result I started to achieve. Close has become acceptable in Cairo, and since when I return to the States, I might open a school and teach a course in patience, I figure I am getting my money's worth from Hazem.

When I gave Hazem the parking ticket, he did not argue because I had just given him hell about the hotel in Luxor where I wanted to spend Thanksgiving. Hazem had waited too long to make the call; It was fully booked.

It took a while but Tom, Hazem, and I sorted out the matter. I decided to go to the ballet after I convinced Tom that even the LA Rams make some of their players take ballet lessons, and it was not a reflection of my masculinity. I invited him and Unan to go along, but he declined.

After Tom left, Hazem and I got down to serious planning. I told Hazem to buy me a ticket and make sure it was a good seat. He asked me what I meant by a good seat. He was ready to take one of Doctor Osmond's plush office chairs to the theater for me.

I caught on and told him my idea of a good seat was one lined up with the center of the stage, about three rows back from the orchestra.

Hazem left to make the arrangements. I started daydreaming about a quiet night away from the confusion and rudeness of Cairo restaurants and traffic. After all, what could be more soothing than a Swan Lake performance by the Russian ballet?

It took Hazem a while. I had time to reflect. I have never been one to go much out of my way for anything except a cold American beer on a hot Cairo day. Most of my cultural experiences have been accidental like the parking ticket turned ballet flyer.

I learned years ago that people in the throes of spring fever often give in and do things they know they are going to hate or go to places to impress those they are wooing or being courted by.

People go to concerts that offend their ears, movies that offend their eyes, cities that offend their sense of smell, sporting events that take two hours to clear the parking lot, and just about anywhere else because love is blind.

I was wondering what the Russian ballet would be like in an Egyptian theater. I was no exception. I gave in once or twice. The current turn of events reminded me of one of those times.

I thought the love of my life said something about going to the chalet. I had been duck hunting all week and my ears were still ringing from the blast of the shotguns. The idea appealed to me because a chalet meant snowbound in the mountains in front of a fire, playing snuggle bunny under a warm quilt. The Woman had been playing hard to get, and the sudden change of temperament made me jump at the chance to be alone with her in a chalet, which, in the end, turned out to be a ballet theater.

I loved it! I never admitted it to my macho friends because I did not want to seem unmanly. In the end, I am glad I did not refuse the invitation, but I should have declined because my lady friend told everyone we went to the ballet after I told the guys we went to the chalet.

I regretted the lie but got over it because after being caught lying to my friends, I switched my attention to a new girl with a horse. The girl with the horse does not belong in this story except that if I had not met her, I probably never would have bought a horse of my own, and I never would have considered riding the Arab stallion. I loved it, the ballet, that is. Oh! Yes, and riding the Arab Stallion, too!

When the confusion of the parking ticket turned ballet flyer was resolved, I was looking forward to the performance. Hazem came in the next day to tell me the day was set for nine p.m. Thursday.

Planning in Cairo had become one of the most important parts of the day. I gave up planning on the construction project; I just took it one day at a time. For the more important things like fishing or ballet, I spend time designing a network so I end up close to the results I hope to achieve in my search for sanity in Cairo.

The ticket was in Arabic. The map Hazem and I worked out was Arabic-English. My driver fueled the car and checked the tires and oil before he turned it over to me for the drive downtown.

The trip from my flat to downtown Cairo is only twenty klicks, but with traffic or one wrong turn, it could take all night. I planned to leave a few hours early. Doctor Osmond knows I am still having problems with directions. He suggested I have the driver take me.

I declined; not only was my driver always late, but I thought my driver and my houseboy had something going on. Since I said something to Tom about it, with our current translation problems, there was always the possibility Tom would hear about me going to the ballet with my houseboy's boyfriend.

On a good day, it was 30 minutes to downtown. I left for the theater at six, thinking three hours would be enough for any diversion, including traffic jams, wrecks, police checks, a wrong turn, and finding a parking place. At seven, I thought I had located the theater. After I found a parking place, stood in line for thirty minutes, and gave my ticket to the attendant, when I entered the theater, I found myself at the circus.

Yes, I know, I should spend more time learning to read and speak Arabic instead of pestering Tom for alcohol. It was 8:00; I still had an hour. However, the ticket attendant had deposited my ballet ticket in the box with the circus tickets. I went back to try to talk him into returning it so I could go to the ballet, which was only a few blocks down the street.

The ticket attendant was giving me a tough time. I was losing my patience. The reason for going to the ballet in the first place was to get out of the circus for a few hours. My ticket was pink. The circus tickets were white; the attendant should have caught that. I could not see any reason why the attendant could not just open the damn box and let me get my ticket to the ballet.

The attendant was not seeing it my way. I was causing a scene when I remembered the method I used to solve some of my other problems in Cairo. I reached for my wallet. I had waited too long. Security arrived because the people who wanted to go to the circus while I stood in the way were losing their patience.

One of the most vocal was a woman who taught Arabic to expats at a private school in Cairo. She broke into the conversation and told me she had heard enough, and since she did want to go to the circus, she would help me sort out the problem. Once I had someone on my side who could communicate, it only took a few minutes to get my ticket back.

Maha, the English teacher, told me if I did not do better with my Arabic, this sort of thing would probably continue to happen. She gave me her business card and invited me to take the next class she was starting. Maha started to give me directions to the school. It was almost 8:30. I wanted to do something. Now that I had my ballet ticket back, I did not think it would be a good idea to try to pawn it off as a circus ticket. I told Maha I would rather she give me proper directions to the ballet.

Maha's directions were better than Hazem's. It was a simple matter of leaving my car and walking a few blocks. I arrived at the Balloon Theater a few minutes before nine. When the usher showed me to my seat, I was thinking that, for a change, my planning had been pretty dammed good.

When I looked around the theater, I began to wonder if, by some trick of fate, I had entered the circus by the back door. The building was made of canvas in the shape of a round tent. It was supported by plastic trusses filled with air giving it a balloon-looking effect, hence its name, The Balloon Theater.

The folding chair I was sitting on was a reject from the last convention. Trash littered the floor; that helped. I used some cardboard to level the broken leg. Barkers were in the aisle and my face every few minutes, hawking soda, peanuts, candy bars, and a smelly sandwich.

I felt sure I had returned to the circus when the curtain started to rise. As the ballerina entered the stage, a cat ran between my legs chasing a rat, which until then had been in the aisle munching on one of the sandwiches someone discarded.

Distracted, I had not noticed there was no orchestra. As the music started, I wondered if they scratched the record clear across or if the damage was only in the prelude area. Five minutes into the first act, they changed the record. Everyone settled, and the barkers moved back into the aisles from between the rows.

I ignored the distractions and watched the show. The ballerina was stunning. Hazem told me it was the Swan Lake ballet, but I knew better. I have seen the Swan Lake ballet. I did not recognize the stuffed goose Robin Hood hung on the door to the ballerina's cottage.

By the end of the second act, the lights were adjusted to the stage, the rats had moved into the shadows, and the cats had taken up residency under the seats. The barkers quit barking and were only moving up and down the aisles, somewhat silently, and I was passing a test in patience.

By the time the curtain dropped on the final act, the distractions had taken their toll on the performers. As for me, it did not matter what ballet it was or that the theater was filthy, and I had to share it with a few stray cats sorting out the rat population. The Russians were simply out of this world. Considering the commotion and distractions, they did a superb job.

The Egyptians made up for their rudeness by presenting the ballerina with a few dozen roses and seven curtain calls. As the curtain lifted for the final time the ballerina looked around the room, the frown of stress had changed to a smile. I had the feeling the young woman knew there were a few of us who, at least for a few moments, were able to imagine we had been to a concert hall worthy of her talents, and we understood.

Chapter 19

Abboud returned a few days later and told me he would be meeting with one of the subcontractors he was considering hiring and wanted me there.

"That's fine, Doctor; when is the meeting?"

"Tomorrow afternoon."

"What time?"

"Eight."

"Doctor Abboud, eight p.m. isn't exactly in the middle of the afternoon. I have to be at the office by eight every morning. It will be after midnight before we're done. Isn't there some way we can arrange some of these meetings during my time of day?"

"Mr. Pat, you are in Egypt. I'll do what I can, but you need to adjust."

"Doctor Abboud, I would appreciate it if you would tell that to Cesar and the COE."

Abboud assured me that if I would be patient a while longer, he would try to get the schedule sorted out. After he left, I decided I had to find a new method of communication. I missed the meeting intentionally. When he returned to the office, I went in to apologize.

"Good morning, Doctor Abboud. I'm sorry I missed the meeting."

"Sarha left you a note. The meeting was changed to Sunday afternoon at two."

Sarha was doing pretty well with the vocal part. She had not taken a writing course.

The meeting took place, but Abboud never showed up. The subcontractor did speak a little Arabic-English. I had finished a four-hour session, and from what I understood, if I were to award the contract to him, he would see to it *that I was taken care of.*

It was a new experience for me. I was the one bribing my way through the system. It appeared if I were so inclined, I could be on the receiving end. Abboud returned the next day and asked me how the meeting went.

"Doctor Abboud, I don't want to use that subcontractor. I think he offered me five percent if I awarded him the contract."

Abboud was not worried. He told me it was standard business practice in Egypt, that I should ask for ten, and that I was to give the money to Doctor Osmond's accounting staff. He never did say how I was supposed to explain the transaction to Cesar.

After the meeting with Abboud, I told Doctor Osmond I was not familiar enough with local laws, and I felt he should have his attorney to draw up the subcontract agreements. Abboud came in later that day to tell me Doctor Osmond had contacted his friend at the local law school.

A few days later, Doctor Osmond told me he sorted out the legal problem. I thanked him and started to leave, but he asked me to wait because he had someone in his office he wanted me to meet.

I left the meeting shaking my head. It was an interesting turn of events. I told Doctor Osmond I did not want to oversee the contracts because I felt an attorney should be drawing them up. Dr. Osmond reminded me all subcontractors had to be prequalified by me and then the COE. To do that, the contracts had to be in English. Dr. Osmond's attorney's staff was not qualified.

He introduced me to a professor from Cairo University Law School. The English contracts were boilerplate. It did not take a real lawyer to fill in a few blanks. Knowing it would be limited exposure, his solution was to get me a law degree in Egypt. That way, I could oversee the legal work. It would only take a few days and cost a few thousand LE, which would be substantially less than an international law firm would charge to draft the documents.

As I was driving to the site, I thought of the mess I was in. It was bad enough that the project was falling further behind; now, I was an Egyptian lawyer who could not read or write a word of Arabic, and Abboud thought I should take a bribe, which I should turn over to my American boss's Egyptian partner.

Subcontractors had to be approved by the COE. That was a matter of paperwork. Labor and material were split. The installation subs were the responsibility of Doctor Osmond and had nothing to do with his financial arrangement with Cesar. However, the cost and profits of the extra work concerned both. I prepared the estimates; I could pad the U.S. materials for Cesar and shave some cost for labor to make up for Dr. Abboud's 10%. There was no reason I should personally be involved until the subs arrived on site.

I met with Abboud the next day and told him the language barrier was too great to expect me to make deals with the subcontractors. I also told him I heard Anwar was coming back and felt I was going to be too busy to deal with the subs other than to review their qualifications and oversee their work.

Abboud reluctantly agreed. Anwar would return *after tomorrow* and manage the subcontract agreements as long as I reviewed them and made sure the scope of work was covered. I agreed if he would explain what a*fter tomorrow* meant and have Hazem translate them for me so I did not have to take a course in Arabic. On the way out of Abboud's office, I ran into Anwar. For a change, *after tomorrow* was actually that day.

****

At first, I tried to maintain an eight-to-five workday. The Egyptians do not start their day much before 11:00. If I am there when Abboud or Doctor Osmond is in, I am trapped in the office until seven, and often, it is after ten before I can convince them it is time for me to go home.

Ceasar's office and the COE operated on an eight-to-five. I tried to get the Egyptians to rearrange their schedules to mine, but

I am ready to give in. Electricity in Egypt is just about as dependable as Anwar. At first, I was not too excited about starting late in the day because I felt it would be difficult to finish the project on time without lights. I am ready to concede because it is easier to deal with the local help in the dark when they are partially awake rather than in the daylight when they are all half asleep.

According to the Arabic calendar, it is still the 14th century, which is probably why sewers and toilets that work for any length of time do not exist. The religious month is a month of fasting, during which no one is allowed to eat, drink, engage in sex, or, for that matter, have sexual thoughts during daylight hours. They are only excused if they are sick or pregnant, which is probably why there are so many sickly-looking kids everywhere.

The people get used to sleeping all day and staying up most of the night for at least thirty days a year. Ramadan is the ninth month of the Islamic calendar, observed by Muslims worldwide as a month of fasting, prayer, reflection, and community. Most of them continue the practice for the other eleven months.

The Gregorian Calendar is a solar calendar based on the Earth's rotation around the sun. It works; we have four distinct seasons.

The Islamic calendar is Lunar; it does not take into consideration the seasons of the year. The seasons shift by ten days every year. That makes our Christmas in July every thirty-five or so years. I am confused enough, that it would be hard to follow.

****

I realize religion is a serious matter to many. I make light of it only because, in the Muslim world, it causes a lot of grief for those of us who are going through life as if life matters, especially when I keep tripping over men who spend the better part of each day either on their knees bowing toward Mecca, or on the floor asleep.

"Anwar, what are you doing on the floor?"

When I left Abboud's office, I turned the corner into mine and nearly broke my neck when I tripped over Anwar, who was on the floor of the hall, taking his afternoon nap. Anwar recovered from the kick and then caught up on his prayers while I went to clean the tea off the front of my shirt.

"Anwar, where the hell have you been, and why did you lie to me about the plans being done?"

I never did get an answer, we spent the next hour negotiating a truce. Anwar would stay off the site, and I would stay out of his office. I gave in when Anwar wanted to make amends. I accepted his apology when he hugged me and, in Islamic fashion, gave me a kiss on the cheek, just as Tom walked in the door.

"Try knocking."

Anwar was leaving. Tom heaved with laughter.

"I don't know about you, Patrick. Maybe you should plan on a trip to the States for Christmas."

Cheek kissing between males is common. Cheek kissing between a male and female is usually considered inappropriate unless within the same family, a brother and sister, or if they are a married couple. Tom has been in the Middle East long enough to understand the customs, but he still enjoys needling a newcomer when he finds him trapped by the system.

Tom was right; I needed some time off. Tom and I discussed the ballet. Tom had a social life with other players from the COE. It was becoming more difficult for me to find anything to occupy my free time. The American college was putting on the play *My Fair Lady.* I was hoping to entice Tom into going.

Once you have been to the pyramids, bazaar, museums, cemetery, and the Citadel, there is little else to do in Cairo. Social life for Americans with single status revolves around hotels, restaurants, or the American college campus in Maadi. If you have the time and money there is lots of action in the surrounding countries. Tel Aviv and Cyprus, where nightclubs and decent restaurants abound, are a short plane flight away.

The Valley of the Kings and Queens in Upper Egypt are worth more than one trip, and the Red Sea for a weekend now and then will be less than four hours away when the new highway is opened in the spring.

Travel and decent hotels take more time and money than most of us have, but traveling by oneself is not a good idea in the Muslim world. I have no idea what to do if the car broke down except to leave it. The phone systems are a mess, and even when they do work, there is no one to call.

Tom and I were getting bored. Unan had returned to Thailand for a month. We both needed a break.

"Tom, Thanksgiving is Thursday. Let's plan a few days off and get out of Cairo."

"The moon is in the wrong place."

Taking time off at Thanksgiving, Christmas, or Easter was difficult unless they fell within a Muslim holiday. Other than Thanksgiving and Christmas, expats were expected to follow local traditions. The best Tom could do was Thanksgiving Day. We decided to try to find a turkey and cook it at my flat.

We could not find a turkey, but Thanksgiving was a success. Andy found a fresh ham in the commissary, which is a rare find in the Muslim world. Tom brought traditional stuffing ingredients and a few cans of apple sauce. We also managed the rest of the trimmings for an old-fashioned holiday meal.

After dinner, the monkey helped clean up the dishes we left on the sink. Tom and I polished off the remains of a bottle of Black Label. In all, it was an enjoyable day spent by men homesick for their own families and friends.

The landlord had still not connected the water heater to the kitchen sink. I did not feel like boiling water on the stove. After Tom left, Andy and I stored the rest of the mess in the kitchen for the houseboy, who would be coming in on Saturday.

"Andy, give the monkey some more of the leftovers and then tie her over the landlord's new car."

After dinner, I sat down to read the mail Sarha sent to my flat earlier in the day. The home delivery started after I found the mail in her desk. She did not want me to accuse her of hiding it again.

One of the letters was from my mother with newsy stuff about the lives of my two dozen nieces and nephews. Political censorship is extensive under military rule. Egyptian censors had opened the letter and mixed the contents up with someone else's mail.

It is not as if the Egyptians care what the contents of a letter are. I doubt if many of their censors can read English. Their reason for opening foreign mail is to steal money. We all know better; I doubt they collect a great deal.

After I sorted out the letter, it appeared they had dropped the pages on the floor and then shuffled them with somebody else's mail. When they put it back in order, it contained two pages marked three, one that said three and was changed to four, a five, and a six, but no one or two. It was good by Egyptian standards but difficult to follow. I decided I should answer all the questions anyway because even though someone else's mother sent them, I knew they would align with Mom.

Dear Mom,

Go ahead and sell the house but forget Phoenix and move to the Red Sea. The weather is better, the rent is cheaper, and even though the chicken is quite foul, the crabs, lobster, and fish are great.

The distance from the States will guarantee you will not be bothered by your relatives' problems. The grandkids will be able to visit more often when Congress reinstates the draft and sends them here to protect the oil fields to keep the White House limos in gas.

You will not have to worry about insurance, taxes, or cars. Twenty grand a year will be enough to rent a villa on the Red Sea; there will be money left over to hire a fisherman to keep you supplied with fresh seafood. You could also buy a water buffalo for milk and cream, and hire a boab to keep the sand out of the house. You will need a housekeeper with a donkey cart to take you to town. All that and you would still have money left over for side trips to the places you read about in the Bible.

Do not worry about my daughter who wants to be grown up at twelve. Like her, I, too, missed my childhood because I thought being grown up was better. Now that I am a grandfather, I am reverting. I am almost mature enough to manage being a teenager in today's society.

Yes, Mother, I do realize it is only a few weeks until Christmas, and I should start doing something about a Christmas list. I paused for a moment; there was no time like the present to start.

- To my children and grandchildren: My words of wisdom infected with sarcasm of the truth they all should but will never have to face.
- To the overprivileged teens of the world: A bucket of sand trampled under the bare feet of Third World children who are bloated with starvation, infected with lice, starved for attention, and neglected out of necessity. They can scatter it on the carpet in their private bedrooms, use it for kitty litter, put their joints out in it, or throw it in the faces of adults who they feel refuse to listen to or try to understand their problems.
- To those who read all the horror of the world for entertainment: My sympathy for their inability to read between the lines and a picture of a sunrise at the Red Sea to mask the reality of a world that is beyond their understanding.
- To my mother: My love, because she will take time to try to learn the truth about that which she cannot experience for herself, and because she knows me well enough to understand that most of my sarcasm is an effort to hide the frustration of my inability to do anything about it.

To those who think we should stay out of politics in the Muslim world, the following questions:

- Would you walk by a starving child or pass by a cripple on the street unable to move?

- Would you wash your dishes, kids, and clothes in creeks infected with polluted waste and raw sewage, or scrape maggots from your food, then eat it?
- Would you ignore and pass by when starving children reach out their hands to you for help?
- Would you think me subhuman because I see it every day, and yes, I turn and walk away?

For those of you who simply shake your heads and believe none of this is true, I send my sympathy and the following poem:

CHILDREN OF THE THIRD WORLD

Alone in a world of indifference and pain,
Set aside and withdrawn from others, they claim.
The children I see with their clothes in shreds.
The money is used for munitions instead.

I walk down the roads in clothes from the West.
Children approach hands held out in a test.
The words are unknown, but the look I can read.
They step back in silence, their eyes simply plead.

When I first came, these sights gave me a start,
I thought back in time, and I opened my heart.
I thought of my children, and I couldn't stay.
I shared what I could and then walked away,

Their bellies extended, mother's breasts dry,
Children weak from hunger, too tired to cry.
We butcher our cows from excessive milk,
We send them money, and their leaders buy silk.

These children are ravaged by war and disease,
Rulers turn west with hands out and say please.
While the children plead and beg us for bread,
We plow under our wheat and send guns instead.

The leaders of both the East and the West,
Fail these children when taking a test.

Come, see these children; you, too, would be sad,
When you realize how this world has gone mad.

Thanksgiving was fine, Mother. We did not find a turkey, but Andy found a ham. I also found time to thank God that you and those I love are safe and comfortable back home, and that I only signed up for one year.

After I finished addressing my mother's questions, I found I had also taken care of most of my Christmas shopping. It looked like I would have a few extra days on my hands. However, I made a mental note to go back to a few of the villages so I would not forget.

Chapter 20

I did not feel like fighting traffic to the site Saturday after Thanksgiving. I went into the office to catch up on correspondence from the States. After an hour of sorting through the papers on my desk, I could not believe how little I could do until the Egyptians delivered the shop drawings.

It was November 26th. I had been in Cairo for almost four months. Based on the COE's schedule I should be busy on the site. Instead, I was like the Egyptians in the villages, just waiting for tomorrow. The most pressing items were:

- A set of drawings so we knew what materials to order.
- The COE to finish the material submittal reviews.
- Tom to get the change orders approved for the gate, phone, and water lines.
- Anwar to get the equipment I asked for a month ago.
- Don to ship the foundation anchor bolts.
- Hamid to finish hooking up the toilets at the site.
- Customs to release my computer.
- My landlord to get the new leak around the bathtub fixed.
- My driver finished with his prayers so I could go to the site and see what I needed to add to my list.

While I was waiting for my driver to get up off his knees, I reviewed some of my earlier notes. I was still searching for some answers. It was a suitable time to fill in some of the blanks of those I had.

- People in the Middle East do not use toilet paper because it sticks to the concrete walls when the sewers overflow.
- Laborers wear traditional dress, so when they squat in the corner for their morning tea, I cannot tell which one shit on the fresh concrete.

- Marriage engagements last two to three years because the parents cannot agree on the dowry.
- The Generals delay the project to keep me in the country because if the expats left, baksheesh would dry up.

I was still working on my notes when my driver finished his prayers. By then, it was time for lunch. I postponed the trip to the site and decided to drop in at Tom's office to see how he was faring after Thanksgiving dinner.

"Hello, Tom; how about lunch?"

"You should have stayed away. General Aziz is back; he wants to see you."

"Let it go until tomorrow. He won't know the difference."

"Yes, he will. He has his spies; our security called the minute you came through the gate."

I sent my driver ahead and rode with Tom. I dreaded going to the meeting. Surprise….! General Aziz was in a pleasant frame of mind. It appeared it was strictly a social call. I did not want to bring up the problems Tom and I were dealing with, so it looked like Tom and I would be going to lunch after all. We finished our tea and were making excuses to leave.

"Ah, Mr. Pat, I have a small problem."

Thought: *Shit, General, you never have a small problem!*

"Ah, General Aziz, how can I help you?"

My turn with "*Ah"* crap. I knew there had to be a catch.

"What's the problem, General?"

"It's these papers, Mr. Pat. They are in English, and the print is too small for me to read. I understand you have a copier that will enlarge the print."

My copier did not have an enlarger, but the COEs did.

"Sure thing, General. I'll take care of it for you."

General Aziz handed me the documents. As I started to put them in my briefcase, Tom and I noticed the bold letters on the top page.

UNITED STATES GOVERNMENT

CLASSIFIED SECRET

Tom started to say something, but I quickly closed the briefcase and left General Aziz's office.

"He gave them to me, Tom. As far as I'm concerned, you haven't seen them."

"Damned right, I haven't. Did you see what they are?"

"No, but since the Egyptian Government has issued me a security clearance, I don't see any reason why I shouldn't look."

Tom and I left for the Sonesta Hotel for lunch; after we ordered, I took out the General's papers.

"Tom, this is the contract between the Egyptian Army and the OMC for the Computer Center."

"I was afraid of that."

Tom told me it was not a problem for him because he had a copy in his office. It was a problem for me because I was not supposed to see a copy, let alone have one in my possession.

"My copier won't enlarge the print. Can I use yours?"

"Shit, why not?"

It would have been futile for Tom to refuse. He knew I would find a way to get it done, and he felt it would be better if no one else knew of the General's request.

When we returned to Tom's office, I made two copies, one for the General and one for my files. I sent Hazem to return the General's original with a blown-up copy, and to tell him I would be happy to do the favor any time. I spent the rest of the day at my flat reading the agreement between the Egyptian Army and the OMC. The next morning, I headed for the Embassy.

"Good morning, General. Is Colonel Baker in?"

After I briefed the General on the progress at the site, he sent for the Colonel. The Colonel started in on me about a complaint the Egyptian Army filed with the OMC about various problems I was causing on the site.

"Not today, Colonel. Why haven't you got my residence visa straightened out? While we're on the subject, you're also supposed to be getting me my duty-free privileges."

"What makes you think it's my responsibility?"

"Because the contract the Egyptian Army signed with your agency makes it your responsibility, along with all the other crap you've been pawning off on me."

"Like what?"

The Colonel was getting upset, and I was getting madder by the minute. He had dumped his problems on me by throwing the *diligently pursuing the contract* clause at me for the past four months.

"Like what? You know damned well what! How about site security, road access, and the mobilization area, for starters? Oh! And don't forget the car shed. Colonel, I not only read the contract the OMC signed, I have a copy in my files."

"That document is classified and requires clearance. Where did you get it?"

"It's none of your business. Besides, I have clearance on this project as long as I'm in Egypt, remember?"

The three of us argued the point until General Olsen decided to take charge.

"The document is not supposed to be available to anyone except U.S. Government personnel and the Egyptian Army. There were agreements by all parties. Some of them we knew were unmanageable, but we agreed to them to get the project started. Your contract with the Corps of Engineers was an offshoot of the one between the Egyptian Army and my office. Your company contracted to perform according to the contract you signed, not to the one we signed with the Egyptians."

"General, with all due respect, the document is the contract between the two Governments. It outlines the responsibilities of the Egyptians as well as mine. I should have had a copy at the beginning. It would have saved me a lot of hassle with the Egyptian Army if I knew what they agreed to. At least we would all have been working according to the same rules. For Christ's sake, General, putting in the fucking gate and separating the site from Sayer's base was the first order of business."

The General and Colonel Baker gave in. We agreed we would all review the contract and each of us would try to do the things outlined as our responsibility. Colonel Baker also agreed he would try to make the Egyptian Army live up to their end of the bargain. As I was leaving, Colonel Baker made one last try.

"Patrick, where did you get it?"

"Does it really matter, Colonel?"

It did not. The fact I had it was enough to get the Colonel moving on my permanent visa, the road access, and a few other headaches that had plagued me from the beginning and were still up in the air.

I left the office wondering what the exercise really was. It was one thing fighting with a bunch of lying players from the other side. It was another knowing General Olsen and Colonel Baker knew most of the issues were sorted out before the contract was awarded and that they could have gone over Aziz's and Sayer's heads if they had wanted to stir the soup.

It was a known fact that American Aid to Egypt was a $3.2 billion-a-year giveaway. To me, that translated into a lot of advantages anywhere, and more so in a country as poor as Egypt; I could not help feeling that if the OMC wanted to apply some pressure, they could have easily gotten both General Sayer and Aziz in line from the start.

I went back to Abboud's office and told him the Egyptian government agreed to make the contract tax-free, not only for the

Americans but for all the contractors and subcontractors involved. That would mean a substantial bonus for Dr. Osmond's company since the tax rate in Egypt was over 25%. He asked me how I knew. I told him the information came from the OMC.

I knew it would land in my lap, so I suggested he check with General Olsen's office and request a copy of the contract, which outlined the tax-free status for the JV and its subs. It would make a significant difference to them when bidding on the work.

On the way out of the office, Sarha handed me a telex. Cesar agreed to let me take two weeks off at Christmas. It was the boost I needed and took some of the edge off the argument with Colonel Baker. I was definitely getting into a better frame of mind.

I left the office smiling for a change. The tax issue would get everyone's attention and keep the players off my back for the time being. It was time to make plans for the trip home.

I knew the Egyptian company would let everything go until the last minute, and Cesar would probably want me to stop at the home office in Portland for a few days. I sent Cesar a telex asking that he ask Don to make my flight reservation. But this time through London and then over the pole to Seattle. It would cut three days of travel off my holiday.

Caesar sent me a telex telling me he would not reimburse me for the trip. The terms of my contract were for a Christmas holiday in country. If I wanted to go home, I would have to fund it myself. He also mentioned he wanted me to stop in at the office for a meeting while I was home. I responded that if he wanted a meeting he could come to Egypt or buy my plane ticket home.

Don sent a follow-up a few hours later.

I don't have time to deal with your shit. Make your own fucking reservations.

Cesar and the Egyptian partners had not been getting along since Cesar found out the Egyptians could not or would not come up with their part of the bonding requirements. I was not getting along with Cesar because after I arrived in Cairo, I wrote to him and told him I would appreciate it if he would find a way to pay my expenses on time.

Cesar responded that since I was new to the company, he was testing my loyalty. Since then, I have been getting my paychecks on time, but Don has been checking my expense reports. My living allowance and expense reimbursements were a month behind because, according to Don, they were having a tough time finding their way into the Egyptian banking system.

Regardless of the in-house conflicts, we were into the fifth month of a twelve month contract with only seven more to go, and we still did not have a workable set of plans from the Egyptians, or any materials in transit from the States.

It was becoming difficult to convince Tom how we were going to finish on schedule if there were no plans or materials to do the work. Tom had been telling me from the onset that one of the prime reasons for requiring American supervision was that the Egyptians had proven themselves incapable of keeping their word or performing to American construction standards on their own.

I was beginning to believe Tom was right, and the people I was dealing with in Cairo were a sample of a system where rudeness, lies, and a failure to live up to commitments were a way of life.

Cesar had his head up his ass and refused to come see for himself. As a result, my ability to communicate with him had developed into a language barrier of its own. I was constantly telling him if he did not resolve the conflicts with his partners the COE might find another contractor to finish the job, and he would have to foot the bill.

I was also having a tough time communicating with the Egyptians. My command of the language, although improving, was far from adequate. I was picking up enough of the conversations taking place around me to know they were not concerned about the time limit or their commitments to Cesar or me.

I hated to admit it, but my initial observations of both company's inabilities to deal with the American Government were underestimated. The next morning, I heard the telex in Sarha's office clicking. Although faxes had recently become available, I still had not been able to convince Doctor Osmond to spend the money.

I was making it a point to come in before Sarha or the rest of the staff because it appeared I was not receiving copies of all the correspondence from the office in the States or from the U.S. suppliers I was supposed to be dealing with.

I was not sure if Abboud and Anwar were the ones responsible, or if it was a matter of the poor communication systems in the country. Whatever it was, I received conflicting information from Tom about our shipments and the delay in securing the bonds.

Cesar told me the bond was issued, and the prefabricated buildings were ordered before I left the States. That was five months earlier. Tom told me the bond issue was still not resolved, and the prefabricated building was not ordered. If he was right. I was managing a contract that was in default from the start.

I sent faxes from the Sonesta Hotel a few days earlier to keep the inquiries to myself. I picked a few companies at random and kept my questions routine so Don and Cesar would not be aware I was checking up on everyone. I also asked the vendors to respond at a time when I knew I would be the only one in the office.

The telexes arrived before Sarha showed up. The telex machine has a recorder on it, so she knew I received correspondence; she wanted copies.

"Sarha, I haven't had time to review them. When I do, I'll give them to you."

"But, Mr. Pat, Anwar told me to give him the telexes before you see them."

Sarha's not very bright, but ever since the letter episode, she's been honest with me.

"Sarha, check Anwar's telex files and make copies of all the telexes addressed to me. Moya seems to have misplaced my copies."

Moya was the wife of a British expat. I hired her as my site secretary. She spoke fluent Arabic and took notes of the meetings at the site. The Egyptians on the site were unaware of her talent for languages. She kept me informed of the deals being made behind my back. Both Dr. Osmond and Abboud had suspicions and would not allow her to attend meetings at the office.

I started to review the information I received earlier. Sarha brought copies of Anwar's files, half of which I had never seen. When Abboud showed up I was aware the bond had not been resolved, the building was not ordered, the foundation materials had not left the supplier's warehouse, and the combination meant I was going to be in a great deal of trouble with Tom. I told him the opposite to get another payment approved.

"Good morning, Doctor Abboud. When will Anwar be in?'

"After Tomorrow."

"What the fuck does that mean, Doctor?"

"I don't appreciate that language."

"That's more bullshit, you were educated in the states. Give me a straight answer."

He was pissed, but Doctor Abboud was not sure. I decided it was time the Doctor and I had a new understanding. I told him about the information I just received.

"Doctor Osmond and I are working on the bond. We will order the building when we get the next payment."

"Doctor Abboud, it's a matter of priorities. Tom and I have had enough of this bullshit. There won't be any more payments if I can't prove to Tom the bond is issued and the building is ordered."

"There's no need for you to change your position. You have papers in your file that say the issues are resolved; use them."

“I can’t do that, Doctor; Tom wants proof.”

“I will have proof *after tomorrow*, Mr. Pat!”

“Shit…. What does that mean, Doctor Abboud?”

“Soon, Mr. Pat! Do what you’re told.”

“I don’t work for you; I work for Cesar. No bond, no more money; make that clear to Doctor Osmond.”

The message was clear on both sides. Dr Osmond and Abboud were wealthy men, and they were Egyptians, not Arabs. Their ancestors built the Pyramids; I should not be concerned about their ability to finance or erect a lousy prefabricated metal building on time. I did not say anymore, but at that moment, I flunked the loyalty class, and I had no intention of reenrolling. The situation I faced was straightening it out with Tom.

Abboud and Doctor Osmond both had a Ph.D. from reputable colleges in the States. What was happening was confusing in that these highly educated individuals could not recognize the warning signs. I was convinced the project would extend long past the due date and was mentally restructuring the schedule while remembering John’s comments the first week I was in Cairo. Two weeks had turned into six months for John. I was beginning to think my contract could be a lifetime.

I headed for Tom’s office, hoping he and I could find a way to get the partners in line. Tom listened while I tried to explain that the company simply did not understand the importance of the schedule, and I may have been mistaken about the status of the bond because of the language differences. Tom responded by opening his desk, taking out the last pay estimate, and throwing it in the round file.

“Patrick, I want a new schedule reflecting what you just told me before I release more money.”

“I figured as much.”

I went back to my office and sent a memo to Abboud and Cesar telling them the money would be delayed until I received a copy of the bond. I explained why and asked for an accurate update on purchasing and shipping schedules.

As a P.S., I added it would be a good idea if the partners would resolve the bond issue before the COE terminated the contract, and that they should get the metal building fabricator started on the drawings. I kept the rest of my thoughts to myself.

Chapter 21

Dr. Abboud was pissed when I left the office. With little choice, I would keep after the partners until Cesar fired me or Tom threw us off the job site. When I got home, Andy's monkey was loose in the kitchen. Cockroaches were one thing; dealing with monkey shit on the countertops was something else. Andy could clean the mess up, but dinner at home was out.

I needed a break; I figured enough time had passed since my episode with the Brit at the Sheraton for me to go back to the German restaurant.

The restaurant was full. Mohammad was not there; the hostess told me without a reservation, it would be at least an hour's wait.

At the time, the Heliopolis Sheraton was the nicest hotel on the airport strip. The food was not bad, the service was mediocre, they put a little liquor in the drinks, and sometimes they had English-speaking entertainers, not bad by Cairo standards.

I stopped in the gift shop with the intention of buying a U.S. or British newspaper. They had a few copies of USA Today, but they were two weeks old. I settled for a Cuban cigar and headed for the lobby bar.

The place was packed. The social secretary at the front desk was fluent in French; a busload of Germans was checking in. I wandered past, looking for a table.

I got lucky as I walked by a group that was leaving. It was the only table available, designed to seat six, with a couch on one side and chairs on the other. The waitress was a little miffed when she realized I was alone.

I ordered a scotch, then settled back in the overstuffed couch. I was enjoying the show. After she brought me *a brandy, shit... what the hell,* and the cigar I was trying to light finally took hold,

I put the project and partners out of my mind and watched the tourist's reactions to their first day in Egypt.

English is a second language in Egypt and most of Europe. However, most of the local restaurant help spoke only Arabic, but some realized that being friendly and coming close when it came to good service increased their tips; some waitstaff make an attempt.

One couple was arguing with a porter. Porters had a habit of grabbing luggage whether you wanted them to or not and would not give it back until you gave them a tip.

The German woman sitting behind me, who ordered tea, was trying to explain to the waitress she did not want buffalo milk. I had ordered a scotch, but she brought brandy; having been there a while, I knew close counts in Egypt.

As I set my drink down, I noticed an American wandering around, picking up napkins. He approached and asked if he could join me at my table, commenting that he had left his key in his room and the clerk at the desk had told him the hotel had misplaced it. He was waiting for security to bring a new one. He was sitting down when he glanced at the newspaper he just bought and realized it was the right day, but two weeks old. He mumbled *something*, then turned to me.

"Will you be here a while?"

"At least an hour."

"I'll be back."

As I turned back toward the room, four Arab men approached my table and then stood staring at the empty seats. The leader was a weasel of a man dressed in a silk thobe and a checkered headdress.

Based on his clothes, I assumed he was a wealthy oil sheik from Dubi in the oil-rich United Arab Emirates. There was a cigarette dangling from his chiseled beak. When he leaned over, his ashes dropped on the table. I reached down and picked up my drink to avoid the fallout. It did enter my mind that it would be best if I got up and looked for another table. As I hesitated, he whispered.

"You must move."

Sorry, *I know I should have moved*, but his arrogant tone pissed me off. I leaned back, took a deep drag on my cigar, looked at him and his three watchdogs, who were pulling the chairs away from the table in obvious determination to sit down, and exhaled the foul-smelling pollutant in their direction.

"Find your own fucking table."

I did not like the look. The Arab did not like the smoke in his face, or my attitude. He turned to his companions, giving them some orders while pointing toward me. I was not impressed, and I did not intend to give up my table. As I exhaled another lungful of Castro's finest, their moods became as clouded as the air. Hollywood has its influence. The word fuck is universal in every language. I know he took offense, but it took a few seconds to register. This time, it was one of his friends, only it was not a whisper.

"You must move! Now!"

Up to that point, as far as anyone in the area was concerned, I had been a gentleman. The only thing the waitress or the other guests overheard was the man yelling at me in Arabic and his loud conversation with his friends. I have no idea what he was saying, but the waitress was concerned enough to go to the security desk and return with Achmed, the chief of security who settled the argument between me and the Brit in the German restaurant. He was standing obscurely in the background along with half a dozen of his guards.

The man and his cronies' attitudes changed from arrogance to smoldering rage. He turned to the three men, pointed toward me, and issued a command that made them move in my direction. I had my escape fairly well planned. The table was between me and the men. The couch I was sitting on had a low back. I was halfway over it and sliding into the lap of the woman behind me when the security guards moved in.

I was apologizing to the woman while Achmed got the situation on the other side of the couch under control. I knew the Arabs had a lot more money than I did. I also knew Achmed was inclined to base his decision of liability on who offered what and how discretely they managed it. In this instance, the Arab was mad enough to forget the basic requirement of successful negotiations in Cairo. Achmed recognized me from the German Restaurant. When he approached, I offered him my hand.

"Ah, Mr. Pat, you are one; they are four."

"I have friends coming, Achmed."

Two ten-LE notes settled the argument in his mind. Achmed turned back to the group. After a few heated words in Arabic, Achmed and his men escorted the men to the security desk.

As I was lighting a new cigar, I looked over at the group milling around the desk. The Arab was holding out a wad of money, but one needs to be discrete, Achmed was ignoring him. He calmed down and then left for the patio to sulk.

Tour buses, some leaving, others picking up passengers were returning. Most of the people who sat through the incident had left. The tables were filling with milling guests.

I had resettled at my table. The American was back. I asked him if he would watch my drink so the waitress did not pick it up and to tell her I would return after I checked with the German restaurant. I returned a few minutes later. They had not put my name on the list the first time. I was at the bottom of the list and back to people-watching.

When a customer approached or signaled to get their attention, the waitstaff would tune them out and stare into upper space. Kids today at home do that a lot when a parent or teacher is trying to get their attention.

I was thinking I should have paid more attention when I was a kid because the teacher in my kindergarten class would not allow me to go on to first grade until I could get along with others. How do you flunk someone in kindergarten? Half the kids who graduate from public high school in the States cannot read or write, and a lot of them are thugs.

You cannot make this shit up; I flunked kindergarten. I needed to be a little more easygoing. Although I do not consider all of the problems I encounter my doing, I am the one responsible for my actions. I also know I could have avoided the situation with the Arabs and the Brits if I had simply moved out of the way.

I decided if provoked in another like situation I would take another approach. I was getting my new resolution settled firmly in mind when I looked up and saw an Arab dressed in traditional dress following a Swiss Air flight attendant who had just checked in and was heading for her room.

At first, I was not positive and thought it ludicrous, but it appeared the man had an erection, and it was holding the fabric of his silk Thobe away from his belly.

The woman he was following was a doll. Tall, blond, about 25-years old. I made a mental note to forget London and have Hazem check with Swissair for my Christmas flight to the States.

The woman was unaware of the drama developing behind her. It was easy to see she was used to crowded lobbies and corridors of international hotels. She was expertly weaving through the milling crowd, careful not to tangle the suitcase trailing behind her in the legs of others crowding the area.

It was also apparent the woman had done a lot of recent traveling. All she was interested in was putting her flight and security problems behind her by heading straight for her room and a shower.

I was having a tough time keeping the resolve I had just made about leaving an unpleasant scene right itself and was thinking about intercepting the man before he could reach her. I thought better of it when I realized the swarm of people milling close by afforded her all the protection she needed. I settled back to watch the show but lost sight of the Arab in the crowd and figured he gave up the pursuit.

I caught sight of him again as I was turning to pick up my drink. He had worked his way through the crowd and was approaching the flight attendant who was stalled in the crowd waiting for the elevator. The scene was only a few meters away. My chuckle caught the attention of the American and some of the other tourists at tables adjoining mine. The Arab moved into plain sight, pushing his way through the crowd. I started to laugh at the absurdity of the situation when he reached the flight attendant.

The woman at the table next to me caught on, let out a gasp, and spilled her drink on her companion. The American yelled an obscenity, which pissed me off because he almost spoiled the show. Our waitress came over to clean up the spilled drink and followed everyone's gaze. She left the mess on the table and headed for the security desk.

I was no longer concerned about the woman; half the tourists in the bar were watching, and security guards were heading in the direction of the elevators. The Arab did not know we were watching; the flight attendant did not know the Arab was approaching. My cigar had become hot in my hand, and without looking, I reached for the ashtray, which the waitress had moved, and I spilled the American's drink.

The flight attendant was reaching to press the lift button when the Arab stepped between her and the door. He turned around to face her and said something, causing her to look down. When she looked back up, she looked around the room to see if anyone was watching. As she did, she let go of the suitcase, let the strap from her overnight case slip off her arm, and took a firm grip on her handbag. She then turned back and brought her purse down across the Arab's thobe, catching his erection like a woodsman cutting a tree limb with an ax.

In the next few seconds, the lift opened, and the flight attendant stepped in. The security guards arrived and dragged the Arab into the toilet while he was screaming obscenities and holding his crotch. I turned back to the crowd in the bar. The Americans were cheering, two of the women were clapping, and I was laughing so hard that I tipped the table and spilled my drink.

While this was happening the busload of French tourists arrived, but the social secretary had been replaced with one who spoke German. I helped the waitress clean up the mess, ordered a drink to replace the one I spilled on my companion, paid my bill, and headed for the restaurant, wondering what the next floor show in the Sheraton would be like.

I also decided to forget about any resolve I may have made earlier. If the young woman could manage an unpleasant situation so easily, it should not be that difficult for me.

When I got to the German restaurant, Mohammad showed up and found me a seat, even though I did not have my name on the list.

Dinner was excellent. Achmed arrived and joined me just as I finished my chicken. We had an Arabic-English conversation, but it was pleasant. I managed to understand that Achmed wanted me to know he was sorry about the incident at my table. He mentioned again that there were four of them. It was not about the number of seats. It was the third incident; he had thrown the men out of the hotel, and they would not bother me again.

I figured I needed to pay the entertainment tax, so I slipped him another twenty LE. You never know what might happen next.

Chapter 22

I was fighting my way back to my flat through heavier-than-usual traffic. I was also thinking the project I was involved in reminded me of someone trying to make love to a mannequin. I was an American in Cairo to build a building for the Egyptian Army with the COE directing traffic. Cesar, a nationalized American from the Philippines who did not know the rules, was running the show from the States. Abboud was giving orders in Cairo. Anwar was finding a reason to disappear every time I needed something. I had been in Cairo for five months and was not any closer to a climax than I was at the start. With everybody trying to screw everyone else, it did not look like I would ever get the job done.

I woke up at two a.m. The jet passing five hundred meters above my flat was rattling the windows. After it passed, I was wide awake. It was a good time to catch up on my letter writing. I went to the kitchen to make coffee.

Andy had used the last of the coffee and had not replaced it. I reached for a cigarette. The pack was empty, which in Cairo is no big deal because one breath of Cairo air is equal to about two packs, and the Egyptian tea I had to settle for would give me the same sour taste in my mouth.

I am addicted to cigarettes, and I am getting used to Egypt tea. I decided to borrow a pack of Andy's. Andy bought the cheap ones they rolled in Egypt, *I think*, made of tobacco blended with camel dung. I preferred American Marlborough. I was desperate; Andy's would do. As usual, my planning was off. I should have gotten the cigarettes first. The monkey was supposed to sleep on the patio. I woke her, and she screeched, which surprised me.

I should have attempted the theft before the tea was ready because I spilled the tea on Andy's bed. Everyone was awake, and I did not get the cigarettes. I walked back to the kitchen, letting things calm down. Andy was in the bedroom cursing and changing his linen.

As far as planning, my choice of peaches and cream for dessert may be one of the reasons I was wide awake. It is best to avoid Egypt dairy unless you boil it; you cannot always trust the hotels. After a quick run to the toilet and a stop off in Andy's room to make peace and borrow a pack of smokes, I went back to the living room to write the letters I started earlier.

Andy and the monkey were back to sleep, and the jets were using the other runway. Things were quiet, which made sense because it was almost four a.m. By six, I had finished the letters but still could not get back to sleep. I laid there thinking I had a lot of sleep the past few nights, so it was not the job keeping me awake.

Monday night I went to bed at eight and slept ten hours. Last night, I went to bed at ten and pulled the covers over my head in hopes that by the time I woke up, so would Cesar and Abboud. No such luck, as usual; I was awake before everyone else and wondering what was going to go wrong that day.

I gave up on sleep and decided to try to catch Tom at the Sonesta Hotel, where he had breakfast every morning. Tom never made it. He called me later in the day to tell me General Aziz had returned from the States. The General requested his presence first thing this morning. I was not aware of what was going on between the General and Tom, so rather than go to the site, I left for the office to confront Anwar, and if I could not find him, Abboud.

There was a telex from Cesar. Abboud and Doctor Osmond had left for Portland, and he wanted their arrival time. I had no idea they were leaving. I rummaged through Sarha's desk. I found a flight schedule for Doctor Osmond and telexed the information to Cesar.

A call came at 8:30. It had to be a problem because nobody was awake at that time of the morning in Egypt except Tom and me. I tried to ignore it, but on the eighth ring, I relented and picked up the phone.

“Ah, Mr. Pat.”

General Aziz was back. I had no idea what it might be about. Things had been going well on the site in his absence, but there was no way he would leave well enough alone.

The General had been gone for two weeks, and many of my problems were solved.

- My security pass did not expire for another month. I have my passport and visa back.
- Andy promised to make sure the monkey would not shit on the clothesline after the houseboy did my laundry.
- Everyone has forgotten about the breach of security. The sewer overflowed and the passing buses plastered the gate with napkins from the hotel so the newly painted gate looks like the rest of Cairo.
- I have also finally mastered local driving, and instead of me giving the taxi drivers the finger, they are shaking their fists at me.
- Hazem taught me how to say no in Arabic. I have forgotten how to say thank you or please, even in English.
- Tom and I made plans for the next fishing trip.
- I found the Arabic school where Maha teaches Arabic. I have not enrolled because I am still flunking my patience class and I do not want to take on too large a class load before I leave for Christmas.
- Yesterday I received a notice from Egyptian customs telling me if I did not pick up my computer, they were going to start charging me storage. What that is all about, I have no idea. Hazem is sorting through the system.

Things have been going pretty well, except for the repeat.

”Ah, Mr. Pat, can you make it to a meeting at ten in the morning?”

“Yes, I will be there for the meeting tomorrow. What is it about General Aziz?”

The line went dead. I had twenty-four hours to figure out what it was the General wanted. In the meantime, I needed to address the unresolved items on the current list.

- Go back to the Sheraton and see if the flight attendant has gotten her handbag cleaned. *That is just an excuse; she was gorgeous*.
- Pass my new course in patience.
- Enroll in an Arabic class or have Hazem translate my itinerary to the States into English because close only counts in Cairo.
- Convince Unan that I want to do the grocery shopping for the next fishing trip.
- Reserve the stallion for the night of the next full moon.

And, the new addition, which Tom just called and added. Convince General Aziz I should not have to pay $15,000 for the mental anguish I caused him and General Sayer during the first 90 days of the project. Tom gave me a list of the pain and suffering complaints that would be the subject of the next day's meeting. Thoughts: *That ought to be interesting*.

The expats I meet in Cairo keep telling me we all have to be nuts to work in the Arab world. Their constant reference to the subhuman, double-digit intelligence we are dealing with keeps entering my mind.

Subhuman? Yes, it is a bullshit, racist label created by dynasties during the two hundred years of colonial rule on the African and Indian continents, America's attitude during the Indian wars, and the brutal regimes in the 20th century as an excuse to enslave or exterminate a population.

As for me, the term subhuman has a connotation. I am unable to accept that one race has less intelligence than any other. I keep telling myself it is simply a matter of a difference in cultures. I have repeatedly had to make an adjustment in my mindset and accept that words have different definitions as cultures vary.

At first, I thought it was a matter of culture shock mixed with a lack of understanding for the local citizens. As days turned to weeks and weeks to months with little or no progress, it does not appear there is any honor in the Middle East.

The people I deal with seem unable to decipher fact from fiction. They are so used to lying to one another and to the rest of the world they lie to me without even knowing they are doing it.

The subcontractors and partners refuse to accept a set of rules, let alone a critical schedule. They also refuse to see Egypt for what it is today as they reference centuries when Pharaohs ruled. I honestly do not think they see the filth, poverty, or pollution, which is matched only by the corruption.

I understand better each day. I no longer pay much attention to trash on the streets, overflowing sewers, beggars on corners, thousands of unfinished buildings, roads driven on, which for the most part, are undrivable, and the fact no one is in a hurry to do anything about any of it, let alone address their immediate and personal problems.

In the span of a few short months, I am finding it bothers me less as each day passes, and it is easier to deal with it the more my mind becomes accustomed to the sights. Reflecting on it makes me wonder if it would bother me at all if I were native to the land and had grown up with it around me.

Ingrained prejudice makes ethnic acceptance impossible for some to attain. I keep trying, but I still have not figured out what global civilization is all about. All I can judge it by is my experiences in the West. It is simply that, like a majority of Americans, prior to my arrival, I was naive when it came to reality outside the confines of my limited space.

The environment and quality of life are of no concern to the leaders of the Third World. Before this experience, it has never been a concern to me. I have spent most of my life in areas free of pollution. Lakes and rivers, still clean and full of fish, are vivid memories of my growing years.

Unlike some, I realize there must be some balance between the environment and man's need to survive amidst an exploding world's population.

Conflicts between sportsmen, property owners, self-serving environmentalists, and pork barrel politicians are the subject of the day. Industry destroys the environment for profit's sake; politicians use jobs as an excuse.

The Green Movement closes our forests, beaches, rivers, and mountains in the name of future generations, denying us the right to the beauty of our land for today's enjoyment.

Forests close to save an owl; when workers protest the loss of jobs and the forced shutdown of their way of life, politicians tell them to move to the city where jobs are plentiful.

Major cities are becoming wastelands, and the jobs are low pay. Who in their right mind wants to live in tenement housing, exposing themselves to inner-city crime and drugs? Those forced from their rural way of life by environmental shutdowns have few options.

I do not have the answers, but I would abandon the owl. However, the military waste I am familiar with reinforces my opinion that all countries should divert some of the trillions they spend in the name of military paranoia to programs that feed and house the masses born, living, and ending their lives in utter poverty.

It also seems to me with a little planning our national parks, scenic rivers, deserts, mountains, lakes, and a variety of other terrain could be made habitable for both man and his environment.

- We force the industry to the verge of bankruptcy by making them comply with laws designed for the handicapped. Yet, we close our national parks to anyone not capable of carrying a backpack and walking miles into the wilderness. How nuts is that?
- We spend billions on a space program racked with indifference and ineptitude to explore an unreachable new frontier, light years away, while waste and pollution litter this planet.
- We force single mothers to live in tenement housing, unable to care for tomorrow's generations. At the same time, we build

five-star prisons to house murderers, rapists, and thieves in a lifestyle of comfort.

- We fund abortions of choice for those wanting to choose the sex of their offspring in the name of convenience.
- We allow illegal immigrants to overrun our borders, bringing drugs that destroy the youth and future of our society.

Plain and simple, the priorities of many of our leaders in the States are, like the leaders in the Middle East, based on their own self-interest and personal gain at the expense of those they were elected to serve.

I spent a day last week sightseeing in a rural village by the Steppe Pyramids. I entered one of the villages by accident and came away with the feeling life in the Third World is a matter of existing in its timespan, and living belongs to those of us privileged to live outside reality.

I have passed the area a number of times. The constant outpouring of polluted waste from the nearby factories fills my throat with a bitter, parched taste. I stopped at one of the many roadside stands selling cigarettes and soda pop. To stop, I turned into a dirt path leading through a farmer's field.

I bought a Pepsi, then sat for a moment, cooling my throat while watching children, toddlers to teens, in a field digging potatoes. I was returning to my car when three farmers approached. They communicated with me in sign language, jokingly, and apparently asking if I would give them a ride into their village.

Yes, I know! It is foolish to pick up a stranger, let alone three at one time. It was something under normal circumstances I would have refused. As they pointed in the direction of the path passing for a road through a field, I instinctively knew they were what they seemed, three friendly farmers asking for a ride home.

The village was out of my way, but I was not in a hurry. The men were surprised when I gestured for them to join me in the car. The one who took the front seat pointed in the direction to take and was openly pleased I understood a few Arabic words, giving basic directions.

My camera was in the front seat. I reached to move it; he pointed beyond the potato fields to the palm trees in the background. I understood he was asking if I wanted to take pictures. I nodded yes. He pointed me to a narrower winding path, which looked unsuited for the car but appeared to be passable.

We meandered through a sparse field where women were gathering potatoes. We reached a grove of palms before I noticed the mud-brick buildings of the village showing through the background of the trees.

Digging Potatoes.

The farmer continued to point in the direction I was to follow. I hesitated to take one of the forks in the road by crossing a narrow bridge. Wood sticks were covered by dirt to form a culvert *of sorts*. It appeared impassable, spanning one of the many ditches feeding foul and smelly liquid to the fields and, in the distance, the village.

He encouraged me forward. I took him at his word and crossed the bridge. It took the better part of an hour to navigate the crossing from the highway of today into the village and life of yesteryear.

As we left the shelter of the palms, we passed row after row of shabby mud-brick buildings separated by narrow paths cluttered with animals, children, and debris. Most passageways were barely wide enough for the car to pass. I stopped at times while my passengers got out to remove the larger obstacles blocking our way, and to shoo children who were approaching with clamoring curiosity.

A girl, about ten, caught my eye. She was dressed in a dingy sweater, passed down from generations, torn in places, and patched with other garments of varied shades and textures.

Waiting for Tomorrow.

She stood transfixed, watching me, her bare feet inches from the waste, her hands crossed in front of her, her hair matted and tangled.

When I entered the village square, my guide signaled me to stop. I positioned the car out of the way of the milling children and animals.

An ancient monument dedicated to a long-past civilization was the focal point. There was a shallow, damp ditch fed by liquid seeping from village huts, cutting through the square leading back to the creek I had just crossed.

The other men left the car. My guide reached for my camera case and then handed it to me. I followed him to an area littered with the young, old, sick, and tired people of the village, who looked as if they were all just waiting for tomorrow. My arrival roused the curiosity of those able to raise themselves from various positions of repose and approach in my direction. My guide explained that I wanted to take pictures. Some enthusiastically agreed, others shrunk back into the shadows of the buildings.

Children, shy at first, clamored for attention as they pressed me back against the car. The men who rode in the back blended with the crowd and disappeared. I was becoming uncomfortable as people from the surrounding buildings poured into the courtyard. I felt sure I was the only foreigner who had entered this village since the days of English rule.

Infidel, leave, now!

A group of angry village elders dressed in ankle-length black thobes entered the square. My guide tapped me on the shoulder, and indicated it was time for us to leave. One man approached and blocked the exit. The discussion was loud and filled with angry gestures. When I started the car, the man pushed my guide aside and directed his attention to me, glaring and pointing me back the way I came.

The farmer ignored him, walked to the other side, and sat down in the front seat. The man turned and left. The farmer paused a moment until the man was out of sight, and then pointed forward in the direction of a path bordering the palms leading from the square.

I picked my way through the people, clutter, and animals. In the mirror, I saw the elders leaving the area, shooing the children ahead of them as the square emptied.

I was surprised when the farmer got back in the car. As angry as the elder was, I thought I would be left to find my way back. When we exited the square onto a narrower path, I hesitated, reluctant to go further into the village. I was not sure I could find my way back to the highway as it was.

We continued along the path separating the fields and palms, boarding the village, stopping intermittently to capture on film the subsistence of peasants, friends of the farmer, and anxious to meet a stranger in their midst. Many of the women and children had never been beyond the village fields, confined for life to a few square meters of land and tiny huts made of mud and straw.

The farmer smiled as he urged me forward, leading me deeper into the village. He then pointed to the camera on the seat, once again making motions with his hands. I took him to mean he wanted me to meet his family and take their pictures. The sun began to set when we entered an area of corrals made of brick and stone. The only signs of life were a ragged-looking donkey, goats rummaging through trash, and scraggly chickens perched on fences and gates.

My guide stopped me at a hut that opened to a hidden courtyard in the back. I got out of the car. He left me standing by the door, wondering where I was and how I was going to find my way back to Cairo.

Home for a Lifetime.

He returned, took me by the hand, and led me to a square behind the hut. The courtyard was filled with women and children. I assumed the farmer was introducing me to his three wives and eleven children and telling them he had brought a guest home for dinner.

I had forgotten about proper planning and had gotten myself into a situation that was not going to be easy to avoid. I knew I was welcome, but I also knew the creek I crossed and the ditches it fed irrigated the farmer's fields.

My body had not built up the immunities to handle the diet of the peasants of Egypt. I was starting to protest that I had to return to Cairo when one of the women brought out a painted mat made of reeds and straw. She unrolled it and then, after herding the children back from its edges, offered me a seat.

The matt was obviously an honored place. My protests dissolved as I reluctantly took my place, wondering what it was I was going to have for dinner.

The Dining Room.

The women busied themselves while the farmer offered me a homemade cigar. He insisted, prodding my arm when I declined and reached for my cigarettes. I sat back against the wall, thought about where I was, and figured, what the hell?

As I smoked the cigar, which smelled of goat and donkey shit littering the corral, the children edged closer to my place of royalty. The man was bone thin, and they all appeared undernourished. Puss packed some eyelids, cheeks smeared by dirt from filthy sleeves as they wiped at snot running from their noses.

Food was an issue, but according to the World Health Organization, in Egypt, as in many other developing countries, most infant and childhood mortality is due to diarrhea, acute respiratory infections, neonatal infections, accidents, and vaccine-preventable disease.

One of the women was nursing a listless, uncrying infant. The child next to me crawled into my lap. The farmer crossly reached for him. I waved him off and resettled him more comfortably. The farmer smiled and offered me a fresh cigar.

When I did not seem to mind the child in my arms, the others edged closer. The one I was holding was older than his frame and attitude. He was one of three from the youngest wife, who was pregnant with a fourth. The farmer indicated his age to be four. He did not weigh twenty pounds, and as my fingers circled his upper arms, I wondered how many of the eleven would survive.

I watched the women finish preparing a meal of boiled eggs, cheese made from milk from goats in the outer courtyard, a green vegetable ground into a fine powder, potatoes, and some kind of brown bean, all blended into a mash.

They served it in a bowl made of rusty tin I knew had been recently washed in the polluted creek running through the field. I hesitated for a moment, thinking about the consequences. I then broke off a chunk of stale Egyptian bread, dipped it in the bland gruel, and placed a bite in my mouth.

One of the boys reached into the bowl to scoop the bitter and sour substance with his unwashed hand onto a piece of bread he snuck out of the fly-covered pile; the farmer lightly tapped his hand.

Egyptian Bread - The Staple of Egypt.

I understood that custom dictated the man and I dine first, and the woman and children could eat only after we had our fill. The first bite was more than I wanted. Not wanting to insult my host, I took a chunk of bread, dragged it through the family's meal, and offered a bite to the child in my lap. The gesture broke the ice. Soon, the children were filling themselves and washing the meal down, as I was, with strong and bitter tea.

His wives and teenage girls never joined us and stayed back in the shadows. I ate all I could and managed to convince the farmer I had enough; the women removed the food and took it to the other side of the courtyard; the rest of the family followed and left us to ourselves.

I offered the farmer a cigarette and sipped on the cooling tea. As I watched his family, I was amazed at a man who had taken in a stranger passing by and who shared the meager substance of his family so willingly.

It was surprising how well the two of us managed to converse. It made a great deal more sense than the conversations I had been having with Anwar and the Generals of Egypt.

I spent a few more minutes saying goodbye, only after I managed to convince him people were waiting for me and they would be concerned if I did not return soon.

I was concerned about my ability to find my way back to the highway. I picked up a stick to draw a map in the dirt showing the roadside stand, the field, and the village as best I could remember it. He led me to the path where the car was parked. We had come in a circle. One left turn would take me to the main highway a mile down the road.

I wanted to do more than simply say thank you. When the little boy who bridged the social gap earlier came out to say goodbye, I pressed the roll of notes I kept in my pocket for social emergencies into the farmer's hand.

It was not until later that I found out multiple families sharecropped most fields with a landowner. Peasants rent a piece of land according to the owner's terms. As a farmer, his typical wage for a year was the right to a shack, a spot for a garden, and a few LE when the landowner sold the crop. It was far less than I had given him. It was only the need of his family that allowed him to accept it without protest, as I did his hug and kiss of thanks. It was little money compared to what I earned, but I felt better knowing that perhaps one more of the eleven might now survive.

If you go back to the picture of the women gathering potatoes, it is the leftovers a family is allowed to keep after the landlord sells the crop. As I was leaving, I passed kids working in a cotton field.

These kids do not go to school, they are working in the fields as soon as they can walk.

Chapter 23

Same shit, different day, continuing my search for sanity in a world enveloped by reality and inhabited by humanity alien to my personal experience. When I returned to the office, I noticed the milestone date on the calendar. It was December 4th, 120 days into the project. Days left, 245, still, very little accomplished.

Anwar failed to show up, *again*. The phone was ringing. I answered it. It was Doctor Osmond calling from Cesar's office in the States. Doctor Osmond asked why I answered the phone. He was also looking for Anwar. It was unusual because I do not speak enough Arabic to ask directions to a working toilet, let alone take an intelligent message.

I told him it was a reflex reaction. I was the only one in the office besides the accountant, and since he did not have a phone, I was acting secretary. Doctor Osmond asked me how things were going. I told him I planned to fire Anwar as soon as I could find him.

"Ah, Mr. Pat, you must learn some patience."

"Doctor Osmond, I flunked patience."

Of all the Egyptians, Doctor Osmond was coming around, but he did not have a clue. He asked if he could help. No one I knew used checks in Egypt. Everything was paid for in LE. Up until then, I refused to carry a briefcase full of cash, which would have made me a target on the streets of Cairo.

Difficult times result in desperate measures. I told him I needed money to buy the things Anwar was supposed to get, and I would appreciate it if he would tell accounting to open the safe.

I tracked him down, Doctor Osmond talked to the accountant for a few minutes and then told me he instructed him to do whatever I asked. He also told me he was sure Anwar would show up, *after tomorrow, inshallah* to help straighten out my problems.

"Doctor Osmond, maybe you can tell me what *after tomorrow* means."

"Anwar will be there when he is there, Mr. Pat."

"Fine, do you mind if I don't do anything, and I just wait in my office for him?"

"You must be patient Mr. Pat. Anwar will return soon."

Dr. Osmond was reading my frustration. I did not want to tell him what had caused my latest riff with Anwar. I did draft a memo to cover myself when Dr. Osmond returned and found I spent 10,000-LE when I scheduled the backfilling a few days earlier, something that was outside my limit of authority when it came to Dr. Osmond's responsibilities under the JV agreement.

I was three weeks late because Anwar could not find the sand. I found it, which was not difficult because a desert surrounds the entire southern end of Cairo. All I had to do was make a right turn when I left the office.

I hired the subcontractor and needed to pay the bill. After I arranged to have the sand hauled to the site, I left a request for some equipment on Anwar's desk so we could put the material in place and compact it to the COE specifications. I told Anwar to order a dozer to spread the material. I also needed a roller compactor, two sections of hose to connect to the new water line and five laborers with shovels.

When I was at the site earlier, I found Anwar had sent, in order of their arrival: instead of the compactor, twenty-two laborers, each with a chunk of railroad iron welded to a ¾-inch pipe, the dozer, six more laborers and two wheelbarrows, the hose, and three rubber buckets.

After Doctor Osmond authorized accounting to open the safe it took the rest of the morning to convince the accountant I needed the money. He finally gave me half of what I asked for, which was okay because it had become a game and I asked for twice as much as I needed.

It took the rest of the morning to find the equipment I had asked for two months earlier. Once I knew the backfilling would begin, I was ready for General Aziz, *or so I thought*.

After the incident with the gate, General Aziz bypassed the local OMC and sent a demand letter for $15,000 to the OMC office in Washington charging me with causing him and General Sayer mental pain and suffering over the tree, the truck, and the utility lines.

The OMC in Washington forwarded it to General Olsen, who sent it to the COE in Washington, who snail-mailed it back to Colonel Baker. Colonel Baker gave it to Tom. Tom ignored it and sent it back to the OMC in Washington. It ended back on General Olsen's desk. He sent it back to General Aziz, telling him it was a personal matter and to take it up with Tom and me.

The General discussed it with Tom on the phone. Tom must have been thinking about the next fishing trip at our last meeting because he did not say anything about it until he saw the equipment Anwar sent to the site. Tom slipped it in before the meeting with General Aziz when he asked if I thought three buckets were enough.

I was reluctant, but according to Tom, we had no choice. We needed to clear the air with General Aziz. I had the premonition a meeting at that moment was going to piss me off. It did, in spades. I let off more steam than I should have before Tom ended the meeting. When we left, General Aziz was pissed.

"Relax; it's not that big a deal."

"Tom, this is bullshit. One of these days I'm going to forget the prick is a general."

"It sounded like you already forgot. Look, he's an Egyptian General, and he is in charge of the project. Regardless of what bullshit he pulls you have to treat him with proper respect in front of his men."

"Fuck him, none of his men speak English, and he's not very damned good at it."

"No, but he got your gist."

"Tom, I have no intention of paying them fifteen cents, let alone fifteen grand."

"Forget it, I sent the letter back to the CO in DC. He's been reading my reports. He bought the feud story. He thinks it's hilarious."

Tom was going to ignore the mess, or I could deal with it. I decided if the COE were going to ignore it, I would too, especially since the letter was back in the channels of red tape entertaining all the players.

The next morning, I met Tom on the site to see how the backfilling was progressing. Some of the equipment had arrived and the work was progressing. Most of Anwar's laborers had nothing to do and were milling around trying to look busy. I told Hamid to lay off the laborers and get rid of the hand tools.

That was above his pay grade and would have to come from Anwar. In the meantime, the laborers were indiscriminately digging in various locations on the site. I was trying to make sure Hamid understood I did not want to tear up more utility lines when Colonel Baker showed up with General Aziz.

It would have been customary for me to offer them tea. Moya, my secretary, told me that Anwar had taken the hose that fed water to the trailer a few days earlier and had not returned it. She refused to pack water from the Army base for tea. I could not prolong it.

"Ah Mr. Pat, we have a dilemma."

The SOB must have bought a dictionary.

"Dilemma? That's a big word General. What's the problem? As you can see, I'm taking General Sayer's advice and using labor instead of equipment to do the work. He should be happy; I am sure he will leave your water turned on."

I was just about to get the General's attention when Colonel Baker broke into the conversation. The Colonel was not happy.

"What are you talking about? We're here to discuss the complaint General Aziz sent me this morning."

Once again, I was caught off guard. After Tom and I left the meeting with General Aziz the General sent a copy of the pain and suffering complaint back to the Colonel with a PS mentioning I was not showing the Egyptian military proper respect. I did not have a clue how to deal with this shit. Tom said something about taking the rest of the day off to look for a new fishing partner.

"I'm sorry about yesterday, Colonel. I was out of line and more than a little frustrated."

"That doesn't cut it, Pat. You seem to forget your position as a representative of the U.S., and that military people are due some respect."

Thoughts: *Shit....! I need a diversion.*

"Colonel, the General, and I have had a few misunderstandings due to the language barrier. I'm working on my Arabic. You may work for the OMC, but I'm not in the military, and this project is supposed to be a civilian construction project. We call a spade a spade."

"You do like hell; you call it a fucking shovel. You need to watch your language with the Egyptians."

Thought: *Fuck you too, Colonel*, but decided to change tactics and the subject. *Besides, Colonel Baker was in the Special Forces.*

"Colonel, I've had enough of this bullshit. Maybe, just maybe if you would spend your time trying to get the Egyptian military to cooperate with me, I might get done, and then you and General Olsen can devote your time to your real business, which appears to be figuring out how you're going to get that plane load of arms sitting on the Cairo runway to the Persians Gulf."

I pulled that one out of the air just to needle Colonel Baker. It had been on the nightly news for two weeks. BBC was spotlighting America's involvement in the war between Iraq and

Iran accusing America of siding with Iran. The subject came up when the Colonel showed up at an earlier meeting with Tom, he denied it, no, more than denied it. He was adamant. The rest of us did not have a clue at the time.

Google the Iran Contra Affair. The scandal was compounded when Oliver North destroyed pertinent documents between November 21st and November 25th, 1986, which was the week we had the discussion with Colonel Baker.

The Brits got it right this time, America was siding with Iraq. However, Oliver North and his friends from the CIA were covertly supplying arms to Iran to prolong the war and to keep Iran's focus on Iraq and away from Saudia Arabia and Israel.

Iraq and Iran had been at war for six years. Estimates of total casualties range from one million to twice that number. The number killed on both sides was close to five hundred thousand with Iran suffering the greatest losses.

The U.S. actively supported the Iraq war effort by supplying the Iraqis with billions of dollars of credits, military intelligence, and advice, and by closely monitoring third-country arms sales to Iraq to make sure that Iraq had the military weaponry required to prolong the war.

From the way the Colonel reacted I thought I hit on something. I made a mental note to go home by way of the airport and see if there was a U.S. cargo plane on the runway.

Iran is Persian and, although they are Muslim, they are bitter enemies of the Arabs. We were off the subject of pain and suffering and into a shouting match about American meddling in the Middle East. At the time I did not give a rat's ass. It was enough that the recent arms shipments to Iran were causing me problems with the Arabs involved in the project.

The Egyptians thought the Americans were siding with the Persians against the Arabs, which gave them an excuse not to trust me. I was ready to file my own pain and suffering complaint with the OMC.

General Aziz was having a tough time following our discussion. I have met a number of Generals, none of them like being left out of a conversation.

"Ah, Mr. Pat, I thought General Sayer solved the problem of the munitions building."

Oh, shit! Where the hell did that come from? It was my turn to be confused. The munitions building was the building on the site I asked General Sayer to empty before the project started.

The General thought I was complaining to Colonel Baker that General Sayer refused to move the arms and ammunition, and that he had posted armed guards around the area to keep my personnel away from the building. The munitions building had caused a delay because the soldiers guarding it cleared the area between it and the foundation area of the new building to plant a new garden for General Sayer.

When I objected to the garden because it was in the parking area for the Computer Center, General Sayer filed a notice with General Aziz demanding I move my fences out of the way so I would not interfere with his men. I nipped his garden in the bud when we excavated the site and dumped the debris on the garden site. That was one of the items listed on the pain and suffering complaint the Colonel was dealing with.

Arabic-English was not working, the General was also confused.

"Mr. Pat, I don't see that you have reason to complain to Colonel Baker about guns on the site, this is a military complex."

"General, I'm not complaining to the Colonel about anything." "Hamid, would you please try to sort the problem out with the General?"

"What problem, Mr. Pat?"

"I don't give a shit, Hamid, whatever you sort out is one less I have to deal with."

The General and Hamid started a conversation about *something*. I turned to the Colonel to find his attention diverted by the sight of Moya carrying a bucket of water.

"Hamid, tell General Aziz we don't have time for this shit, find out what the pain and suffering complaint is really all about."

The cloud in the room was pretty thick. It was time to calm it down.

"Colonel, it looks like Moya is either planning on making tea or flushing the toilet. If it is tea, would you and General Aziz like to join us for a cup?"

The Colonel mumbled something about, *how did I know so much about fucking airplanes*, and finished with:

"Tea, shit…., why not?"

I convinced Moya I would have Hamid send one of the laborers for another bucket of water to flush the toilet if she would use the one she brought for tea.

Hamid had a knack for confusing anyone. By the time Moya brewed the tea Hamid had confused the General enough to get him off the pain and suffering complaint. The General gave up the conversation with Hamid and joined us at the conference table in my office.

The pain and suffering complaints were off the table. It looked like I would have a little more time to figure out how I was going to keep from adding to the General's retirement fund. General Aziz remembered some appointment and rose up from the chair to leave. As he was going out the door, one of his aids came in and handed him a file; he turned to me.

"Mr. Pat. I need a favor."

He pulled the file out of his briefcase. Thoughts: *Son of a bitch! He is not pissed about anything. This is all a fucking game, a game I do not know how to play.*

"Sure, General. How many copies would you like?"

"Just one and be sure you use the machine that makes the print bigger."

I waited for General Aziz to leave the room so he would not hear the Colonel's reaction when I opened the file. The Colonel was engaged in a conversation with Moya about why she was carrying water instead of using the sink when I turned the documents over so the red classified stamp from the OMC was in sight. I was just getting into the second paragraph when the Colonel noticed the stamp.

"What are you doing with that?"

"I'm going to copy it for the General."

While the implication of it began to register, I asked Moya if she returned the other documents to the General. Before Moya could answer the Colonel reached over to pick up the file.

"What do you think you're doing, Colonel? This is classified."

"I know it's classified. It came from my desk."

"Don't get excited, Colonel. After all, you're the one who keeps telling me to cooperate with the General. Besides, this has nothing to do with our project."

The Colonel was livid. The document was a schedule of spare parts arriving in Alexandria destined for the Egyptian tank corps. It was part of the arms for Aid package to Egypt. General Aziz was in charge of the division of the Egyptian Army responsible for moving arms and munitions to wherever they were supposed to go in Egypt.

The General had been giving me documents to reproduce and enlarge for him ever since I copied the contract for the building. I knew better. I never kept copies and always returned them intact within 24 hours.

I had not seen any documents about arms shipments to Iraq or Iran, but there had been a number of landings by U.S. C-130 aircraft in the past two weeks. The scuttlebutt coming through British expats was there were shipments in transit bound for the Persian Gulf. From the Colonel's earlier reaction, I might have hit on something touchy. The Colonel tried to insist I give him the documents.

"Colonel, I have an idea. I don't care what's in this, any more than I care whether I ever copy another one for the General, but I'll copy this one and you return it to him."

We took the papers over to Tom's office. As the Colonel was leaving, I thought it was time to settle the pain and suffering complaint.

"By the way Colonel, what do you want me to do with the pain and suffering complaint?"

"Ignore it, the General may have some problems with his own pain and suffering for a while."

"Colonel, if you go storming back to the General's office and make a big deal about some lousy tank parts, you'll cause more headaches for all of us. There's nothing in the rules that says I can't copy papers pertinent to the project for the General. Tracking this shit is the goal of the Center when it's finished. The General and I are going to take the position that it's an early step in the scheme of things. Take them back to Aziz. When you do, ask him if he really wants to pursue the pain and suffering complaint. I think you can solve both problems at the same time."

I was hoping I had heard the last of both subjects. I knew the Colonel could not do anything about Aziz's lack of security. I also knew he had been around long enough to know the more he stirred the soup the messier the table was going to get.

After Colonel Baker left, I stopped in to see Tom and let him know Colonel Baker agreed to take care of the pain and suffering complaint. I then headed back to Abboud's office and Anwar.

"Hello, Sarha. Is Anwar in?"

"Yes, Mr. Pat."

"Did you give him my memo?"

"Yes, Mr. Pat."

"Thank you, Sarha, find Anwar and ask him to join me in my office."

Anwar showed up an hour later with my memo in his hand. He was cheerful; that was not a good sign.

"Anwar, did you read it?"

"Yes, Mr. Pat."

This was not going according to plan. Sarha followed Anwar into the room.

"Sarha, call the travel agent and book me a flight tonight."

Sarha looked confused; Anwar responded.

"Where are you going, Mr. Pat?"

"Home, Anwar. Where did you think I'd be going?"

Anwar gave me a quizzical look. Sarha chirped in with something about breaking off her engagement, and then.

"I thought you were leaving on the sixteenth, this is only the seventh?"

"Not now Sarha!" "Anwar, did you read the memo?"

Sarha does not like it when I raise my voice; she headed out the door.

"Anwar read the memo. Never mind! It says: You don't work for me so I can't fire you. But, if you don't stay away from Genera Aziz and off my site, and start doing what I ask, I quit. That's what the memo says. Now, since you're so cheerful, which do you agree to?"

Anwar did not say anything, I tried again.

"Look, Anwar, it's simple. I want you out of my office, off the site permanently, and if possible, out of Egypt until I finish this project. Doctor Osmond said something about some warranty work on a job you did in Pakistan. Why don't you go and see what the problem is, and don't come back until after tomorrow?"

"But, Mr. Pat, I was just trying to help."

"Please, don't try, Anwar."

We spent the next hour going over my complaints. Anwar did not understand, and, since Anwar has a heart condition, I did not want to upset him any more than I already had. I tried to make a deal.

"Anwar, do us both a favor. Find something else to occupy your time and leave General Aziz, Hamid, and me alone."

It was a useless exercise. Anwar was not aware I canceled his orders and hired the site work subcontractor. When I gave him the voucher from accounting he was upset, in his mind that was his job, and I paid too much. He lapsed back into Arabic.

It was after ten and past my bedtime, but it would be a while. I excused myself. The equipment was scheduled for delivery that night. I did not trust Anwar. Hamid would be at the site when the equipment arrived. I needed to make sure Anwar would not send it back.

The traffic had settled into a crawl. I noticed a large compactor parked alongside the road a few blocks from the gate. I let myself dream. I ordered a twelve-ton machine. Most of the equipment in Egypt would be considered obsolete in the U.S. The one parked alongside the road was a new thirty ton Cat.

Anwar was not there. Hamid and I were going over the schedule when the compactor I saw parked alongside the road showed up. It was a bonus I did not expect, and it would speed up the process.

Shit….! More Egyptian excitement. The compactor was approaching the site when the taxi in front of it lost a wheel and slid to a stop blocking the gate. The driver got out to open his trunk and took out a jack. The compactor was stopped in the road blocking traffic. Impatient drivers trying to pass were leaning on their horns and yelling at the operator to move on. The taxi was not going anywhere, at least not for the next hour.

We still needed a ramp from the curb to the site. I told Hamid to tell the equipment operator to pretend the taxi was not there and drive over it. Hamid said something about patience and then signaled the operator to take the compactor around the block. Hamid then rounded up a couple of laborers to help the taxi driver change the wheel.

The block meant the army base. It took the operator an hour to make the trip. I was wondering why I had not insisted on a new ramp when Hamid came in to tell me the Cat was on site. Hamid also mentioned something about a water leak. I was not quite into the Arabic-English and asked if it would interfere with the backfilling. Hamid's one-word answer, malish. (*no problem*)

When I arrived at the office the next morning Mohammed, one of Dr. Osmond's engineers assigned to the site was there. All of the roads into the area of the army base were closed.

We still did not have a phone at the site. Mohammad had no idea what was wrong, but it was apparent there was a major problem somewhere in Cairo. I decided to wait another hour and let the traffic clear up. When it did not, I tried calling General Aziz. No one picked up the phone.

I never did get to the site that day, or that night, and still had not made it by the next morning. The office and a whining Anwar in the background were not going to help the disposition I was trying to reacquire before my Christmas trip to the States.

It was getting close to my time of departure and Moya would also be going home for Christmas. She was at the office because she could not get to the site. Moya suggested we spend the day in a place on the other side of the city where there were we would find shops loaded with suitable Christmas presents at half the price as those in the shops in Cairo.

My driver said he knew a way around the traffic, and that getting to the bazaar was not going to be a problem. We left with the thought in mind that the evening schedule called for me to be at the theater for My Fair Lady by 8:30, and for Moya to join her husband for darts at eight.

The 20-klick drive took a little over two hours. It appeared all the drivers in Cairo knew the same route my driver knew, and they too were trying to avoid the traffic jams downtown.

The Impatient American

Moya and I spent the afternoon haggling with the local shopkeepers and filling the car with Christmas gifts. When we finished, we had plenty of time for the trip back to Heliopolis and our scheduled appointments for the evening.

However, my driver also takes a wrong turn now and again. One of the overcrowded buses forced him off the main highway and onto a street we were trying to avoid. Three hours later Moya was on her way to take her frustrations out on a dartboard, and I was on my way back through Cairo traffic to see if I could make it to the theater in time. I seriously considered giving the idea up, but I told Jim, Moya's father-in-law, that I would meet him for the show and dinner afterward.

I arrived at the theater at 9:30 for the 9:00 show figuring that if I missed the performance, I would still be in time to meet Jim for dinner. My timing was close and close counts in Cairo. The performers also faced the same traffic jams. There was a poster in the lobby; the show would start at 10:00.

Jim never did make it. I assumed he had more sense than I had and stayed off the roads for the night. With or without Jim I was looking forward to the performance.

The cast was made up of students and teachers from the American school in Madi. The theater was neat, orderly, and exceptionally clean by Egyptian standards. The play was excellent. Two glorious hours of organization later it was time to call it a day. When I left the side street where the theater was located, I found myself back in heavy traffic. It was another torturous trip. By the time I entered the open streets of Heliopolis, my nerves were shot, the lights of the trucks had nearly blinded me, and I was once again flunking my patience course.

As the traffic thinned, I was writing the day off and making plans for my trip home: daydreaming about clean Oregon air, even hoping for one of the winter rainstorms I dreaded in the past. I was a few klicks from my flat when one of the locals decided to test the resolve of a lone foreigner on a dark night.

I was traveling about 80-klicks an hour when a car started to pass. His partner opened his window, waved his middle finger, and then pointed to a bus a few hundred meters ahead. The driver was trying to force me to the inside lane where a bus was stalled.

He slowed, matching the speed of his new Mercedes to my wreck, crowding me closer to the side of the road. He did not intend to give way and allow me to escape into the clear. By the time I realized what was going on it was too late to make a safe stop.

Thought: *It is only metal and a few more dents in the side of my car would be better than the engine in my lap.*

I have always been of the opinion playing chicken with cars is a stupid game. In this case, I did not have much choice. I moved the car toward the other driver's lane as if he were not there. He veered off giving me clear access around the bus.

He was pacing alongside. When he looked over laughing, I gave him the universal sign of peace. His passenger objected to my sign language and started yelling out his open window. I ignored him and continued down the road. I *really* thought that would be the end of it.

The driver of the other car moved his Mercedes in on the back bumper of the piece of junk I was driving and started flashing his lights. I had had enough, it had been a long, *long* day and I wanted an end to it. I checked to make sure my Egyptian security pass was in my pocket and that there was only one car behind me.

I increased my speed, opened my window, stuck my arm out, and gave them the finger, *again*. He took the bait closing in on my bumper as I increased my speed to 120-Kph, 75-Mph. I then braced myself and planted two hundred pounds on the break.

The kid driving the other car had not realized I had been in Cairo long enough to know there were no rules. Trying to avoid my taillights he grazed the side of the new Mercedes off a concrete wall.

I thought that would be the end of it, but the driver managed to get his car under control and back on the road. I had slowed; it did not take him long to catch up. I ignored them but took the next turn off the main road to my flat that would take me past an army base. He was not inclined to give up. I waited until the last second. I looked in my rearview mirror hoping my sudden turn would leave them on the main road. Sliding sideways he managed to follow me through the turn. I decided to put a stop to the nonsense.

Shit….! I know. It was not a smart move for an infidel anywhere in the world, but lighted streets in front of an Army base and a dozen soldiers close by were a better choice than the dark alleys around my flat.

As I was getting out of my car I thought about Paul Newman and the movie Butch Cassidy and the Sundance Kid, and I formed plan-A. I also took out my Egyptian military security pass along with a few ten LE notes in case plan-A did not work, and I needed to go to plan-B.

The other driver slid to a stop a few meters behind my car. I looked over at the Army Base. When the other driver stopped the police were about a hundred meters away but were now closing.

I got out. The two men were in their late teens or early twenties, and probably driving daddy's car. The driver was having a fit, pointing to the car where the side was caved in, and the molding was dangling in the street.

I was leaning on the hood of my car waving back, giving two of the soldiers' time to approach. The driver of the car understood sign language, he took it personally and headed my way. Most of the affluent in Cairo spoke English. When he got within a hearing distance, I held up my hand.

"Wait, let's discuss the rules of engagement."

He was pissed and continued to walk towards me.

"What rules?"

He was a big kid, eighteen, maybe, but on the fat and sloppy side. He stopped a few feet in front of me, planting his feet wide apart. Thought: *big fucking mistake! You are no Mohammad Ali.* I kicked him in the balls.

Thank you, Paul Newman. The passenger ran up to help his friend. As soon as the kid hit the ground the guards heading for us accelerated to a run. I was reaching for my security pass and a few ten-LE notes, which were plan B. I confused the guards with my Arabic-English, then offered my Egyptian security pass for their inspection, along with 20-LE for clarification.

The driver's friend was looking as if he wanted to go home. I took the opportunity to hold out my hand to retrieve my pass. When I did, I passed a few more LE to the soldiers. By the time they handed back my pass the driver had recovered. He and his friend were arguing with one of the guards.

Still in my hand, the guard was pointing to my pass. It appeared the LE was making an impression because the big guard was stepping between me and the men, and he was smiling.

Egypt is mostly a paper army: ineffectual and unable to withstand challenges. These guys were regular army, not like the kids on Sayer's and Aziz's base, they meant business.

Room and board were provided, but military pay was a meager seven-LE per month. I had given them the equivalent of four months' wages. I reached back into my wallet and made it six for each of them. I figured the other driver could explain the mess to whoever was in charge.

I got back in my car and started to drive off. The kid had recovered and tried to stand in the way. They took him by the arm, leading him back to his car and pointed him back the way he came.

By the time I got to bed, it was almost four a.m. It was Friday and was supposed to be my day off. I set the alarm for noon. Andy's monkey had other ideas, and at about eight she decided to use the shutters on my balcony doors for a playground. Andy had gone out for breakfast and apparently forgot I had told him I was getting a craving for monkey stew.

I was looking for something to use as a club when Andy returned from breakfast carrying the morning English paper and hot coffee. The coffee and the newspaper diverted my attention from the monkey. I was beginning to relax until I read the feature story on the front page.

A 30-ton compactor is a vibrating machine that exerts tremendous force on the soil beneath it. When it is operating on a paved surface that was not properly compacted to begin with something has to give. Looking back, what Hamid meant by no problem was that the Nile River was not going to be affected by the flood.

On the way around the base the operator tested the vibrator on the pavement. Something did give, the 24-inch water main that supplied water to downtown Cairo. It was late. I was tired, and since the equipment was on site I decided to leave it in Hamid's hands. As I was driving out the gate I remembered Hamid's reflex response to the question of the water leak. I had a premonition, but it was late. I ignored it and headed for home.

I did not read the paper until the third morning because they had not arrived at the hotel where I had breakfast. I figured it was someone else's problem. The only good thing about the mess was Hamid and the crew were trapped on site with nothing else to do except get the work done.

I hate to repeat myself, but *you just cannot make this shit up*. I still have the clipping from the paper.

THE EGYPTIAN GAZETTE

12 DECEMBER 1986

MAIN WATER PIPE BURSTS, HALTS TRAFFIC

"The main water pipeline feeding Aggassia, Ani Shams University, and Manshiet Elbakbi burst yesterday, causing a traffic jam for several hours. Orders were immediately given by the Cairo Governor, Mr. Yussef Sasbri Abu Taleb to supply equipment to get rid of the water, which reached a depth of two meters. The Director of the Central Traffic Department, Major General Reda Abdulla, supervised the process of putting up traffic barriers to secure an easy flow of traffic and to prevent vehicles using Khalifa El-Mamum Street."

Thought: *Shit...., fuck!*

"Andy, I'm going to the site."

"I thought after you read the headlines you might want to change your roundtrip ticket to one way and move up your departure a few days."

Andy was laughing as I started to leave the flat.

"Andy, the monkey's hanging over the side of the balcony by her leash. She slipped off the clothesline."

Andy ran for the balcony. I headed out the door.

Hamid told me it was *no problem* when the water line started leaking. The water washed out a hole under the asphalt and a truck fell through crushing the 24-inch water line feeding downtown Cairo.

It took the Egyptian Army until noon the next day to find the valve to turn the water off. By then the water was standing seven feet deep in the underpass by the site and had flooded the local streets, which closed the main road into Cairo. The President's Palace is across from Sayer's base. He had to take an alternate route, which closed the other main highway.

The Presidential Palace in the area accounts for the brief time of ten hours it took the Army to shut the water off. The streets were not reopened until four a.m. this morning, which explains the traffic jams of the last two days.

Overall, the get-even week did not turn out too bad. The water line broke in front of the gate leading into the construction site when the operator turned the vibrator on before he entered the site.

I will not need as much water to compact the sand. The hole in the street is a plus because, until they fix it, it will slow traffic and make it easier to get in and out of the site. The contractor with the compactor does not dare leave for at least a week, so I know the work will be done. Best yet, I got even with all the Cairo drivers at once.

Chapter 24

How do you fire your boss? I was back in my patience class. Anwar wanted to give me *his new schedule* and go over the construction methods he wanted to use that had no resemblance to the contract specifications the COE expected me to follow.

At first, I said proposal A was not acceptable. Neither was B, C, D, or E. When he got to F, I started thinking it was not the conversation I wanted to end the get-even week with. I tried a novel approach. It took a few minutes for Anwar to realize the tone of the meeting had taken a turn. He was talking, and I was agreeing.

"Yes, Anwar." "That's fine, Anwar." "Good idea, Anwar." "Anything you say, Anwar."

Anwar quit talking. I called Sarha and asked her to ask Abraham to make me a cup of tea. Anwar was brooding over the paperwork. He started to say something; I interrupted.

"Whatever you say, Anwar."

Anwar was confused. The answers I was giving were the ones I had been hearing from him for the last five months. Anwar was brooding. Sarha brought me my tea. Anwar started with another question; I cut in.

"Anwar, let's discuss it after tomorrow, inshallah."

Sarha had been trying to get me to work on my Arabic; it appeared she felt I was in the mood because of my *inshallah* comment. She decided it was time to tell me why she was going to break off her engagement *again*.

Anwar was always interrupting our meetings with off-the-wall conversations with anyone who walked in the room. I did not see any reason not to engage in some chitchat with Sarha.

Sarha and I continued our discussion for about ten minutes while Anwar stewed in the background. This time, Anwar was upset because I was ignoring him.

I have never figured out why Sarha wants to break off her engagement, but she seems to feel better every time she tells me.

Sarha went back to whatever her duties were. I went back to the conversation with Anwar. I told him I had other things to take care of and was out of time. Anwar said he wanted to discuss a few more items.

"Fine, Anwar, after tomorrow, inshallah."

"Are you tired (sick), Mr. Pat?"

"Yes, I'm tired, Anwar."

"Ah, Mr. Pat, what has made you tired?"

"I'm sick and tired of your bullshit, Anwar. But I have a cure. When I leave, I'll have Sarha go to the doctor and get me a plane ticket."

Anwar was confused; to him, tired meant sick; he did not have a clue what sick meant. The doctor bit and the plane ticket was over his head. I gave up on Anwar for the day. Anwar left the office and disappeared. That does not mean a thing because there have been many times in the last five months when Anwar disappeared until *after tomorrow*.

Sarha came in a few minutes after Anwar left and told me I looked tired. I told her I was sick and tired of the whole mess and then asked if she had seen Doctor Abboud. Sarha was still on the sick and tired subject and said something about me going home. I told her I intended to, but the plane did not leave until Tuesday. Sarha then told me she thought Anwar was also *tired*, and she did not expect him back for a few days.

Abboud came in and started where Anwar left off, suggesting building the concrete forms out of mud bricks instead of plywood or steel as the COE specified. I was tired and sick of these types of conversations and decided to take Sarha's advice.

"Doctor Abboud, I don't feel well today and would like to deal with this later. Would it be all right if I didn't mention anything about brick forms to Tom until I see if I can find some steel or plywood?"

Abboud mumbled something about steel and plywood costing a lot more money.

"Doctor Abboud, I'll see Tom tomorrow. I don't feel well, I'm going home to get some rest."

Sarha had returned.

"But, Mr. Pat, your plane doesn't leave until Tuesday."

"My home in Heliopolis, Sarha."

Sarha and Abboud left. I called Tom and asked him if the meeting was still on for the next day. I was going out the front door when Abboud caught up with me.

"Mr. Pat, I set up meetings with the subcontractors for the first of the week. Can you delay your trip for a few days?"

"We've had four months to meet with the subcontractors, Doctor Abboud. I'm leaving Tuesday."

Abboud went on about how he had promised Cesar he would replace Anwar after the first of the year and was going to start overseeing the work himself. He asked me again if I would put off my trip for a few days or at least until I approved the plumbing and electrical subcontractors. Thought: *More bullshit, Abboud, not a fucking chance!*"

"Sorry, Doctor Abboud, but all flights are full, and my tickets can't be changed. Schedule the meetings for tonight and tomorrow morning. We should be able to finish by then."

As I opened the door to my flat, I was looking forward to a hot shower and a long nap. It was time to go back to bed, pull the covers over my head, and hope someone would wake up while I was asleep.

The houseboy was in the flat. I showed him to the door and told him not to come back until the next day. I then stripped out of my clothes to take a shower and wash the last of Abboud's conversation out of my mind.

It was a promising idea, but more poor planning. When I started to rinse the soap out of my eyes the houseboy let himself back in. He forgot to empty the washing machine and hang up the clothes.

I have never been able to get the plumber to reroute the clothes washer discharge from the shower head to the drain. When the houseboy discharged the water from the washer, the white soap in my eyes turned brown.

I escorted him out the door. I took another shower and headed for bed and a nap. Andy's monkey started using the shutters for a playground. I took my pillow into the living room and sacked out on the sofa. I had just fallen asleep, and then a banging on the door. The houseboy was back, he forgot his key. I gave it to him and pointed to the stairs. This time, he took the hint and did not return.

I was wide awake. The water buffalo I had for lunch was finding its way into my intestines; the Egyptian dinner from the night before was finding its way out.

I moved the monkey to the clothesline because it was Andy's clothes the houseboy had just washed. I took another shower and then started the nap routine over again.

I returned to the office at seven. For a change, a meeting took place on schedule, but it did not help the score in my patience class. The meeting was the same as the hundreds I had attended in Cairo. Everyone was making deals in Arabic. I was wondering what the hell was going on.

By four p.m. Tuesday, Abboud hired the plumbing, electrical, and mechanical subs. It did not seem to matter that I kept telling him that he should not sign the contracts until Tom and I reviewed their qualifications and approved them.

Abboud ignored me and said that by the time I returned from the States the plans would be finished, and the subcontractors would have hired the English-speaking supervisor the specs required. I was not convinced, but my plane left at two a.m. I wanted out of the office. Sarha broke into the meeting to say goodbye.

"What time does your plane leave, Mr. Pat?"

"At seven, Sarha."

I lied because Abboud was listening. I knew if I told her I still had ten hours before my flight, I would be in the office the rest of the night. I had not eaten that day, and I could use a drink. Dinner would take two hours, and it would take at least two more to clear security. My suitcases filled with Christmas presents were by the front desk.

"Sarha, ask Abraham to flag a taxi."

The cab arrived a few minutes later. I said goodbye to the staff and left for the Sheraton, a relaxing dinner, and a glass or two of wine before I had to face airport security and the grueling thirty hour flight home.

Try the perch.

I had never eaten in the seafood restaurant at the Sheraton because the prices were more than my budget allowed. I was going home, and on holiday, I would treat myself. The restaurant had a seafood display where you select your protein. Once you pick it out, the waiter brings it to the table and prepares it. The cooler contained an assortment of whole fish, shrimp, and lobster.

I picked out a half dozen jumbo shrimp, a fish that looked like a sea perch, and a small squid. I then found a table. I knew it would be a while, so I settled back with a glass of wine and mentally began preparing for the trip home.

The waiter brought what I picked out. That was a plus. I expected a mix-up of sorts and was pleasantly surprised they got it right. He also brought along what looked like a can of Sterna, a frying pan, and a bucket half-filled with water.

I did not pay attention while he was setting up the banquet until he cleaned the fish in the bucket and threw the shrimp in the frying pan, heads, hides, and all. It looked like I had made another mistake in the Sheraton. But I was also becoming curious. That lasted until the he put the fish in the pan without bothering to remove the head, gills, or blood membrane running the length of the backbone.

As he reached for the squid, *stop!* I calmly reached over and took the pan off the fire. I was trying to be pleasant and explained I thought it was a shame he was going to ruin my appetite before he ruined my dinner. He was upset, mumbling something about tourists, and as much as I did not want to, it looked like I was going to cause another scene in the Sheraton.

It did not take long. Achmed came over with one of the English-speaking customer relations people. It was no big deal to me. Before the conversation started, I offered to pay for the meal I had not eaten and leave quietly. Achmed said something to the waiter, then turned to me. We were on a first-name basis.

"Ah, Mr. Pat, you again."

I palmed a 10-LE note and shook his hand.

"Malish, Achmed."

I turned to the translator.

"Please tell the waiter I meant no harm. I'll pay for the food and go to another restaurant."

The woman translated. While Achmed was debating what to do, a group of Dutch tourists walked into the room to look at the seafood display. The waiter was telling Waffa, the public relations woman, that I insulted him. I was looking for a way out when one of the Dutchmen approached, and in English, he asked.

"How's the seafood?"

Waffa overheard the question, said something to Achmed, and then she stood there waiting for my answer. *What the hell!*

"Great, try the perch."

The tourists sat down at a table a few meters away. My plane did not leave for six hours. Meanwhile, my dinner was still in the bucket where I had emptied the frying pan.

The waiter had moved to the Dutchmen's table. I explained to Waffa that I had an idea. I told her if she had no objection, I would like to prepare my dinner on the equipment the waiter left at my table.

At first, the suggestion was unacceptable. I tried another approach and explained the new rage in the States were restaurants that had displays just like the Sheraton where people picked out their seafood and cooked it themselves. I also told her I was homesick and that it would make me feel better. I did not tell her that once you selected it in the States, you took it home to prepare it. The homesick line and a ten-LE note were a convincing approach.

Waffa and Achmed talked about it for a few minutes. If I did not mind paying the full price, and as long as I did not interfere with the other guests it was all right with her.

Since I had already invested twenty LE, I would try to make it the kind of meal I would prepare back home. I told Waffa, if she did not mind, I would like her to accompany me to the kitchen so I could get a few things. She told me that would not work, but if I gave her a list, she would see what she could do.

I needed a sharp knife, a cutting board, a large spoon, butter, garlic, a lemon, and another glass of white wine. Waffa told me the additional items were not included in the price; five-LE would cover it.

I gave her the note and sent her on the scavenger hunt while I headed for the salad bar. By the time Waffa returned, I had picked through the veggies and selected mushrooms, green peppers, onions, and a few miscellaneous I did not recognize but sampled and tasted surprisingly good.

After I laid everything out, Waffa and the restaurant crew thought they made a mistake. Waffa held up her hand for me to pause, then disappeared for a few minutes and came back with a white apron and a chef's hat. She asked me to put them on so other guests would not get upset about someone in cowboy boots and Levi's cooking in the dining room. I put them on and went about preparing my dinner.

Next order of business: clean the fish, peel the shrimp, and tenderize the squid. By the time I completed the tasks, my table was a mess. Waffa came to the rescue with a helper carrying a trashcan and new linen for the table.

By then, the waiter was plopping a perch into the bucket by the Dutchman's table. Achmed returned and joined Waffa at my table. It was not long before I had the butter, garlic, lemon, and veggies, along with white wine, simmering in the pan.

As I added the protein, the restaurant manager showed up. He was a little baffled, Waffa explained. After inspecting the pan simmering on the stove, he joined Waffa and Achmed at the table. The next thing I knew, the waiter was setting three more places.

I went back to the display to pick out another half kilo of shrimp and a small perch. Waffa frowned and pointed me toward the kitchen. This time, I was allowed to clean them at the kitchen sink before I brought them to the table.

It smelled and looked great. The only problem was, when I dished it up, I had only cooked enough for three servings. I never had seafood that night, but the wine and company were great, and the restaurant manager picked up the tab. I had a few hours before my plane boarded. I went to a German restaurant; Mohammad greeted me.

"Sorry, Mr. Pat, we're out of chicken."

Chapter 25

I had to clear security before entering the ticketing area. Security x-rayed and then inspected suspicious luggage. It is a delay I never object to.

The trip home was my first departure from Egypt. I thought it was just a security check. I was not aware customs also checked luggage for contraband. My two oversized suitcases drew their attention.

At the time, I still considered the restaurant on the coast of Oregon to belong to my wife and me. It had an area set up as a gift shop. The suitcases were the largest allowed by the carrier. I told him I had a big family and many friends. He was not buying it. There were fifty cotton sweaters and eighty small jewelry boxes. He did not believe they were gifts. I would have to pay export fees, which entailed a trip to customs.

My plane boarded in two hours; I did not have time. We spent the next 15 minutes arguing the point. It was going nowhere. I mumbled something about storing the gifts with my computer and that I would deal with the problem when I returned.

I turned to head for the ticket counter. The officer pursued me; he did not want to take responsibility. I kept telling him it was no big deal. The gifts had only cost a few hundred dollars, and I did not intend to miss my plane.

In the end, it had nothing to do with export fees. It was a currency issue. While I was waiting in the check-in line, he called another official who spoke better English. He asked me to prove I had exchanged foreign currency at a bank or a hotel and legally purchased the gifts. For a change, it was easy. I still had the receipt from the banker in my briefcase for the extra transaction when I was sorting out my visa.

I was lucky to be going at all. Hazem waited too long, making my reservations. The only flight available was on Yugoslavian Airlines, YAL for short. It meant an additional stop in Belgrade with a six-hour layover before a connecting flight to Paris. It added eight hours to the trip, but it was better than not going at all.

I gave my ticket to the attendant to claim my boarding pass. He told me I was #13 on the waiting list. Not only was I surprised, but so were the twenty or so other passengers who were told the same thing. YAL had overbooked the flight. Like American carriers, YAL did not give a shit.

I was arguing with the attendant when an American woman who was quarreling with the clerk in the next line tapped me on the shoulder.

"Do you speak Arabic?"

"Sorry, no; he understands English; he doesn't want you to know that."

Karen introduced herself as a teacher assigned by a missionary agency in the States to the Coptic Christian school in Cairo. She booked her flight before Thanksgiving but was also on standby. Karen was number nine.

Karen arrived a few hours earlier and had made calls to find another flight to Europe with a connection to the States. There were not any that she could get space on until after the first of the year. Karen was an American, and like me in a jam, I did not want to usurp her place in line.

"Karen, give me your ticket."

"Why?"

"I have a method that works in Cairo."

I had given up on traveler's checks and was carrying cash. I had receipts, so there was no risk of breaking another law. I simply wanted to go home so I gave in to the system.

I approached one of the supervisors standing in the background at the ticket counter and flashed a $50 bill, which was enough to divert the attention of any Arab in Cairo. Another $50 got our tickets on top of the pile of standbys. However, it took another $200 to get the boarding passes belonging to two others waiting in line to claim their seats.

We cleared the ticket counter after I paid $200 for shipping the extra luggage, which was supposed to be included in my original fare. With a boarding pass in hand, we left for the gate and, hopefully, an uneventful flight home.

Karen and I paused at the coffee shop while I cooled off enough to deal with the last security check before entering the final boarding area. Karen told me she was a first-grade teacher at one of the Coptic Christian schools, but it was more a missionary post than a teaching job. Her salary was a modest 80-LE per month with room and board. Karen was flying YAL because it was the cheapest ticket she could buy.

We spent the next hour becoming acquainted while we waited to board the flight. Karen was a nice woman. I was looking forward to the company going as far as New York, where Karen would be changing planes for Boston, and I would be heading to the West Coast.

They called our flight at three a.m., only an hour late, not bad by Cairo standards. We cleared the final security check without incident when Karen agreed to a body search after they found a female attendant, and I spent a few minutes on my knees repacking my carry-on after security emptied it on the floor.

I mentioned the carry-on search to Tom when I returned. He laughed. He and other ex-pats leaving Cairo, or for that matter, any airport in a Muslim country, leave their dirty undergarments on top of their clothes. It works. I guarantee you that *no Muslim is going to sort through your soiled shorts or panties*.

We boarded the flight and found our seats just aft of the forward bulkhead. Karen had an aisle seat; I had the window. After we settled, a rotund French passenger took the center seat. He was out of breath. He spoke fluent English. He and I chatted for a few minutes while the rest of the passengers found their seats.

As I was fastening my seat belt, the Frenchman grabbed me by the arm and made a frantic gesture toward his briefcase on the floor in front of him. He was having a seizure. I pressed the call button on the panel above me and then reached for the briefcase.

His body filled the space around him; I was struggling to prop the man back into his seat. The last of the boarding passengers came through the door. The boarding gate was closing when the flight attendant arrived. By that time, the Frenchman had succumbed to a heart attack.

"I don't have a problem, but I think this guy is dead."

The flight attendant called for the captain. By that time, the door to the plane was sealed, and we were backing away from the gate. The plane came to a halt. A few minutes later, the captain arrived. He examined the passenger, muttering something about wishing the man had died before he boarded the plane. He turned to the flight attendant and told her to announce we would be returning to the gate.

We sat at the gate for about 30 minutes before the captain returned with a doctor and someone from airport security. The doctor pronounced the passenger dead. He then turned and left with the captain. Another hour passed before the captain and flight attendant returned. It appeared that once we left the boarding gate, we were officially out of Egypt.

The man was French. She told me the Egyptians refused to allow them to remove a dead foreigner from the plane, and they would have to deal with the matter when we arrived in Belgrade. I told the captain I would prefer not to travel with a corpse in the seat next to me. The captain told me the plane was full. There was nowhere else they could put the body. He also told me if I wanted to get off the plane, he would call airport security and make the arrangements.

The Egyptians had no intention of dealing with a foreign national who died on the plane. Once the boarding gate closed, he was outside their authority. I did not intend to give my seat up to a corpse, especially since I just bribed the airline crew to get me on the plane.

"Captain, I'd prefer to stay on board. But if you don't mind, he's spilling over into both our seats. Can we move him to the window and strap him."

Karen had not said a word. After we moved and strapped him upright in the seat, she mumbled something about a sleeping pill in her purse. Since she would be sleeping and I would need to use the toilet, I asked her to trade places. She told me she preferred I remain the buffer between her and our traveling companion.

The flight to Belgrade was uneventful. The stiffening figure did not seem a lot different from Karen and other passengers taking the opportunity of a long flight to catch up on their sleep.

A meal was never part of the deal. There was not a restaurant open in the airport. Even after our delay in Cairo, our connection to New York through Paris was three hours later.

Belgrade is home to five of the fifteen most polluted districts on the continent. Foul coal plants, vast landfills, junk vehicles, and outdated heaters spew a cocktail of toxic particles. It was raining when we arrived. I looked out at a city painted gray by a mixture of soot and rain. Still, we could have left the airport and found a restaurant in the dingy city. Karen mentioned the possibility of doing so.

I was not interested and told her to go without me. Although we had both become accustomed to rampant pollution, I was not interested in trying to obtain a visa and taking a chance to miss my connection.

"The rest of the world is not like Cairo."

"I flunked patience, Karen. I have no intention of enrolling again until I return from the States after Christmas."

Karen had no idea what I was talking about. I was too accustomed to dealing with the Egyptians to realize Americans like to understand what you say and why you say it. Karen got a little testy after my patience comment, thinking I was referring to her. She said as much as she picked up her overnight case to find a more sociable area.

I am a little dense, but in this case, I caught on in time to convince her my state of mind had nothing to do with her. I did not think it was a good idea to take off on a sightseeing trip while we waited for the only connecting flight to Paris until after the first of the year.

We were still flying YAL and would need new boarding passes. My last session with their ticket counter in Cairo depleted my foreign currency. We might need what I had left until we were safely in New York; Karen understood the economics.

We switched to TWA for the crossing. We had dinner at a restaurant in the Paris airport during our layover. Karen and I parted company in Washington, DC, after we exchanged our Cairo phone numbers. She was to return about the same time I was. We agreed to make contact and perhaps get together for dinner.

I boarded United Airlines for the cross-country flight to Portland with an unscheduled stop in Chicago. I arrived in Portland four hours late. Same shit, different country.

Cesar relented and paid for my tickets, but on condition that we had a meeting when I arrived and another before I departed. I spent the next eight hours at the Airport Sheraton catching up on my sleep and preparing for a meeting with Cesar and Don before I could leave Portland for the coast of Oregon.

When I left the meeting, I felt as if I was still in Cairo. Don had not shipped the foundation materials, so they were going to be late, and Cesar, well…., Cesar just asked me when I was going to be done and when the COE was going to pay the next invoice.

I spent a few hours on the phone clearing the foundation anchor bolts for shipment by air so they would be in Cairo when I returned. I explained to Cesar that he could count on completion by August, but I was not sure what year.

Because of Don's lack of planning, I gave up an extra day and stayed in Portland one more night before heading for the coast. I had been away almost five months. Portland is a three-hour drive from my home. I called and suggested my wife pick me up at the hotel where we could get reacquainted and then make the drive together.

She felt it would be better if I rented a car so she would not have to drive me back after my holiday. It made a little sense, but the handwriting was on the wall. I could tell the separation was taking a toll on an already fractured marriage.

I spent a great deal of time during my holiday talking with friends about Third World life. I tried to explain what it is like to live and work in a world without rules and where no one is visibly in charge. I also tried to explain the filth, poverty, and the plight of the farmer and his family. The discussions reminded me of the ones I had with Anwar and Abboud. We simply did not speak the same language. My friends shook their heads as if I were making the stories up.

Christmas day spent with my own family had a sobering effect. As I watched a nephew struggle with the wrappings of his presents I wondered if all of the farmer's children lived through another month.

When my wife told my son to clean up for dinner, and he hesitated, I reflected on the pus in the eyes of the farmer's children and the snot smeared on their sleeves as they scooped mush out of a rusty tin bowl washed in creeks polluted with factory waste and sewage.

I was home but for a few short days. I almost convinced myself I was making up some of the stories. My family was healthy, as were my friends.

Our restaurant was a gathering place. In the dimly lit bar, I had difficulty seeing the garbage on the streets and the puss in the eyes of the village children.

It is no wonder our politicians cannot see the truth Third World leaders hide from them to maintain the status of military aid. I live in Cairo. I do not believe half of what I see. How can I expect those who have not lived it to understand narratives tempered by sarcasm and personal inflections?

The holiday was over quickly. I did not have enough time to adjust to the time difference, let alone clear my head enough to fully realize things were not the same at home as when I left in August. Mary, my wife, mentioned she was *growing*. I took her comment to describe the few pounds she put on while I was away.

Reflecting on the week, I should have pursued the conversation when she mentioned that *just because people love each other does not mean they can stand living together*. A comment I took at the time meant she was upset at our youngest daughter, whose room has always looked like a Cairo rubbish pile.

The phrase, *close counts* had become something I was accepting in daily life. The five-month separation gave my wife time to reevaluate our lives together, and my errors and omissions of the prior twenty-three years. My inability to deal with domestic confrontation had rubbed off. Although she neglected to tell me at the time, she concluded she had made a mistake staying with me as long as she had, and she was looking forward to a continued separation.

Before I left, I reminded Cesar about the language in my contract. I was entitled to business class. I refused to repeat a forty to fifty hour grueling trip in the back of the bus. Since I had three days, I rebooked business class on British Airways: Twelve hours over the pole through Paris with a two-night layover, and then five hours to Cairo.

By the time I arrived in Cairo, after two days of French cuisine, excellent wine, and Paris nightlife, thoughts of my domestic situation at home had faded.

Chapter 26 - January 7th, 1987

The plane approaching the Middle East caused me to reflect on the changing status in America. During my waking moments, I reflected on my conversations with friends in the States. I wondered how long it would take them to realize they were only a few short years away from reality themselves.

My homeland, a country of vast cities and plains.
Known for its beauty and people's high aims.
Some cities are now a wasteland of trash,
Some rivers polluted, some forests just slash.

Will the leaders of home ignore the world's past?
Will we let them, as it creeps up on us fast?
What will it be in a few short years?
Will the legacy we leave be just a few tears?

How long will it take those who are there,
To see what is real and to understand fear.
I looked all around, and I saw the blank stares.
I wonder how many of them really care.

Was it just me, or are they so out of touch,
They will never believe, it's simply too much.
I can't say that I blame them; it's a faraway land.
If I hadn't been there, nor would I understand.

I would like to explain and for them to know,
I send photos, to them it's just show.
They are simply pictures, truth not in the least,
Perhaps it's better to leave them in peace.

You can't open a mind that has never been there.
Will they ever believe the stories I share?
Would it be best to leave them alone?
I wonder why I feel a need to atone.

As the plane settled into its final approach, I thought about how little I was doing to make up for the lack of caring by the leaders I dealt with every day. I also thought back on some of the philosophies I have developed over the years. I was having strong doubts about my convictions.

I try not to preach, nor do I attempt to impose my views on others. As I look out on the polluted and wasted city, I must accept reality. I had managed to escape for a time. I did not relish the thought of having to accept things, not as I wanted them to be, but as it is for those forced by birth to live in the Third World.

I am still not sure what troubles me the most. My inability to understand the circumstance that placed me here merely as an observer, my refusal to accept responsibility for what I see, or my inability to see a change in the future of those caught up in a world alien to where I call home.

As I left the airport and reentered the streets of Cairo, my mind was cluttered with thoughts. The construction problems were business. The sights in the slums and villages were another matter and much more difficult to deal with.

I know it is impossible to solve the world's problems in the short span of one man's lifetime. After all, none of us can offer more than we can give without draining that which we have acquired. For some reason, I felt detached from the world I had reentered, and therefore, I should not regret my inability to solve another society's problems.

I know my sanity is attached to reality by a thread of personal experiences, sometimes combined with my concern for others. I also know if I put too much strain on my mind, then, like a donkey hitched to a Cairo cart with a worn harness, something is bound to snap.

Perhaps if I could convince those I left behind to take time to read between the lines of the publications in the world, they would find that most of their problems are minor. In that event, then perhaps they, like me, will accept the pictures of the starving world as real and conclude living is better than simply existing. If they do, they might take the opportunity to make the best of the few short moments they have.

I wrote the above thirty-five years ago. Today, as I write this, reflecting on that day, as sad as it is, it was a prophecy. Millions of destitute refugees are pouring across our borders. Yes, mixed with rapists, murderers, and drug dealers.

The inner cities of the U.S. are filled with homeless. Drugs are rampant, trash and human shit litter the streets. What were pristine neighborhoods forty years ago are now growing pockets of slums.

One only has to walk the streets of New York, Los Angeles, San Francisco, Portland, or Seattle, which are only a few of the major cities in America that have succumbed to the apathy of many of the rich and powerful unaffected by America's changing tide.

Those who live in the suburbs refuse to see the cities as they are. Pollution is a stark reality and not far from that of the back streets of Egypt. Trust me, it is coming your way.

As I entered my flat, I made a mental note to take time and go back to the farmer's village. I also decided to start my new patience class first thing in the morning. Andy was gone; the monkey was sitting on the mirror ledge in the bathroom.

It took twenty minutes to catch and tie her on the balcony over the landlord's clothesline. I left a note telling Andy the monkey, or I would have to find new quarters. I then left for the office and my New Year meeting with Dr. Abboud.

January 8, 1987. Same shit, new year.

Doctor Osmond told me he had sent Anwar to Kuwait for six months. At least this time, I knew what after tomorrow meant.

Abboud had officially taken over Anwar's duties. I was to work with him to see to it the Computer Center was done on schedule, and within budget. Thought: *fat chance.*

"Doctor Abboud, have the subcontractors delivered the plans?"

"The subcontractors called and said the plans will be done by the twenty-fourth.'

"Doctor, when I left for Christmas, you assured me the plans would be ready when I returned. The twenty-fourth is two weeks away."

Abboud told me to have patience and not to worry about it the first day I was back. I spent the rest of the day in my office with the staff, welcoming me back and avoiding conversation about the project.

The revolving door was working. There were changes in the few weeks I was away. Hatem and Hazem found employment elsewhere. Hazem was my assistant and dealt with local agencies and ministry offices. Hazem and I had also developed a friendship *of sorts*. Hazem went to work for the Egyptian Government in some training capacity. I was going to miss Hazem.

I had not seen much of Hatem since the first meeting with General Aziz. Hatem left to start his own export business. *Good riddance, I say.*

Andy chose not to go home for Christmas. He was saving his money to buy a place back home. Although it was supposed to be in-country, my Christmas holiday was in my contract. Andy had not been on board long enough to earn a paid vacation.

"Good morning, Andy. Have the anchor bolts arrived?"

"Yes and no."

"Andy, I just got back; what the hell does that mean?"

"They arrived, but they're still at the airport."

"That's better; making sense helps. How long have they been there?"

"A week."

"Why doesn't someone go get them?"

"It's a long story."

"Make it short."

The story took up the rest of the morning. I paid a premium to have them shipped by air; the anchor bolts arrived a few days after I placed the order.

It was against the law to import steel bolts because they manufactured them in Egypt. Andy, Tom, Abboud, and the Egyptian Army all tried to explain to Customs the materials for the contract were, according to an agreement in hand with the Egyptian Government, duty-free.

Customs would not buy the story and insisted on a letter from the Ministry of Defense. Once we got the letter from the Ministry of Defense Customs wanted a letter from the OMC because I instructed the freight forwarder to address the bolts care of the OMC. Once we obtained the letter from the OMC customs turned the problem over to the Ministry of Trading and Imports because it was their law we were trying to circumvent.

The Army and the OMC addressed the letters to customs. The Ministry of Trading refused to accept them. They insisted we obtain new letters addressed to them before they would allow customs to release them, which took a while, but we managed. For some unknown reason, Customs still refused to release the bolts.

"Tom, this has been going on for three weeks. What am I supposed to do now?"

"Give the shipping documents to Gary."

I gave the papers to Gary, who left for the Embassy to pick up Colonel Baker and see if they could sort it out.

"Tom, don't you think it would be easier if the COE waived the Buy American Act on this one item so we can all go back to work?"

"Can't be done; I already tried."

Tom was as frustrated as I was. The Government freight forwarder had misplaced the materials, and the project had been at a standstill for thirty days. It was February first. Six months were remaining. The work was only 5% complete with no materials on hand to proceed. I had not addressed the cost of the delays because the COE would not pay if we delayed the project ourselves concurrently with the delays the Government and Egyptian military caused. The big issue came to a head.

"Patrick, where are the fucking plans?"

"They'll be here on the fifteenth."

"You told me the twenty-fourth of last month."

"I know. Abboud brought them to me. Truthfully, they were shit. I rejected them."

Tom and I were having the same problem. Neither of us could figure out how the subcontractors could do the work if they could not prepare a legible set of plans.

"Pat, you're lucky the freight company delayed the shipments. That's out of your control. If the materials arrive before your plans are approved, I won't be able to grant you added time or the cost for the shipping delays. Glen will take the position you're running late concurrently and place you on liquidated damages the day the contract is scheduled for completion. Find a way to get the fucking plans done."

"I'm working on it, Tom."

I sent Cesar a telex telling him to either hire a firm Stateside or send a qualified engineer from the States to oversee the engineering of the project. Cesar answered the next morning, insisting that the JV agreement stipulated the Egyptians were to supply the plans.

I responded by telling him it was fine with me, but the COE was adamant. Unless I found a way to get acceptable plans or at least a definite schedule for them, the COE would not pay for any more materials shipped from the States. Both he and Dr. Osmond would miss out on reimbursement due to the initial delays caused by the Egyptian army and now the shipping delays caused by the COE freight forwarder.

The pipeline was full, and bills were past due. Without a legitimate basis for a time extension, it was going to get extremely expensive for both Ceasar and Dr. Osmond, very soon.

Cesar and I had been arguing for months. Dr. Osmond and Abboud simply ignored the warnings. We were six months into the contract. Liquidated damages loomed on the horizon, as did the continuing cost of managing the project past the twelve month deadline. I prepared an estimate as to what it would cost. It came to $8,500 a day and change without Dr. Osmond's Egyptian personnel.

Dr. Osmond had refused to pay for American engineers. I do not know what kind of deal they cut, but with the money cut off and the project going down the toilet, they both conceded, *almost*. Not one, but three men were on their way from the Philippines. I sent another telex asking Cesar if they spoke English.

Cesar sent me a return telex asking me why I was telexing so much. They would arrive in a week, and yes, they spoke English *a little*. He also noted that the freight forwarder found the materials they misplaced earlier. The shipment was stored at a military air base in South Carolina. They would be leaving the port of New York in two to three weeks, *maybe*.

The next morning, I went to Tom's office to see if Gary and the Colonel made out any better than I had on the anchor bolts. Gary and the Colonel were there when I arrived. Gary told me it was going to take at least another two weeks to get the paperwork sorted out and the bolts released.

"Patrick, if you had shipped the bolts through the freight forwarder instead of by air, we wouldn't have the problem."

"Colonel, get off my ass. If I had shipped the fucking bolts through the freight forwarder, they would still be in South Carolina with the rest of the material we shipped in November."

Tom sent me back to my office to cool off and work up a new schedule. On the way out the door, I turned to Gary and the Colonel.

"Colonel, it's my understanding the American Government is giving the building to the Egyptians, and all we had to do was buy it and build it. How come you always seem to think I should be the one to solve your problems?"

Colonel Baker did not have an answer.

"Colonel, I'll make you a deal. If you somehow manage to get your people to cooperate and deliver the materials to the site by March 4, we'll finish the building in the five months we have left."

"Tom, I don't need to change the schedule. I'll assume the Colonel will solve the delays and the materials will arrive on time. I'll do my job and see what I can do about some plans so I can start the work when the materials do arrive."

"Pat, it's February, you don't have any plans, and your people in the States still haven't ordered all of the materials. Even if you had plans and the States catch up, you haven't hired qualified subcontractors to do the work, and if you have, I haven't seen the paperwork. How do you expect us to feel?"

"Colonel, I have foundation drawings, and that sub is approved. That material is sitting in Cairo. The OMC is responsible for getting it released. It appears that isn't going to happen in a timely manner. When I get the rest of the materials, I'll figure out a way to get them installed. In the meantime, see if you can do something about relaxing the Buy American Act so I can at least get the fucking foundations done!"

"Forget it, I already tried."

"They're fucking bolts, Colonel. They're in Cairo; payoff whoever you have to." "What the hell, Tom? Six months is a good estimate. The way I see it, the materials will start arriving sometime in late April, *maybe*. We'll be lucky to be out of here by Christmas."

"You need plans before you can do anything, Pat."

"I know, but they wouldn't be much good without the materials. Cesar is sending three engineers from the Philippines. It's a lousy pre-engineered metal building. That will settle the issue with the plans. The Egyptian freight forwarder is your problem, Colonel."

"Do they speak English?"

"How the fuck do I know, Tom?"

Chapter 27

Chico, Deo, and Amonte would arrive on schedule. They all had master's in engineering. *Yes, they all spoke English.*

"Tom, there won't be much for me to do on the site until the anchor bolts arrive and the plans are caught up. I'm going to take a few days off. What about you? Can you manage another fishing trip?"

"Let's try next month. The fishing is best from mid-March through the end of May. By the way, don't leave Cairo until you get an Aids test."

"Now, what the fuck are you talking about?"

"It's a new rule. Expats assigned to a military post in Egypt must have a current test showing a negative result. You have a week, or your security pass and visa will be revoked."

"Where in Cairo are we supposed to get it done?"

"At the Embassy if you like. If not, you can always opt for one of the Egyptian hospitals, but I understand they use the same needle for all the tests."

"Thanks, Andy, and I will settle for the American method; anything else?"

"Yes, Colonel Baker is aware of Andy's monkey. He wants her tested, too. I understand she has bitten you, Andy, and a few of the Egyptians. According to medical research, the disease originated from her species. I've taken the liberty of setting an appointment for the three of you with the Embassy nurse at four p.m. today."

"Thanks; how long will it take to get the results? I hear it takes two to three weeks in the States."

"They have all the equipment at the clinic. The preliminary results will be ready in twenty-four hours. I'd appreciate it if you and Andy would stick around until those results are in."

Tom called the next day. All three tests came back negative. Andy and I breathed a sigh of relief. We had not said much to each other during the testing and the waiting period that followed. The monkey was a concern. Andy bought her from a vendor at the bazaar. We had no idea as to her origin or, for that matter, the state of her health.

It was no one's fault. HIV had only recently reared its ugly head in the States. It was not something neither Andy nor I had considered when he bought the monkey. Still, it was a major relief for both of us.

After Tom's call, I told Andy I was taking a few days off. I stopped at the flat long enough to take a pee and shower. The monkey was sitting on the back of the toilet. Andy was in the bathroom soaking in the tub.

The embassy clinic insisted we quarantine the monkey until the results of some additional tests came in. They did not have the equipment and the blood samples had been sent to the states. It would take another week. They had no place to keep her and did not want her put down for reasons unexplained to me. She had bitten both of us on numerous occasions; they did not see any harm in us keeping her.

"Andy, the engineers will arrive in a few days. I'm going to have them share this flat with you and the monkey. I'll move back into the hotel until I find a new flat. I'll be out of here by the time they arrive."

Andy did not have a choice. My contract gave me the option of living alone. Andy had neglected to read the fine print. He had to share quarters if more personnel arrived.

By the time Andy finished his bath, cleaned up the monkey shit in the bathroom, and the hot water tank recovered, it was too late to leave that day. I went to bed looking forward to the trip and a change of housing.

The next morning, I headed toward the main intersection in Heliopolis. When I got to the roundabout, I would take off in the direction of least resistance. That way, I would end up in one of three places: Alexandria, Suez, or Ismailia.

I prepared for any type of accommodation. I brought a can of Raid, bed linens, and towels in case I ended up at one of the Egyptian three-star hotels. The roads were jammed with morning rush hour. For a change, the snarl of traffic and honking horns did not bother me. I was not in a hurry. Normal check-in for a hotel in Egypt was around three p.m.

I let traffic guide me through the roundabout. When I exited from the maze I was on the way to Ismailia. It was a good sign. I took time the night before to check hotel accommodations. I was able to make reservations at the Etap Hotel in Ismailia and the Sheraton in Alexandria. Other than dodging a few buses and some of the larger potholes on the highway, the trip was uneventful. I checked into the Etap at 2:45. My room would be ready by six.

When I returned to Cairo, I downloaded my notes and prior correspondence to the States onto disks and erased them from the hard drive. It was a somber moment. My writing had been entertaining and often my only touch with reality during my first seven months.

I made it a point to send my stories home. I was receiving letters each month from the few friends I had in the States. For the first six months, I savored the mail from home. The ones I looked forward to most were those from my own family.

Sarha gave me two letters the day I left. When I arrived in Ismailia, having a few hours while I waited for my room, I took a seat by the pool to breathe fresh air and read the letters from my wife and daughter.

The contents were unexpected and more than unnerving. It seemed I was guilty of new errors and omissions. As a result, the letters had a major effect on my life. They changed my future and, in so doing, the future of those I cared about back home.

The hours I spent writing were my way of dealing with the culture shock and daily frustration of dealing with the JV. Putting my experiences in writing and sharing them with family and friends helped keep it in perspective.

I intended the stories to be entertaining and, although a little sarcastic at times, educational. The stories were true, but I had taken some literary license. I offended my daughter. My wife believed I was having an affair with Sarha. I did not know it then, but it gave her the excuse she needed.

It never occurred to me that what I was experiencing would be so foreign to those back home that they would not be able to accept the truth, and they would take my sarcasm as a personal attack on them.

Quoting from my Christmas correspondence, "*Overprivileged children*," who are you to talk? The bucket of sand for Christmas was too much. My daughter felt I was disappointed in all my kids. She reminded me they were a product of their upbringing. If something was lacking in them, I should look in the mirror for the one responsible.

After chastising me for hurting my daughter's feelings, Mary concluded I was physically involved with Sarha. It had come up, I blew it off, and she did not press it while I was at home.

My being there had caused a great deal of stress. There was a lot of tension in the air. By the time I left, I was depressed and frustrated. I let it slide, chalking it up to the pressure of the business Mary was running while I was away and the personal relationships in my daughter's life, which I felt were causing her typical teenage growing pains.

The letters made clear subtle comments I had not taken seriously. I had been naïve and made excuses because I still did not have the integrity to face reality in my own life. I thought my midlife crisis was behind me, and we were working on a fresh start.

I had let myself believe I had taken the project to give my family room. We also needed the money. They were used to better things in life. My financial setback happened at a crucial time in all their lives; it was difficult for them to adjust to having less.

I believed what I was doing was atonement for the past while trying to establish some security for the future. I also thought most of our issues were dealt with and we all agreed the job in Egypt was in our best interests. I know now it was narcissistic.

I read the letters twice that day and again after breakfast the next morning, and then I dumped them in the trash. I did not realize it then, but looking back, it was at that moment when I moved on.

It is never easy to accept personal responsibility, let alone simply apologize. I had rationalized my leaving was not only to get away from the IRS and redeem some of the financial losses of the past but also to allow them to, as they often put it, grow without my authoritarian personality smothering their day-to-day lives. Based on the contents of the letters, I had succeeded.

My ability to accept reality was like the Egyptians around me. *Second thoughts: sins of the past, always second thoughts, crept back in.* My kids, like my wife, were unable to read between the lines. Neither my wife nor my daughter understood the overprivileged I was referring to was more a reflection of my past.

I was injecting more into the letters and stories than I thought. I enjoyed my time in the evenings and my time off writing. I did not want to have to pick and choose what I said or to whom I referred. When I returned from Ismailia, although I kept a personal journal, I quit writing newsy letters and stuck to specifics. It was not fun anymore; my letters home dwindled to one or two a month.

By the time I returned to Cairo, I had slipped back into denial. I simply refused to accept the situation for what it was. I knew the contract was going to take a great deal longer than anticipated. If I wanted a home to go to, I had to do something different. I chalked it up to the length of time we had spent apart.

I decided my wife, and I just needed to spend some time together. I called and asked Mary to spend a few weeks in Cairo.

She agreed *reluctantly*. We scheduled her trip for the first week in April.

When I returned to Cairo, the engineers had arrived from the Philippines and moved in with Andy. I moved back into a hotel and looked for a new flat. I managed to find what I thought would be acceptable housing. It was not up to the standards of the U.S., but it was close. The only problem was it might not be ready to move into when Mary arrived.

In the interim, I made a deal with the property owner to rent her flat. It was furnished and nice by Egyptian standards. The furniture was not to my taste, but it was clean, the toilets did not leak, and the closest Mosque was a half-mile away. If mine was not ready on time, the property owners would suffice.

I was arranging for Mary's arrival while the engineering staff were busy drawing the plans. I had waited eight months for the Egyptians to start. Tom was off my back because we were caught up and turning them in regularly, and now that materials were arriving on the site, the building was taking shape.

The Middle East and the American Military are revolving doors. Fresh faces surface, and old ones disappear without a trace. Colonel Baker transferred out. General Olsen was preparing to leave for the States and attend his retirement party. I never heard from Anwar again.

The building was progressing per our original schedule. It appeared it would take twelve months. They would start from the time the materials began arriving on the site, which was the middle of March 1987, eight months after the original start date.

Mary arrived as planned. We took the usual tourist trips to the Pyramids and some of the other local sights. We also took a two-day trip to the Red Sea and a fly-swatting excursion into the Sinai, the land of Moses. Mary made an outward effort to enjoy herself.

A few days before her departure I mentioned we might reschedule her flight for a week or two later. It was apparent she was reluctant and anxious to leave. I did not question her. She was relieved when we let the schedule stand.

Letters from home grew distant. Phone conversations became more intense. Reality aside, I rationalized that my presence at home was more important than my loyalty to the project or my fight with the IRS.

It appeared the major headaches were solved, or soon would be. I called Cesar and told him I would not be renewing my contract; he, too, seemed relieved.

The next few months filled again with renewed frustration and aggravation. I was anxious to leave, but Abboud was up to his old tricks, and Don forgot where Cairo was. Tom was becoming anxious. There was progress, but there were many unanticipated delays.

Distracted by what was going on at home, I was not paying as much attention to the project as I should have. I continued to address day-to-day, but my mind was on phone calls and letters from home. I reckoned I had done all I could, and the new headaches belonged to the OMC and the new PD.

I spent the better part of July cleaning up my files and settling outstanding issues that were my responsibility. Tom was calling me a quitter. I could see he was disappointed because I was making Cesar change horses in the middle of the stream.

Carl arrived on August 9, a week late; at least, I thought he was late. I asked Cesar to send him a week before my departure, which was August 10. Tom was anxious, and I thought he would need to break in before he tried to tackle General Aziz and Abboud.

I was the only one from the JV concerned. The money was flowing again, and I had negotiated a time extension and a healthy reimbursement from the COE for the delays. Abboud convinced Cesar the job was going smoothly and that the transition would be simple. Muhammad's birthday was coming up, which would give the new man at least ten days to adjust to the culture.

Carl would be taking over my flat. My driver picked Carl up and brought him to Tom's office, where I was saying my farewells and going over the last open change order with Tom.

Carl arrived on the scene fresh and overly aggressive. Without waiting for introductions, he asked what I was doing. I told him I was settling a change order with Tom. Carl told me my responsibilities were finished, and he would handle business matters left undone. I did not much care. Tom did not like his attitude.

"Who the hell are you?"

"My name's Carl. I'm the new Project Director."

"Not on this job, you're not."

"Fuck…., now what? Wait a minute, Tom. What's going on?"

Tom was guilty of errors and omissions of his own. He knew Caral would arrive that day.

"I don't know who this guy thinks he is, but until I get a letter from the JV rescinding your authority and his resume, I have no intention of dealing with anyone but you."

"That's fucking bullshit, Tom. You've known for a month I'm leaving. Why wait until the last minute to start an uproar?"

"You said he would be here last week. I've been gone. I don't know a thing about the man. Glen and I have no intention of accepting him as your replacement until we know he's qualified to take over."

"I thought Cesar sent you his resume, and the issue was settled."

"More bullshit from your outfit. We were supposed to receive it before he left the States. I never received it, or any formal notice you were being replaced. No one is going to cram someone down my throat just because you have a plane to catch. Tell your boss I'll shut the fucking project down first!"

"Fuck…….! Carl, let's talk."

There was more to this. Tom had been gone for three days. I had never seen him that pissed. Carl started to interject, but I took him aside. He did not have his resume with him. Shit…...! I told him that unless he wanted to be on the next plane west, he had better wait outside and let me deal with Tom.

"Tom, what the hell is this really about."

"You, we finally see the light at the end of the tunnel, and you bail. The guy is in his sixties; he looks eighty, and he's a fucking mouse. From the looks of him, Abboud and Aziz will have him for lunch. I need his resume, or you need to stick around."

"Tom, I'm going home; Abboud has Carl's resume."

"I'll be here until five."

I called Abboud and asked him to have someone deliver Carl's resume to Tom. Abboud asked me what the problem was. I tried to explain. He told me he would deliver it personally. Abboud wanted me gone as much as Cesar. I figured that would settle the issue. I took Carl over to the site to introduce him to Andy and the staff.

Andy was at the gate with the Filipino Engineers. Chico, Amante, and Deo had been in Cairo for six months. They renewed their visas after a trip home. The visa had expired again, and they were in the grace period.

"Andy, where the hell are you going? I told you I'd be back."

"Immigration called; we have to get their visas renewed."

Andy caught me off guard. Carl was standing off to the side. I forgot he was there and failed to introduce him to Andy.

"Andy. I'm leaving. Abboud assured me he would have it taken care of by the end of the week."

"When did you start believing anything Abboud says? I called him. Their contract ends in two weeks. Abboud said his engineers would finish the plans."

I was running late. I was leaving the next day, but until then, I was still in charge.

"That's fucking bullshit, and you know it. Tell them to go back to work. I'll straighten it out with Cesar."

The Engineers were not having any part of it. Immigration had contacted them and told them their grace period was running out. They would soon be in the country illegally and subject to fines and imprisonment.

"Deo, please, have some patience. You have another two weeks; stick around, at least until then."

"Same shit, different PD, Andy. He's green; the two of you will need to stand up to Abboud and Cesar, or this project will go down the toilet. By the way, I want you to meet Carl."

"That's another issue. Tom just called; he wants you back in his office ASAP. He has a problem with Carl."

Carl was not saying much. Tom's comments had taken the wind out of his sails. He was reluctant to discuss his resume with me on the way back to Tom's office. All he would tell me was that he spent a few years working as a PM for the COE in Riyadh, Saudi Arabia. I thought it strange. Tom and Glen had been in Riyadh until just before their assignments in Cairo; I thought they would have known the other COE personnel assigned to the area.

Glen had just left his office when we arrived. Tom was getting up.

"I have to use the head."

Tom was pissed. He was gone longer than he needed to be. I sat there reflecting. Carl sat off to one side. Tom returned, sat down, leaned back, cupped his hands behind his head, sat there a moment with eyes closed, and then let out a big sigh before he opened his eyes.

"Tom, this isn't like you, what's up?"

Tom ranted for a while. For starters, I knew he despised Abboud and his constant interfering bullshit. When Abboud attended one of our meetings it was always the Egyptian army's, the COE's, or mine, or Andy's fault.

Abboud personally delivered Carl's resume and fed Tom a load of crap about how qualified he was. Abboud told Tom Cesar had fired me, that I made up the story of having resigned, and that everyone was going to be happy with a change in management.

Abboud left before Tom read Carl's resume. The fact was Carl was not going to be an acceptable replacement for the project.

"Abboud's a prick, Tom. I don't give a fuck what he thinks."

Tom made it clear he was not going to allow the project to continue without qualified American supervision. As far as he was concerned, Carl was off the project. It was no longer my problem. Still, I was at a loss for words. Tom broke the silence after Carl and I turned and started for the door.

"Pat, read this shit. Abboud thinks he's running the show, and I'm going to accept Carl because you're leaving, and I have no other choice. That's bullshit. You can tell him and Cesar that the project shuts down the minute you exit Egypt, and it won't resume until I have a qualified American replacement on site, one whom Glen and I approve in advance of his arrival. You can also tell them I will be instructing DC to hold all funds."

We had been through that a few weeks earlier. When I gave my notice, Cesar sent Don's resume to the Washington COE office. He did not have the experience; he was rejected.

Ceasar did not bother to send Carl's resume before he left the States. It was not necessary to read past the first page. Carl did not lie. He had been a PM for the COE in Saudi. His assignment was material procurement and distribution. Carl had managed procurement contracts, but he had never been a construction manager.

Cesar had not reviewed the latest update which showed the construction work was only 60% complete, with the most complicated issues of mechanical and electrical still ahead.

Tom and I discussed the turn of events with Carl. Carl was also upset. Cesar told him the construction work was 90% complete, and it was a matter of finishing the paperwork and closing out the books.

“Pat, what are the chances of you staying on until Cesar can send a qualified replacement?”

“My plane leaves at nine tomorrow, Tom. As far as Cesar and Abboud are concerned I’m off the payroll at the end of today.”

“Look, Tom…., settle. Hold the payment, but everyone is gearing up for Muhammad’s birthday. There isn’t going to be anyone working on the site for at least ten days, that’s in the current schedule. I will be in Portland the day after tomorrow and talk to Cesar. Let the rest slide until the end of next week. By then, Cesar will come up with somebody.”

A bottle of Jack and two glasses were sitting in the open. Tom and I were friends, good friends. He reluctantly agreed, that is, after we asked Carl to give us a few moments, and *Jack* joined the discussion.

I had quit. There was no doubt about it. As far as Cesar and Doctor Abboud were concerned, there was no turning back. Had Cesar hired a qualified PD, the issue would have been muted. But the sudden turn of events might be beneficial for me.

My plans seemed up in the air again. That morning, I placed a call to the States to give Mary my arrival schedule. We had been married for twenty-three years. I was finally beginning to realize she preferred I stay in Cairo, or anywhere else rather than return home.

Carl and I left Tom’s office and headed for the Sheraton. We settled ourselves in the lobby bar. As we were waiting for the bartender to find some scotch I watched Carl’s reactions to the local scenery. From the look on his face and his refusal to look me in the eye, I knew there was something more than he told us.

“Carl, what are you doing here?”

Carl was 63 years old. Tom was right; he was a mouse. He looked like he had been ridden hard and put away wet a few times, and this current turn of events was about to put him around the bend. The waiter brought our drinks. I did not take a sip. Carl’s glass was empty, and he was signaling the waiter for a refill.

"Carl, truthfully, what is going on?"

It took a while, but I pried the story out of him. He was a civil engineer. He had always worked in procurement or a review and design capacity. He had no firsthand experience in construction.

After college, and during the first thirty years of his professional life, he worked in a small city's engineering department. City budget cuts mandated changes. It meant a small pension with kids in college. He refinanced his house but was out of work for almost two years before he landed a job with the COE in Saudi Arabia.

He was hoping to finish his career with the COE. When oil money started to dry up in the 1980's and construction projects were cut back he found himself displaced. He answered an ad Cesar placed when I gave my notice. He had experience with the COE. Cesar felt he could swing this job, and the COE would buy off on him.

During my conversation with Carl, I began liking him. I also understood his attitude. Like me, at the onset of the project, he was lied to. When he saw the site and realized how much work was left to be done, he had reservations of his own about his ability to manage the project.

It would have been difficult for Cesar to know what went on. It had been a year. He still refused to come to Egypt. I got the impression from Carl that Cesar felt I made mountains out of molehills and that the COE would welcome just about any change in site management.

At the time, I was not sure what my concern was. I had long since failed my loyalty class and I knew my patience grades were not much better. I did have reservations about leaving the project in inexperienced hands. Somehow, I retained some pride in my accomplishments, and I did want to see the Computer Center finished without it turning into a can of worms on my resume.

I called Tom before departing Cairo and told him I would be contacting him later in the week. He wished me well and told me that even if I was a quitter, I was the best fishing partner he ever had. I was going to miss Tom.

I arrived home on August 14th, 1987. One year and two weeks from the date of my first departure. Surprisingly, Mary met me at the airport. The past year had allowed her to grow into the person she wanted to become. Based on our discussion on the four-hour drive home, I was convinced that, not unlike the project in Egypt, I was no longer high enough in the management structure at home for my opinion to count for much.

Reflecting on the discussion, I can only say that for a time, I believed I had passed a real patience course. However, in the end, as usual, I simply was not ready to deal with reality.

A few days after my arrival, the phone was ringing in the bar. I answered it; it was Cesar.

"Hello, Cesar."

"I want you to go back to Cairo."

"It's nice to hear from you too; what about Carl?"

I expected the call from Cesar. Tom called the day before. Carl was not going to work out; Cesar was stalling. He mentioned to Tom that he knew Tom and I were friends and suggested Tom call me. Tom wanted to know if I would consider coming back. I was waffling; I had not made up my mind.

After Tom's call, I gave Mary a loyalty test and asked what she thought about me going back for another six to eight months. The cloud on her mood lifted when she told me we could use the money, and she had proven she was capable of handling the family business while I was away.

We were at a booth in the bar at the restaurant. I thought about that for a minute. The restaurant was barely breaking even, and the decor I had taken pride in was covered with graffiti.

Mary was bartending. I made my mind up when she left me and went to the bar to pour some guy a drink. She leaned over and whispered something; they both looked back at me, smiling.

Cesar strayed from his normal short and to the point long enough to tell me Carl was not going to work out, and he felt since I started the project, I should go back and finish it. He also told me that since he had already signed a contract with Carl, he wanted Carl to stay on and help with the final paperwork.

“I don’t think the finances will justify the added overhead.”

“Yes, Doctor Abboud and I talked about that. Carl can do part of your job; we thought you wouldn’t mind sharing some of your salary.”

“Fuck Doctor Abboud, Cesar, and don’t you bullshit me. Let’s you and I put our cards on the table for a change. I talked to Tom. You can’t come up with a replacement in time, and he’s going to shut the project down. Even if you find a replacement, he won’t give you more time. Glen will put you on LDs if you don’t meet the current schedule.”

“Go back for a month; we’ll find someone by then.”

“Not a chance, Cesar. If I do go back, it’s for the duration, and I want a twenty-percent raise and my housing and car allowance adjusted to the American standard we agreed to when I first signed up.”

“We can’t afford it with Carl on the project.”

Cesar and Abboud had faced reality. There were a few million dollars of materials in the pipeline, and bills were past due. The bond they finally managed to provide was at risk.

“More bullshit; the time change bailed you and D. Osmond out. I’ll handle Carl. If I go back, you won’t have to pay us both. One more thing. Chico, Dio, and Amante remain on board until the as-builts are finished; it’s not negotiable.”

“All right, call Tom and tell him you will be returning.”

Chapter 28

I know; most would think I am nuts. Given another out, I was not ready to confront the situation at home. I did not see a reason to delay my departure. I left the following day for Cesar's office in Portland.

Don booked me on a marathon flight through Atlanta with connecting flights through Paris and Madrid. It meant at least forty-plus grueling hours of security and custom headaches if everything went without a hitch.

I had only been home a few stressful days, I needed some rest, more to get my head on straight. I called Tom to tell him I was on my way, but it would be a few days. After meeting with Cesar, I put my personal life on the back burner and rescheduled my flight from Seattle over the pole to Amsterdam with a layover and a few days of R & R before having to face Abboud and Carl.

As luck would have it coincidence happens, even in a city of twenty-two million. Andy met me at the airport; at least, I thought he did when I saw him standing on the sidewalk when I exited customs. Same shit, nothing changed. Andy was not there to pick me up. He was there with Deo. Abboud had not resolved the visa problem. The Filipino engineers planned to leave the next day. They needed to exchange their tickets; Andy was alone.

"Andy, where is Deo?"

"He's at the check-in desk."

"Let's go talk with him."

"By the way, what are you doing back here?"

"It's a long story."

I was not in the mood to relay it to Andy at the time. I was more concerned with keeping Deo and the other engineers from leaving Cairo, and me having to deal with Abboud over the rest of the drawings. Andy and I caught up with Deo while he was still in line.

"Hello, Mr. Pat. What are you doing here?"

"Let's go back to work, Deo."

Deo was reluctant. I cannot say I blamed him. I asked him who paid for his tickets. He told me they had open return tickets home, and he needed to change the date.

I convinced Deo to return to the flat where Chico and Amante were busy packing. Everyone was surprised to see me. Cesar had not told Abboud to tell them I was returning, or Abboud did not want to believe the telexes Cesar was sending. I had no idea which, and at the time, I did not care. My concern was keeping them around long enough to finish their work.

As third-country nationals and the requirement of U.S. personnel, the OMC could not get them work permits. However, living with Andy and not needing military passes, the engineers were under the local radar.

Abboud was anxious to see the last of them. He and Cesar never settled on the responsibility of keeping the men in Cairo. Abbood had refused to fund a second holiday.

I was not concerned with the cost. I knew Abboud's engineers were incapable of finishing the work. I was going to see the project through to the end; I wanted staff I could rely on. The men were used to the back of the bus and staying in one-star hotels. If I sent them out of the country for two weeks, they could reenter and start their visas over. Everyone was agreeable.

I had $800 in my pocket. A little short for two weeks.

"Andy, how much cash have you got, dollars?"

"About six hundred."

"That's enough, get it. I'll pay you back."

I gave Andy Cesar's American Express card and told him to take them to the airport, buy round-trip tickets to Cyprus on the first plane out, and have them back in two weeks. It was time to visit Tom.

"Hello, Tom. How about planning a fishing trip?"

"It's about time you got your ass back. How are things at home?"

"Bad subject, what's happening on the site?"

"Not a thing. Carl's lost, and the locals are running him in circles."

The Feast was over. I could not believe I was away less than two weeks. When I thought about it, I had been off the project longer. During the six weeks before leaving I had taken a one-day-at-a-time attitude. I had not planned on coming back.

"Pat, I need a schedule update."

"What's new, Tom? Remember the one I prepared last October showing a completion date of next March?"

Tom did not remember. It was hard to believe the session I spent drafting it in frustration turned out to be a reality. Neither of us liked the idea, but the project would not finish until after the first of the year, and that was if everything went according to the current schedule, which it probably would not.

Tom knew my heart was not in the project the prior two months. Some areas progressed simply as a matter of course. There were fresh players, most were revolving through the country. The only original members of the staff were Andy, Hamid, and Doctor Osmond's relatives. Cesar and Don were in the States, and for the time being, Abboud was still conducting sessions with Doctor Osmond.

It was the beginning of the second year. We sorted out the major issues in the first eight months. Tom and I knew we could get the JV back under control by managing their money; it should only be a matter of time.

Tom had put a hold on the money. He had not been to the site since I left. He thought we should both get up to speed before I met with Carl or Abboud. The only one on the site when we arrived was the guard at the gate. There had been two deliveries since I left, but with the Feast in process, there was an obvious lack of progress.

Abboud did not want me back, but Cesar had felt pressured by the COE when Tom held up the payments. I suggested approving the last pay estimate would be a step in the right direction and make the pill easier to swallow for the JV partners.

"Where will you be living?"

I relinquished my flat to Carl when I resigned. With my new allowance, I felt I could do better. Until Tom mentioned it, I had not thought much about where I was going to set up housekeeping. I was staying at the Sonesta Hotel, where I had breakfast most mornings during the first year. I was comfortable, but I knew Cesar would soon be objecting to the expense.

"I'm not sure, Tom. I thought I would face the nightmare of finding a flat next week."

"There's one available in the building where I live. From what the last tenant told me, the flat is clean, and most everything works."

Maadi was the high-rent district for the expat community. My prior housing allowance was not enough for me to live in the area. My increase would be enough to allow me the luxury of close to American standards. The only problem was the COE might frown on one of theirs and a contractor's PD living in the same building. I asked Tom to check with Glen and, if it were all right, ask his leasing agent when I could view the flat.

Same shit, still no phone on the site. Tom and I decided to meet at the Sonesta and have a celebration drink. Tom stopped in the lobby to make the calls. Glen was agreeable; the flat was available. I could see it that evening.

I had not slept since I left Amsterdam. I took a shower and decided I would let my reunion with Abboud and Carl wait until the next day. For the time being, I would make housing my number one priority. Clean, air-conditioned flats were a rarity in Cairo. I did not want the opportunity to slip by.

It was rush hour. Traveling to Maadi meant an hour by way of Downtown Cairo or forty minutes through the City of the Dead. I was in a hurry; I chose the latter.

I was driving Andy's car. I was not sure where my old one was. Andy's was no better than the one Abboud had given me. The Egyptians treated it with the same inshallah attitude as everything else in Cairo. If Allah willed it, it ran. Halfway through the City of the Dead, Allah figured it was time for a Western infidel to contribute to the local Aid program. The car quit in one of the most congested areas of the cemetery.

I made it a policy not to ride with a taxi driver who started our conversations off with *ten Pounds*. These two words were universal when it came to setting taxi prices for tourists in Cairo.

A taxi driver's English vocabulary was limited. No amount of arguing would convince him you wanted to pay the going rate of two-LE he charged the locals for the same ride. The secret was not to ask the fare in advance. Expats do not negotiate until after they reach their destination. They handed the driver what was fair after getting out of the cab. Usually, it was more than he would have received from a local citizen, and the argument was limited to some mumbling.

I did not have a choice. I did not have ten-LE. During my absence, Egypt had floated the Pound to the dollar to put the black market out of business. They also dropped the law requiring the conversion of foreign currency into LE. The change in regulations saved me two hours, but in my haste to exit the airport, I neglected to exchange money. I bumped into Andy at the airport. I did not need a taxi. I checked into the hotel with Cesar's American Express card. Money had not been a problem, until now.

I did have six-LE from earlier days. The trip to Maadi would cost two, and the trip back to my hotel would cost about three more. It was not that I was concerned about a few extra LE. I had developed some habits while I was in Cairo, and proper planning had become a top priority. On this day, I was lucky. I only had to flag down three taxis before I was able to enter one without the usual haggling.

I had learned enough to deal with most of the day-to-day situations an expat encounters. I knew my way around the city and learned enough basic Arabic words like right, left, forward, no, stop, slow down, and here, along with a few hand signals to direct a taxi driver to almost anywhere I wanted to go. The Arabic also helped because the driver knew I was not a tourist. When it came time to pay, haggling was minimal.

I was accustomed to the reckless actions of the drivers in Cairo. Like the garbage on the streets, I did not notice it any longer. I settled into the front seat.

Now…., I have mentioned a few times that *you cannot make this shit up*. I also realize that thousands of tourists travel to every corner of the globe daily, some for extended periods. The majority never step in the shit I routinely find myself ass deep in.

No tourist in their right mind would intentionally cross the City of the Dead any time of day, let alone during rush hour when swarms of humanity were leaving the fields and changing shifts at the factories. The right mind thing may be debatable, but I was not a tourist. I settled back, looking forward to viewing the flat.

We were navigating our way around donkey carts and pedestrians at a slow but steady pace. The driver was preoccupied, following the crowd without the usual horn honking, arm waving, and yelling at people in the streets to move out of the way.

Things were calm. I was reflecting on things back home and that I was once again on the other side of the world, this time for an indefinite length of time. The driver's sudden surge to the left in his attempt to pass a congested area woke me from my trance. Vendors had set up a vegetable market in the middle of the street. When we swerved around them, the donkey never had a chance.

We hit it head-on, lifting it, throwing it back into the garbage cart it was pulling, and into the laps of three kids in the seat. I was too startled to remember the rule of an expat leaving the scene of an accident. More excitement in Cairo. I waited too long to exit the taxi and leave the growing crowd.

The driver was out of the car when I regained my senses. An angry mob had surrounded the taxi and was reaching for me through the open window. The kids in the cart concerned me. I tried to open the door to get out. The crowd was not having any part of it. From what I could gather, we were waiting for the police to arrive.

The kids appeared to be all right, and it did not appear I was in immediate danger from the crowd. I figured it was smarter just to lock the door and wait.

They must hide in the shadows; a police officer arrived a short time later. He moved the crowd back from the car and then gestured to me to get out. I did, but he was becoming impatient with our inability to communicate.

I could see the kids in the cart were unscathed. The donkey, on the other hand, was dead, and the cart was going to need major repairs. I did not see how it was my problem. I was becoming impatient myself and had to keep reminding myself that it was in my best interest to behave and stay calm.

I had just returned and had not been to the embassy. I realized I no longer had my military credentials. I did not think the accident was my problem. My patience ebbed a little more than it should have, considering the situation.

I was a lone tourist in the wrong part of the city. It was time to try to exit myself from the crowd. When I turned to walk away, the police officer caught me by the arm and escorted me to the front of the taxi, where the driver was arguing with the man who owned the donkey and the cart.

I understood enough to understand the taxi driver was making his problem mine. I was at a distinct disadvantage. I still did not have enough grasp of the language to defend myself in the argument. One word I did understand was money. I stepped back to wait for things to calm down and for what I thought was going to be a trip to a police station.

As minutes passed, I resigned myself to a long and tedious situation. The best I could hope for was that I could get to a phone and make the inevitable call to the Embassy.

More excitement. I was the focus of attention; the police officer, taxi driver, and cart owner were in one of the modes often seen in Cairo. A driver of another car held up in the traffic approached me, and in clear English.

"What the fuck is going on?"

"Are you American?"

"No! I'm Egyptian; I went to school in the US, Stanford."

That accounted for the word *fuck*. Maybe I could get this sorted out after all. I explained to him what happened. I was not hurt, and neither were the kids. I would like someone to explain to the police that I would like to be on my way. The man approached the threesome to explain my logic. He returned a few minutes later.

"How much money have you got on you?"

"I wasn't driving."

"That makes no difference. It's your fault."

"Why the fuck is it my fault?"

It took a while. In the end, I understood the logic, at least the logic of a situation where I was the only one involved who was financially able to pay damages.

He explained the accident would not have occurred if I had not asked the driver to take me to my destination. That makes sense, I guess. I resigned myself to the inevitable. I asked if he would negotiate a settlement, he agreed. We approached the police officer, who was still engaged in a conversation with the owner of the cart.

The four of them wandered around the conversation for a few minutes. It appeared there was 500 LE damage to the cart, and the donkey was worth another 250. I told them I was not a tourist; I could buy a donkey at the local auction for 50 LE and the cart for 250.

“The donkey was pregnant you must pay for the offspring.”

“Really, how many fucking generations?”

Cairo Livestock Auction.

My negotiator recognized sarcasm and realized a call to the American Embassy would take a lot longer. Still, they would probably straighten out the mess without it costing me a dime. He was in a hurry, and we were blocking his way. He returned to the group to explain I was not prepared to pay 750 LE, but I was willing to negotiate.

“How much will you pay?”

Things were looking up. The ceiling was 750. I got the message across. If the price were too high, I would let the police and Embassy sort it out. If they became involved, I would not be the one paying the bill. I did not want to involve the Embassy on my first day back. I also did not want to spend the night in an Egyptian jail. It gave me some confidence to know there was enough money in my wallet.

"Tell him one hundred for the damage to the cart and fifty for the donkey."

We negotiated back and forth another half-dozen times until we settled on a price of 280 LE for both, $140. I counted out the $20 bills.

More excitement. I do have to start remembering the rules. It was still against the law to pay local bills with foreign currency. When they floated the pound, they allowed the hotels to change currency and pass the receipts to the government.

"I just got off a plane; I don't have LE; tell the officer to take me to a hotel. I'll change the money and pay him in LE."

"You know that's not going to work."

I opened my wallet. Another $20 settled the problem with the police officer. It was not worth the hassle. I did not want to lose the opportunity to lease the flat. Maadi was still on my agenda, and I was already two hours late. I turned to leave the group and find another taxi. When I turned to leave, my negotiator grabbed me by the arm.

"You must pay for the damages to the taxi."

It took me a minute. We already established fault. I looked over at the taxi and wondered if I had enough money to get out of the fix. The taxi, like most cars in Cairo, was a wreck before the accident. The accident caved in the front end. It looked like a total loss. I had another $200 in my pocket. This was going to be hard to explain on my expense account.

We negotiated back and forth. I paid the taxi driver $130, the police officer another $20, and the man who negotiated the deal $40, which left me with $10 and six LE.

By the time I found another taxi willing to take me to Maadi, it was after eight. I was late. Tom was home when I arrived. Two hours is not too late for a meeting in Egypt. Tom told me the property owner called and told him he would meet me at nine.

I told Tom what happened. Tom was pissed that I gave into the system. He forgets I do not carry a diplomatic passport that keeps him out of all the scrapes I get in.

Unan was in the kitchen preparing some of her delicacies for Tom. When I arrived, she doubled up the portions and brought us a tray of *something*. Tom knew my stomach's adversity to the spicy hot side of Thai food; he offered me a scotch. It had been a long day. I never had a chance to stop and eat. I was hungry, so long as I did not know what was in it; after the last year in Cairo, I could eat almost anything if I had scotch to wash it down.

Tom and I have never convinced the Egyptians to adjust to our schedule. We were into the third tray of snacks and a fourth scotch when the landlord showed up. It was after ten.

In my condition, the flat was nice and close to American standards. It was probably the scotch that kept me from noticing the missing hot water faucet in the kitchen and the pile of garbage under the balcony in the alley. I also missed the ten or so stray cats who called the alley home, the bathroom door that would not close, and the lack of a light switch in the hall.

One unpleasant experience kept me from falling into another. The accident depleted my cash. I was not in a position to give the landlord a deposit. I told him I liked the flat and would return the next day to settle the rent and sign a lease.

He was asking for 1200 LE a month or about $500. I have no idea how they circumvent the law about paying in dollars. I was offering 800 LE. We were close, considering we were in Cairo. I had no doubt we would settle somewhere in between.

Tom and I returned to his flat; it was past one a.m. Tom offered to drive me to the hotel in the morning. He also offered a nightcap. The one turned into the rest of the shared bottle and reminiscing about the tuna trip the year before. I am not sure what time we went to bed, but at five, the loudspeakers from the Mosque next door shattered the silence with morning prayers.

Prayer time lasts fifteen minutes. I was sound asleep when Unan woke me for breakfast at seven. Tom needed to be at work by nine. I should have been at the office the day before. I squashed my inclination to crawl back under the covers.

Tom dropped me off at the hotel and asked me to meet him for lunch. It was time to get on with the project. By the time I showered, cleared my head with a pot of coffee, replenished my LE, found a taxi, and arrived at the office, it was 11:30, about normal for an Egyptian.

Sarha, my old driver, and a few members of the accounting staff were in. Cesar was still saving money on telexes. They were surprised when I walked in the front door. Abboud arrived as I was leaving for the site.

"Hello, Doctor Abboud."

"Welcome back, Mr. Pat."

I could tell he did not mean it.

"Doctor Abboud, Andy's car broke down in the middle of the City of the Dead."

Abboud was used to our breakdowns. We left the cars wherever they occurred. After the first two or three times, I quit worrying if it would be there when somebody returned to get it. Now, I do not bother to roll the windows up. Abboud did not seem concerned. He called his driver and translated directions. I did not bother to explain the accident. I would do that when I prepared my next expense report.

"Doctor Abboud, I need a dependable car."

"Patience, Mr. Pat. Someone will bring you the one you had this afternoon."

"Doctor Abboud, I drove that piece of shit you call a car for a year and spent more time in a taxi than I did driving it. I want a car I can depend on."

"I don't have another car."

"Your deal with Cesar says you provide cars to American standards. If you don't have one, I'll lease one and charge it to your account."

"Give me until after tomorrow, inshallah."

"Doctor Abboud, what does that mean? Forget it; I know what it means. I'll give you until Saturday."

Abboud was not used to my ranting or making demands on him for personal convenience. I had spent the first year trying to keep peace between him and Cesar and get the project done. I was not in the same frame of mind.

Leasing a car in Cairo was an expensive undertaking. Abboud was holding out on me. He sent one of the office staff out, who returned a few minutes later and handed me the keys to a 1984 Buick. It was in the garage below the office; the registration was in the glove box.

Abboud was not used to giving in; he was miffed. I knew it was not a good time to bring up the subject of the engineers, but I figured I might as well while I was in the mood.

"Doctor Abboud, I sent the Filipinos to Cyprus for a holiday. When they return, they will be able to remain in Cairo for another three months. I intend to keep them here until Tom signs off the engineering and the final as-builts."

"The Filipinos are too expensive. Our Engineers can finish the work. "

Abboud was not happy, and in a way, I could see his point. That is, if I was inclined to look at it from the standpoint of an Egyptian. The engineers each made $1,000 a month and had a $500 a month living allowance. It amounted to three times what Doctor Osmond was paying his entire staff. I was not in the mood to argue.

"You and Anwar had a year to get the drawings done. Your men are still working on the few I let them keep when Cesar's engineers showed up six months ago.

"Mr. Pat, Doctor Osmond will refuse to pay them."

"That's up to him. I know Doctor Osmond doesn't believe the cost is his responsibility, but that's between him and Cesar. Cesar will continue to fund their salaries and living expenses. I'll deal with it when I sign the authorization for the payment distribution."

"Tom stopped processing the payment when you left Cairo."

"I was only gone a couple of weeks. Tom approved the last pay estimate yesterday. One of his issues was engineering. I will deal with the construction issues and the COE, but from now on, I refuse to be in the middle of the JV's arguments. You and Doctor Osmond work out the company issues with Cesar. I have to get to the site. Let me know when it's sorted out."

The discussion ended, but not before one of the staff came into the room to discuss some expenses.

"I don't have time, Doctor Abboud."

"Mr. Pat, we need to charge Cesar for the duty on your computer."

"What are you talking about?"

I had forgotten about the computer. I billed Cesar for it months earlier. He refused to pay the bill and told me to file a claim with the COE, and that he would pay me when he was paid. I wrote it off when I quit.

"The computer is in the accounting office. Hazem came back and told us he kept in contact with the customs agent. He found a way to get it released."

"Which was?"

During the first six months, the computer had been one of my pet peeves. Customs would not return it, and Cesar refused to pay for it.

Tom suggested I pay the duty and file a claim. Whatever duty I paid on materials used on the project was reimbursable, eventually the COE would get it back. The COE rejected the claim because I had not paid the duty. That did make sense, but I tried to explain the duty was twice what it was worth. I wanted to recover the replacement cost. The COE told me the contract only called for duty reimbursement, and unless I had a receipt, there was no way to process the claim.

Duty and penalties came to $9,000, which I did not have. I asked Cesar for an advance, but he refused to advance me three times what it was worth. He told me it was a personal item; I would have to deal with it.

In the meantime, Hazem left. He was my only contact with the officials who held the computer. When everything else went sour, the computer fell to the bottom of my priorities. I was not sure I wanted to deal with it now. Abboud told me Hazem negotiated a payment of 500 LE.

“Doctor Abboud, when did Hazem make the deal?”

Doctor Abboud lapsed into Arabic in a discussion with the accountant, then turned back to me.

“I don’t know. Hazem delivered it to accounting after you left for the States.”

“Interesting timing, Doctor Abboud.”

I could not help thinking how upset he was when I insisted on leasing one to replace it; he and Cesar had argued about responsibility. It looked like Cesar would recover the 500 LE from the COE, and Abboud intended to keep the computer. Same shit, same companies, same players. Cesar had not said anything about the computer when I discussed the settlement of the first contract I signed.

“Doctor Abboud, charge the duty off to site office equipment and split it with Cesar, then have accounting put it in my office. I’ll sign the voucher.”

I found the Buick in the parking space under the building. It was in fairly decent shape by Egyptian standards, but someone had a flat, and the factory mini spare was still on the car. I went back upstairs and gave the keys back to Abboud.

“What now?”

"The car needs tires and a thorough cleaning before I'll drive it. Saturday, Doctor Abboud, please."

Abboud mumbled something about picky Americans. I turned and headed out the door to flag down a taxi.

Chapter 29

We started in the second year. The same guard who I conscripted, when I put in the gate, was at his post. He saluted me as I passed by.

Two weeks passed. The metal building arrived on site. It was an erector set, one even the Egyptians could not screw up so long as someone laid it out for them. The frame was up, the roof in place. It was time to start underground plumbing and electrical. There were pallets of electrical conduit and plumbing pipe laying alongside crates of fittings for both disciplines. I was thinking it would not be long before the building was closed in.

Andy and Carl were in the office arguing with Hamid, Mohammed, and Schmir. Schmir was a new player. He was the English-speaking representative for the primary subcontractor who showed up a few days after I returned.

Schmir had his own construction methods, which were a lot like Anwar's and Abboud's. Andy grabbed me by the arm as I walked past.

"Pat, didn't you have an electrical contracting business in Oregon?"

"Yes, we did plumbing, too, but it's been years. That was before I became a general contractor. Why do you ask?"

"It's time to start the plumbing and electrical underground."

"So, tell Schmir to get on with it."

"He doesn't know where to start."

"When we hired him Abboud said he's an electrical and plumbing contractor, among his other trades. Tell him to follow the plans and the schematics. It's not rocket science."

“He can lay out the work out, but he’s not familiar with U.S. materials.”

“For god’s sake, Andy, it's pipe, conduit, and wire. ....Fuck!” “Schmir, what’s the problem.”

“Pipe no good.”

Arabic-English, here we go again.

“What pipe?”

“All pipes.”

“Andy, help!”

“They don’t know how to bend conduit, and they aren’t familiar with what plumbing fitting goes where. I shut him down because we don’t have a lot of extra materials, and everything they put together is now with the scrap.”

“Tell Hamid to fire the son of a bitch and get a plumber and electrician who knows what they’re doing.”

“Carl and I checked. We would need to hire a British or German firm, which will cost a fortune.”

“Ok, so now what?”

It had never entered my mind until Andy brought it up. There were modern hotels, high-rise apartments, and international office facilities scattered in Cairo, for that matter, all over the Middle East. However, they were constructed by foreign firms with expat tradesmen using imported materials.

Egyptian commercial, midrise flat buildings, and most everything else in Egypt were built the Egyptian way, using whatever was cheapest and handy.

I walked a few local construction projects. Any rubber hose would do when it came to running electrical wires. When it came to a turn or a corner, a kink did not matter; they would cut the hose and plaster over the wires. Electrical device boxes for fixtures, switches, and plugs were set in concrete voids and then plastered in. Plumbing was a nightmare of pipes feeding fixtures without traps, duct tape used as clamps, and an occasional piece of scrap formed and welded into a T or a Y.

"You were an electrician and did plumbing on the side."

"Andy, you're not thinking what I think you're thinking."

"It's a solution."

"Andy, I'm the PD, not some fucking traveling trade instructor."

"So, you could use some exercise, why not show Schmir the ropes when it comes to bending pipe and laying out plumbing fittings."

Thinking: *Fuck.....! Why me? I should bite the bullet and hire the Brits. It would serve Abboud and Dr. Osmond right.* More thought: *Then again, it was not their fault; Cesar had brought them on board knowing Abboud's engineers could not read the plans.*

It was 1987. Egyptian labor was twenty-five cents an hour. British or German expats would charge $30 or $40. Hiring expat electricians and plumbers was a moot question. There simply was not enough money to pay that bill. I talked myself into it. *How tough could it be? I learned it.*

Schmir's crew.

Truthfully, you have to hand it to them. These kids were the best!

"Okay, I'll give it a try, but this could turn into a real shit show. Electrical and plumbing apprentice programs are four years. We've got a month. Try to keep Tom off the site for a few days and tell Schmir to have his crew here at eight tomorrow. No bullshit excuses. Tell him to be on time, or I will fire his ass. Also, tell him to have somebody here who speaks English; sign language isn't going to work."

I had assumed the Egyptians would be short on modern tools. It never entered my mind they would not know how to use them. I arrived at seven to check the supplies. There were a few sticks of conduit Schmir had tried to bend using an abandoned frame of an army jeep. There were also a dozen or more plumbing fittings glued together that would work in a hamster cage.

I checked the shipping documents and found the crate containing conduit benders. It was all there, plus a few extra tools that would help down the road.

Bending pipe is a young man's game. I spent the next month losing ten pounds teaching Schmir and his crew the tricks of the trade. Subhuman, my ass! Mostly kids and teens, they were eager to learn. By the time we were finished, when it came to installing conduit and pulling wire, I would match them against any electrician I knew in the States.

Plumbing, well, that was another matter. It took a while to convince Schmir traps mattered and that they needed to watch the bubble on the level because water and shit runs downhill.

Andy and I were busy with the electrical and plumbing and were not paying attention to the wall. There was no spec for the concrete wall between the bases. The instructions were to use local materials and match what was there.

Schmir's crews were working on the wall during our off hours. By the time we finished the electrical and plumbing, the wall had magically appeared and was painted. It looked better than the existing walls. The wall was built, it looked fine, and we signed it off. *Little did we know what was under the paint*!

We were past the plumbing and electrical rough. Same shit, new discipline. We were into laying concrete blocks between the building frames. There was a rigid spec for the walls of the building. Andy wanted him to follow the guidelines and the specs, but Schmir was bowing his neck.

The Egyptians manufacture an assortment of blocks. The strength depended on the amount of cement and the quality of the sand. The concrete blocks were for the infill walls of the building, which held up part of the frame, and the firewalls, which had to have a two-hour fire rating. They were one of the few locally made materials allowed on the project. We needed the top-of-the-line. Andy had stopped work because Abboud had a bunch of crap delivered and refused to buy the specified materials.

Schmir was caught in the middle. He had installed some of the blocks Abboud had given him. Abboud and I had discussed the blocks when I put in the requisition. I thought we got by it. The current problem was easy to deal with if I wanted to make an example, and at that moment, it was time.

"Andy, give Hamid and Schmir a copy of the specs." "Hamid, tell Schmir to tear that shit out and do this one by the book."

"We can't, Mr. Pat. Doctor Abboud told us to buy the cheaper blocks. They are already on site."

"Hamid, how many blocks do we need?"

"Over thirty thousand, Mr. Pat."

"What's the difference in price between the cheap blocks and the right ones?"

Andy joined in.

"Ten piasters, we've been arguing the point for three days. Doctor Abboud isn't going to give in."

I did a quick calculation. While I was gone, the Egyptian government floated the pound. Its value had dropped like a stone. Thirty thousand at ten piasters each, which was a little under three cents at the current exchange rate, came to a difference of less than $900.

"Andy, Doctor Abboud's not in charge of the project; I am. The contract says we turn the defective materials over to the Egyptian Army." "Hamid, tell General Aziz Doctor Abboud has solved the problem of rebuilding General Sayer's car shed."

"But, Mr. Pat, we have over five thousand on site. Doctor Abboud will have to pay for them if we don't return them."

"Hamid, I've had enough of this shit. Order the right materials so you can start the walls; don't come back until they are on site. It's time Doctor Abboud started paying attention. Once material is unloaded on this site, it cannot be removed. Tell Doctor Abboud what I've said and remind him the liquidated damages on this contract are three thousand dollars a day."

Tom stayed out of the conversation. He should never have been in the room. Carl or Andy should have nipped this one in the bud before Hamid ordered the blocks, or at least prevented them from being unloaded when they arrived on site. Now I was pissed.

"Schmir, go to work." "Andy, why don't you and Tom do a safety inspection?"

Andy had taken over the added duty of safety when it became apparent Doctor Osmond's nephew, Mohammad, was not up to the task. Andy and Tom took the hint and left me alone with Carl. I had not had an opportunity to deal with Carl. He had been checking inventory and materials as they arrived on site. Payroll was coming up; Cesar was asking questions.

"Carl, this isn't going to work. The blocks are an issue you should have dealt with. Andy told you the samples were out of spec."

Carl knew something was coming, but he was not sure what my approach was going to be. He signed a contract for one year, or when the project was complete. Carl was established in my old flat and his wife had joined him.

"My wife's here, we signed a lease, we're settled?"

"Carl, the JV signed the lease. If you go home, what will you lose? I'll give you a month's severance and pay your expenses home. Take a holiday; stop in Europe on the way."

"I can't afford to do that."

"You're in over your head. Consider this to have been a paid holiday."

"What if I refuse and insist you pay off my contract?"

"Get serious, Carl. Don't make me play hardball. I'll fire you for incompetence, and you can pay your way home. I've read your contract. One of the conditions is that you're acceptable to the COE. You weren't, and you're not. You can sue Cesar when you get back to the States. I doubt you will win, and even if you do gain more than I'm offering you now."

"I don't think you have the authority; it has to come from Cesar."

"Carl, Cesar has his head up his ass when it comes to Egypt. My title is Regional PD. For the time being, Cesar has you listed as Project Manager; you work for me. Tom will shut the project down if I tell him I intend to leave you in charge. Why not admit everyone made a mistake, take a holiday in Europe, and then go home?"

Carl reluctantly agreed. I did not blame him for negotiating the best deal he could get, but in my heart, I felt he was glad to be off the project. Tom and Andy returned just as Carl and I settled. It was a relief; I liked Carl; he was just in over his head.

"Andy, ask Moya if she wants to join us."

"Moya's gone. The project her husband was on is finished."

I was sorry to hear the news. Secretarial help who could deal with a contract in English was rare in Cairo. I did not like the thought of having to put up with Sarha or another Egyptian who could not deal with English documents.

"Have you found a new secretary?"

"I may have. Someone who said she knows you. She said she met you on your trip home at Christmas."

"Karen?"

I had forgotten about Karen.

"She's a nice lady, Andy, but I thought she was teaching at the Christian school. We need someone full-time."

"She only works four hours a day. She has a friend who could split the work up.'

Andy was being too persuasive for this to have just come up.

"Andy, what's going on?"

"Nothing, they're Americans, they need the job, we need a secretary, it fits."

"I take it you made a deal."

Moya had given notice right after I left. Carl interviewed some applicants but did not find anyone satisfactory. Andy dealt with the problem when he met Karen.

I gave Karen my phone number but did not hear from her after I returned from the Christmas holiday. I had moved, so I was not surprised.

Although there are over twenty-two million people in Cairo, it is a small, tight-knit community for American expats. Andy met Karen at a shindig some Americans were having, and the subject of the COE came up. One thing led to another, and someone introduced Karen to Andy. My name came up. Karen relayed the story of our flight home. Andy gave Karen the office number because she said she and a friend of hers would like to earn some extra money.

"I don't see a problem, Andy. When do they start?"

"Tomorrow."

Andy had worked the schedule out. The hours varied, but the paperwork was Andy's problem, not mine. I felt solving two problems in one day was more than I could hope for. I did not see a reason to push my luck.

"Andy, let's all go to lunch. When we finish, I want to go back to the flat in Maadi and make sure I didn't miss anything."

"Where's the car?"

"Mine or yours?"

I explained and asked where Carl was. It seemed he was also still on foot.

"Tom, how about a ride?"

We piled into Tom's car and left for the Sonesta Hotel. By the time we finished lunch, I did not feel up to a trip to Maadi. Tom went back to work. Andy and Moya took a taxi back to the site. Carl and I went back to the bar.

Carl had been thinking about it since he found out I was returning. We needed someone for the Operation and Maintenance close out of the project. I had not gotten around to dealing with it. Carl had a proposal of his own and had sent it to Cesar. When Cesar did not respond, he thought it was off the table.

"Carl, Cesar isn't paying attention to Egypt. O & M is going to be a pain in my ass; run it by me."

Carl offered to remain in Cairo until the end of the project at a reduced salary. He had leased out his home in the States, and an extended holiday in Europe would have been more of a financial burden than he could afford. He did not have any place to go. He would stay and complete the O & M manuals, do the onsite training, and prepare the paperwork for the final turnover.

I had been requesting information from Cesar about that phase of the work and who would be performing it. It was going to be an expensive part of the project. Cesar passed it on to Don. Don had been ignoring my correspondence, which Carl had read.

Carl and I reviewed the requirements. O&M data and training manuals came with the equipment. It was a simple matter of going through the tedious motions, which neither Andy nor I would have time for. We had a budget for the work. I offered to pay him an amount equal to the budget, which would take the place of his salary and living allowances. It was within pennies. Carl would not have to take a cut in pay.

It was a better compromise than mine, and it settled a big issue I was going to have to deal with before the contract was finished. I did not see how Cesar could refuse. He was saving whatever settlement Carl would be entitled to, and it was a guaranteed amount to finish a phase of the project that was going to be a real pain in the ass, not only for me but for all of us. Andy and Don were both delighted because they knew Cesar would not pawn it off on them; everyone agreed.

Chapter 30

I dedicated today to arranging for relocating from the hotel to my new flat. I had made an appointment with Tom's property owner to discuss the lease and review items I felt needed attention.

I picked up the Buick Abboud had repaired and cleaned. It had a set of close-to-new tires, and they moved the trash from the front to the back seat. I threw the trash on the floor of the garage. My driver could take it out and deposit it in the rubbish pile.

The Buick was a three-speed stick-shift. It had a notch or two missing in the transmission, but when I shifted gears, it worked.

I was two hours late when I left for my appointment but arrived a half-hour before the landlord showed up. I was finally adjusting to Egyptian timing.

During my second inspection, I noticed issues I missed the night Tom and I became reacquainted. I made a list of repairs, but the landlord insisted they were *upgrades*.

After haggling about the cost, we settled on a price of 900 LE per month. I refused to pay in dollars because the pound was dropping daily. I signed the lease and paid the deposit but held the first and last month's rent back until he completed the *upgrades*.

I spent the next two weeks catching up. Most expat contracts are for a year, subject to review. The construction part was winding down. The students in the States had become moot; none of the Egyptians would be returning. We had a number of fresh players from the U.S. Government who would be assigned to the Computer Center after turnover.

Karen and Cathy started on an alternating schedule. So far, Andy seemed pleased with their performance.

The landlord performed better than expected. All but a few minor issues were repaired. The landlord assured me the rest of the work would be completed within the week. I moved in under his protest without paying the last month's rent. I told him he would get the money when all the items on the list were done.

It was inconvenient the first two nights because the landlord wanted to work between 11:00 p.m. and 4:00 a.m. On September 5th, they completed the punch list, and after 13 months, I settled in a flat close to American standards.

The only things the landlord did not resolve were the cats in the trash pile under my balcony and the chanting from the mosque next door. I settled the cat problem with a bag of balloons. Before going to bed, I would fill a half-dozen with water and bomb the rubbish pile until I drove the cats into the alley. I did not have many direct hits, but close counts in Cairo. A few days after I moved in, I bought earplugs to block out the early morning chanting from the mosque next store. As a bonus, the flat came with a resident boab.

Doctor Abboud left a few days later to find Anwar. Sarha said they would both return *after tomorrow, inshallah*. I never saw either of them again. I did not miss them!

Abboud was gone. After the concrete block incident, I passed out new business cards. On the back in bold Arabic print: Do it right or do it over! The concrete block incident convinced Doctor Osmond to give up the fight; he instructed Hamid to follow my directions. While I was overseeing the workers at my flat, everything was progressing smoothly on-site. I was not only surprised but I was also impressed.

The Engineers returned a few days later than expected from the semi-nude beaches in Cyprus. They were no longer concerned about my getting them long-term visas and were looking forward to another holiday in Cyprus 90 days down the road.

The engineers were turning in drawings faster than Tom could review them. Carl was busy pestering Cesar and Don for O&M data. Doctor Osmond sent me a memo telling me to instruct Carl not to use the new fax machine and to continue to use the telex because the paper and toner cartridges were expensive. I ignored him but bought a supply of paper myself, which satisfied him.

Andy followed my lead and renegotiated his contract with Cesar when his first year was up. This time, he read the fine print and had the luxury of living in his own place. He found a flat down the street from mine a few days before I returned.

Andy gave up the monkey because one of his new friends lives in the flat below him, and he does his laundry twice a week. Andy brooded about the monkey for a day or two, but Karen and Cathy were showing up most of the time, on time, so he had company most days.

Andy is spending his leisure time banging on my door, complaining about the lack of hot water in his kitchen. We have the same landlord and some of the new amenities used to *upgrade* my flat had been *borrowed* from his while he was at work. I told him he would have to take it up with the landlord, which resulted in a comment about *paybacks being a bitch*.

Andy merged into the expat community better than I had. He had also passed the patience course I flunked. However, the aggravation of his job had put him in a get-even mood of his own. I should have heeded the warning. When I arrived home in the evening after the argument about who owned the water heater, Andy, Karen, and Cathy were sitting in my living room.

The boab who took care of my flat had a spare key and knew Andy and I were friends. I made a mental note to check the water heater and get the key from Andy before he left.

"Andy, what are you people doing here, and how the hell did you get in."

"Egypt's rubbed off on you, Pat. You weren't nearly as rude at Christmas."

"Hello, Karen; who's your friend? Wait….! Shit…! Give me a minute."

Yes, it was a curt answer. I was a little miffed. Thoughts: *Rude, really? Give me a fucking break. It is my corner of the world. It had been a long day; I was tired and ready for a toddy. I am not ready for more fucking problems on the site,* which in my mind, was the only reason for them being there.

The room settled. I went to the kitchen and poured myself a drink. Fortified, I returned to the living room. Karen introduced me to Cathy.

Cathy, not what I expected, but reason enough for Andy's recent concern for his looks, which, like mine, had deteriorated since I arrived in Egypt. Andy was sporting new clothes and had recently gotten a haircut.

Karen was, as I remembered her, a nice-looking woman with little makeup, the missionary schoolteacher type, between 35 and 40. Cathy was much younger. She was about the same age as my oldest daughter and looked much like Elizabeth Taylor in her early twenties.

Karen and Cathy started work a few days before I returned. I had not seen either of them because I was busy running between the COE office, Doctor Osmond's office, and the American Embassy. My timing at the site had been such that I kept missing them.

We got through the introductions and then spent the next hour becoming acquainted over a couple of bottles of wine. It appeared it was strictly a social call. Andy's get-even threats were fading until I asked Cathy how she happened to be teaching at a Christian school in a Muslim country. Cathy burst into tears, fleeing into the bathroom, with Karen trailing after her.

Regaining…., I sat there for a moment.

"All right, Andy; what the fuck is going on?"

"Watch your language; the girls are missionaries."

"Andy, this is my space; I can scratch anywhere it itches. If they haven't heard it before, they won't know what it means. Apparently, this isn't a social call. Tell me, what the fuck is going on?"

"The girls were fired from the school. They are being kicked out of the complex where they live."

I did not have time to respond. Karen and Cathy were reentering the room. Cathy had regained her composure. Karen was, well, I am not sure what you would call the expression other than the fact that they would not be there if I were not being dragged in.

I spent the next hour listening to their side of the story. Cathy had taken up with a Muslim. Karen was spending her free time at the local American pub enjoying cold imported beer and the company of Americans with the UN who were assigned to the peacekeeping forces in Egypt.

It was a Christian school. Karen's problem would have been easier to sort out if she had not taken sides with Cathy. All Karen had to do was give up the after-hours beer parties and return by curfew, which was nine p.m. She was a Christian missionary; it seemed reasonable to me.

Cathy committed the unforgivable sin for a Christian woman in the Middle East. She was engaged to a Muslim and would not give him up. This was against every acceptable rule on both sides of the aisle. The man's family insisted she give up her Christian faith and become a Muslim. The Christian employers at the school demanded she give up her Muslim boyfriend. Neither solution was acceptable to Cathy.

Thought: *Just what I needed, two women who thought the entire world was liberated and that they should be able to do anything they damned well pleased. Cathy, well...., she was a naive product of a liberal education and overindulging parents.*

Karen should have known better. She had traveled the world enough to realize the rules she grew up with do not apply in the real world. After a year in Cairo, I did understand that both had been willing to take some chances to find company and pleasure in the alien society they chose to live in.

"Okay, Karen. Sorry, I was a little startled when I got home. So, you're here because you lost your jobs. I would think you should be going home."

"It's not that simple."

Karen and Cathy were to vacate their rooms by Friday. Since they broke the rules, they were fired and would have to finance their own plane fare home. On the wages they made, neither could afford a decent meal in a Cairo restaurant, let alone plane fare back to the States.

I did not see there was a great deal I could do. I was living on an allowance. My salary checks were going directly into a trust account out of the reach of the IRS and then filtered back to my wife.

I still was not sure I was willing to give up on a reconciliation with Mary. I could not see how I could call her and ask her to send money so I could buy two women's plane tickets back to the States. I was also starting to think that somehow something had gotten lopsided in the conversation. Andy and the women were trying to make their problem my problem, and I was falling for it, *hook, line, and sinker*. It was time to figure out how to sort it out without causing me trouble.

“All right, let’s begin again. Andy, what’s really going on?’

“They need a place to stay until they can raise the money for the flight home.”

“It’s your idea; let them stay with you.”

“I have a one-bedroom flat. Besides, my wife is coming over for a visit in a few weeks, and she wouldn’t understand.”

“I’m sure she wouldn’t, Andy. What makes you think mine would?”

“She doesn’t have to know.”

Andy was aware of my domestic situation and that my correspondence with Mary had diminished considerably since I returned to Egypt.

I was weakening. Andy was right. The flat was much more than I needed. It had three bedrooms, two bathrooms, a dining room, a big living room, a den, and a balcony. The furnished flat included all the linen, bedclothes, and appliances for a family of five.

"Karen, I never did like the series Three's Company. Let me think about it for a day or so.

"What's to think about? You have plenty of room, we won't be any bother, and we are willing to help keep the place up."

"I already have a housekeeper. I told you, Karen. I'll let you know after I sleep on it."

"But….."

"Subject's closed. We'll talk about it tomorrow."

'Pat, we won't be any trouble."

"Karen, if you want an answer tonight, it's a big no! Please, give it a rest until tomorrow."

The women and Andy left. It was not that I was totally against the idea. It had been a long year, and I was tired of living alone. I had quit writing in the evenings, and I was not socializing with the expats. My only entertainment since I returned was a nightly 15-minute English news broadcast by the BBC.

Although my personal life was in the toilet, I was not in a hurry to throw twenty-three years away and end it altogether. I doubted if I could explain the situation to Mary, regardless of how desperate the girls might be.

I opened a new bottle of scotch. I slept on it but woke up a little fuzzy and rationalized. *Cairo was 10,000 miles from Oregon. How much trouble could I get into with a couple of missionaries?*

I was willing to deal with a temporary situation. I was not prepared to commit to a long-term arrangement. To shorten the time, we had to find a way to resolve the girl's financial situation so they could buy tickets home.

That was going to take some planning; I intended to set the rules in advance. I called Karen the next morning and told her to bring Cathy and meet me at the Sonesta for lunch.

When they arrived, I gave them a letter I prepared for their school Administrator. The gist: Since the girls' contracts were canceled, they should be paid through the end of the school term, which was another six months. This amounted to 480-LE each, but far short of what they needed for a return flight to the U.S.

The demand also included transportation back to the States, just as the original contract called for, and a letter of recommendation so they could seek other employment without having to leave the experience in Cairo out of their resumes. I signed the letter noting my title as a lawyer in Egypt. I figured I might as well take advantage of the degree.

Karen read the first page.

"Pat, they have no intention of giving us more money, let alone the price of tickets to the States; they were pretty adamant."

"Karen, read the rest of the letter…., please."

Karen was a lot like Abboud. She had made up her mind the Egyptians were in charge and no amount of persuasion was going to change the outcome.

I noted it was not only unfair, but it was also illegal for a Christian school to dismiss an American teacher because she wanted to marry a Muslim. I also mentioned that it was wrong to fire another teacher because she had taken sides with her friend who was in a relationship with a Muslim. The last paragraph said if they refused, I would file a complaint with the immigration authorities in Cairo.

"Pat, this isn't true!"

"So, what! It's half-true and close is acceptable in Cairo, Karen. Egypt may be a sham republic, but the laws are based on Islam's Qur'an. The Government will do more than just frown on Christian school authorities for disciplining someone because they stood up for the Muslim faith. The letter won't go beyond the administrators at the school and the sponsoring agency in the States."

I hoped the letter would solve the problem. The girls only had a few days before they were to vacate the premises. I figured the money for their plane fare would have to come from the sponsoring agency. That would take at least two weeks. I thought the school would postpone their eviction, but I agreed they could move in on Friday if the school forced them out.

I did not doubt that if the first letter did not resolve the problem, a follow-up letter to the proper agencies would have the desired effect. I was convinced the arrangement should only last a month at most.

We needed a set of rules for unattached women living in my flat; this was crucial. If anyone questioned the arrangement, they were to stick to the story that Karen was my sister, and Cathy was my niece. The women's male friends could not come to the flat. I had no idea what Karen's status was, but Cathy would have to arrange to meet her boyfriend off the premises.

The girls had resources if they were desperate enough to want to use them. If the school did not come through with their plane fares, they would have to ask their families to fund the trip home. I did not think that would be a problem, but I understood their reluctance to explain they lost their jobs because of what amounted to a morals charge. They signed on as missionaries to tutor young girls in a Christian school within a Muslim country; they both should have known better.

There also had to be living arrangements that made sense, and I did not see any reason for the arrangement to cause me any inconvenience. I would establish an allowance for groceries. They would do the shopping, prepare meals, and keep the place clean.

I did not want the JV to find out about the arrangements and have it somehow filtered back to my wife. Dr. Osmond was a devout Muslim. I would have to discharge my houseboy because of his relationship with my driver, so the laundry and ironing duties would fall to them. They agreed. They took the letter to the school that afternoon.

Karen and Cathy were waiting for me at the flat when I arrived home. Their luggage was on the floor of the living room.

Cathy's makeup was on the shelf in one of the bathrooms, and Karen's was in the other. I would nip that in the bud at the first opportunity. I started to address the issue, but I got sidetracked.

Dinner was on the stove; Andy was sitting on the couch with a paybacks are a bitch grin on his face.

"What's going on, Karen? I thought they gave you until Friday; this is Wednesday."

"Your letter worked. Close, that is, and you did say close counts in Egypt."

The school administrators did not want to explain their religious intolerance, but it also convinced them that Karen and Cathy should depart as soon as possible. Karen decided when they offered them a compromise. They agreed to pay them 480-LE each. They would also provide letters of recommendation and give them their return tickets home, which were purchased by the agency in the States when they were hired.

There is always a catch. They could not change the date without paying a substantial penalty. The school refused to cover the foreign currency needed to change dates or buy new plane tickets. That money would have to come from their sponsoring agency in the States.

They told them they had to leave as soon as the letters and the money were available. Karen agreed; twenty minutes later, the letters and the money were in their hands. The boab also brought their suitcases; they were to leave immediately.

Karen did not see a problem. After all, they had a place to stay and enough money to see them through until their next payment from Doctor Osmond. The only problem I saw, I painted myself into a corner and I was going to get to live the soap opera Three's Company. Thought: *What the hell?*

"Andy, give Karen the boab's key."

Andy handed her the key and then mentioned he was hungry. I got up to pour myself a drink. Cathy was in the kitchen stirring something on the stove. I was reaching over her into a cupboard. Cathy, shy at first, and I had not quite bonded, she ducked back into the living room. I bent over the pot; it smelled good.

"Karen, what's on the menu?"

Karen took my question to mean the issue was settled. The women busied themselves with dinner while I broke the seal on a bottle of Black Label and then tried to catch up on some work issues with Andy. From Andy's lack of attention and the comments about the smells coming from the kitchen, it was apparent he was looking forward to a home-cooked meal.

Dinner was ready; the table was set for four. Andy's participation was predetermined. He funded Cathy's trip to the shopping district in Maadi before I came home.

Karen was a good cook. She also knew the secret to preparing Egyptian vegetables was rinsing them in potassium permanganate and then spinning them dry. Fresh, crisp salad, country-fried chicken, baked potatoes, green beans, and strawberries in cream for dessert made the arrangement a lot more palatable than it was when I first walked in the door.

We spent the rest of the evening reminiscing about our experiences in Cairo. I enjoyed the company and when the evening ended, I thought the arrangement was not going to be at all disagreeable.

The next morning when the alarm went off, I headed for the toilet for my morning pee and a shower to start another day in Cairo.

Karen was soaking in the tub; she grabbed a towel.

"Try knocking!"

I went to the other bathroom; I knocked; Cathy was in the shower. I stepped out onto the balcony and relieved myself over the railing into the trash pile below, disturbing a big tom I missed with the water balloon the night before.

I dressed without a shower and went into the kitchen. Fresh coffee was brewed. A few minutes later, Karen and Cathy joined me at the table.

Cathy was warming up to the arrangement.

"You're out of hot water."

"What's this, I'm out of hot water crap? I have to be at work ladies, from now on I get first crack at the shower in the morning. By the way, Karen, you, and Cathy can take turns with the makeup; you don't need to use my sink."

"It takes an hour. You're not the only one who has to be at work."

"Karen, neither of you have to be at the office until ten. Besides, only one of you comes to work at a time.'

"We have other jobs."

"What do you mean, other jobs?"

"We're teaching English to refugee families."

"Who hired you?"

"A Canadian-Christian relief agency."

There were thousands of refugees from the Iraq-Iran war and sub-Saharan African countries in flames, finding their way to Cairo and looking for a way to migrate to the U.S. or Canada, two stable countries allowing refugees to apply for citizenship.

In addition to the wars, Christians were under siege throughout the regions and were unwelcome in the refugee camps springing up along borders. Christian agencies were funneling people through safe houses. Local law enforcement, anxious to reduce the numbers, frowned on expat involvement in the program because it encouraged more illegals to enter the already overcrowded country.

"Karen, where are your refugees from?"

"Ethiopia."

"Are they here legally?"

"They're working on getting permits."

"In other words, no, right?'

"Yes, I mean no. They aren't in the country legally; we're working on their visas to Canada."

"You know this can't work. I have an Embassy endorsement, and they frown on our meddling in local politics. You two are going to have to give this up."

"We're not meddling, as you put it, and there is no reason for you to get upset. It's only for a few more weeks, and then the families we're working with will be gone."

"Karen, you know dammed well nothing happens in Egypt according to schedule. I was supposed to be done a month ago. I'll be here for at least another six months. I have no idea what you two are engaged in, but I do know it will not go according to your plan."

The conversation ended. I still was not up to domestic confrontations, and in the end, I figured it was none of my business. They had been working with the refugees for over a year, and no one had bothered them.

The Canadians and Americans involved in the illegal refugee program established their presence in Cairo by whatever means. Unless the girls became involved in local politics, the agencies would probably leave them alone. Besides, the plan was for the girls to leave in a few weeks.

Chapter 31

The second year settled into a routine. Everything was progressing at the Egyptian pace, but even I was beginning to believe all things do get done, even in Egypt.

Don found a quicker way to get material to the freight forwarder; the materials started to arrive on schedule at the Port of Alexandria. Now that Abboud was out of the picture, Doctor Osmond's expeditor in Alexandria got his act together, and the Egyptian Army was getting the materials to the site timely.

Carl was doing an excellent job with the O&M data. He was also attempting to conduct training courses with the Egyptians; it was a challenge. The O & M manuals were in English. The COE refused to pay to have them translated. The Egyptians were not showing up for the classes, but Tom allowed us to count the hours if the time was scheduled, and we delivered a notice to General Aziz.

Carl had to show up. Carl did not mind. Since grades did not matter, it was easier teaching someone who was not there than students who could neither read nor speak the language.

Chico, Deo, and Amante finished the plans. Doctor Osmond wanted me to send them home when their visas expired. I kept them on the payroll and sent them to Cyprus. When they returned, they started the as-built drawings.

Andy was busy, as were Karen and Cathy, sorting through the paperwork and putting it in order for the COE. It was taking more time than it should because Andy had kept notes of his safety meetings, and the girls were having trouble filing while they were doubled over laughing.

Andy's descriptions were graphic. At first, I thought we should trash some of the reports because no one would believe someone would weld a pipe to a chunk of railroad iron and expect laborers with bare feet to compact the site. Few people would, but then there was Anwar.

I had to laugh myself when Karen handed me the notes about the day we tested the water lines. There was not a water line in Cairo that could maintain a pressure above fifty pounds without turning into a sprinkler system. Tom was being a jerk that day. Forty-five would work; our specks required a test of seventy-five.

Schmir was having a tough time because, having never heard of them, he refused to install thrust blocks in the ditch to prevent the pipes from shifting under pressure. It was not spelled out in the test requirements. Andy and I gave up arguing; it could be a lesson. Tom and I took our cups of tea and settled in the shade to watch the show.

Schmir managed to pump sixty-five pounds of pressure into the lines. I could see the belly of the pipe rising from the ditch. I thought that should be sufficient and tried to talk Tom into accepting it.

Tom was turned the other way. Emphatically, *No!* Tom did not notice the pipe lifting out of the ditch when the gauge reached sixty-eight pounds. I made an excuse to move out of the way. I was on my feet and backing up when Tom saw the pipe rising out of the ditch.

"Too late, Tom."

"Fuck…., you could have warned me!"

Tom was drenched. When the gauge reached a little over seventy psi, three sections of six-inch pipe left the ditch quicker than Robin Hood's arrows left his bow. As a twenty-foot length sailed out over Tom's head, the stream of the water from the end of the pipe still in the ditch drenched Tom with Cairo water before he could get out of his chair.

"What now, Tom?"

"Where's Andy."

"I don't know, Tom, why."

"He's supposed to conduct these tests."

"I'm right here, Tom; I've been taking notes."

Andy went off to write his report. Tom conceded to a pressure test of sixty pounds if Andy would lose the report, and after Schmir reinstalled the pipes, this time with thrust blocks. That was one of the more fun days.

There was one report Andy had hidden from me that I found after the work was complete. I conceded that he could lose it since Tom had not pressed the issue. I mentioned it earlier.

The design called for concrete block infill between the building frames. I was gone, Andy was on holiday. Hamid did buy the right material, but Egyptians have a unique way of mixing mortar and grout to fill the cells. They pile sand on the ground, fill a fifty-gallon barrel with water, and then build what looks like the cone of a volcano.

They add water and mortar to the center of the cone. Now I understood what the ropes were for. One man held the shovel while three others dragged it around, mixing the sludge. There is a line of men with tin pans, much like a Japanese cooking wok, but half the size. They put a shovel of mix in the pan and carry it to the mason, who lays the block; he then fills the cells with what is left while he waits for the next pan. Then there's prayer time. It can take a while between mixing and filling. By then, lumps form, and it does not flow.

And then there are the blocks themselves. They did not use concrete saws; they used whatever was available for a hammer, chipping, and breaking blocks to fit at corners, doors, and windows.

When Andy got back to the site, the masons were skimming plaster on a wall that looked like a disheveled honeycomb. I arrived as Andy was explaining to Schmir that it was unacceptable and would have to come down.

Hamid had been in charge while Andy and I were gone. Schmir was arguing that Dr. Osmond would make him pay for the wasted materials, and he would not pay to have him do it over.

I had grown fond of Schmir. I looked at the new wall Schmir had built between the bases when Andy and I had been busy with electrical and plumbing. Then I remembered how easy it was for the loader to punch a hole through the old wall. Schmir's wall was definitely an improvement.

"Andy, it's Thursday, take the weekend off." "Hamid, tell Schmir to finish and paint it before Andy and Tom get back on Monday."

Later, when Cathy took exception to Andy's notes explaining to Schmir that the men had to clean their shit off the fresh concrete and use the outhouse, I left for the day.

The design was faulty in many areas and incompatible with the available utilities in Cairo. Because of the pending changes, the timing turned in our favor once the plans were finished. Tom approved the pay estimates and change orders regularly.

I had made a lot of promises the first year, but even so, Doctor Osmond and Cesar were surprised we were being paid for the past delays caused by the Egyptian Generals and the freight forwarder. Black ink replaced red, which kept the partners happy and off my ass, and with the women in the flat, my standard of living had significantly improved.

Karen had the boab put a lock on the bathroom door. I switched to taking my shower at night. Dinner was ready by the time I finished my evening scotch. If I was late, no one seemed to mind.

There was always a clean-pressed shirt in my closet. I was getting hot showers, and since the day I washed my blue sweatshirt in the same load with Cathy's frilly pink nightgown, the grumbling about me taking a turn at the laundry had subsided.

When Karen and Cathy started work Andy managed to convince Gary to get them duty-free privileges. Neither consumed much more than a glass of wine with dinner. My scotch and Jack supplies were always stocked, and my disposition had mellowed.

I had not heard much from home since I returned to Cairo. The few letters I did receive were mostly bad news. Once in a while, a friend would write; it was apparent Mary was having a fling; who could blame her? I had been gone for over 14 months.

Things were not going well with two of my daughters or at the restaurant. I was 10,000 miles away and not available to deal with it, which was adding to the bitterness I detected on my last trip home. I could do little about it. I could not go back until Christmas, which was three months away. It seemed much further.

There was an underlying tone in the letters and Mary's voice during my occasional phone calls. Still, I refused to face reality. I was content with my new status. Without realizing it at the time, I had accepted that my old way of life was at an end, and once the project was finished, I would have to make major adjustments in my life. I had a job and a place to live for now. It was easier not to deal with it.

General Aziz returned after finishing his training in the States and constantly wanted special items that were not in the contract. With all the changes, we were pushing the OMC's financial limit on the project.

When I entered the office, Andy, Carl, General Aziz, and a stranger I had not met were sitting at the conference table. Andy was going over some drawings with our visitor.

"Pat, meet Mike. He's the PM for the agency that will be training the Egyptians after we turn it over to the COE."

"Hello Mike, are you just here for a visit?"

"No, I'll be here until the fifteenth of December and the turnover ceremonies."

Someone had not kept Mike appraised of the progress, or if they had, he was acting like his Egyptian counterparts and ignoring the facts. I turned to the General.

"General Aziz, you know we won't complete the building before the first of the year?"

"Mr. Pat, you must finish by December fifteen. We scheduled the dedication ceremonies and can't change the date."

"I don't care who you've invited, General Aziz. I have time extensions until January fifteen; there isn't any possibility the building will be ready before then.'

"Pat, it has to be ready. Otherwise, we are going to have to pay IBM for the delays you will cause in the follow-up contract."

"I'll cause? That's bullshit, Mike. I don't give a shit about IBM. I told your office not to award the contract if it meant we had to be done before the first of next year. The COE has granted us the time. Whatever it's going to cost is no concern of mine."

"Patience, Mr. Pat. We need to work together and find a way to get it done on time."

"Ah, General Aziz, it's time you showed a little patience yourself. You know what the schedule is. Tom and I met with you just last Sunday."

"Mike, why not tell Pat the real reason you're here.'

"What is this, Andy, another snow job?'

"No, just bad news."

"Let's have it, Mike."

They wanted December 15th but were working the issues out with IBM. IBM's engineers had been to the site and told Mike the plans for the switchgear and layout in the building would not be compatible with the IBM equipment. IBM insisted we change it to meet their specs.

IBM had a point; they sent the specs to General Aziz and Mike's office six months before Cesar signed the contract with the COE. The documents were misplaced before they reached the COE and had been overlooked. They resurfaced at a meeting between Mike and the IBM engineers after IBM's visit to the site.

Mike and the General were trying to cover their ass and slip the change in.

"That's too bad, Mike. You get what we're building unless the COE decides to issue another change order."

"I was just out in the building. The electrical work in the computer room isn't finished. It wouldn't be a big deal to change it."

"You're right; it wouldn't if I had a set of approved drawings and the materials to make the changes were in Cairo. This is the middle of September. If I knew what IBM wanted, which I don't, it would take two weeks to get new shop drawings to Tom. Electrical plans go to Washington for review. Figure another thirty days for the COE to review the plans, two weeks to purchase the material, and another hundred twenty days to get it to the site. That adds up to five months plus install time if everything were to go right, which history says won't happen."

"There isn't an option. There has to be some way to expedite it. It won't work as is; it has to be changed. I want you to stop the electrical work until this is resolved?"

"You don't have the authority, Mike. What the hell do you want me to do, mail it through the diplomatic pouch at the Embassy? This is your problem. Don't try to pawn it off on me. If it's that important, take it up with Washington; my orders come from the COE." "Andy, is Tom in his office?"

"Yes, and he's aware of the problem."

"Shit….! Why am I always the last one to know?"

I spent the rest of the afternoon going over it with Tom. We were both of the same opinion. Neither of us wanted to let Mike make his problem our problem.

"Tom, even March doesn't look like a good date."

"Why not mail it through the Embassy?"

"I was joking, and you have got to be fucking kidding. There's no way the Ambassador would go for it."

I did have Embassy mailing privileges, but the limit was one ten-ounce package per week. I had not yet seen the IBM plans, but Mike would not be there if it were not a major issue. It was ludicrous to think we could get away with mailing electrical materials through diplomatic channels.

I could protest all I liked, but Tom and I knew if IBM wanted the change, we were going to have to find a way to make it happen. Tom told me he would discuss it with Mike and Glen. The time would work itself out. Tom did not seem too upset. He just signed a contract with the COE for another two-year tour in Cairo.

Less than twelve hours earlier, I was on schedule, looking forward to finishing without more screw-ups and leaving Cairo in time for winter steelhead fishing in Oregon. I was depressed and tired of the whole affair when I opened the door to my flat.

"Karen, what the hell are all these people doing here?"

My living room looked like a refugee camp. There were about twenty people in various positions of repose on the living room sofa and floor.

"We lost the classroom we were using. I didn't think you would mind if we used the flat for a few days until we could find another."

"Damned straight I mind, Karen. This is the only place in Cairo where I can get away from the bullshit of this society. Besides, if I'm caught with a bunch of illegals in my flat, I'll end up being the one deported. Get them the hell out of here, now!"

Karen had the sense not to argue and quietly asked Cathy to escort the refugees out the door. I headed for the liquor cabinet and a healthy glass of scotch.

"You wouldn't be so cranky if you didn't drink so much."

"You're wrong; I'd be a hell of a lot crankier. Three's Company is one thing, Karen. I never agreed to twenty-three. By the way, have you had word from the agency in the States about your plane tickets home?"

A half-hour later, I heard Cathy reenter the flat. I was lying on my bed, feeling guilty for the way I talked to Karen. Besides all the housekeeping work, the girls had added a few touches of home, which did a lot for my morale.

I was being more than a little testy. I walked back into the room to apologize and overheard Karen tell Cathy to stay out of my way. She also said she did not think it was the right time to tell me.

"I heard that; tell me what?"

The women had been in Egypt for a year, but they had not been exposed to the same people I had, which made lying easy for me.

"We have our tickets to the States."

"Great! When will you be going home?"

"Sorry to disappoint you, March twenty-third."

"Karen, that's six months away?"

The sponsoring agency purchased tickets with specific return dates when the women signed up. The agency considered the girl's leaving a resignation, which in their contract meant them paying their way home. The agency was willing to give them the no-change, nonrefundable tickets. It was up to the girls to buy their own earlier flight.

"Pat, we want to remain until the refugees we're working with are accepted into Canada.'

"You told me when I agreed to this they would be leaving in a few weeks."

"This year's quota is filled. The Canadian Government put their applications on hold."

"I can't guarantee I'll be here in March. It's time you bite the bullet and ask your families for help."

"Andy told us there will be another change order that will extend the contract until at least then. Cathy and I are going to stay until the families we're teaching have their visas. If you want us to move out don't make up excuses. Just tell us, and we'll find another place."

The women's salaries were Egyptian standards for English-speaking help. Between the two of them, they were making the equivalent of $500 a month. With living expenses, the best they could hope for was in a slum. A slum in Cairo for two white women is a dangerous garbage dump back home. I had come to know Karen well enough to know if she made up her mind not much was going to make her change it. I ended up doing what I normally did in a domestic argument: I put it off.

"What's for dinner?"

"Nothing, the refugees have been here all afternoon. We haven't had a chance to start dinner. Besides, you have been taking advantage. You should take us out to dinner; we think we deserve it."

Karen was catching on. A good offense was better than a logical defense. Karen may not have been right about my taking advantage, but she was right about us needing a night out.

"All right, get ready. Where did you have in mind?"

"We heard the Ramses Hilton on the Cornice would be nice."

For a woman who could not afford Egyptian beans, Karen had good taste. The Ramses was the newest five-star hotel in Cairo. I had not been there, but Tom had. According to him, they had a magnificent restaurant overlooking the Nile where the food and service were excellent. It was also extremely expensive.

"Why not?"

The roads into downtown Cairo at that time of evening would be jammed with traffic approaching the downtown area. I knew the chances of finding a place to park within five klicks of the hotel were nonexistent. I poured another scotch as I was debating, car or taxi.

"You shouldn't drink if you're going to drive."

"Karen, if you two are staying, one of the new rules is for you to quit being such a pain in the ass. I don't intend to drive into Cairo this time of night. We'll take a taxi."

"I only mentioned it because you detest Cairo taxis."

"You sure as shit aren't going to drive. There are a lot of things I don't like, but in Cairo, we learn to cope. When it comes to driving through Cairo traffic, and then finding a place to park in the evening, a taxi is the lesser of the evils."

The mood mellowed. The girls got dressed; I showered and changed, by then, it was after 8:00. Finding a taxi in the evening meant a walk from the residential area to the main highway that runs through Maadi. The taxi drivers in the area are used to dealing with the expat community that expects clean cars with working headlights. Karen was not yet used to dealing with Maadi taxi drivers.

The first taxi was one of the Peugeot station wagons that prowled the more affluent neighborhoods. I opened the door and told the driver we wanted to go downtown. He responded with the normal *ten pounds*. I expected it and did not feel three bucks was too much to pay for a 20 klick drive downtown. Karen had other ideas.

"Ten-LE is too much. It only costs two when Cathy and I come from downtown to the flat."

"I'm not in the mood to argue, Karen. I just want to go to dinner."

"We'll get another taxi."

With that, she closed the door and told the driver to move on.

"Karen, it's three dollars. All the taxi drivers in this area will ask the same amount."

A few minutes later, I stopped another. Karen decided to handle negotiations. This time it was Karen losing her patience. When the third taxi pulled to a stop, I told Karen to get in, or I would go alone. She did, but then gave me a lecture on how Americans in Cairo screwed things up for the working class.

Cathy was young and still trainable. She made it a point to take the Arabic classes Karen and I kept putting off. The classes, combined with her relationship with her boyfriend, gave her a fluent grasp of the language. Cathy was telling the driver where we wanted to go.

Cathy told us she renegotiated the fare down to four LE. Cathy was coming out of her shell; she mentioned something about me learning to speak Arabic and to quit throwing money around. I mentioned something about Herfy's instead of the Hilton, which put an end to the discussion.

The Ramses had not been open long enough to absorb the smells of the surrounding areas or the attitude of the local labor force. When we entered the lobby, the aggravation of the ride into town melted with the magnificence of the sparkling new hotel. I felt I had left the city of Cairo and entered another world where organization and social graces were the norm rather than the exception.

The host seated us at a table surrounded on three sides by glass with a panoramic view of the Nile. The confusion on the streets below was in the shadows of the buildings. The only reminder I was still in Cairo was the loud, shrill at times, Arabic wedding party at a table behind us. I thought about asking the waiter to move us to a quieter location, but Karen and Cathy were absorbed in the violin group that was approaching our table.

It was a little noisy. I decided to do some homework for my patience class. The thought was lost as I tried to make the waiter understand Karen and Cathy were used to the local white wine priced at six LE a bottle in most Cairo hotel restaurants. The waiter gave me a sleazy look when I insisted on the same wine priced at twenty-two on the menu.

I ordered scotch. It appeared the first order of business was complete until the waiter came back and asked if I wanted the special or the regular scotch. When I answered regular, he gave me the same look as the one over the wine. When he left Karen picked up the menu and then turned to Cathy.

"Shit, Cathy, this is expensive. We can settle for Hors d'oeuvres."

"Such talk for missionaries, Karen. You knew it was expensive when you suggested it, I agreed. I'm looking forward to a pleasant meal and more music. Put it out of your mind; you will spoil the night if you concentrate on the cost."

Based on the 80-LE a month each of them had been making at the school, they would have had to work six months to pay the dinner tab. My budget anticipated eating out at one of the more conservative restaurants two or three nights a week. This was my first night out in the last two weeks. Karen had done the grocery shopping for the coming week. Allowing for one of the Cuban cigars after dinner, I would still end the month with a surplus.

Thought: *Two weeks? Actually, unless I was stuck at the office, which seldom happened after Dr. Abboud disappeared, I was having dinner at home regularly. Karen had a point. I had not thought about it. When I was at home, and the girls were around, I was content; maybe I was taking advantage.*

When we finished a three-course meal, topped it off with one of the pastries from the dessert cart, and the girls finished a second bottle of wine, it was almost 2:00. The noisy group of Arabs left hours before. The girls managed to put the price of the dinner and the frustration of Cairo behind them; I was in no hurry to end the evening.

It had been a long time since I felt relaxed and enjoyed myself with anyone of the opposite sex. The conversation of the past hours did not reflect the brother, sister, and niece set of rules we established at the onset.

I am not sure what the bill came to. I paid for it with Cesar's American Express card. He could deduct it from my last month's allowance that was still trying to find its way into my Cairo bank account.

The liquor had an effect. The three of us weaved out of the hotel arm in arm. Cathy and Karen were giggling. Parked at the entrance was a line of horse-drawn carriages. It seemed a perfect way to end the evening. When I asked the driver if he was available and the driver answered with the usual ten Pounds, neither of the girls said a word.

Karen stepped into the carriage. We settled back, adjusting ourselves to the seat designed for couples touring Cairo on their honeymoons or holidays. I took the middle and allowed Karen and

Cathy to cradle in my arms. It was comfortable and a very pleasant place to be.

Settling back under the soft cotton quilt, we lost track of time. By the time we circled the majestic lions standing guard at the entrance to the Sixth of October Bridge, the hassles of Cairo routine were the furthest thing from our minds.

Traffic on the Cornice diminished by the time we turned the corner and returned to the main street that follows the Nile to Maadi. The wine was wearing off, and the realization that finding a taxi at three a.m. might be difficult entered our minds.

Cathy suggested we walk along the Nile while we waited for one to pass. The only other pedestrians were soldiers stationed every one hundred meters and security guards posted in front of homes for the affluent of Cairo's society.

We had come full circle and were across from the hotel. We stopped at a viewpoint jutting out over the Nile that afforded a view of fishermen settled on the decks of their boats warming their morning tea. They would soon be setting their nets for an early catch so they could be at the market when it opened to sell to buyers from restaurants who paid more than the locals in the afternoon.

The reflections from streetlights masked the sewage and other waste floating in the river; it had disappeared into the shadows. It was chilly; Karen shifted closer, as did Cathy. I reacted to the moment by putting my arms around them, drawing them in, warming us from the morning breeze.

I was intoxicated by the smells and feelings that come from the closeness of a woman a man finds himself caring for. Suddenly, and without warning, the quiet was shattered by shouts from a soldier. He grabbed me from behind, spun me around, and forced me back against the stone column and railing, which kept me from falling into the polluted and wasted river.

Reason was lost in the shock of the sudden interruption. Karen and Cathy were huddled in the background as other soldiers joined the first, yelling at us in Arabic. I reached out to protect myself from the rifle butt jammed against my chest, but contained myself in time, trying not to give the soldiers cause for further roughness.

Cathy was in the background pleading with one of the men, trying to find the cause of the sudden disturbance. Her grasp of the language calmed the others; they relaxed their hold on me.

I asked quietly.

“Cathy, what’s going on?”

“Pat, let me deal with this.”

Cathy had a way about her that could relax most men, the soldiers were no exception. They were not used to dealing with assertive women in their society or a beautiful young foreigner who spoke their language.

Karen and I began to relax as the tension in the soldier’s stance took on a look of nervousness. Cathy was getting through. I started to butt in; she gestured to me to keep my place. I did; there was no reason other than a chauvinistic belief that it was I who should be protecting her, not her protecting me.

Karen and I were bewildered when the soldiers turned to us and apologized for their mistake. When they left, I settled back, lit a cigarette, allowed my heart to regain an even tempo, and waited for an explanation.

One of the soldiers saw us leave the hotel and followed the carriage. When we started walking arm in arm back toward the hotel, he was convinced I was a tourist who had picked up two women. Public affection by members of the opposite sex is not allowed in the Muslim world. Adultery is punishable by death. It seemed I made my gravest mistake to date, disrespecting the laws of Islam.

Cathy stuck to the story. Karen was my sister; she was my niece. We had shared a couple of bottles of wine and had forgotten the rules; she apologized. The public display of affection was, if not common, acceptable for tourists in Cairo.

I shook my head wondering if there was any possibility I would ever adjust to the society. I was sinking into thoughts of reasons why and how I came to be in such a strange land when Karen flagged a passing taxi. She was subdued. The *ten pounds* by the driver did not affect her. We settled into the backseat, and as the sun started to rise over the city, I mentally prepared for another day.

Chapter 32

I was questioning Mike's ability to read a set of plans. The changes were substantially more than Mike's notes indicated. Mike was a bureaucrat assigned as a negotiator to the IBM contract; he was not an engineer. Mike was concerned more with covering his ass than assisting field personnel who have to deal with unscheduled or unanticipated delays.

"Andy, have you heard from Mike or General Aziz?"

"No, but Schmir's complaining. We're holding up work that can't be done until the wiring is finished."

"Tell Schmir to relax until Saturday. Tom promised me some answers today."

Schmir had a point, one Mike would never understand. Delaying electrical work may not have appeared critical to Mike, but it was having a far-reaching effect on the HVAC, ceilings, sheetrock, flooring, and painting. Schmir was running out of things to do, but there was a great deal of work remaining.

"Andy, notify the staff I want a meeting this morning, and then call General Aziz, Mike, and Tom. I would like to meet with them this afternoon."

Andy was leaving to round up the players while I prepared for the meeting.

"Andy, is Cathy here?"

After Moya left, Cathy was an immense help in dealing with the Egyptians and the General. Like Moya, she was fluent. I asked her to pretend she did not understand Arabic when she was on the site.

Moya was British and had no qualms. Cathy agreed. However, she told me she did not think spying was part of her job description when Andy hired her. Cathy was still young, and, as I mentioned earlier, she was trainable. She agreed to attend meetings and take minutes of the conversations, including the Arabic comments in the background.

The exercise was enlightening. What was happening on the site was not always in line with the discussions taking place in English. Once Cathy realized the Egyptians were ignoring the rules in the documents, she understood the need for me to know what was going on.

The process was working. Hamid and Schmir were surprised when Andy was able to pinpoint areas on the site where they were cutting corners, trying to hide defective workmanship and substandard materials.

I called the meeting to review other delays the electrical work was causing. After the meeting, I asked Andy and Cathy to join me for a cup of tea; Cathy was beside herself.

"Are you nuts? How long has this been going on?"

"Enlighten me, Cathy?"

"Hamid told Mohammad it was your orders."

"Cathy, what the hell are you talking about, and when did you start believing anything Hamid says?"

"Sorry, after you and Andy left the site yesterday, Hamid and Mohammad moved some electrical materials to Doctor Osmond's warehouse. They think they will be left over because of the changes; they don't want to give them to the Army. Andy asked Mohammad for an inventory. Hamid told Andy and Mohammad you gave the orders."

My team knew the rules; if I was breaking them, Andy was not going to confront me; he was along for the ride. Cathy had scruples; she was more direct.

Electrical materials like pipe, wire, and boxes are generic. They would work with the IBM change. Others were specific to the design but useless on the project when the design changed. However, they could be sold and incorporated into local projects with less stringent specifications.

Normally, it would be a windfall for the contractor. Mechanical, plumbing, and electrical materials had an extremely high value in Egypt, where imported materials were assessed up to 100% duty. Ours was a duty-free project. It was clear in the bid documents that once the materials were turned over to the government freight forwarder, the company billed the government and they belonged to the Egyptian army. It was a criminal act to remove them from the site.

It was apparent Dr. Osmond intended to sell the leftovers on the black market. Cathy knew the rules and, for a minute, thought I might be involved. She also knew that would put all the Americans at risk.

"Cathy, just for the record, I'm not. But if Hamid is selling them and is caught, I will be the one held responsible. Since it appears Mohammad is not involved, see if you can con him into telling you which of Dr. Osmond's warehouses Hamid is using."

It could be my biggest and much more than a headache to date. All foreign contractors in Egypt must JV their projects with an Egyptian firm. A few months earlier I had been in the Sixth of October City to pick John up at the factory where he was still working. His site was shut down, and he would be returning to London until work resumed; it would be a while.

The German contractor who did the site works for the industrial park also had a contract with the Egypt military to work on a nearby airbase. In addition to military work covered by the duty-free clause, they prepped a private company's site that was subject to civilian laws and duties.

The Germans purchased $2.6 million worth of new equipment and shipped it through the military facilities at Alexandria to be delivered to the Egyptian air base. Before the Germans finished the work on the base, they moved half the equipment to the private company's site.

The duty-free clause was not part of the private contract. A British firm also bid on the Sixth of October project. After the German firm underbid them, the Brits notified Egyptian customs that the Germans were using duty-free equipment that they imported for the military projects. The military threw the German PD in jail. Customs confiscated not only the equipment on the private site but also on the military site.

Duty on cars and heavy equipment was 100% of its value. Customs levied an additional 50% penalty. Once the money was paid, Egypt sold the equipment to the British company, deported the PD, and barred the German company from working in the country.

I contacted Don and asked him to send me the cost of the materials on our site. Don resented me butting in and refused. *I had the budget; use it.*

As it happened, it was not Hamid and Mohammad's fault. Material gets lost and damaged in shipment, so it was customary practice to buy a percentage more than you will need. Cesar and Don neglected to read the fine print. When the money was tight, Cesar asked Abboud to sell leftovers and obsolete materials, and he would split the proceeds with Dr. Osmond.

Abboud was gone. Dr. Osmond assumed Cesar informed me and that the request to Dr. Abboud came from me. Dr. Osmond gave the instructions to Hamid when it became apparent there would be valuable materials left over because of the defective plans.

What Dr. Osmond thought did not matter. Both he and Abboud knew the rules. I did a quick calculation of what I thought the materials were worth and compared it to what the Germans paid in fines. Cesar nor Doctor Osmond would pay that much ransom for me.

"Andy, let's try to keep this under wraps. Tell Hamid Cesar changed his mind and to return the materials to the site. Then send a fax to Don telling him we're short materials in other areas and we don't expect any leftovers."

Andy was not happy getting dragged in.

"Doctor Osmond won't be happy; I'm sure Cesar agreed to split the proceeds?"

"Andy, you're the second American in command on this project. That puts you in jeopardy alongside me. You and I are not going to jail."

"I hadn't thought about that."

"Think about it. Tell Hamid they have until Saturday to bring the material back without anyone finding out."

Andy left to find Hamid. A few minutes later, Hamid entered my office.

"Mr. Pat, we will bring them back after tomorrow, inshallah."

"Cathy, Arabic-English isn't going to work. Come over here and translate."

"Hamid, tell Doctor Osmond bookra inshallah doesn't fucking cut it. You or Doctor Osmond had better find Allah. This time, after tomorrow, better mean Saturday. Also, tell him you are responsible for security. If we come up short, I will back charge his account and give your name to General Aziz. General Aziz and Tom will check our inventory against the shipping documents on Sunday, Hamid. Get it done!"

Hamid stood glaring and then mumbled something in Arabic.

"Cathy, what did he say?"

"He's upset about the Allah crack."

In the past, it had been sarcasm due to frustration. Up until the time I write this, I cannot remember any time in my life ever being that angry on a job site.

"Fuck him. Cathy, translate me to him; use Arabic, verbatim!" "Hamid, don't fuck with me on this. Tell Dr. Osmond Andy and I are not going to jail. Bring back the materials, all of them, and then do an inventory before General Aziz and Tom get here Sunday!"

When he left, Hamid was as angry as I was. I stewed for the next hour. Hamid and Mohammad moved the materials the night before. I had a feeling it was coming. Later that day, General Aziz summoned Mike, Tom, and me to his office.

"Mr. Pat, my soldiers told me your staff took materials from the site."

Shit! Bleeding hearts do not survive long in the Middle East. Neither do expats in prison. *Thank you, Cathy, for the warning.* I had had time to cool down and come up with a story.

"General, we're running short on warehouse space. I told Hamid to inventory the redundant electrical materials and store them until we settled the change."

"We've been through this before. Nothing is to leave the site unless you arrange it with my office."

"Tom, it's that fucking electrical change. They should have been installed by now. They were in the way. We need space for an incoming shipment. It was a slip-up in translation. I told Hamid to sort the materials and move the excess. We don't have a spare secure area on site. Mohammed and Hamid thought I meant off the site. Andy discovered the shortage this morning and brought it up at our meeting. Cathy will send you a copy of the minutes. They will return the material by Saturday and then take inventory. It's all there, but General Aziz is welcome to lend one of his soldiers when they check it off against the shipping documents."

"General Mike, will you excuse us for a minute? Mr. Pat and I need a few minutes." "Let's step outside."

"Pat, you fucking well know better. If you come up short, we are all in one hell of a mess."

"I know, Tom. Hamid hasn't had time to sell them; we'll get them back. Let's deal with the change. It will get Aziz's mind off it when he realizes how much it's going to cost, and it will give me time to fix this."

"Saturday, no later. I mean it, Patrick. If you come up short, the COE can't fix this!"

"Got it. Aziz and Mike will wonder. Tell them we were discussing the change order."

"Better you bring it up."

I knew it was far from settled and the tally better match. Tom warned me many times about residual materials. He was adamant about making sure to document leftovers and that we turn them over before the project closeout. This was something Tom could not bail my ass out of.

"Mike, we need to settle the change. I've stopped working. If we don't settle it soon, we will have to use what we have."

"That will never work. Tom has the authority; let's get it done."

Mike, Tom, and I returned to my office. I gave Tom and Mike a copy of the cost estimate for the changes, along with the new schedule showing the completion date extended to April 1988.

"Pat, there has to be another way."

Tom and I had been fighting over the schedule for fourteen months. Although most of the delays were a result of the Egyptian Army or delays by the COE's freight forwarder, the partners had caused their share. This was easier to deal with, knowing it had nothing to do with our responsibilities. This was strictly General Aziz's and Mike's problem.

The IBM revisions caused an unanticipated delay, Mike's negligence in pursuing changes with the OMC, and the COE's delays during the review would get us off the hook for good and guarantee a tidy profit for Cesar and Doctor Osmond.

The time had come for honesty between the players. Up until now, the liquidated damages were hanging over my head. It was a pleasant change to be in control.

"Mike, BS aside, what's reality?"

"I've rescheduled IBM. They have to be done no later than March fifteen, or their programming crew will lose their window for next year. That means you need to be done by mid-February so IBM can install their equipment. We extended IBM's contract to coincide with the return of the Egyptian students from the States; they won't be coming back. It will take at least eight to ten months to train new personnel and program the computers. Our first shipments for the F-Sixteen base and the Tank Core facilities will arrive in January 2009. If the equipment gets lost in the system before the tracking programs are in place, we may never find it."

"Pat, what do you suggest?"

"Let's try the mail, Tom. If we manage it, it will only inconvenience the Ambassador for a few days, but get the OMC on board just in case.'

"How much material are we talking about?"

"A lot, close to a ton, and there are no guarantees. Write the change order to reflect a completion date of February 15 with the understanding that if the mail scam doesn't work, the liquidated damages will be waived."

"I can't do that; it's going to be tough enough getting the date adjusted and include the cost for air mailing the material. How much of a gamble are you willing to take?"

"Jesus Christ, none…., shit…, Tom, it's not my problem. I don't give a fuck when we get done as long as it doesn't cost my company any money. I'll agree to February-fifteen if you let me include enough money to cover liquidated damages through May first."

"I can't do that. That's almost a-hundred-forty-grand. By the way, how much is the work going to cost?"

"If we count the postage fees a little over two-hundred-fifty thousand, that is if we settle it today so I can have Don start sending the material."

"The Government estimate is one-fifty."

"So, what the fuck's new? I don't give a shit what the Government estimate is. The Government estimate when this Contract was awarded was twelve months. It's been fourteen and I still have three months or more without this change. If you don't agree, I'll finish the project per the plans and let IBM sort it out when the equipment arrives."

"You know that isn't going to work. I don't like unilateral changes; they're a can of worms, but my orders are to get it done."

Thought: *So, What? If I refused to do the work, he would order me to do it unilaterally, and the Government would be on the hook for whatever time and money it actually took.*

However, unilateral meant we had to perform without question and settle the money later or face the LDs. Settling the money could take years. There was no way I was going to convince Cesar to spend more money without knowing when and how much he would be paid. It was in everyone's best interest to cut a deal.

"Tom, Andy, and I need to check something on the site. Give us a half-hour. Maybe I can come up with an alternate."

"Andy, let's take a walk."

Andy was out of the loop. He was confused at the sudden adjournment and our unscheduled inspection trip to the site.

"What's up?"

"Does Tom know the Egyptian Government hasn't made arrangements to hook up the water and sewer lines to the mains in the street?"

It was our last major hangup. We had run utility lines to the edge of the property line; our responsibility ended there. It was the Egyptian Army's responsibility to hook them to the mains in the street. We could not finish testing and complete the project without fire protection, water, and sewer.

"I'm not sure; I've sent a number of letters to General Aziz and an FYI to Tom a few weeks ago. I was going to bring it up again today."

"Don't. It's the last ace we have. Let's go back to the meeting."

Tom and Mike had been discussing money.

"All right, Tom. Let's settle the money first and then the time."

"The most I can go is two hundred thousand and an extension to February first."

It did not surprise me. I was not supposed to know it, but alcohol loosens lips. Tom's limit of authority on changes was $225,000. If the change costs more, it will have to be sent to a higher level; that would take weeks.

"Tom, Mike said the middle of February, two-hundred-twenty-five-K, and the fifteenth."

"The fifteenth is cutting it too close. Two-hundred twenty-five and the fifth is the best I can do.

"Tom, you're making the Government's problem my problem again."

"If you want to play hardball, you'll never finish on time even if we don't make this change. If you force me, I'll put you on liquidated damages the day your current time extension runs out."

It was business, and it was not our money. If Tom wanted to revisit the first year of the contract, he would argue my own company caused sufficient delays to offset any delays the government caused. I did not want to reopen that can of worms. I still had the water line. It was no time to get into a pissing match with Tom.

"February fifth it is." "Mike, is that agreeable?"

By the time we finished, it was after six. With the Electrical held up, work on the project had slowed. I looked out the window as Mike and Tom passed through the gate. Schmir and his crew were gone. The only one left on the site was the guard at the gate.

Andy and Cathy had stuck around sorting through the records, getting ready for Andy to take inventory, if or when Hamid returned the materials.

I was not anxious to go to the office after the session with Hamid. Dr. Osmond would be furious. There was a bottle of scotch on my desk. Andy and Cathy came through the door as I was pouring a drink. It was a little somber in the room.

"Sorry, Cathy, I didn't mean to drag you in."

"What the language, for Christ's sake, Pat, I've been living with you. I've heard it before, and besides, they had it coming."

Cathy was not as naive as I thought. She turned around, left the room, came back with two more glasses, and then poured both herself and Andy a couple of fingers of scotch. *What the hell?*

"When did you two start drinking scotch?"

"Our nerves are shot too. That was quite a session with Hamid. Do you think he will bring them back?"

"I don't know, Andy, but if Doctor Osmond has any brains, they will. He can't buy his way out of this one."

The three of us sat there for a while. I looked at my watch; it was close to seven. I was putting the bottle away. When I looked up, I was facing the window. A truck was coming through the gate.

"Andy, are we expecting any deliveries."

"Not until next week."

"In that case, it looks like Doctor Osmond and Hamid found Allah."

Hamid and Mohammad had returned. I assumed they had it all. There was no sense in me or Andy getting involved until it was time to take inventory. We left the site and the unloading to Hamid.

I avoided the office to give things time to settle. Having been caught, Doctor Osmond would eventually realize he and Cesar had made a mistake.

I stopped by the Sonesta Hotel and called Tom. He would be relieved. Then I sent a fax to Cesar and told him we had settled the change and for him to consolidate the material and make sure it all came in no more than four shipments.

Cesar responded a few days later with questions about when we would be done when the COE would pay for the added materials, and why I was spending money sending a fax from the hotel.

Floating this by the Ambassador was going to be difficult. He eventually agreed, but we had to keep the disruption to his mailroom at a minimum. I do not think I mentioned it was a ton or more of material.

A week passed. Hamid had been absent from the site. I waited until after the inventory results were in before going back to the office. The books balanced; Doctor Osmond was gone until *after tomorrow*. Hamid was also taking a few days off.

Chapter 33

Twenty-three settled into a routine. When I finished my day before 6:30, I stopped off at the Sonesta for a drink and conversation with the British expats. This gave Karen and Cathy time to finish the lessons with the refugees at my flat, which they had turned into their regular classroom after they managed to get temporary visas for the students.

I usually got home by seven. Evenings were family-style meals, BBC news, and a game of Scrabble. Dull by American standards, but pleasant and relaxing away from the constant conflict between the partners and the pollution of Cairo.

I was at the Sonesta bar reflecting; it had been a quiet month on the home front. The correspondence between my wife and I had diminished to once-a-week phone calls when the connection could be made, and she was there to take the call, which was becoming less and less frequent.

There was an occasional letter when something was wrong in the lives of one of the kids. I was tired of hearing bad news. We had been avoiding the inevitable my returning to the States in a few months was bringing it to a head.

I was wondering if I should schedule a trip at Christmas or simply wait until the project was finished. Ron, a British expat, interrupted my thoughts. Ron asked if I wanted to join a group of expats who booked a weekend at the Movenpick Hotel in Luxor.

Luxor is six hundred klicks south of Cairo on the upper Nile. It is within a taxi and boat ride to the Valley of the Kings & Queens, one of the last on my list of places I wanted to visit in Egypt. It was Thursday; they had a cancellation and needed a replacement to offset the fare.

"Bring Karen along."

I was not able to keep the three's company situation quiet in the expat community. Karen knew some of the expat's wives, and although I tried to ignore the background comments at the bar, people were following the soap opera with interest generated from a lack of anything better to do.

"It's late notice, Ron. I'm going to have to pass; I have worked to catch up on."

It was not true. The work was progressing as rapidly as possible while waiting for the first mail shipment to arrive and the resulting furor I knew it would cause at the Embassy. I eventually had to come clean. The Ambassador was livid after I approached his staff with a warning as to the quantity and gave them the shipping documents.

It took the OMC and the COE to convince him. The shipments were not due for another week, and that could change if back-ordered material did not arrive at Cesar's warehouse. Andy and the staff could manage the work on the site until then.

"If you change your mind, the train leaves at seven p.m. tomorrow; I'll have tickets on board."

It did sound like fun. The group booked a Pullman on a first-class train. They had a private club car and a party planned for the evening. The train would arrive in Luxor at eight on Saturday. Bungalows were reserved at the Movenpick, which was the only five-star hotel in Upper Egypt. They were going to stay three days.

Tours of the Valley of the Kings and the village market were scheduled, but the hotter part of the days would be spent lounging around the pool. They would fly back on a chartered flight with Egypt Air. The fare was a modest 215-LE per couple, all-inclusive.

It sounded inviting, too inviting. I mulled it over for a while and decided I could not take Karen, and I did not feel like going along as the only unattached person in the group.

I had decided. As I left the bar I stopped off at the office and called to tell Mary I was planning a trip home for the holidays. The ten-hour time difference meant she should be at the restaurant. I reached my daughter instead. She said her mother was out of town visiting friends for a few days. She had not left a name or alternate number.

I arrived at my flat at seven. Cathy was coming down the stairs carrying an overnight bag. She was spending the weekend with her fiancé and his family at their country estate. Karen was sitting on the couch in her bathrobe, munching on leftover chicken and working on a crossword puzzle. She looked up when I came in the door.

"Why don't we take Ron up on his offer?"

"Karen, how the hell do things like this always beat me home?"

The news reached the flat before I did. Donna, Ron's girlfriend, called Karen and told her Ron had invited us to go along on the trip. Karen wanted to go.

"Come on, Pat; it will be fun. We've been cooped up in this flat for a month."

"That's hardly true, Karen. We've been spending two nights a week at restaurants."

"That's the point. We need to get out of Cairo. Cathy's will be gone for a few days, and I don't feel like sitting around the flat alone."

"What about your refugee classes?"

I knew the girl's work was voluntary, and they could plan their schedules as they wished, but I was looking for excuses.

"We gave them a holiday until Cathy gets back."

"I'll think about it."

Karen knew I was married. She also knew I was feeling less and less that way. It was impossible to live this close without the subject coming up. I also knew Karen was becoming attached. Although I did not want to admit it, I was enjoying the arrangement myself. I had not brought up the subject of the women leaving since the day I came home the first time the refugees were in the living room.

"Cathy will be leaving before Thanksgiving."

"I thought she and Mohammed were planning a wedding."

"The wedding's off. She's gone to his village to break the news. His family insists she joins the Muslim faith. If she doesn't and they marry, the family will disown him. His family has lots of money. He doesn't want to be disinherited; he wants a decision."

"Why go to the village to tell him?"

"Do you want him to come here for the weekend?"

"No, I think she's a lot better off. Cathy is too liberated to be a slave to a Muslim. What about you? Will you be leaving with her?"

"That's up to you. I will if you want me to, but I would like to stay, at least until your project is finished and you go home. You are going home, aren't you?"

Karen was getting a bit testy; it was not like her. It was obvious there was more to this.

"Yes, Karen. I'm going home."

"Why? You could easily get another post overseas?"

"I told you; I'm going home."

"For God's sake, what the hell for, and to what?

"To whatever's left."

"Which is?"

"How the hell do I know?"

"I've heard the story. Your marriage has been over for years. Why don't you face it and get on with your life."

"Karen, I told you to stay out of it."

"Why should I? Every time you get a letter from home or place a call, and no one answers, I have to listen to the dissertation. You know damn well there's nothing left for you to go back to."

"I told you I'm going home; the subject's closed."

"Yes, I know. At least until you open the next bottle of scotch and want to talk about it again, give me a break."

"Fuck you, lady!"

I have been told using the term lady in reference to a liberated woman was a four-letter word substitute for bitch. Karen sulked for a minute or two and then.

"Okay."

Karen slumped back on the couch, stirring a glass of wine with her finger.

"What did you say?"

"I said, okay. What's the matter with you? Have you been in Egypt so long you can't understand plain English? Cathy's gone, and even if you're too cheap to take me to Luxor, we have the next five days to ourselves."

"I thought you didn't believe in casual relationships, and what would your missionary friends think?"

"I don't, and you can hardly call this causal. I cook your meals and wash your shorts. As far as my friends, they all think we're sleeping together, wouldn't you?"

"Probably?"

It was not happening the way it does in movies. I liked Karen, but I was not in love with her. I did not think she was in love with me. Circumstances had thrown us together in a polar opposite culture 10,000 miles from our homes and families.

"I'll think about it."

"Think about what, fucking me? You are an arrogant bastard."

"Jesus Christ, Karen. What happened to your missionary upbringing?"

"Your language is rubbing off. So, answer me. You'll think about what?"

"Luxor, all right!"

"You don't have to. I told Donna we would meet them at the train station. In the meantime, I thought it would be nice to go back to the Ramses Hilton for dinner, just the two of us."

"Where's my scotch?"

"In the kitchen cabinet, pour me one too…., please?"

"When did you start drinking scotch?"

"There has to be a first time for everything. It might as well be with the same person."

"Now, what the hell are you talking about?"

"I'm thirty-eight. Until I met you, I never drank or swore. I'm still a virgin. I think it's time I made some changes in my life."

"Karen, the only virgins left in the civilized world are twelve-year-old girls who outrun their brothers."

"Cathy's right, you are a sarcastic asshole, you know that?"

"It is what it is."

It was an argument I was not expecting and one I was not going to win. Karen was actually angry, and it was rubbing off on me. We needed an intermission. I left the room and the subject and went into the kitchen to fix a stiff belt. I poured Karen a like amount and then rejoined her in the living room.

"Let's play it by ear, Karen, but you have to understand, this is a transitional period in our lives, and there is no guarantee."

Karen was brooding. I settled back to sip the scotch and reflect on the conversation.

"That I can handle, but I'm not cooking. How about the Ramses Hilton and another carriage ride."

"Why not."

Things settled. We sat for the next half-hour, sipping our drinks in silence. As I sat watching Karen grimace with each sip as it burned its way down her throat, I thought about the conversation and the earlier call to Oregon. Luxor sounded like a great idea.

Karen finished her drink and then went to shower and dress for dinner. I poured another and rationalized the current situation against another blank phone call to the States. Dinner, Luxor, and most of all Karen, why the hell not!

We arrived at the dining room at nine. I asked; they seated us by the window overlooking the Nile. Maybe it was the scotch; then again, perhaps it was that I was comfortable with Karen and her honest approach to what was happening in our lives. I wondered what was going on at home, but I shed my anxieties when my thoughts turned toward the sound of violin music.

Karen had mellowed. Our discussion during dinner was frivolous; a conversation between two people caught up in a culture a long way from our normal who cared about each other. After dinner, we took a carriage ride along the Cornice. It was a warm evening. Nonetheless, we took the quilt and the opportunity to hide ourselves from the looks of soldiers we passed by.

Forget novels and movies that lead us to believe passion overshadows reason. The feeling was one of warmth and comfort, a man and woman who simply liked being close to one another. The carriage ride ended uneventfully, as did the taxi ride back to our flat. The streets were quiet, the flat more so. I fixed us a drink and then joined Karen in the living room.

Earlier moods were forgotten, much like a new beginning in a stable relationship. The conversation centered on the evening and the day-to-day activities of our jobs in Cairo. I looked at my watch; it was past two.

"It's time for bed, Karen."

"It's long past time, Patrick."

Karen turned to me a while later.

"So, what the hell's the big deal?"

"Go to sleep."

It had been a while. Maybe I tried too hard; who knows? After a time, I felt a caress on my back and turned to find Karen restlessly awake. Sometime later, she realized what the big deal was all about and then fell asleep cradled in my arms.

The next morning, I agreed to the trip to Luxor. Karen left for the marketplace to pick up food to stock a cooler for the 12-hour train ride. I left for the site to make sure everything would remain under control while I was away. Andy met me at the door.

"Tom wants to see us."

Although everyone realized that changes are inherent in construction projects, and more so when in the Third World, it was budget time in Washington. Overseas military contracts were in the sights of the congressional committees.

Tom introduced me to Lloyd. Lloyd was an independent mediator sent by the COE office in Washington, DC, who was not supposed to take sides. He arrived that morning to help Glen's crew resolve some difficult open change orders on mine, as well as the other COE projects in Cairo.

"Tom, you and I don't have any unresolved changes."

"Yes, we do. The electrical charge for the IBM equipment needs to be resolved today."

"Can I see you in private?"

Tom and I moved into one of the other offices and left Andy and Lloyd to become acquainted.

"Tom, we settled this."

"Sorry, the paperwork hasn't been processed. It's not up to me. Bean counters in Washington are making the rules. You have to renegotiate it with him."

There was never a doubt the work had to be done. It was always just a matter of settling the price. I started the process when I first received the revised drawings. I lit into Tom about reneging on the deal; Tom closed the door.

"I gave the JV the numbers, we've bought the fucking materials."

"You know the rules. If you start without a written change, you do so at your own risk."

"That's fucking bullshit! I acted in good faith, just as I have on all the other changes you and I settled. If we had waited for the paperwork on every item, we would be here another two years, and you damned well know it!"

I was pissed; my voice carried beyond the door. Glen was in the hall; he entered the room and the conversation.

"Sorry, Patrick, this one is out of our hands. We're pushing budget limits. They sent Lloyd to review all changes over two hundred thousand. It's not just on your project, so don't take it personally. You'll have to renegotiate the electrical change with Lloyd."

"What's his limit of authority?"

"Lloyd's an arbitrator, he doesn't have a limit, but I don't see what difference it makes. You've already agreed to the price and a three-week extension."

"That's the fucking point, Glen! How can Lloyd negotiate with me in good faith if he already knows the maximum he must go to satisfy me?"

"I told you, it's out of our hands."

"This is bullshit! It's not out of my hands. The material hasn't been shipped. I'll cancel the orders, and you can negotiate the change with IBM."

"You know I can force you to do it with a unilateral change order."

"I'm aware of that, but then I don't have to start until the paperwork is signed. A unilateral has to be approved in Washington, which will take a month. That alone will delay the project, and I don't think you want to do that."

"Don't try to play hardball with me. Your company caused enough delays to justify me putting you on LDs if you don't finish according to the current schedule, and you and I know that can't be done."

"Glen, you can't put me on LDs if the COE and the Egyptian military are delaying the project. I thought you knew the sewer and fire protection connection to Cairo's water system is still unresolved, which the Egyptian Army is supposed to arrange?"

It was out of the Egyptian Army's control and in the hands of the local municipal bureaucracy, and it could take weeks to resolve. Glen did not know. The discussion turned heated. Glen accused me of not keeping the COE aware of the issues.

It was not my responsibility; our work ended at the edge of the army base. It was up to General Aziz to deal with the local agencies. They were not cooperating. When the water department repaired the line going by the base, they failed to stub out for the computer center. It meant tearing up the streets they had just repaired. It was going to be expensive.

General Aziz did not have money in his budget for work off the base. That would take a revision to his contract with the OMC; that alone would take weeks. He suggested we tap his lines. I told him no, his sewer and water line leaked like a sieve, and his water pressure was too low. I told him he had to bite the bullet and settle it with the utility companies. He gave me the *after-tomorrow, inshallah* answer.

Even if Aziz got on it the next day, it would be weeks before they would make the connection. Once the line was installed, we had a week of testing before I could move forward. I was no longer concerned about liquidated damages.

Tom stepped in to call a truce. He told Glen he was aware of the utility issue and had been in touch with the Egyptian agencies. Everyone connected with the problem was doing what they could; Glen looked skeptical.

"If I didn't know better, I would think the two of you are in collusion. Patrick, why don't you make the connection yourself?"

I ignored the barb. Tom was informed and was doing what he could.

"The water line is in the middle of the street and outside my scope of work. It's off the military base, and the only way I could make the connection would be to bootleg the work in the middle of the night and without the proper permits."

"You've done it before."

"When it was in my best interest, Glen. This isn't; the longer it's delayed, the better off I am."

"All right, what do you have in mind? This isn't getting us anywhere, and it isn't in anyone's interest for us to start fighting now."

My personal experience, which is what caused my IRS headaches, was most contractors cave in rather than go through the unilateral process that can tie their money up for years. I made the mistake of forcing the issue by not settling in the past; I would avoid it if possible.

"Glen, give Lloyd the background, but don't tell him we discussed price or time. I'll renegotiate it with him if you agree to honor the results and pay the bill."

"Are you kidding me? Do you think you can get more out of Lloyd than Tom agreed to? I think you inflated the numbers; Tom settled to keep the project moving. Lloyd's the expert; it's all he does."

"I don't know, but Tom has limits, and Lloyd doesn't. I settled time and money based on Tom's limits. If I have to do it over, Glen and I start from scratch."

"Fair enough, however, he's a pro, and if you aren't careful, you will get your ass kicked. If you can't convince him, and he says the figure is lower and the time is less, and you or your company don't agree, I will have no choice but to order the change unilaterally. Utilities or not, you will have to perform or face the LDs, and Tom won't be able to interfere."

"Agreed, we take what we get, but only if you make it binding on both sides."

No contracting office worth his salt wanted the contractor to lose money; it created more problems for both sides. Tom and I were friends. Alcohol opens doors to things that should be kept private in these circumstances. Tom knew I had spent many hours in negotiations with government attorneys and had schooled myself on changes.

Prior to coming to Egypt, I had worked for a law firm and had been accepted by the U.S. Board of Contract Appeals as an expert on the effect of plan errors and omissions when it came to pricing changes.

Tom had always been fair. The settlement for the electrical change was pushing his limits. Tom knew I had inflated the figures when I settled at his limit of authority without a fight. He and I were not that far apart; we both conceded to move forward.

My problem was I had passed the settlement to Ceasar without the paperwork and ordered the material. It was going to be damned hard to convince Dr. Osmond and Cesar to accept less. I was mad, no, really pissed. Lloyd had the background and some of the correspondence, but it was my ballfield, and I was in control.

Tom and I went back to where Lloyd, Hamid, and Andy were reviewing the drawings. Tom briefed Lloyd on IBM's concerns and told him we needed to resolve it that day.

I sent Andy and Hamid home. Lloyd was a qualified engineer. It was up to him to evaluate the scope of work without input from my staff that might weaken or distort my arguments.

I have been in the construction business my entire adult life. I have my method. Most construction estimators dealing with changes consolidate work into trades, solicit numbers from multiple sources, and apply the low subcontractor's bid and the vendor's price. That is the uncomplicated way, and for the most part, it is simple to explain and hard to argue with.

When dealing with a difficult client I inflate the cost in order to be able to reach an amicable settlement. To do that, I separate parts from the end product; when you break it down far enough, the actual total cost gets lost in the maze.

In 1986, you could buy a top-of-the-line Ford 150 with all the bells and whistles for $13,000. However, if you patronize a local auto parts store and build it piece by piece, you pay six to eight times what Ford pays for parts, and without robotic assembly, labor will cost thousands of dollars more for the finished product.

It is impossible to price the total of what something might cost when they are looking at the end product. It is easy to convince a client what a 10-cent wire nut or a $2 fuse costs that is incorporated into that product.

I gave Lloyd a list of the parts and their cost as if we were buying the parts and assembling them ourselves. He took one look and focused on some conduit fittings. Some were a few cents higher than you would pay at Home Depoe, some a few cents less.

He picked out a dozen or more items, checked them against the drawings, and when he was satisfied the numbers were comparable to what a contractor would pay for them in the States, we moved on. Lloyd and I spent the next few hours reviewing the drawings and discussing methods of construction and Egyptian military politics.

I gave Lloyd my list. When we left the office to walk the project. I suggested the synergistic effect the change would have on the other work and pointed out the delays it was causing. I neglected to tell him of the possibility of mailing the material through the mail.

Lloyd and I bounced it back and forth. We adjourned while Lloyd prepared his estimate. Tom and Glen arrived at the site just as Lloyd finished adding the column of figures. Lloyd showed me the bottom line as Glen walked through the door. I smiled and gave him a thumbs-up. Glen was getting anxious, and I needed to meet Karen to make the train on time.

"Have you two settled?"

"Lloyd's tough, but we have a deal I think I can sell to my people."

"Which is?"

"Four-hundred-sixty-thousand and a completion date of April first."

I turned to Tom. It was not his money; he was having trouble controlling his grin.

"A deal's a deal, Tom."

Tom agreed. I had hoped to bump the figure but at least break even. We were past that now.

Lloyd was the arbitrator in a binding situation. I agreed, as did Glen. To my surprise, Glen did not mention the money agreed to in the earlier settlement, but the finish date was an issue.

"Lloyd, maybe I can help. I understand the concerns the COE and the OMC have regarding the IBM start date. The material will weigh approximately two thousand pounds. If the Embassy agrees there will be some additional material handling and packaging it to Post office specs. If you add air freight and packaging, I will agree to a new date of February 5 and reduce the cost for added time."

A quick calculation brought the total to a little under $500,000, two & ½ times what Tom and I agreed to. However, with nothing in writing, there was a chance Glen might have second thoughts and have a discussion with Lloyd before the paperwork was done.

"Glen, this time, I'll do it by your book. Why don't the three of you discuss this and let me know your decision when I get back on Monday. In the meantime, I'll tell Cesar to hold the shipments. Oh, Lloyd, don't forget to add one day of time and overhead to the schedule for each day it takes to get the paperwork done."

"Patrick, sit the fuck down!"

Tom, Glen, and Lloyd left, returning a few minutes later. Tom was shaking his head; Glen was as serious as a bird dog on point.

"Tell Cesar to ship the materials; the sooner, the better."

"Thank you, Glen, but it's Friday. The office in the states will be closed until Monday. I'm leaving this evening; I'll be back on Monday. I'll make the call, but only if I get written notice to proceed from your office."

I started out the door and then turned back. The utility connections had fallen by the wayside. I was going to wait until the last minute, but with Lloyd in play, I needed to address the issue.

"By the way, Glen. In case it slipped everyone's mind. Our time limit assumes that the Egyptians will make the connections in the street by the time we need to do the final testing. I seriously doubt that's going to happen. I think we need to deal with that reality."

"You outright rejected doing the work; I've passed it to the OMC. We're waiting for a response."

"Good luck with that, Glen. I didn't reject it; I said it wasn't in my best interest. I want to finish and get the fuck out of here. Now that we have that route, it's in my best interest."

"You've got our attention; what do you have in mind."

"We give the OMC and General Aziz thirty days to resolve it and get the connections made. If it's still up in the air, we'll make the connections. That's going to be expensive."

"How expensive?"

"Lloyd expensive. Lloyd, how long are you going to be in Cairo?"

"I'm here until next Wednesday, then I need to be in Saudia Arabia."

"Glen, you can write a provisional change. If Lloyd can work up his numbers, we can sit down when I get back on Monday and settle it before he leaves."

"Hold on, I can't put it together without drawings and a list of materials."

"Lloyd, I've been here long enough to know this was going to end up in my lap. Our engineers have done their part, and I've got my numbers." "How about it, Glen, Tom?"

"You will have to close the road; how do you plan to float this by the Egyptians."

"I can't tear up the street or shut off the water, Tom. We're going to have to tunnel under the road, which means shoring and tapping the lines hot.

"That's ludicrous; the President's palace is across the street. If they catch you tunneling in that direction, if they don't shoot you on sight, they'll throw you all in jail, and the OMC will wash their hands."

"I've got that covered, but it's above my pay grade, and Tom, you don't want to know; let's just say Dr. Osmond has friends in high places and let it go at that." "Glen, I have a train to catch, yes, or no?"

"On one condition, both General Aziz and General Sayer have to sign off."

"Forgone conclusion, but that means them going upstairs. I've already had a discussion with Dr. Osmond. Lloyd will find it under dewatering. Are we done here, Glen?"

As for the electrical charge, it was not their money. Tom did not give a shit, and no one in DC was aware of the earlier settlement. It was a third-party deal, binding on both sides. Having Lloyd negotiate the change covered Glen's ass. Tom and Glen would be over it by the time I got back.

Chapter 34

I arrived at the flat later than expected with little time to pack for the trip. Karen had the ice chest, her suitcase, an overnight case, and a duffle bag with linen and bedclothes packed when I entered the flat.

A few minutes later, I had everything we needed, including my clothes repacked into one suitcase and the ice chest. We were only going to be gone for three days. It was still over 85 degrees in Luxor. I did not intend to fight porters, taxi drivers, and beggars on a 600-kilometer trip carrying stuff we did not need. I had repacked our bathing suits and two casual outfits for each of us.

It was pushing 5:30. One thing that did run on time was the train carrying the Egyptian elite to their weekend retreats. The argument ended when I told Karen the train departed at seven sharp and it would take at least 45 minutes to get to the station.

I had not traveled by train in Egypt, but I heard horror stories about Egyptian trains and expats trying to track personal belongings through the system. I did not want to check and then try to recover luggage. The suitcase and ice chest, along with our camera cases, were all I wanted to deal with.

Karen had done some sightseeing and had spent her time off traveling with Cathy on their schoolteacher's budget. She was used to hotels that only knew what a star was by looking toward the heavens on a clear night.

Karen was still grumbling on our way to the station. When I told her we would be traveling on a first-class train and staying in a five-star European hotel, she resigned herself to my having left the bedding, soap, towels, hair dryer, coffee, napkins, silverware, and toilet paper at home.

Traffic was congested. The station was a crowded nightmare. I was settling with the taxi driver. I looked for Karen; she was trying to pry our suitcase away from one of the local porters who was dragging it on the sidewalk while trying to balance the ice chest on his head.

I caught up with them after they went in the wrong direction. I tore a five-LE note in half, handed half to the porter, took Karen by the arm, indicated the porter follow, and headed for the landing where our train was waiting. By that time, the other expats had boarded, but we were fifty meters from the train. The train's whistle was going off; it was getting ready to depart.

We fought our way through the crowd and passed our luggage into the waiting hands of the steward assigned to the Pullman. Once on board, the steward stood blocking the hall until I could fish a five-LE note out of my pocket.

The club car was crowded with other expats sorting out baggage. Thirty minutes later, Karen and I stowed our luggage in our compartment. The steward came by and gave us a dinner menu. It was in English. *Isn't it amazing how first-class money talks?*

The menu noted the dinner hours assigned to each compartment. Our reservation was at ten p.m. It was 8:15 before we finally settled. Karen was fishing through the ice chest while I was rinsing some of the Cairo dust off my face and hands.

"Dinner is less than two hours; I can wait."

"I thought you might like a drink."

Karen was more thorough than I anticipated. She set a bottle of Black Label and a baggy full of ice cubes on the counter.

"I told you; you shouldn't travel by yourself."

"Open the suitcase and take the other bottle out before it gets broken."

"Smart ass, I could have brought my hair dryer."

Karen fixed us a drink while I settled back and watched the traffic and lights of Cairo blend into the farmland of the Nile delta. We moved steadily through the suburbs, passing through various stations where the multitudes of Egypt were huddled, waiting for the commuter trains to take them home from fields and factories.

Our train would only stop a few times that night depositing the more affluent of Egypt's society at their various weekend retreats. We passed the next hour in small talk, reflecting on some of our travels in Egypt and wondering what we would find in Luxor.

The steward came by just before ten. Tables would be available in the dining car in fifteen minutes. This was an Egyptian train run by the Egyptians. In my haste, I neglected to remember one of the more important aspects of traveling in Egypt. It was always better to be safe than to have a trip spoiled by a lack of foresight.

"Karen, did you pack the Kaopectate?"

"Yes, it's in the ice chest, along with some fried chicken, potato salad, rolls, strawberries, and a bottle of wine. There are also boiled eggs, pastry, and instant coffee for breakfast if you're interested."

"I am."

Karen was settled back, sipping a scotch, when Ron knocked on the door to tell us the expats were meeting in the club car for a picnic and cocktails.

"Aren't you glad you didn't leave the ice chest too?"

Karen was in contact with Ron's wife. Some in the group had been this way before. Although first-class trains were a cut above the regular trains, the food was apt to cause indigestion, or worse.

The picnic was an enormous success. We spent the next few hours swapping stories about our experiences in Egypt. We all had our favorite tales to tell, and as unbelievable as they were to my family and friends back home, they seemed ordinary when discussed among a group that lived as we did, within the society.

It was a strange feeling, camaraderie of sorts. Something I had missed out on in Egypt, which was my fault. I had not taken advantage of the society within the society. The expat community keeps things in perspective; it was a warm feeling.

"See what you've been missing?"

Karen was in a reflective mood when we returned to the sleeper. She knew I had isolated myself from most expats in Cairo. My existence to date focused on the project with some of Tom and Andy thrown in.

"I didn't come to Egypt to socialize, Karen."

"What did you come for?"

It was an interesting question. I thought about the IRS and my failures of the past. Perhaps it was an opportunity to make up for some of them or to get out of a marriage that my wife and I had stuck with for twenty-three years that was never meant to be.

I had enough time in Egypt to reflect on my first forty-six years. I was finally beginning to realize I simply did not have the courage to face my life for what it was. It had been simpler to find an excuse to run away.

"I ran away, Karen."

"Will you ever stop running?"

"Someday, perhaps."

"Are you sure you will be going home when you leave Egypt?"

"I'd like to, even if it's just to spend some time with my kids."

"What are the chances you can stay in the States?"

"Slim, at least for a while. The IRS is lying in the woods and will be until the statute expires. The law's a little vague. I'll have to wait and play it by ear."

Karen fixed us a nightcap. There were two bunks, each thirty inches wide, one folded against the wall directly above the other. I started to lower the upper but stopped when I saw it would leave no place to sit.

Karen was leaning back on the lower bunk, offering me a fresh drink with one hand, adjusting her pillow with the other, and then patting it, inviting me to join her.

"There's hardly room for one, let alone two."

"We'll make do."

"From the looks of it, it will be limited to the missionary position."

"It wasn't in my job description, but I was told there would be some inconveniences. My days of missionary service are over; come to bed."

The Luxor depot was crowded with departing passengers, and those waiting to board for the trip to the last stop on the rail a few hundred klicks further south.

The train had arrived at nine, an hour late, but acceptable by Egyptian standards. The sun was up; the air hot and humid from the moisture rising from the Nile. The weather forecast was wrong. It was going to be a blistering day.

Like the rest of Egypt, there were no lines, just a mob of humanity crowding to the same exit, which was jammed with taxis and horse-drawn carriages. The drivers had hawkers on the landing trying to lure the arriving tourists. Karen and I bypassed the aggressive taxi drivers and carriages pulled by old and worn horses. We walked toward the entrance to the square, all the time fighting off porters who were grabbing at luggage as people passed by struggling to work their way through the crowds.

"Your choice, Karen, taxi or a carriage?"

"A carriage would be nice."

There was a group of carriages a hundred meters from the station. They were carved of wood, ancient and worn, unlike the plastic and steel models blocking the steps leading from the depot. The drivers sat quietly, waiting for customers. I picked what looked like the oldest but the cleanest looking of the lot. The driver and obviously well-cared-for bay stallion, both gray with age, seemed well matched.

"How much?"

"What you like."

The driver knew expats were tired of haggling. If he had said ten Pounds, I would have haggled. Now, I would give him twenty. The carriage meandered through the streets before coming to a narrow road paralleling the Nile. The Movenpick is located a few miles out of the poverty, dust, and stifling heat of downtown Luxor.

The Movenpick was an out-of-place retreat in Egyptian society. It was clean, spread among towering shade trees with roomy bungalows fronting the river. On the surface, the river appeared unpolluted. I would not risk a swim, but the smell was fresh, and the water was clear without the Cairo sludge floating on the surface; it was inviting.

A porter showed us to a cottage nestled among date palms and bananas. The entrance fronted the river. The rooms were neat, air-conditioned, and secure from mosquitoes and flies affixed to the outer walls, shading themselves from rising temperatures.

We would spend the first day lounging around the pool, soaking up some rays and stretching our bodies from the confined quarters of the 15-hour train ride.

Karen and I showered, then changed into our swimsuits and headed for the pool. The area was crowded with expats escaping from Cairo for the weekend. Some were lying in the shallows, eight inches deep, which extended twelve feet from the water's edge. The design afforded a tourist the luxury of escaping the heat of the day by lying in shallow, cool water without having to dodge the more playful guests in the deeper areas.

It was Egypt's autumn, but the temperatures were still in the nineties. Karen picked a chair at the water's edge, sheltered from the sun by one of the umbrellas littering the area. I settled for the shallows and a chance to work on my tan.

"You'll burn lying out in the sun."

"Not to worry, Karen, I'm used to it."

Later.

"That hurts!"

"I tried to warn you. It serves you right, four hours in the sun; I thought you had more sense."

It had taken over a year to get a decent tan, an hour at a time, one or two days a week. Karen was right; in just a few short hours, I turned it into a blanket of blistering sores, which, when healed, would leave me looking like a spotted calf.

The burns put a damper on extracurricular activities, but they did not prevent us from enjoying a trip into the Valley of the Kings and Queens, and a visit to the aging past.

The Tombs are nestled in a valley made up of sandstone and granite. Cliffs surround the tombs, dwarfing rubble still mounded at the entrance, left over from centuries of grave robbers.

The Tombs, unlike the one-room Cheops Pyramid, are a maze of hallways and covered courtyards. The walls are cluttered with ancient writings; the granite floors silk-smooth from the shuffling feet of thousands of tourists who had preceded us.

Some Egyptians believe the flash from a camera will lift the writing from the walls. Signs, some in Arabic, some in English, forbid taking pictures. Forbidden, that is, until a ten-LE note left a tourist's hand and found its way into the palm of one of the guards.

On the evening of the second day, Karen and I took a carriage into the heart of the city to browse among the shops and dine at what the tourist magazine advertised as one of the best restaurants in Egypt.

The guidebook also mentioned it was the only five-star in Luxor. In fine print, at the back of the book, they noted in Arabic that the Egyptian government owned and operated the hotel. Five-star, my ass! But, then again, why else bring Kaopectate?

Chapter 35

Sixteen months passed, but still another four, *inshallah*, from finishing a building Acme Construction could build in the States in three to four months. Cathy was packing for her trip home. She would be leaving in a few days for the States.

Cathy's breakup with Mohammed was not that traumatic. It appeared Cathy was guilty of a few omissions of her own. Her family was affluent, and if she had wanted to ask for the fare earlier, they would have gladly sent it to bring their wandering daughter home. Cathy would be delayed again. She had met a Middle Eastern student whom she was planning to visit and holiday with on Cyprus.

Andy was counting the days. He was also counting the money in the bank that had made his journey worthwhile. He could pay off the mini ranch and the video store he made a deposit on with his first year's salary. Although Andy had done a great deal better than I did mingling with Cairo expat society, he missed his wife. He was anxious to go home and get on with his life.

Carl was finishing the O&M training and was getting on well with all the players. His job was simple; besides, he was a diplomat. All he had to do was raise hell with Don once a week and remind him where Cairo was so he would continue to send the information from the American manufacturers.

I insisted the Filipinos remain until the as-built drawings were finished so it would not hold up the final payments to the partners or keep me in Cairo a day longer than necessary. The Egyptian engineers were not up to the task, and I did not intend the responsibility to fall back on them. It was time to renew their visas again. Chico, Amante, and Deo were looking forward to another trip to Cyprus. Doctor Osmond was still not happy with the arrangement.

Cesar continued to telex once a week asking when Tom would approve the next pay estimate, and as usual, asking when I would be done. He was convinced I was stalling and dragging out the project. Where he got that idea was beyond me. Cesar had never bothered to make the trip to see for himself. After the Generals, Don and the material shipments had been our biggest holdup.

General Aziz was in the States trying to talk three Egyptian students into coming home. They were planning to marry Americans so they could convert their temporary status in the States to permanent residency but had not found women who were willing. Their visas had expired, and U.S. immigration did not seem to care.

General Sayer was on his side of the new nine-foot block wall and had not reentered the picture since we closed off access to his base. The car shed was forgotten once the wall was completed.

IBM followed our lead. Mike was in Cairo waiting for the mail from the States so he could oversee the final electrical connections for IBM.

My motto has always been, *do it right or do it over*. Although I won most of the earlier battles and educated the Egyptian workforce on the requirements, I was tired of the sessions, burnt out, anxious to finish, and forced myself to deal with the day-to-day problems. The brown hair I started the project with had turned mostly gray. I felt and looked a great deal older than my 46 years.

Karen and I were making do with what was available in Cairo. She continued trying to get me involved in the social activities of the expat community. I was still avoiding them and most other social gatherings as well. Karen took over Cathy's duties at the office but was getting bored.

"I hear Tom wants you to go on a fishing trip?"

Tom and I never made the second trip. We had promised ourselves one more before I left Egypt.

"Who told you?"

Tom and Unan lived in the flat below mine. Karen and Unan had become friends.

"Well, are we going or not?"

"Karen, you can't stand Tom. I can't see the two of you on the same small boat for three days."

Karen was still involved with the refugee community. Tom's persistent comments about subhuman Arabs offended her. Karen did not understand Tom. I felt as though I did. I saw through Tom to his gentleness with the boab's family at the flat. I had also seen him deal with members of the working class. He was always pleasant and a great deal more patient than I. However, like me, he had a genuine dislike for the middle and upper class, who treated the people Karen cared about like slaves.

Tom's subhuman comments were like mine when Karen was not around, based on his contact with the greed and corruption he faced daily to accomplish even simple tasks.

"Yes, Tom and I are planning another fishing trip, and you have been invited."

I did not add the reluctant part. Tom was still reluctant. He had not agreed to Karen coming along. Tom had not married a Thai woman by accident. He had a problem with liberal American women who have an incessant need to voice their opinions on subjects they know little about. Karen fit the bill as far as Tom was concerned.

For a woman who had traveled a great deal, Karen was naive in many ways. We all have opinions, and many of us have little knowledge about some of the subjects we feel most strongly about. I figured Tom and Karen should be getting along pretty well.

Karen and I discussed the trip. If she went along, she would have to follow the rules. She wanted to know what they were. There was only one to concern her. Tom was in charge. As long as we did things his way, everyone would get along. Karen did not believe I was serious. She knew me not to give in when I thought I was right on any subject. I told her fishing trips were different.

"I don't care who's in charge just as long as we get where we're going, close to the time we're supposed to be there. It would also be nice to catch a few fish without having to referee the two of you, which means if you go, you stay off politics and go along for the ride."

Karen was aware that I was still miffed about the last time she and Tom were in the same room together. The heated discussion got out of control on the subject of refugees, meddling American missionaries who would not leave well enough alone, and American expats who threw their money around.

I mentioned it. Karen took the hint and agreed that she would find a way to get along with Tom. I left Karen to ponder the rules while I went down to Tom's flat to tell him if Karen could not go along, I would have to pass the trip, knowing he would agree.

"I told you I don't want that woman along!"

"Tom, give me a break. She promised to keep her opinions to herself."

Tom gave me a look of skepticism, but he did not want to make the trip alone. Sharing the cost was one issue, but he also wanted male company on the trip.

"Alright, tell Karen to call Unan and help get things ready for the weekend."

"I'll ask her, Tom; telling Karen anything would not get us off to a good start. By the way, I understand we won't have to take the road through Helwan or across the open stretch of desert. Ron told me he went to Suez last week, and the new highway to Hurghada is open."

The Egyptians had finally finished the road to Suez and along the shore of the Red Sea. It would cut four hours off the trip.

"I've heard that too, but I haven't talked to anyone who's actually taken it to Hurghada. We'll schedule an extra four hours. If we get there a few hours earlier fine, but if we have to backtrack and then take the desert road, we will lose a full day of fishing."

Tom was off the subject of Karen and into the fishing trip. We spent the next few hours planning and reminiscing about the trip a year earlier.

“Friday it is, Tom.”

I returned to my flat a little later than expected.

“The trips on, Karen. Tom said he would be delighted if you came along.”

“Was that before or after the bottle of scotch?”

“What the hell’s the difference? It’s settled, and you’re going. Tom asked if you would help Unan pack groceries.”

Karen was ecstatic. It got her off the subject of our rapidly approaching departure from Cairo. I met Andy at the Sonesta the next morning for coffee. It had been routine since Karen and Cathy moved in. When Cathy left, I did not see a reason to revert.

“What are you going to do about the toilet problem at the computer center?”

Muslims face Mecca when they pray and generally do not believe they should do the same when using a toilet. The designers did not have a clue, and I did not catch it until the plumbing and tile were done. It meant tearing up the floor and changing the stall layout. I refused unless the COE approved a change order for the added cost. General Aziz was determined and had made it an issue before he left for the States. He also wanted us to install the ass washers.

“Andy, the tile is installed, and the General doesn’t want to pay the bill; ignore it.”

“He claims you agreed to take care of the problem.”

“I did, after tomorrow, inshallah. We are going to install the toilet paper holders, just like the plans show.”

The subject of turning the toilets and installing ass washers came up many times between Tom and me. Tom was not interested in issuing a change order for something he could not explain to the office in the States. Since I was unwilling to do the work for nothing, we were at a stalemate. We quit discussing it. General Aziz could deal with it after we left.

"Andy, what headaches do I need to deal with before I leave for the Red Sea on Friday?"

"Just the Embassy; we have their mail system plugged up."

"How upset are they?'

"Not bad, considering the mess and inconvenience. Mike is managing it through the OMC. It looks like things are working for a change, but the Ambassador wants an end to it."

"Don't hold your breath, Andy. The project's been going too well lately. Something is bound to get messed up soon. By the way, Christmas is a few weeks away. Are you going home?"

February 5 turned out to be just another milestone. This time, it was IBM's faulty design. We had to make some changes to the change.

Thought: *When I brought it up to Mike, since it was their mistake, IBM managed to shift their schedule on another project to accommodate this one.*

"No, we should be finished by the first of March, April at the latest. Cesar has agreed to pay me a bonus in lieu of paying for a ticket. I can use the extra money. I don't have anything lined up after this project.'

"I wouldn't worry about it, Andy. You'll find something soon enough. Besides, it will take some readjusting when you get home."

"How about you? Are you going home for Christmas?"

"No."

"Is Karen the reason?"

"No, some on the other side of the world would prefer me to stay on this side. Besides, even the Egyptians can't screw things up enough to make it last past April. I think it'll be easier to deal with it all at once rather than piecemeal."

Andy left for the site. I stuck around for another cup of coffee and reflected on my situation. The project was finally a piece of cake Cesar promised sixteen months earlier. The lessons of the past taught the Egyptians it was easier to do it right the first time rather than continuously having to do it over. Although the progress was still slow by standards in the States, it was adequate, the end was in sight.

Doctor Osmond, Don, and Cesar had accepted that the project had to be done to the COE specs on some sort of schedule. I was simply monitoring progress, coordinating shipments, and observing the material installation. Unlike Andy, I was convinced March was attainable.

I was looking forward to the end but not to going home. My errors and omissions of the past were creeping back into my life. The time was rapidly approaching when I would finally have to deal with reality. I had spent a year and a half in the Third World and like the local peasants, I was living my life day to day.

My IRS problem was hanging over my head. It was late November 1987. The statute of limitations would run through the fall of 1988, still a year away. It would take another year to clear the lien. Catch-22: if I went home, I could not work, and the longer I stayed away, the more difficult returning would be.

Letters had diminished to once a month. I continued to attempt a once-a-week phone call, more out of a feeling of responsibility than anything else. On many occasions, even at the prescribed hours, there was no one there to take the call. As the project wound down and the day of my departure rapidly approached, the handwriting on the wall became a reality.

Karen thought she was in love. My inability to return it hurt. The subject of what was to come afterward came up often. I was becoming irritable. My answer was always the same. I did not want to discuss tomorrow.

I told Karen she should be going home to get her life in order. She was willing to accept the situation, but she wanted it to last as long as possible. I was not looking forward to the time I knew I would have to end it for good. My mention of an earlier departure for her usually put the conversation on hold.

Any discussion about a completion date, while Karen was around caused the time between unpleasant scenes to grow shorter. In a way, I was not looking forward to the fishing trip. It seemed the more our lives took direction away from our life in Cairo the harder it was for Karen to deal with reality.

As always, when confronted with domestic arguments, I took the easy way out. It seemed the habit I had gotten into had become a way of life. I was not in love, but I did like Karen. I decided to make the best of the holiday.

Chapter 36

A clean pair of shorts work for me. Why do women have the incessant need to pack everything in the closet for a three-day trip?

"Karen, we're going fishing, not to the French Riviera!" "Unan, what's all this shit?"

Tom was sitting on the steps drinking a beer. He looked up when I approached and then towards the women, shaking his head.

"I told you this was bullshit."

"Lighten up, Tom; it looks like Unan packed more shit than Karen."

It was a toss-up. Tom had replaced his station wagon with a sedan. The fishing gear, firewood, camping gear, and foodstuffs left little room for the ice chest and suitcases. There would not be room for more than two in the car.

"Unan and I decided we should take two cars."

Karen had taken charge. Tom was sitting on the front porch of his flat, sipping a beer and swatting flies. When I looked over, he tossed me a can, shrugged his shoulders, and pointed to my car.

"What the hell, two cars it is. If we're ready, let's go."

We were taking an unfamiliar route. I figured it best if the man with the diplomatic passport hit the roadblocks first. Tom took the lead.

There were no military checkpoints once we left Suez and headed south on the newly paved highway. We were also able to travel without fear of dodging oncoming trucks or detouring through the desert and hidden minefields.

The grueling ten-hour trip through the desert by way of Helwan we took the previous year was cut to a pleasant four hours along a scenic highway that paralleled the magnificent and unspoiled gravel beaches of the Red Sea. Unspoiled, that is, until we came to the Gulf of Suez and started passing Army outposts and coastal villages serving the oil rigs dotting the horizon.

The new highway connected with the road we had taken the year before a few hundred klicks from Hurghada. The old road had been widened and resurfaced since our last trip.

It was dark when we crossed this stretch before. In the daylight, it was another environmental nightmare in the midst of an unselfish act of God. The Sea itself still maintained the multi-colored surface of the Hurghada area. The seashore and the surrounding rock outcroppings appeared covered with a thin layer of black oil.

Karen settled into the trip like a local tourist. She was on a picture-taking kick. She wanted me to stop every few klicks when she saw so much as a lone tree in the desert, or sidetrack into one of the villages dotting the seashore.

"You can take all the pictures you want once we board the boat. In the meantime, try to content yourself with watching the scenery. Tom is not about to stop, and I prefer we have company in case this car decides to quit on us."

The transmission started howling an hour after we left Cairo. I mentioned it to Tom when we stopped at the last gas station a hundred klicks back. The puddle of liquid settling into the sand under the car was a sign of the maintenance abilities of Doctor Osmond's mechanics. The gas station was a remote outpost at the crossroads of the new Suez highway and the old desert road. Diesel fuel and gas were the only commodities available.

Transmission fluid and a check on the seals and pan would have to wait until we reached Hurghada, if the car made it that far. It was not a comforting thought. We continued with the premise that if worse came to worse, we would abandon the Buick and cram ourselves into one vehicle.

By the time we reached Hurghada, I had the car in neutral, coasting whenever possible. I knew from the burnt smells and heat coming through the floor it was going to be more than just a matter of adding fluid.

Tom led the way to the hotel where we would spend the night. The Global Hotel is a seedy minus-two-star, even by Egyptian standards. But, compared to the others in Hurghada, except for the Sheraton, it was a palace.

"Why didn't you make reservations at the Sheraton?"

Karen found some tourist brochures and was aware there was a Sheraton in town, and that it was nestled in a sheltered cove high enough to have a panoramic view of the Red Sea. We were looking over the rooftops of neighboring slums.

"Tom made the reservations. This is only a stopover. We board the boat first thing tomorrow morning."

Unan, well…., compared to her village in Thailand, it was a palace. Prices changed when the highway was completed. I would have preferred the Sheraton. Tom felt that 60-LE a night, compared to 240, was an acceptable arrangement. Besides, the Global included breakfast.

"Can we at least have dinner at the Sheraton?"

"Karen, this is a fishing trip. We'll be camping on a deserted island. You'll appreciate this hotel by the time the trip's over. Try to make do. In the meantime, help Unan with the linen and our overnight bags. Tom and I have to find a mechanic to get the car fixed if we want to get it back to Cairo."

"You should leave it here."

I had been cussing Abboud the last two hundred klicks. Leaving the car in Hurghada would not be a big enough problem for Dr. Osmond. He would send someone to patch it up and return it to me.

"We will have room in Tom's car on the trip back. I would rather leave it in the desert on the way back and let the nomads strip it. To do that, some repairs are in order. Tom and I will find a mechanic."

Tom and I planned dinner at the Sheraton to surprise them. It was going to be a peace offering for leaving them to the cleaning while we arranged to get the car repaired and met with Captain Abbas, our fishing guide.

Captain Abbas was unavailable on my first trip with Tom. Tom became acquainted with him on one of his earlier trips. He was an exception to the rule. According to Tom, he spoke fluent English, maintained his boat, and did not mind traveling to the better fishing grounds one hundred klicks from the port.

Tom and I found a mechanic willing to fix the car, and then spent an hour drinking tea with Captain Abbas. It was past nine when we returned to the hotel. Karen met me at the door.

"Why don't we spend tonight camping on the beach?"

Karen and Unan were both in a foul mood. They chose the lesser of the tasks to perform first. The toilet room doubled as a shower, with the showerhead in the middle of the room and the drain in the center of the floor. They had scrubbed the scum off the walls and floor before they made the beds and cleaned the rooms.

After they cleaned the bathroom, they cleaned the bedrooms. Once they finished, they decided to shower, freshen up, and, when we returned, convince us to take them to the Sheraton.

It was a good idea except for planning. They should have cleaned the bedrooms first and then the shower. The time it took to clean the bedrooms was all a dozen German tourists needed to turn the clean shower into a room covered with soap, salt, and pubic hair. Karen was livid and refused to clean them again.

"Wear your tennis shoes and stand in the middle of the room."

I thought it was humorous. I had taken many showers in Egypt wearing my tennis shoes. It saved the effort the women took to clean a shower to acceptable standards.

"If you don't get ready soon, we'll be late for our reservations at the Sheraton, and you'll have to settle on cold cuts for dinner."

"The Sheraton, I only brought one pair of shoes."

"Use mine."

Dinner at the Sheraton took the edge out of the women's mood. I was wearing cowboy boots. My tennis shoes would be dry by morning. A pleasant dinner, the cool breeze coming off the Red Sea, along with a few brandies after dinner, took the edge off everyone; we were light years away from Cairo.

We re-entered the dimly lit hallways of the hotel sometime after eleven. The scurrying cockroaches faded from our minds as we settled between the clean sheets.

"Breakfast at six, Karen."

"That leaves seven hours."

"I'm getting old."

"Not that old, and you have three days to rest up."

The front of the hotel faced east. Dawn lit the room at five. Karen was asleep, content for the moment. I was still somewhere between sleep and wakeful recognition that the day-to-day life I was living had to end soon, but I was not yet willing to face reality. Tom's knock on the door brought me back to the day and the fishing trip ahead.

"Let's meet for breakfast on the roof; Captain Abbas has the boat parked in the harbor. We sail in an hour."

My tennis shoes were still damp from the night before. It did not matter; they would get wet again. I headed for the shower. Soap and fresh water would be scarce for the next three days.

"I'll meet you on the roof in ten minutes."

Karen and I stepped out of the musty hallway onto the patio. It was a beautiful morning.

"Not bad, Tom, sixty LE for a room, breakfast, and a magnificent sunrise."

She had enticed him over with a morsel from her plate. The ragged tom crossed to our table from his shaded bed. Karen reached down to pet him.

"Karen, leave the damned cat alone."

Ignoring me, she was enticing him with a scrap from her plate. He took a swipe at her hand; she retracted the tidbit. The cat was aggressive and latched onto Karen's leg with his front claws.

I was not quick enough. There was a trickle of blood coming from one of the scratches. Many of the domestic animals in Egypt are rabid. This was not the time for one of us to get bitten. As the tom made another pass at Karen's leg I made a grab for him. He did not see me coming, so I got lucky. At least for a second, I thought I did. He was a big cat, twelve, perhaps fifteen pounds, and he was snarling mad.

The cat twisted, latching onto my wrist with his front claws while digging at my upper arm with his hind legs. I managed to keep my forearm out of his teeth, but I was not having much luck keeping his claws from digging into my wrist.

Tom and the group of German divers at the table across from us were cheering for the cat. The Germans blocked the opening to the stairs. The only available disposal site was on the roof across a narrow alley. I aimed between the Germans as I tossed the cat toward the other rooftop, hoping to clear the heads of the men cheering at the adjoining table.

Poor planning, the big tom's hold on my arm caused a late release. He landed short, turning in the air to land on his feet. One of the nearby Germans was too close. The cat managed to get in a few more licks before he exited at a run for the staircase leading to the floors below.

Karen and Unan spent the next twenty minutes cleaning our wounds. One of the divers muttered something that sounded like *chivalry's not dead* while Tom brought us a beer to signal the start of the fishing trip.

By seven, our gear was stowed in the forward cabin; we were on our way to the tuna grounds. When we crossed the point of the island at the harbor entrance into gale force winds it reminded me of the year before.

"Same shit, different year, Tom."

"Patience, Pat. We'll be out of the wind in a few hours when we reach the islands, but even if it blows, this boat can handle it."

Tom came out of the cabin with a bottle of Jack and a beer chaser.

"Your perch on the roof is laid out with a deck chair."

"Thanks, Tom, but don't you think it's a little early."

"It wasn't last year. Besides, this time, you've been wounded defending a woman."

"Right on, toss me the beer."

"Bullshit, if you hadn't grabbed the cat's tail, none of us would have been bloodied up."

Karen was probably right. I did not have my glasses on at the time. Perhaps I just thought I saw blood on her leg before I grabbed the cat's tail.

"Karen, the best place on this boat for the next few hours is upstairs, and if you don't mind, bring us another beer."

"I'm not into beer for breakfast.'

"You weren't into a lot of other things a few months ago; give it a try. Besides, Tom makes the rules, and tea won't be available until we make camp tonight."

It was obvious from the speed we were traveling we would not start fishing until the Captain and Tom were satisfied we were far enough from port to justify wetting our lines. The boat was bigger than the one the previous year. Captain Abbas kept it pointing into the wind, heading north to the islands where we would spend the next few days.

Karen and I climbed to the sundeck while Tom broke out the fishing gear and then joined us with a bag of snacks Karen and Unan had packed for the six-hour boat ride.

"Five bucks on the first, five on the biggest, and five on the most."

"You're on, Tom."

When we reached the warmer tuna currents, we set the poles in holders and settled into our designated places on the back deck. Tom and I toasted each other as we let our tuna jigs drift twenty meters behind the boat.

Chapter 37

I was searching for something, but not sure what. A reason for it all, *perhaps*. My memories of my last trip to the Red Sea pale to those of my first. Although I have tried a number of times since, I have found going back to places that created fond or pleasant memories and improving on the original experience is usually anticlimactic.

We had planned a fishing trip, which was all. We did find tuna, plentiful and adequate by most standards, none as large as the one Tom caught the year before. The Red Sea was just as beautiful, the winds as strong, and the crabs plentiful. It was a good trip for me. A great one for Karen after she and Tom called a truce.

Tom and Unan did their crab thing and argued about how to prepare the catch. Same shit, but it was all fun, and the show was entertaining.

The project was at an end. Mailing the materials through the Embassy worked. Doctor Osmond and Cesar quit bugging me about money. The $500,000 for the electrical work was a $300,000 bonus they did not expect. I had not told them I had renegotiated it until I billed the COE. Cesar forgave me for past sins and sent me a generous bonus when the check arrived.

As for the utility lines, Dr. Osmond did get involved, but we did not do the work. A few weeks after Lloyd's visit Dr. Osmond told me I needed to get a change order for $20,000 for *dewatering*. It was a great deal less than either mine or Lloyd's estimate.

I told Dr. Osmond I would turn it in to Tom when the work was done. A few weeks later, a city crew showed up. It took a lot longer than it should have and caused delays when they blocked the gate. It was a slam dunk; the annexation was complete. General Aziz let me use the old entrance between the two bases, so the work progressed.

In order to test the lines, we had to dig a hole. I stuck a pump in it, and when we finished the testing, I gave Tom a bill for $20,000 plus a 10% markup for *dewatering*. We all felt it was a bargain. It was also a relief to all, mostly me. I was not sure either Dr. Osmond or General Aziz had the connections to put my deal together.

I was leaving Cairo a changed man, and a true expat. I was on the high side of the social scale and light years above those subjugated to the will of the elite. Like most visitors unaffected by their sufferings, I had adjusted to the ills of society, accepting them as preconceived and unchangeable.

Looking back on my observations of the people in Egypt I could not help feeling I interjected some of my feelings. I had become like those in the villages, living day to day, simply waiting for tomorrow.

We were done. Andy had the option; he did not have to stick around. He was heading home to his family. The experience had been a success for him. His bills were paid. He had gained insight into reality; he had also learned to speak Arabic.

Andy's plane would depart in a few hours, mine a week later. I still had a few last things to sort out with Tom and General Aziz. The final walkthrough and dedication ceremonies would take place a few days later.

"What now, Pat?"

"It's time to go home, Andy."

Things had gone well in the final month of the project, but I had a hunch we would not make it to the final ceremonies without another incident. I was wrong; we had two.

General Aziz's staff never attended the training sessions. On the day Andy left, one of the Egyptian technicians pulled the fire alarm handle, which also sealed the computer room. Fifteen seconds later the Halon fire suppressant discharged. The canisters contained twenty-five gallons and cost $3,000 each; there were eighteen. General Aziz thought I should replace them free, but I disagreed.

I also disagreed that it was our responsibility to clean up the mess. The raised floor system and ceiling tiles damaged by the high-pressure discharge were a disaster. It took around-the-clock efforts to repair them in time for the dedication. The American taxpayer paid the bill.

I had managed to sneak a camera in now and then, but it was usually on a Friday when the Egyptians were off. In the last four months there was always too much brass around. I wanted a last look at the finished product. On the morning before the dedication ceremony, I walked through the project.

The General private bathroom had polished granite floors and marble walls. An ornate wall-hung sink matched the décor. The Egyptian laborer sitting on the edge of the sink washing his balls before he prayed did not match anything. The added weight pulled the fasteners through the marble; the sink was hanging off the wall.

You could say that it was at that moment my patience course paid off because I did not kill the man. I did drag him off by his cotton thobe, and I might have killed him, but Tom came around the corner.

A few hours later, the ceremony took place. It was anticlimactic. Tom bought off the project. General Aziz agreed to have his soldiers reinstall his sink when they installed the ass washers and turned the toilets.

There was lots of fanfare. The Egyptians took turns telling the rest of us how grateful they were to the Americans and, surprisingly, to me. General Aziz presented me with a computer printout thanking me for furthering cooperation between the two countries. Tom almost gagged on his tea.

I was flattered. Both sides forgot the pain and suffering complaints. The paper the General presented to me was nothing more than a piece of plain bond printed by one of the new printers. There were a few misspellings noticed by General Aziz. He offered to have it redone. I declined; it meant more to me in its original form.

The project was finished. Regardless of the length of time it took I was proud of it and the Egyptian laborers who, in the end, met or exceeded the American standards set for them by the COE. That is, except for the honeycomb block walls hidden behind the plaster and paint.

Doctor Osmond invited me to his home before I left; it was the first time. Hamid, Mohammed, Schmir, and Hazem showed up, along with some of the other players from the Egyptian side who had come and gone during the eighteen months I was in Cairo.

I told Doctor Osmond my plane departed at one a.m., and I had to be at the airport by eleven. I lied; I planned to stay a few more days, and planning had become second nature. Tom and Glen invited me to a gathering of the American players for the following evening and I wanted to be sure to be on time.

Dr. Osmond walked me to the door, then stopped when I tried to shake his hand, and in Egyptian tradition, he put his arms around me and kissed my cheek. I was at a loss for words and stood there for a moment. Dr. Osmond stepped back with a smile.

"Thank you, Mr. Pat. You will always be welcome, but if you return, you must learn some Arabic."

"I laughed, and for the first time, he offered, and I shook Dr. Osmond's hand."

"Thank you, Dr. Osmond, it's been a pleasure."

He held my palm in his for longer than protocol, thinking. His turn to laugh.

"By the way, Mr. Pat, you really did not want to dig that tunnel, and neither did I."

I left, shaking my head. *It was their country, their rules; it* will always be that way.

Tom was in a somber mood. We had developed a deep friendship, and the odds of us ever crossing paths again were slim to none.

“What now, Pat?”

It was a small community. No one had any secrets. I was reluctant to head home.

“Paris for a few days to clear my head, then home.”

“What about Karen?’

“Karen leaves the day after tomorrow. I promised her one more dinner at the Ramses Hilton and a last carriage ride.”

Karen dealt with reality better than I had. I owed her a great deal, my sanity perhaps. We established the rules at the onset, and we were both aware Cairo was an interim and passing part of our lives.

“By the way, Pat, I had a call from a vice president at AMCA, an American contractor I’m working with who needs a manager for an offshore project. I gave him your name and a recommendation. I have his card if you’re interested?”

“Not right now, Tom, but I’ll take his card just in case I need to make new plans.”

I said goodbye to the American and British players. Some had become friends and family of sorts. I knew I would never be coming back to Cairo or, sadly, seeing them again.

I gave in to Karen one last time. We spent four days in Paris. The weather was as gloomy as her mood. The rain was refreshing. My lungs cleared from the months of Cairo air.

Karen and I parted company in New York. We spent two short hours at the airport. Her connecting plane flew north, mine west. I arrived in Portland, Oregon, seven hours later.

Epilogue

This book was about Egypt, that is behind us. Just in case some of my readers are curious how it all turned out when I returned to the States.

The IRS was looming in the background. I had six months left before the statute would expire. Even then, I would have to make the appeal and prove I met the conditions before the IRS would release the lien. That could mean another six months, possibly longer, before I would be able to go back to work in the States.

I was underfoot, hanging out at the restaurant, taking it day by day, *just waiting for tomorrow*. A week after I arrived home I received a call from a recruiter for the company on the name of the card Tom gave me. Before I left Cairo, I did some research. AMCA (American Canadian International) was a billion-dollar player in the international construction market; they were a stratospheric step up from EGICON.

After I hung up, I debated; it was not going well. There was someone else hiding in the shadows. Mary was distant, but neither of us had gotten up the courage to discuss it. After the call from AMCA, I decided to try.

Like all in the past, it was an emotional lost cause. Mary's reaction then, as it had been since the day our first child was born, was to burst into tears at the slightest confrontation. I had gotten to where I could not handle it and would simply turn and walk away. At that moment, I knew I had flunked my patience course. The domestic confrontation was postponed once again.

I went to the bar and called Steve, the managing director for AMCA. He was anxious; they had a problem and an immediate need for a Quality Assurance and Safety manager for a new U.S. embassy on the Island of Cyprus. My initial reaction was that it would be a step-down. I was used to running the show. He countered that it was a $70 million project, the pay was exceptional, and it was an interim position. They had a number of projects in the pipeline. If I accepted the Cyprus position, I would be next in line for the project of my choice.

Six months made sense, even if I did not take a new project. If I left the States, I would retain my tax-free status and be out of reach of the local agent from the IRS until the statute expired.

As in all the past situations Mary had quickly regained her composure the moment I walked away. Things had settled. I brought it up more as a question than a fact, leaving out the part about it being an *interim position until the next project*. I was not sure she was ready for that.

She thought it was a great idea and, after I explained that Cyprus was a playground for the rich and famous, and five-star all the way, she agreed to join me at the end of the season for the restaurant, which was four months away. I believed she meant it. That was promising, possibly a fresh start.

The next day, I flew to AMCA's office in Ohio and accepted the offer. I left for Cyprus the next day. Over the next month, I tried a number of times to reach Mary; two out of three, she was either busy or out of town. Three weeks passed after the last call before she picked up the phone. It was one-sided and short. She was in love with someone else and wanted a divorce. It really was not a surprise.

Remarkably, it was not a relief. If you were to ask me today, I could not tell you why, other than one does not just throw twenty-four years and four kids in a trash can. I decided to fly to Oregon and give it one last try. I walked into the restaurant and found her in her office.

"What are you doing here?"

Mary was a beautiful woman; she looked wonderful, better than she had in years. Obviously, whoever, whatever, she was happy. It gave me a reason to pause. I changed my mind and confessed an old sin before I asked her.

"Are you sure?"

This time, there were no tears; Mary was finally liberated from me.

"Yes, I'm sure."

I turned and walked out the door. I returned to Cyprus and started where I left off. My youngest daughter joined me. Angie was a wayward child. At fifteen she had run off with a cook at the restaurant and ended up on the streets in Florida. She and I settled in, each with our problems, trying to get our lives in order. It was working.

AMCA was having issues with the PD on the Embassy. They were behind on all fronts. The State Department had shut the flow of money off until the Quality Assurance and Safety manuals were submitted and the plans were in place, that is why I was there.

I finished the QC and Safety issues in six weeks. I was inspecting the work and conducting meetings on the site. The money was flowing again.

Keven, the PD, and his wife were wining and dining the U.S. Ambassador. Keven was ignoring Dave, the Project Manager. Dave kept dragging me into other aspects of the project outside my scope of responsibility. I soon found myself drafting letters for Keven who could not be bothered with the day-to-day.

One of the day-to-days was a change order Keven gave to Dave after telling him it was a non-issue. Dave brought it to me. Not only was it an issue, it was a mind-blowing issue. AMCA was just starting site work. The change involved major electrical, mechanical, and plumbing upgrades, and a rearrangement of several rooms. The synergistic effects were so complicated that the only way to price the change was to rebid the entire building.

I told both Keven and Dave this was over our heads and that Keven needed to get the home office involved. I was drafting Kevan's letters. When Keven brought it up to the CO from the State Department, the CO went ballistic. Keven decided it was beyond my pay grade. He told me to stick with safety and quality control. They would work through it as the project progressed.

I took it upon myself to send Steve the drawings with a suggestion to have his estimating department look it over. Steve dumped it back in my lap.

Steve called Keven and told him I would be dealing with the change. Keven was not happy I went over his head, but he called a meeting with the State Department CO and the Ambassador. We got into one hell of a pissing match. Steve was on the intercom listening. A week later, Keven left Cyprus.

The Ambassador and the CO were putting up roadblocks and threatened AMCA with a unilateral change order telling them to build it by the new plans.

Dave was the interim PD. Dave was a young man; it was early in his career, and it was a real mess. To give Dave credit, he felt the job was over his head and voiced that to Steve. Steve asked me to step in, and I agreed.

Truthfully, I do not know how it all turned out. A week later, Joe, my attorney, called. There was an unresolved issue with my divorce. The restaurant was just breaking even. Mary was getting married; alimony would not work, and neither would her new husband. She wanted a settlement. I was to give her $5,000 a month until the restaurant could support them both; it was open-ended.

I refused; I needed to appear before the judge. It was an argument I was going to win, which put Mary in a get-even mood. A few days before my flight, Mary called the IRS agent and told him where I was.

Before I accepted the offer, I told Steve the story. He was working on a solution as to how to pay me in Cyprus in order to keep the IRS at bay. At that time, I was on AMCA's payroll. It was not difficult for the IRS to find an American on a U.S. embassy project on the island of Cyprus. I received a call from Steve telling me the IRS had slapped a lien on my salary.

I told him paying the IRS anything was out of the question. The statute would start over, and I would have wasted the past six, almost seven years. I had little choice. I quit the project and asked

Steve to offset any monies due against advances for deposits they had made on a flat and furniture. Steve was sympathetic; the IRS did not get a dime.

Angie and I left Cyprus for New York. Angie's friend, the cook, was working. She took a flight back to Florida. I headed for Seattle, found a place to live, and settled, waiting for the statute to expire. That does not belong in this story. You will find it in the full-length version of my time on this planet, less Egypt. The book, My Yellow Brick Road, A Trainwreck, Without Regrets.

When the final divorce papers were ready, Joe, my attorney, called. I arrived in Portland a few days later. Joe met me at the gate. He was there to bring me the divorce papers from Mary's attorney.

What was left of my prior life was stowed in the back of Joe's car: a cardboard box of old clothes and a few pictures.

Joe and I spent an hour in an airport restaurant discussing what I needed to do to expedite the divorce and what plans I might have. One of the issues was the $5,000 a month. I figured the fox in the hen house, who had been drinking my liquor and sleeping in my bed, could pick up his own tab. It was when I refused that Mary called the IRS.

Joe had explained to her attorney that Mary had shit in her nest. I was out of a job and had an IRS lien hanging over my head. It would be a futile effort and would delay the divorce; Mary dropped the demand.

I do not think Mary had a clue when she placed the call. With accruing compound interest, the bill was well over a million dollars. The statute had an addendum, the seven years would be extended by the number of days it took from the time I filed bankruptcy until it was discharged. My personal Bankruptcy took six months. But that started after Chapter 11 for the shipyard. That could add another year and a half.

The agent assigned to my case had recently called Joe's office; he wanted a copy of the settlement. If he could collect one dollar, the statute would start over. It was a futile effort. The bank accounts, the restaurant, and the cars were all in Mary's name.

"What now?"

"The bar's open."

We did not have cell phones, and I was wandering. Joe was my contact in the States. Joe had received a call from Steve at AMCA, who wanted me to call him ASAP.

I left Joe to pee and make a few phone calls. My kids were on my mind. Then I remembered Joe told me to call Steve.

"You're chipper; what happened?"

"Looks like things are settled, Joe, at least until the statute expires. Canadian Bridge, AMCA's subsidiary in Canada, is bidding on a project in Egypt. They need someone to lead the bid process. My Cario experience makes me the top candidate. If they get the job, I told him I would take it on. If they don't get it, I'll be in line for AMCA's next one. I'll be taking the redeye to Washington and then to Montreal."

"What about the divorce settlement?'

"It's settled, Joe; get the papers signed, and don't let her drag it out. Let me know if you hear from the IRS."

Joe stayed with me for another hour. I thought back on Cesar's description of Egypt and the one-year, piece-of-cake contract I signed two years earlier. It was not my first choice, but I could do another tour in Egypt.

Turning back to Joe, I wondered how long I would have to stay away and if there was a possibility of ever coming home. As Joe was getting up to leave, I thanked him for the undeserved sympathy.

"What's the possibility of settling with the IRS so I can return for good?"

"Settling is not an option, Pat. They want their pound of flesh. I'll file the papers when the statute expires. It may take a few months to a year to convince them to issue the release, but it will happen. When it does, you will be free to come home.

Past errors and omissions finally caught up. The current turn of events was predictable. I was carrying a thousand in cash and an American Express prepaid debit card I purchased in Paris using the bonus I received from Cesar. It was enough to tide me over, but it was not much to show for two years overseas, let alone 46 years.

I had one last issue. I opened my briefcase and handed Joe an envelope.

"Joe, I can't be in the States more than 30 days in a calendar year, or I'll lose my tax-free status. I'm pushing my limit. I won't be able to deal with this. The instructions are in the envelope."

"The foal will drop in late January or early February. The ultrasounds say it's a healthy colt. Send the buyer the papers when the money is in my account."

A final note.

Canadian Bridge did not get the Egypt project. Canadian AID canceled it when all the bids came in too high. The Statute expired. I stayed with AMCA traveling for a few more years, mostly in the

Third World, from the borders of Afghanistan to the southern tip of Africa.

I returned to the U.S. for good after having been thrown in prison and deported *Persona Non-Grata,* meaning *an unwelcome person* from Botswana, Africa, for an infraction that would go unnoticed in the U.S.

When I returned, I tried to reassimilate. It was a redundant exercise. On the surface, going about my daily business, I seemed normal. That lasted another unsettled thirty years.

Poverty means different things to different people. In America, poverty means a lack of a car, wide-screen TV, refrigerator, stove, soap, a connection to the internet, or a cell phone. Enough said, you get the picture.

Now that I am retired and reflecting, I have become mostly a recluse watching people. As a result, I have little sympathy for anyone blessed to be living in America other than for those incapacitated through no fault of their own.

My definition of poverty as it applies to the Third World:

> Insufficient nourishment to maintain health. A lack of cloth to make clothes. Inadequate shelter to keep the elements at bay. A sword hanging over your head. Abject inability to change your status in life. Lots more, but once again, you get the picture.

For the rest, we all have choices; they are ours to make. No matter who we are or what our status, in America, at any given moment, we are far better off on our worst day than a peasant born in a village in the Third World is on their best day. Make the best of it.

Mr. Pat

Made in the USA
Columbia, SC
27 June 2024

fa89d162-a0ba-4e81-b49b-f1fa8eee241fR02